Globalizing Interests

SUNY series in Global Politics

James N. Rosenau, editor

Globalizing Interests

Pressure Groups and Denationalization

Edited by

Michael Zürn with Gregor Walter

State University of New York Press

Published by
State University of New York Press, Albany

© 2005 State University of New York

Printed in the United States of America

For information, address State University of New York Press,
194 Washington Avenue, Suite 305, Albany, NY 12210-2384

Production by Michael Haggett
Marketing by Susan M. Petrie

Library of Congress Cataloging in Publication Data

Globalizing interests : pressure groups and denationalization / edited by
Michael Zürn With Gregor Walter.
    p. cm. — (SUNY series in global politics)
  Includes bibliographical references and index.
  ISBN 0–7914–6509–8 (hardcover : alk. paper)
 1. Globalization—Political aspects. 2. Globalization—Research. 3. Globalization
—Political aspects—Europe—Case studies. 4. Globalization—Political aspects—
North America—Case studies. 5. Pressure groups—Europe—Case studies.
6. Pressure groups—North America—Case studies. 7. Internet—Government
policy—Case studies. 8. Carbon dioxide mitigation—Government policy—Case
studies. 9. Immigrants—Government policy—Case studies. I. Zürn, Michael.
II. Walter, Gregor. III. Series.

JZ1320.G564 2005
327—dc22

2004017951

10 9 8 7 6 5 4 3 2 1

Contents

Acknowledgments

Ralph Waldo Emerson is attributed to have said that one should never read a book that is not at least a year old. If this rule were reversed, it would urge the reader to study this book because it is not only the outcome of several years of work, it also took more than a year to finalize the manuscript. The book is based on a collective effort in the context of a six-year research project located at the University of Bremen, Germany. The project was financed by the Deutsche Forschungsgemeinschaft (DFG) and carried out at the Institute for Intercultural and International Studies (InIIS) at the University of Bremen. Both institutions proved to be more than just necessary preconditions for our work: The DFG provided the financial resources and—not least thanks to Helga Hoppe—efficient administrative supervision. The InIIS in Bremen supplied the necessary infrastructure and at the same time constituted a very stimulating intellectual environment for our work. Special thanks, therefore, to the members of the InIIS research colloquium, and most notably to Dieter Senghaas and Bernhard Peters. From the Bremen team, we would also like to mention Ryan Kalinko and Vicki May who are responsible for the Australian and British glitches in the otherwise smooth "Denglish" of the authors. Peter Arnhold, Julia Moser, and Jana Rosenboom provided support as research assistants and Stefan Walter significantly refreshed our memory on vector mathematics.

The book is a study of the reaction of various political groups to denationalization challenges, and it would have been impossible to finish without the cooperation of the groups under consideration. Almost all of the selected groups assisted us in various ways. They provided the necessary primary materials and identified numerous interview partners in Canada, Germany, Great Britain, and the United States, who had the patience to answer numerous questions on the groups' perspectives and activities.

Our investigations were carried out over a number of years, and so many people have supported our efforts that mentioning them all would take up far more space than even the most patient reader would be willing to bear. We will thus only list the events which led to significant refinements to the project.

In 1998, members of the Amsterdam RECIPE group commented most helpfully on our research questions. Our thanks go especially to Gerd Junne and Henk Overbeek. In 1999, Beate Kohler-Koch and Michèle Knodt joined us in an intensive workshop on methodological aspects of our study. First tentative conclusions were presented at the 1999 Arnoldshain meeting of the Deutsche Vereinigung für Politikwissenschaft (DVPW). The participants of this meeting, in particular Edgar Grande and Thomas Risse, provided valuable input. The next major step was reached following a workshop in 2000 during which Helmut Breitmeier, Rainer Eising, Nico Dose, Markus Jachtenfuchs, Andreas Nölke and Klaus Dieter Wolf proved to be both critical and constructive. In the same year, Danish scholars working on globalization issues commented on our research. We thank Morten Ougaard and, most cordially, our friend Georg Sørensen, who was very supportive during the whole project period. In 2001, members of the colloquium of the Wissenschaftszentrum Berlin (WZB)—especially Hans-Peter Kriesi—helped to hone our perspective on the conclusions. In addition to these events, we are indebted to various individuals from the American scientific community, especially Peter Katzenstein, Robert Keohane, Gary Marks, and James Rosenau. Last but not least, we would like to thank the anonymous reviewers and the staff of SUNY Press, especially Michael Rinella, who have helped to considerably improve the readability and quality of the manuscript. We hope you will like the ultimate outcome of a long intellectual journey.

Chapter 1

Globalizing Interests—An Introduction

Michael Zürn

It is widely believed that globalization as a process is well under way and destined to fundamentally affect various aspects of political life. Some people go so far as to argue that globalization will be nothing less than the defining characteristic of the century to come: the global age. Be it the nation-state or the international system, democracy or the welfare state, modern political institutions are assumed to be altered, undermined, challenged, or otherwise affected by the process. Yet, despite all these claims, most institutions are still alive and well and the dire as well as the bright social consequences of the process still await comprehensive empirical substantiation. Is this because the effects of globalization have not yet fully unravelled? Or is it because—as we want to argue—the bulk of the globalization literature, being both bound to methodological nationalism and inappropriately narrow in its appreciation of the political aspects of the phenomenon, has produced predictions which are much too simple?

This book aims to overcome these limitations by focussing on the politics of denationalization, that is, the actual political processes set in motion by the phenomenon of globalization. Specifically, it provides an analysis of, and seeks to explain, the policy preferences and lobbying activities of nationally constituted pressure groups faced with governance challenges in the globalization hotspots of climate change, migration, and the Internet. We distinguish between leftist and rightist groups as well as between groups that are considered as protagonists of old and new politics, respectively. This research thus asks whether, to what extent, and whose interests are globalized and thereby creates political processes that cannot be captured in terms of politics as we know it from the national constellation. Our conclusion is that the politics of denationalization and the political cleavages that accompany it differ significantly from politics as usual as it may be termed.

This general introduction consists of six sections. In the first section, the limitations of current globalization research are discussed in the context of a critique of scholarship dealing with the race to the bottom hypothesis.

1

Against that background, section two elaborates on our modified under-standing of what the globalization process actually entails. Section three introduces the focus of our study, while section four examines the conceptual framework of our approach and the case studies. Together, these sections establish an analytical framework we believe addresses the weaknesses of dominant globalization research. Finally, in section five, the hypotheses and findings of the study are presented, and in section six, their implications, for the development of a postnational polity, are discussed.

ON GLOBALIZATION: BROAD DEFINITIONS, METHODO-LOGICAL NATIONALISM AND STRUCTURAL SHORTCUTS

The literature on globalization attributes to the process far-reaching conse-quences of epochal proportions. Raising issues such as the future of the democratic welfare state, transnational civil society, political fragmentation, and multilevel governance, the process is said to be responsible not only for a decrease in national autonomy and the likelihood of interstate war, but also for the disabling of democracy and the decline of legitimacy of national political systems. It is also regarded as having altered the nature of sover-eignty and the fundamental structures of politics.[1] In many of these illumi-nating studies however, the way in which globalization is conceptualized is still somewhat shaky; many of the attempts to define the process invoke extremely broad categories. Accordingly, it has been said to represent "the stretching and deepening of social relations and institutions across space and time" (see e.g., Giddens 1990; Held and McGrew 1993, 263; Held 1995, 20; Elkins 1995; Rosenau 1997). On this understanding, globalization denotes all (individual as well as the sum total of) globally oriented practices and pat-terns of thought as well as the epochal transformation which is constituted by them (Albrow 1996, 89). Such a broad definition, however, hinders an empirical assessment of globalization's consequences; if globalization is everything, there is nothing left to explain. And if the conceptualization of globalization allows no distinction between the process itself and its assumed consequences, then the proper empirical probing of hypotheses becomes impossible. Perhaps it is no surprise, therefore, that the amount of systematic data on the driving forces behind the changes is still remarkably scarce; despite the tremendous change in world politics that is ascribed to globaliza-tion, systematic measurement of globalization is still mostly uncharted terri-tory. This deficiency provides the first point of reference for the approach adopted in this volume: the development of a clear and inter-subjective mea-surable conceptualisation of the globalization process.

Two further weaknesses in much of the globalization literature can be pointed out in an examination of a field of research that does not suffer from this lack of an empirically based measure of the phenomenon under study. This field of research, namely, that on the effects of globalization on social and welfare state policies, is among the most advanced in the globalization literature, its methods representing the typical approach to how external influences on national political systems are studied. Measuring globalization by the degree to which national economies are integrated into the world market, scholars studying the process from this perspective foresee "the end of the social democratic era" (Scharpf 1987), the "retreat of the state" (Strange 1996), the "misery of politics" (Narr and Schubert 1994), the "trap" of globalization (Martin and Schumann 1997), a "race to the bottom" or at least a "competition of the obsessed" (Krugman 1994a), a "competition state" (Hirsch 1995), a "Schumpeterian workfare state" (Jessop 1994) and a "residual state" (Cerny 1995).

Common to these studies is the notion that increased capital mobility leads to an increase in competition between states to attract capital, with the result that states, in order to remain economically viable, must endorse economic and social deregulation programs and cut back on social welfare. Contrary to these expectations, however, the level of state expenditure has not decreased with the rise of globalization, and clear-cut convergence processes are yet to be observed.[2] In addition, a redistribution of state expenditure from welfare to the security and R & D sectors as predicted by the notion of a competition state also has not yet occurred on a broad scale (Zürn 1998, 153–157).

One may argue that social policies are currently in transition and that the relevant indicators will soon vindicate the predictions of theory. This position is supported by the fact that the data used in most studies comes from statistics on state and social expenditure, which for the most part derive from the early 1990s. This is still very early, especially since very recent data shows the first signs of change (Stephens, Huber, and Ray 1999; Kittel, Obinger and Wagschal 2000: Pontusson 2001). In addition, there is already evidence that while the level of unemployment expenditure in fact grew in almost all G7 countries, the amount of money received by individual beneficiaries dropped, suggesting a relative reduction in state expenditure in these countries (Neyer and Seeleib-Kaiser 1995). Moreover, some of the findings could be a result of institutional inertia. Sweden, for example, clearly made extensive cuts to its social benefit system, but expenditure initially grew faster compared to other states because the sudden rise in unemployment activated the welfare state. Thus, whereas the figures for Sweden indicate neither convergence nor deregulation, a significant movement in that direction can be discerned. Another possible reason for why the early data does not really reflect the influence of globalization pressures may relate to common low denominators: since social spending is measured as a percentage of GNP per capita, slow growth in many OECD countries in the early 1990s may have kept the social quota artificially high (Pontusson 2001). Finally, studies focussing on specific policy areas can easily demonstrate a marked convergent trend towards deregulation: the postal and telecommunication services are a strong case in point (Grande and Schneider 1991; Vogel 1996).

Yet—in our view—the shortcomings of this race to the bottom hypothesis go much deeper; the predictions reflect what we believe to be a somewhat apolitical notion of politics in the global age, characterized by structuralist thinking and methodological nationalism.

First, these studies seem to rest on the quite problematic assumption that structural pressures translate directly into political outcomes. To the extent this assumption is relaxed, an absence in convergence processes cannot be equated with an absence of constraints. In other words, pressures such as globalization have their first impact on the political process, and it is the complexity of this process (rather than the pressure itself) that determines which outcomes are borne out or not. Thus, case studies examining the political processes currently occurring in many welfare states reveal that economic pressures imposed by global constraints are strongly felt, often translating into uneasy compromises (Seeleib-Kaiser 2001), and often resulting in a reconfiguration of politics and political cleavages. For instance, the global call for greater economic openness has seen an increase in the demand for domestic policies, which offset the less desirable effects of world market integration. In this sense, social policies and state intervention can be seen not only as cost-intensive burdens on efficient production, but also as a form of risk insurance in the face of increased economic openness (see Garrett 1998a; Rieger and Leibfried 2003; Rodrik 1997). Moreover, new growth theory suggests that many instances of state intervention are still economically efficient and thus effective even and especially in times of global competition (Krugman 1994b; Barro 1996). Hence, higher levels of economic interdependence and globalization may well lead to more rather than less state intervention—depending on the political choices that are made.

Accordingly, it may be said that globalization leads to new political challenges, which still, however, leave much leverage for a variety of different outcomes. On this analysis, then, what globalization does change is the power and influence of interest groups, the societal coalitions and cleavages associated with certain policies as well as the policy instruments used to meet the various challenges that arise. In this sense, globalization does not lead to the dissolution but rather to a reconfiguration of national politics (see also Grande and Risse 2000).

Second, globalization processes call into question the premises of methodological nationalism. Because political actors have a choice when faced with challenge, they may not only develop new policy instruments but also change the level on which policies are formulated. Faced with economic globalization, states can respond in two principal ways: downwards, by restructuring state-society relations, or upwards, by establishing interstate relationships. Consideration of this second option, however, is analytically prejudiced wherever the focus is exclusively on the national sphere. Paradoxically, the most important strand of the globalization literature—the race to the bottom hypothesis, which builds on the state-theoretical notion of the competitive state—contains this very bias.

Methodological nationalism sees the nation-state as the basic unit of all politics—within nations and between nations—and looks at competition between nation-states in an interdependent world as a fundamental driving force.[3] This double premise precludes the simple option of a competition between the political and the economic sphere and thus a pooling of state sovereignty in order to strengthen governments vis-à-vis economic forces in the transnational sphere (see Beck 2003). It also rules out the option of collaboration between governments via international institutions in order to shield certain policies from domestic resistance (see Wolf 2000). Similarly, organisations other than multinationals can also develop transnational alliances, but again, the presumptions of methodological nationalism prevent analysis at this level. To be sure, nation-states are still important actors in world politics and national societies are still important units for analysing social and political developments. Hence, differences between nations will be an important explanatory variable for differences in social and political behaviour. An appropriate conceptualization of politics in the age of globalization may however not exclude by definition other loci of collective action and coalition-building. It cannot assume the nation-state is the basic unit of all politics. In order to maintain or even step up a given level of intervention, states as well as political groups may or may not collaborate at the international level and retain the possibility of establishing common policy-making institutions; thus, they may or may not evidence behaviour in opposition to the analytical premises of methodological nationalism. Keeping this question analytically open is equal to avoiding methodological nationalism.

While our study does not contribute directly to the debate about the effects of globalization on the welfare state, our aim in this work is to avoid the three shortcomings, identified above as typical in globalization studies, namely, an unspecified causal agent, structural shortcuts, and methodological nationalism. Our intention is to move beyond the simplistic notion of the external force, which alters national policies, in order to understand the more complex political effects occurring in the wake of globalization challenges. To this end, we attempt to define precisely what we mean by societal denationalisation as well as fine-tune the means by which the consequences of denationalization are studied. For this purpose, it is necessary to be conceptually open to processes that transcend methodological nationalism and systematically take account of transnational and intergovernmental coalition-building and policy formulation on a level beyond the nation state. More particularly, our aim is to contribute to a better understanding of the way in which globalization unfolds within and across national political systems. In our view, globalization poses challenges for politics as usual in some (but not all) issue areas. We see globalization as a structural restraint, which is consequential politically, only to the extent that, and according to the manner in which political groups respond. We believe an increased focus on agency is a necessary prerequisite for a more accurate understanding of globalization-induced policy change. Globalization does not directly affect political outcomes; policy outcomes are mediated through political institutions, political actors, and political struggles. In a nutshell, we maintain that a much better understanding of the effects of the phenomenon can be gained by looking at the politics of globalization instead of the policy changes caused by globalization. What is required is an examination of processes, not outcomes.

This book offers such a focus by comparing the policy preferences and lobbying activities of nationally constituted pressure groups in various industrialized countries in response to a variety of globalization challenges. Given the state of research in this area, the purpose of this study is, to a large extent, the generation of (not the testing of preexisting) hypotheses.

First, the patterns of responses made by interest groups to globalization challenges are compared with what we know about regular national politics. This comparison of the politics of denationalization with (an ideal type of) politics in the national sphere leads to a number of general inferences about the political effects of globalization. Second, we aim to account for the variance in the responses of the groups under review. On the basis of some conceptual and theoretical reflections, the study contains a "structured and focused comparison" (cf. George 1979) of six cases, which overall, offer a sufficient number of observation points to carry out a quantitative analysis. This allows a blend of qualitative and quantitative methods to be applied. The overarching interest behind this exercise is, however, theoretical: our aim is to contribute to a better theoretical account of politics in the context of the postnational constellation.[4]

FROM INTERDEPENDENCE TO GLOBALIZATION AND DENATIONALIZATION

Interest in both interdependence and globalization can be seen as an expression of a "poorly understood but widespread feeling that the very nature of world politics is changing." (Keohane and Nye 2000, 104). Interdependence describes a situation of mutual dependency; it rests on the notion that national political actors (most often governments) are structurally affected by the behaviour of others (most often societies in other countries) while at the same time remain essentially autonomous. In this sense, each state "decides for itself how it will cope with its internal and external problems, including whether or not to seek assistance from others."[5] Such a notion of interdependence still implies the opportunity to choose between unilateral and multilateral strategies, even if the effectiveness of a unilateral strategy (the degree to which the purposes of the strategy are achieved) is likely to be less than a multilateral endeavour.

Globalization goes further than interdependence. Richard Cooper (1986, 1) argues that "the internationalised economy of the 1960s was characterised by a sensitivity of economic transactions between two or more nations to economic developments within those nations." By contrast, the process of economic globalization describes a movement towards one integrated world market in which "buyers and sellers are in such free intercourse with one another that the prices of the same goods tend to equality easily and quickly" (Cooper 1986, 71). This distinction between an internationalized economy and the global integration of markets can be generalised to draw a distinction between interdependence and globalization. Globalization can thus be described as the process by which the world moves away from merely internationalized societies and towards an integrated global society. Accordingly, globalization, by calling into question the parameters of national societies, can be seen as challenging the distinction between domestic and foreign relations. This view recognizes that distant events of all sorts have immediate consequences, not only for states but for individuals' daily lives, both in terms of their basic living conditions and how their local communities operate (Rosenau 1990: 78, Holm and Sørensen 1995, 4–5; Hirst and Thompson 1996, 7; Held et al. 1999, chap. 1).

We use in this volume yet another term: societal denationalization. As with the term globalization, societal denationalization points to a higher level of interconnectedness between formerly separated societies than the term "interdependence" At the same time, the term "societal denationalization" avoids some of the problematic meanings that are conveyed through the term "globalization" and, moreover, is defined in a more precise and less ambiguous way.

While we agree that we have, at least in some areas, moved to something that is more than just interdependence, the term "globalization" seems not to be really adequate. Even if it is true that transborder transactions are on the rise and in some fields transcend national borders completely, the term "globalization" goes too far and conveys a problematic meaning for two reasons. First, the transcendence of national border of societal transactions does not encompass the whole world. Over 80 per cent of world trade is carried out between countries inhabited by a little more than 25 per cent of the world's population. This narrow focus is even more evident if one looks at direct investment worldwide. Over 91 per cent of all direct foreign investment between 1980 and 1991 was shared between the OECD countries and ten threshold countries (Hirst and Thompson 1996, 67).[6] Communication flows indicate a similar pattern. A world map highlighting the distribution of Internet connections is particularly informative. It makes clear that even within the OECD world there are clear gravitational centres the borders of which, however, do not coincide with national borders. Even in the United States there are extensive networks only along the two coastlines, including also parts of Canada (see Beisheim et al. 1999, 65). Second, territory remains important. The "place-boundedness" of social transactions has not yet been completely transformed. Sassen (1998) is absolutely right to ask why, after all, if knowledge workers can telecommute so easily, so many of the world's most important desktops are to be found in a few square miles in New York, Tokyo, London and a few other places? Space and the borders of spaces will remain of the utmost significance for some time to come, at least for reasons of path dependence. It is therefore more appropriate to use a term that points to a process of transformation from a world of national territories than one that points to an endpoint without any meaning for territory.

Rather than the word "globalization", we therefore use the term "societal denationalization." This term is used in reference to the classic works of Karl W. Deutsch (1969) and Eric Hobsbawm (1992) on nationalism, according to which a nation is a political community sustained by intensified interactions; this community stands in a mutually constitutive relationship with the nation-state and is thus an expression of the national constellation. Societal denationalization, therefore, represents a weakening of the linkage between territorial states and their corresponding national societies. Societal denationalization can be defined as the extension of social spaces (i.e., areas constituted by dense transactions) beyond national borders, noting that this extension need not necessarily be global in scope. The scope of most of these cross-border transactions is indeed not global, yet they still cause a problem for national governance for the simple reason that the social space to be governed is no longer national. To the extent that these problems are resolved by an extension of the validity of political regulation either in the form of political integration beyond the nation state or through international institutions, we speak of political denationalisation.[7]

With this distinction between the process itself and its assumed consequences, the proper empirical probing of hypotheses becomes possible. The word "societal" refers to a measurable process of social change which, in turn, may have certain political ramifications. Societal denationalization, however, is neither identical with, nor does it necessarily lead to, an extension of political space and governance beyond the nation state (i.e., political denationalization). Nor does it necessitate the formation of a world society[8] or transnational political communities.[9] It is conceived as a socio-structural challenge that provokes responses from those engaged in the political sphere. The range of conceivable responses is wide and includes an orientation to the status quo, a reconfiguration of politics within nation states as well as transnational strategies. Which path is chosen is a question of politics. In this way, our conceptualization brings politics back into the globalization debate.[10]

Critics have questioned the significance and uniqueness of the phenomenon of globalization and societal denationalization. It is repeatedly pointed out, not least by economists, that the degree of societal denationalization existent in some transboundary processes today only marginally differs from the time prior to 1914. In his comprehensive literary review of international financial systems, Zevin (1992; 51–52) concludes that "every available descriptor of financial markets in the late nineteenth and early twentieth centuries suggests that they were more fully integrated than they were before or have been since." Similarly, Stephen Krasner (1994, 14) comments that discussion and literature on globalization and the flurried claims of "new, new, change, change" are as substantial as the declarations made in American election campaigns. These objections question whether societal denationalization is really taking place and whether it is different from the age-old phenomenon of international interdependence.

These objections point to empirical issues and to questions of measurement. Indeed, in our understanding international interdependence and societal denationalization are to be measured by the same indicators, the different terms therefore refer to different values of these indicators. We use the interconnectedness of societies as an indicator. The interconnectedness of societies is neither a direct measure of interdependence nor of societal denationalization, even though it has often been used as such. That having been said, interconnectedness of societies can be measured by the amount of transboundary transactions relative to transactions that take place within a national territory.[11] While an increase in the ratio of transboundary to national transactions is often assumed to indicate a rise in interdependence, the notion of societal denationalization is more properly indicated by a rise in interconnectedness with a threshold value at which societal borders no longer mark the space of a critical reduction in their frequency (see Deutsch 1969, 99).[12]

The degree of societal denationalization can thus be operationalized as the volume of cross-border transactions relative to transactions taking place within national borders. Social transactions take place whenever goods, services or capital (constituting the economic sphere), threats (force), pollutants (environment), signs (communication) or persons (mobility) are exchanged or commonly produced.[13] This notion of societal denationalization is not restricted to the economic[14] or cultural[15] sphere. A society is denationalized in a given field when transactions relevant to that field are no denser within the society's national borders than across those borders. The term "societal denationalization" thus has the advantage of defining a starting point (national society) but leaving the endpoint indeterminate. Moreover, if cases can be singled out that show a clear trend towards globalism, there is no problem in interpreting such cases as special instances of a more general trend towards societal denationalization. Seen in this way, the transboundary pollution of the Rhine is just as much a phenomenon of societal denationalization as global warming, although the latter is genuinely global.

In an empirical investigation that we carried out against the background of this conceptualization it became clear that denationalization is not uniform, but rather a somewhat jagged process that differs notably between issue areas, countries and over time.[16] The process of denationalization, defined in terms of a growing significance of cross-border transactions, has been taking place, albeit in a mild form, since the 1950s. While it is correct that levels of economic interdependence were lower in the 1950s and 1960s than in the decades prior to 1929, interdependence grew again in the Western World in the decades after World War II (Katzenstein 1975; Rosecrance and Stein 1973; Rosecrance et al. 1977). From the 1970s onwards, the growth of cross-border exchanges accelerated with respect to goods and capital, information, travel, migration, and regional environmental risks in all of the OECD world. Whereas with respect to some indicators— such as trade quotas and the proportion of international telephone calls— growth rates levelled out slightly in the early 1980s, the latter part of the 1980s brought about a sharp increase in transborder transactions in many areas, such as trade, foreign investment and other capital flows, communications, and culture. This period can be seen as marked by a surge in the interconnectedness of societies that made the term globalization fashionable. In most areas, the level of interconnectedness from that time on clearly surpassed the levels of 1914. Veritable denationalization thrusts, however, occurred in a number of very specific issue areas only in the 1990s. They most often took the form of common production of goods and bads. The most notable developments took place in relation to global financial markets, global environmental dangers, the Internet, migration, and organized crime. In these areas, the notion of interdependence becomes meaningless, since the line between the domestic and the international is erased. It is not the exchange of goods and bads across borders, it is the common production in a common space that is at issue in those cases.[17]

In sum, we believe that our concept of denationalization avoids the shortcomings of the globalization literature by providing a clear-cut variable that can be used for proper empirical research and that grasps the central elements of the process without conveying any problematic meaning. It is sufficiently precise to enable the use of intersubjective measures geared towards assessing the magnitude and scope of the phenomenon. And it does not convey false messages of a borderless world without any role for territory. By employing the distinction between societal and political denationalization, moreover, the concept allows to avoid both structural shortcuts and methodological nationalism. Societal denationalization points to the weakening of the links between "nation states and [their] corresponding national societies" (Beck 1997, 44), as well as to the "deborderisation of national societies and the nation state" (Kaufmann 1997, 119), thus calling methodological nationalism into question. Basically, societal denationalization is conceived here as a challenge which awaits a response by political agents. In this sense, it triggers political processes, but does not determine their outcomes.

AVOIDING METHODOLOGICAL NATIONALISM: SOCIETAL RESPONSES TO DENATIONALIZATION

The transition from interdependence to globalization research is not only the result of different levels of interconnectedness between societies, it also indicates a significant extension of the issues that are affected. While interdependence between territorially defined states mainly involves issues of interface management, or border issues, globalization and societal denationalization raises "behind the border issues."[18] If policies formerly made by national institutions are now made on the international level, it is reasonable to expect substantial changes in the pattern of politics. In other words, globalization research expands the themes of interdependence research, in particular by focussing on changes within and across nation states and on the reconfiguration of societies. Globalization research raises thus the issue of governance beyond the nation state (Haas 1964; Zürn 1998).[19]

This reconfiguration of the political from national into what may be termed multilevel network governance cannot be studied within a framework that is subject to methodological nationalism. An analysis of the politics of denationalization must not conceptually preclude either governance by government as we know it from the modern nation-state, nor multilevel network governance. What is required is an approach that brings into play the concepts of both comparative politics and international relations.

We see our focus on interest group responses to societal denationalization as a contribution that overcomes the shackles of nationalism and thus as a contribution to the study of politics in the age of globalization. Whatever politics in this new age will look like, it will still be a matter of translating divergent interests into effective policy choices and assuring compliance with the law (see Kohler-Koch 1999, 14). Our focus on the organisation of societal interests is based on the assumption that states are not completely autonomous from societies. If there is a fundamental change in both political processes and the concept of statehood, then it should be reflected in the responses of those active within society. By focusing exclusively on "state strategies"[20] one runs the risk of overlooking one of the most important aspects of denationalized governance challenges, namely, a growing disregard of the state as the locus of problem solving and an extension of the political in both spatial and organisational respects. The dependent variable of our study takes these considerations seriously. Among other things we want to find out the conditions under which domestic actors are willing to substitute international for domestic institutions as well as which domestic actors are better at making use of the new politics (see also Martin and Simmons 1998, 747).[21] We therefore compare the policy preferences and lobbying activities of national pressure groups when faced with governance challenges caused by denationalization. In our view, there are at least three reasons why such a focus promises to be useful.

First, the responses of political groups seem to be a much more appropriate means of understanding the consequences of globalization than the convergence or nonconvergence of national policies. If denationalization is taken as a process of melting units, then there is little reason to assume that so-called competitive states will necessarily engage in a race to the bottom as if they were unitary and independent units in a perfect market. Instead it is necessary to look at the responses of political groups first, rather than focussing directly on political outcomes. We need to study the politics of denationalization before we can explain the policies of denationalization.[22]

Second, examining transnational civil society also requires one to look at those politically sensitive groups that are already formed at the national level. Studies that already transcend methodological nationalism by analysing new transnational entities such as multinational corporations (MNCs) and nongovernmental organizations (NGOs) are one-sided in another sense. As fascinating as the rise of these new transnational organisations may be,[23] these studies seem to presume that MNCs and NGOs are the only way of organising social interests beyond the nation state. They do not take into account the internationalization of those pressure and interest groups that have been nationally constituted and entrenched within the modern state. To a large extent, interest groups dominate national decision-making, providing an indispensable source of policy alternatives, and shaping outcomes in their reactions to the proposals of other groups. Perhaps it is not surprising, therefore, that the twentieth century has been called the century of interest groups. Postnational politics cannot be adequately comprehended by the formula intergovernmental politics plus NGOs; rather, it is to be seen as an interplay between governments, other internationally active organisations such as NGO's and MNC's and internationalized national groups.

Third, the democratic legitimation of international policy choices cannot occur from within a framework of intergovernmental negotiation only. Societal interests need to be channelled into decision-making bodies via means other than territorial representation through national governments. The democratization of international institutions thus also requires a functional organisation of interests beyond the nation state.

For these reasons, pressure group responses, as a dependent variable, promise to offer an important contribution to the study of the political consequences of societal denationalization. It is an approach which enables a deeper understanding of both national and transnational strategies in the face of denationalization challenges.

In order to ensure a comprehensive analysis of this dependent variable, the term "political response" is conceptualized here as being made up of three different dimensions. These dimensions may be labelled spatiality, intervention, and activity. The first two look at the regulatory demands of the relevant groups; the last one takes into account how these demands are articulated. Although each of these dimensions is explained in more detail in chapter 2 of this volume, it is worthwhile to provide a brief outline of them here:

- The first dimension, spatiality, looks at the spatial scope of each group's recommended policy solution to the particular problem confronting it. Spatiality in this context refers to such issues as the geographic coverage of the groups' preferred regulatory approach as well as the strength and powers of any envisioned international institutions vis-à-vis national sovereignty.
- Intervention looks at the question of regulatory intensity (i.e., the degree to which the demands of each group permit of intervention in the free flow of transactions) as well as the mode of governance (what steering mechanisms the groups think should be brought to bear).
- Activity as the third dimension looks at the way in which the groups tried to further their political demands: when did they respond to the challenge? How intensive was their reaction? Did they act at the national level only, or also at the international level?

It is necessary to take all of these three dimensions into account in order to overcome methodological nationalism. Looking at the content of group demands (intervention) is necessary in order to understand what kind of policy instruments and tools are perceived as being available to deal with the relevant denationalization challenge; looking at spatiality and activity is required to allow for the possibility of political denationalization.

AVOIDING STRUCTURAL SHORTCUTS: CONCEPTUAL FRAMEWORK AND CASES

Having moved beyond methodological nationalism, we need a conceptual framework that allows the avoidance of structural shortcuts. For this purpose, we look at the most prominent denationalization challenges and the responses of those nonstate actors that are most representative for the national constellation. In this way, we conceive of societal denationalization as a structural challenge to which political actors, old and new, respond. The determinants of these political responses then explain the outcome.

The study of the political consequences of globalization is part of what one may call research into the "future consequences of ongoing transformations" (FCoT), which needs to be distinguished from standard research (StR) (see Walter and Zürn 2003). The label FCoT already describes two of its critical features:[24] First, the dependent variable lies in the future and thus cannot be directly observed empirically. Second, the causal agent under consideration (i.e., the independent variable) lies in the immediate past (carrying on into the present) and is assumed to have transformative potential. This second feature creates two problems. First the independent variable is relatively new and it is therefore rather likely that our theoretical understanding of it is limited. The result of this is that difficulties may be encountered in its correct observation or measurement. Second the independent variable is assumed to have significant and far-reaching consequences; in this case, the potential to transform the international system as a whole. The difficulties of FCoT are thus even more pronounced than those of simple prediction, since established theory may be useless in the new context. It is helpful to recall Gilpin's (1981) differentiation between change within a system and system changing transformations; whereas the former leaves the system intact, the latter fundamentally alters the rules of the game. FCoT-based research deals with the latter type of change, challenging the applicability of established theories and our ability to correctly interpret events as they occur. Most research on the consequences of globalization has to take into account of these features: globalization is an ongoing process, with the potential to fundamentally affect political systems, and where the repercussions of major shifts in those systems will only become apparent in the future.

One strategy for coping with the methodological difficulties of FCoT in the present context is to compare a stylized version of traditional politics (viz. politics in the national constellation) with the politics triggered by extreme denationalization challenges (viz the politics of denationalization), and then seeing to what extent the latter differs from the former. This is the strategy adopted here. We deal with the first difficulty of FCoT, that is, the fact that changes in the dependent variable lie in the future, by focusing on current political processes rather than future outcomes. Furthermore, we investigate political groups that are traditionally active within the national political sphere, thus introducing a clear benchmark against which the influence of the global nature of the problem can be contrasted. These design features make our dependent variable much more sensitive to change. The second difficulty of FCoT, (that is, the first problem relating to the second feature of

FCot as explained above) that observation and measurement is of a causal agent that is just unfolding, is addressed by choosing extreme examples of denationalization as case studies.[25] The third difficulty of FCoT (that is, the second problem relating to the second feature of FCoT as explained above), concerning the absence of sufficiently tested theories, is met by the hypothesis-generating thrust of our study that draws from both Comparative Politics and international relations, and uses an abductionist logic. It is with these methodological considerations in mind that the selection of cases and response units has been carried out.

Governance Challenges as Cases

Climate warming, the Internet, and migration have been chosen as extreme examples of denationalization dominant in the 1990s. The selection of these three denationalization fields emphasises that societal denationalization is much more than an economic phenomenon. It covers a broad range of different transaction fields. The selection of these cases is an endeavour to counter the economic bias of most globalization literature. For this reason, we therefore focus on positive regulations beyond the nation-state, that is, regulations which correct market outcomes on a level beyond the nation-state. Negative, that is, market-making regulations, by contrast, have a deregulating effect on national policies. Whereas negative international regulations contain an agreement, which states refrain from certain activities, positive international regulations oblige states to actively undertake certain activities and intervene in line with a coordinated strategy.[26] All the six case studies carried out in these fields focus on regulative policies, with the Migration Cases and Resource Transfers in Climate Policy having, in addition, redistributive components.

Extreme fields of societal denationalization challenge the capacity of the nation-state to unilaterally achieve its procedural and material governance targets. This is because effective governance depends on the spatial congruence of political regulation and socially integrated areas of activity. Spatial congruence, as a precondition of effective governance, has been emphasised in a number of theories that rush to account for the interrelation between state-building and nation-building (see, above all, Breuilly 1994; Rokkan and Urwin 1983).

The extension of economic and cultural spaces beyond traditional political boundaries, therefore, leads to both a decline in political control and to a reconfiguration of political resources. Thus, in times of increasing transnational societal interconnectedness, national governments are no longer in a position to implement their policies smoothly (Reinicke 1998, 65). As a result, societal denationalization often leads to situations in which traditional national regulations are no longer effective. We talk of a governance challenge if those prominent in the political sphere appreciate this ineffectiveness of a policy and attribute it to societal denationalization. The character of a governance challenge can vary. It is possible to distinguish three causal mechanisms through which spatial incongruence can lead to a governance challenge.[27]

1) As national borders no longer encompass sufficient territory to function as self-contained markets for large companies, all protectionist national legislation cuts against the realities of economic movement. Any national measure that is not consistent with international standards separates markets and creates a barrier for the efficient development, purchase and sale of goods and services. As the barriers between different markets dissolve, R & D costs rise and product cycles grow shorter. Larger markets and unhindered cooperation with other enterprises become essential if competitiveness is to be maintained. In other words, in a denationalized world the "static efficiency costs of closure" increase (Frieden and Rogowski 1996, 35). If, due to tariffs, imports are more expensive in one country than in another because of the second country's more liberal trade policy, manufacturers in the first country, who need to import parts from foreign countries will be at a significant (comparative) disadvantage and will thus press for liberalization. This kind of pressure, where what is sought is nondiscrimination in global markets, is due to what may be called efficiency problems.

2) Governmental regulation has little impact if it covers only a part of the relevant social space. Thus, for example, national action by Australia alone would do little to prevent rising cancer rates due to the depletion of atmospheric ozone. Along the same lines, authorities in Germany, where restrictions on the distribution of racist propaganda are more severe than in many other countries, cannot prohibit the setting up of an Internet site in the United States containing racist material, nor prevent someone in Germany from accessing that site. One may label these kinds of challenge to the effectiveness of national policies externality problems.

3) Policies that may work well at the national level may become too costly if those who are affected operate within a wider social space than that encompassed by the policies. For instance, and in particular, policies that increase the cost of production may turn out to be self-defeating, if the competitiveness of those it affects is compromised, thereby affecting the economy as a whole. Accordingly, manufacturers' associations throughout the indus-

trialized world complain at every opportunity that the social and environmental costs of production are too high. In their view, it is essential to cut wages and corporate taxes, restrict social welfare policies, and remove the blocks put in place by environmental policies. The backlash against this, from the other side of the political spectrum, is the widespread fear of a downward spiral in national social and environmental standards. This challenge derives from what we term competitiveness problems.

Each of the three denationalization fields chosen for this study—the Internet, climate, and migration—is responsible for governance challenges through a variety of these three causal mechanisms. For each denationalization field we have chosen to present two such challenges.

Responses of Nationally Constituted Interest Groups in the OECD World as Units of Analysis

For each of the resulting six cases we look at the responses of nationally constituted interest groups in different OECD countries. Our focus is on the richest and largest liberal democracies in the Western World. These "G5 countries" (United States, Canada, Great Britain, France, and Germany)[28] are those in which the national constellation has been most clearly developed. They can be characterized by a highly developed political arena and strong government, as well as a competent and independent executive. In short, these countries are recognised for their effective governance. We do acknowledge, however, that by focusing on these countries, our ability to generalize from the findings of the study is limited. We do not claim that our results apply directly to political responses to governance challenges in other countries like India or Tanzania.[29] On the other hand, we work on the premise that if societal denationalization affects the politics of the G5 countries, such denationalization challenges should be even more consequential for politics in smaller and less developed countries. For the purposes of this volume, nationally constituted interest groups, the subjects of the study, are defined as organizations, set up to influence public policy, that have some autonomy from the government and the major political parties.[30] Although group selection in general will be discussed in more detail in chapter 2, a few words on the subject are apposite here.

The political systems of the G5 countries have a long history of institutionalized societal division, shaped by a series of historical conflicts over state building, religion, and class that took place between the Protestant Reformation and the industrial revolution. According to Seymour Martin Lipset and Stein Rokkan (1967), these conflicts created distinct and highly durable political identities, social institutions, and patterns of social contestation. Of these three major conflict lines, class differences produced the most stable cleavage with little variance between countries. Thus, as Kitschelt et al. comments: the "chief cleavage in most Western societies was between workers and employers, and this was reflected in the arrangement of major parties along a left-right spectrum" (1999a, 2). The older divisions, reflecting attitudes towards state building and religion, are today somewhat less important, producing more institutional variation between countries (see Flora 2000, 59–71). In the last few decades, however, a new cleavage has arisen, brought about by several challenges particular to the postindustrial age. This cleavage is particularly relevant for these most developed countries that are the focus of our study and sets apart traditionalists from libertarians (Inglehart 1990; Kitschelt 1994). It has resulted in essential and indelible associations with particular issues and policies that show remarkable similarity across countries (Klingemann, Hofferbut, and Budge 1994, 24). This cleavage is becoming particularly important in the context of European integration (Marks and Wilson 2000, Marks, Ray and Wilson 2002) and is expected to be especially relevant with respect to denationalized issues (Kriesi 2001, 17). The organisational representatives of these new social movements, dividing on issues such as ecology, peace, racial tolerance, and woman rights are, on the one side of the spectrum, the Green parties, and on the other, the radical right (Kriesi 1999).

Selection from the endless number of interest groups in the G5 countries is thus based on the notion that modern societies are characterized by two main cleavages, the industrial (representing old politics) and the postmaterialist (representing new politics). Political groups were selected to represent both sides of both cleavages. Organized groups from old politics are divided along the lines of capital and labour with employers' associations and industrial organizations as against trade unions as the corresponding political groups. The postmaterial, or postindustrial cleavage (new politics) is represented by new social movements with a focus on civil and social rights as against those with a rather authoritarian focus on law and order, limits to immigration, etcetera. In addition, we distinguish between umbrella groups and issue-specific groups in order to obtain a comprehensive account of the parallelogram of power operating within the relevant spectrum. The criterion for selection of the issue-specific groups is whether the particular group is specifically affected (negatively or positively) by the denationalization challenge under scrutiny.

In sum, we sought interest groups historically entrenched within the national political system. Our aim was to focus on hard cases, for if the politics engaged in by these groups in the face of denationalization proved different from the more familiar politics associated with the national constellation, our hypothesis that the politics of denationalization is unique would be all the more appreciable. By looking at a good number of carefully selected interest groups in each of the studied cases, moreover, we enable the generation of a sufficient number of units of analysis, allowing both a qualitative and quantitative investigation to take place.

The Cases

Illegal Content and Cryptography on the Internet

When American researchers under the auspices of the Department of Defence's (DOD) Advanced Research Projects Agency (ARPA) started in the late 1960s to develop a communication network that would allow the shared use of computing resources, they certainly did not anticipate that one day millions of people all over the world would communicate via the very same technology. They certainly didn't anticipate that this network would grow to challenge the very national security they were trying to protect. Yet, this is precisely what has happened. Communications technology today connects an estimated seventy-two million computer hosts worldwide, translating, at the time of writing, into an estimated 260,000,000 users worldwide— and figures continue to rise exponentially. The so-called distributive design of the Internet, the very design that makes it so robust, also makes it extremely difficult to control. There is no central server that can be monitored. Data packets originating from the same transmission simultaneously flow over the various nodes spread all over the world, meaning that a message is never in its whole form once it is in transmission. The result of this is to render national rules and regulations over communication almost entirely ineffective. It is extremely difficult to track down the sender or recipient of a transmission, and even if either could be identified it wouldn't be clear which legal jurisdiction applies to the transmission. In fact, given the structure of today's Internet the very notion of territorial jurisdiction is virtually meaningless. Ultimately, on the Internet, almost anyone can communicate almost anything to almost anyone else. This, of course, implies a significant challenge to all policies attempting to control communication content.

There are numerous laws restricting communication content, many of which emanate from guarantees of other rights. The case studies presented in this context focus on two aspects of Internet content regulation. The first study, on illegal content, deals with more direct prohibitions on communication content, such as, for example, the ban on (child) pornography and certain forms of radical political propaganda. The second study deals with cryptography and legislation that allows the state to legally infringe, for the purpose of law enforcement or criminal prosecution, the otherwise guaranteed privacy of post and telecommunications. The Internet serves as a perfect pathway for the distribution of strong cryptographic algorithms and software that makes it almost impossible for the state to exercise these interception rights.

Migration and the Nation State

Migration can be defined as the transfer of a person from the jurisdiction of one sovereign to another, be that temporarily or permanently. In contrast to the Internet, it represents a rather old problem. However, the presence of borders and territorial states distinguishes modern migration flows from the migration of peoples in pre-historic times. Today, migration flows are characterized by the fact that migration has become a global process. An increasing number of countries today take in migrants from an increasing number of sending countries. Recent immigration history of Germany and the United States bears testimony to this statement. Both countries, since the mid-1980s, have experienced impressive immigration flows in comparison with other countries in their respective regions, and in both countries debate on immigration has been prominent in the political arena.

An important distinction exists between politically induced (and therefore involuntary) migration and economically induced (voluntary) migration. The first category comprises those who escape from violence. The second category comprises those who want to change individual or familial circumstances by migrating to another country, which offers more opportunities. The responses of states vary between these two types of migration processes. The first case study, therefore, deals with voluntary migration, and in particular, a new form of labour migration characterized by the fact that such migrants—in contrast to guest worker migration (in Europe) or legal temporary labour migration (in the USA)—are not given basic social citizenship rights because their stay is assumed to be temporary (Germany), or because they are illegal (United States). The second case study deals with involuntary migration, and more specifically the increase in asylum applications correlating to the surge in refugees worldwide and the resulting discussion on the future of political asylum after the end of the Cold War. Both migration processes constitute external challenges to the nation state, and question the role of borders.

CO_2 Targets and Resource Transfers in Climate Politics

The two case studies presented in this section of the book investigate the challenges to the nation state brought about by anthropogenic climate change. Since climate change is global in its causes and consequences, no single country is capable of dealing effectively with the problem on its own. The first case study examines the specific challenges involved in implementing an effective regime of carbon dioxide (CO_2) emissions control by industrialized countries—at present one of the main causes of climate change. Climate change mitigation strategies involve considerable cost and therefore, if there are some countries that undertake such strategies, while others do not, the former countries are likely to suffer in terms of international competitiveness. As a result, one of the issues confronting the international community, and in particular, industrialized countries, is binding international CO_2 emissions targets and timetables, including efficient measures for their national implementation. The second case study deals with the further industrialization of developing and newly industrialized countries. While per capita emissions in developed countries are likely to stabilize (at well above the world average), emissions levels in developing countries continue to increase and are expected to represent some fifty per cent of the global total before the year 2025. If these countries continue to develop in the future as they have up until now, their growing CO_2 emissions will more than offset the reductions achieved by industrialized countries and consequently further advance climate change. Therefore, one of the issues discussed, is how international financial and technological transfers help developing and threshold countries move towards sustainable development.

HYPOTHESES AND FINDINGS

Although the general thrust of this study is the generation of hypotheses, it is of course not completely inductive. The generation of hypotheses has been informed by a number of theoretical approaches which are set out in detail in (see also chapter 2). These hypotheses are separated into two clusters. The first type relates to the process of transformation from the national to the postnational constellation. Because what is in question is the difference (or similarity) between the politics of denationalization and politics as usual, it is first necessary to elaborate what we regard as the features of politics in the national constellation. The second type of hypotheses is of an explanatory character. Because our purpose is to understand why national interest groups respond to denationalization challenges the way they do, we look at possible explanations and hypotheses that have been developed in other contexts and adapt them to our field. These explanatory hypotheses derive primarily from either the study of interest groups within the national constellation (Comparative Politics) or the study of intergovernmental institutions (International Relations). If it is true that these two fields merge in the context of multi-level network governance, they still provide guidance in terms of theoretical concepts and working hypotheses.

The Politics of Denationalization

In order to understand the evolving specificities of the politics of denationalization, it is necessary to delineate a clear-cut null hypothesis, that is, an ideal type of interest group politics as it operates in the national constellation. This null hypothesis is that all interest groups' demands and activities in the national constellation are characterized by three features, each of which relates to the three dimensions of group responses we used, that is, spatiality (i.e., group demands with regard to the appropriate level of governance), intervention (i.e., group demands relating to market regulation), and activity (i.e., patterns of group activities)?

(1) *Spatiality:* Nationally constituted interest groups share a vision of governance that holds the nation state as the principal locus of governance. That is to say, the goods of governance—be it security, identity, democratic participation or social welfare—are considered to be the responsibility of national governments to deliver. It is national policies that are the focus of all politics.

(2) *Activity:* Nationally constituted interest groups share an unconditional orientation towards national policy-making forums, even if the problems at hand are of an international character. If it becomes apparent that specific problems cannot be solved by national action alone, interest groups within the national constellation request representation by their national governments in intergovernmental negotiations. The national government is thus the exclusive target of all lobbying.

(3) *Intervention:* The issue of intervention most strongly reflects the class conflict and thus reveals a binary opposition between groups over issues concerning market intervention. In general, Leftist groups demand strong state intervention into market processes with clear-cut, hierarchical provisions. By contrast, groups located on the Right consider state intervention generally as inefficient and agree to policy measures only if they are strictly in conformity with market conditions, or if they are intended to prevent social deviance.

In short, politics within the national constellation is characterized by a vision of governance by government, unconditional orientation towards national policy forums, and binary cleavages with regard to the intervention into free market exchanges and the available policy tools. These features mark what we call politics as usual.

The politics of denationalization as a phenomenon, exists to the extent that a systematic deviation from politics as usual can be observed. Where there is a deviation, we expect the actions of interest groups to approximate that of postnational politics, or as we labelled it, multilevel network governance. One might say, therefore, that the politics of denationalization represents a significant transformation in politics to the extent that the notion of governance beyond the nation state achieves predominance, or, in other words:

- nationally constituted interest groups call for the strengthening of political institutions beyond the nation state;
- nationally constituted interest groups act in different forums on different levels;
- binary opposition concerning market intervention dissipates.

These features of the politics of denationalization go along with the features of the post national polity.

Explaining Societal Responses

More than just investigating whether there is a difference between politics in the national and politics in the postnational constellation, we are also interested in why this might be so, in other words, why groups respond the way they do. Thus, we link the politics of denationalization to explanatory theories common to political science. In this context, our aim is to translate these general theoretical approaches into practical hypotheses that can be applied to the study of interest groups and their reactions to denationalization challenges. These hypotheses will not be tested in the strict sense of the term. Rather, we follow an abductionist logic, which emphasizes the dialogue between theory and data. In an abductionist logic the meaning of a given data is explored with the help of different theories and then extended to a generalization, which in turn can be tested again.[31] The theories serve to structure our inductive reasoning and thus contribute to the hypotheses-generating thrust of our study. These explanatory factors fall into three categories: problem structure and structural strains, institutions, and political opportunity structures and group specific properties and resource mobilization issues.

Problem Structure and Structural Strains[32]
Intensified societal denationalization can manifest itself in a number of different ways. Exchange between partners in different countries, for instance through international trade in finished products, is one example of denationalization. Yet, some goods are no longer produced in one country and then traded on the international market. They are manufactured in transnational chains and produced in transboundary production processes. Most cars, for example, no matter where the car is assembled, are made up of parts roughly fifty per cent of which are manufactured in other countries. There is thus a distinction that can be drawn between transborder exchange and transborder production. This distinction can be applied to other issue areas as well. For example, ozone depletion could be characterized as a commonly produced form of environmental damage while the pollution of a river upstream from represents an example of transboundary pollution exchange (see Beisheim et al. 1999). A further distinction is that between externality, efficiency, and competitiveness challenges. That externality challenges occur when national regulations are ineffective because the relevant problem is produced within a social space which is more extensive than the space covered by any one nation state. Efficiency challenges occur when national regulations imply trade barriers, while competitiveness challenges occur when desired policies

are renounced because they endanger capital investments. Finally, one may distinguish between problems that are truly global in scope such as climate warming, and those that are more of regional character such as acid rain in Europe.

The strength of denationalization challenge, consisting of the dimensions created by these distinctions, can be expected to influence the political responses of groups. The more the challenge is truly global (as opposed to merely regional) and externality (as opposed to efficiency or competitiveness) oriented, and an instance of transborder production (as opposed to transborder exchange), the greater the deviation from politics as usual is expected to be. In an extremely strong case of denationalization challenge, social actors should be especially aware that traditional, in other words, national responses may not work. This awareness leads to an increased willingness to probe new ways of political organisation. The politics of denationalization can thus be expected to differ from national politics to the extent that it represents a strong denationalization challenge.

Institutions and Political Opportunity Structures
The response of a particular interest group depends also on that group's institutional environment. One important aspect of the institutional environment is the national political system in which the group acts. That is to say, the politics of a given national political system produces certain features within, and socializes distinct types of, interest groups. This distinct national style of interest mediation may also be reflected in interest groups' responses. Similarly, different national political systems create different political opportunity structures that also affect how interest groups respond to any particular situation (e.g., Kitschelt 1986; Kriesi 1991). One way to categorise different states is according to the way in which state agencies and interest groups interact and how state-society relations are structured (Katzenstein 1978; Krasner 1978; Müller and Risse-Kappen 1990). On the one hand, there are pluralist political systems such as the United States or Great Britain with fragmented policy networks frequently accompanied by a decentralized organization of societal interests and a relatively weak national bureaucracy. On the other hand, there are corporatist political systems with a medium degree of state strength and with a relatively high degree of centralization in the organization of societal interests. In these settings, typical for Austria, Germany, and to some extent also Canada, the state is constantly negotiating with a limited number of general associations which enjoy a large degree of representational power and control of membership (Schmitter 1979, 13). A final type are statist political systems such as Japan and France, with tightly integrated policy networks and more centralized, but state-influenced, forms of societal organization. A more recent, but similar typology distinguishes between business coordinated market economies (CMEs) such as Germany

and Japan and liberal market economies (LMEs) like the United States, Canada and Great Britain (see Kitschelt et al. 1999b; Hall and Soskice 2001).[33] On the basis of these distinction, we expect that statist and corporatist political systems with CMEs socialize actors such that they are very strongly tied to the national political system and thus more likely to respond to new challenges by adapting relationships within the state to these challenges (Weiss 1998, 212). By contrast, interest groups in pluralist states with LMEs act more independently of the given institutional context and are thus able to adapt more easily to the postnational constellation. The causal mechanism behind this hypothesis is easy to follow and derives directly from collective action opportunity structure theory. According to this theory, the major determinant behind interest organization is in the structures of political opportunity.[34] As long as interest groups believe that it is most promising to influence the national level in order to achieve their ends, there is little incentive to move beyond the nation state, especially since access to European and international institutions is often exceedingly complex.[35]

There are many other ways of distinguishing types of political systems in a theoretically meaningful way.[36] For our purposes, the argument put forward by Georg Sørensen (2001, 54) according to which Germany is the first and foremost postnational state is of special interest. Due to its restricted sovereignty after World War II, the subsequent role Germany played in the process of European integration and its federal constitution, it can be considered as a state that rejects traditional notions of Westphalian sovereignty and integrates itself relatively smoothly into larger multilevel governance-systems. To the extent that interest groups reflect the attitudes of their particular national political system to postnational politics, we would expect German interest groups to behave in a way which is closer to the politics of denationalization than interest groups from other countries such as the United States, Canada and Great Britain.

Another important institutional feature directly related to the logic of political opportunity structure is the maturity of the international policy cycle. An institutionalist perspective suggests a coevolution of political denationalization and the denationalization of national interest groups (see Eising 2000; Grande and Peschke 2000). In other words, political denationalization produces new channels of political representations (Della Porta, Kvesi and Rucht 1999). Even the activity of transnational NGOs seems to be dependent upon the degree to which international regulation is already institutionalized. As Thomas Risse-Kappen (1995, 30) puts it: "The more regulated the inter-state relationship by co-operative international institutions in the particular issue area, the more are transnational activities expected to flourish." (see also Nölke 2000). Thus, a mature international policy cycle indicates authority beyond the nation state, and where that authority exists an increase in interest group activity can be expected—activity which, given that countervailing interests exacerbate each other, feeds itself at a certain level (see Aspinwall and Greenwood 1998). To be more precise, it may be additionally helpful to distinguish two dimensions of the variable policy cycle: while the maturity of a policy cycle should be reflected in the intensity of the group responses, the level of the policy cycle should be reflected in the level of activity of the concerned group.

Group-Specific Properties and Resource Mobilization

Features particular to the groups themselves may also go towards explaining the response patterns that emerge. Two group-focused factors are of special importance here: available financial and informational resources and the interests as well as ideas of the interest group.

The more financial and informational resources an interest group has at its disposal, the more denationalized its response will be. This expectation can be directly derived from resource theory, which sees the scarcity of resources as a major restriction on interest group activity. The privileged access of business groups to national political systems has always, at least to some degree, been the result of superior resources (see e.g., Lindblom 1977, chap. 13). Interest groups with abundant resources are assumed to be capable of acting simultaneously on different levels. On the operational level, we would expect on the one hand that those groups defending business interests do have more resources, especially if they are general in purpose, than groups from the Left and thus are much better represented on levels beyond the nation state. On the other hand, we would expect the Old Left to be more resourceful than the New Left and thus to be better represented beyond the nation state. In sum, we would expect an even more asymmetrical representation in favour of economic interests than we are used to from politics as usual.

By contrast, we may expect that the groups on the New Left, which often pursue universal norms and thus nonmaterial interests, are especially akin to the transnational level (Gorenburg 2000). Accordingly, norms of exclusion are most often found on the side of the New Right, whereas the New Left often pursues universal norms. Some of these universal goals of the New Left such as sustainable development and a worldwide recognition of human rights almost by definition require transnational action. According to this logic, it can be expected that especially groups from the New Left demand regulations beyond the nation state and also often act on those levels.

A further hypothesis is that the more an interest group's interests and ideas point towards deregulation, the more denationalized its response will be. In general, it can be said that international institutions work in favour of deregulation, since, for structural and institutional reasons, it is easier to develop market-making rather than market-correcting regulatory structures on the international level. According to this view:

political measures aimed at changing or correcting market outcomes can only be implemented within the boundaries of the
nation state. Economic globalization undermines the conditions of
such intervention and allows only de-politicised, privatised and
market-induced forms of economic order.[37]

This supposition rests on an assumption as to class relations according to
which the nation state provides a unique institutional setting for the balanc-
ing of economic interests. This setting depends on strong labor unions,
national solidarity and majoritarian decision making, all of which are nonex-
istent at a level beyond national societies.[38] We can thus expect business
groups and libertarian interests to employ the transnational level for their
purposes, while unions and authoritarian groups remain focussed on the
national level.[39]

Interests not only structure the cleavage between left and right.
Sectorally, defined interests are strongly influenced by societal denationalization as well. Given that mobility can be seen as the factor most relevant for
stratification in a denationalized age (Baumann 1998), the difference
between market-protected sectors and sectors that are directly affected by
transnational markets becomes more important (see Iverson 1999; Schwartz
2001). The sectors that are directly affected by transnational markets aim at
putting the market-protected sectors under the pressures of market discipline
as well in order to reduce production costs. Subsequently, sectorally defined
conflicts gain in importance (Frieden 1991).

Findings

The major result of our study is that the politics of denationalization is
indeed special and potentially transformative. The null hypothesis, according
to which the politics of denationalization is not that much different from
politics as usual in the national constellation, can be rejected. The politics of
denationalization is not a matter of governance by government, nor is it orientated towards national policy forums only, and it transforms the binary
cleavages related to state intervention in market processes.

One can identify three ideal types of response patterns to denationalization challenges, namely, (1) national intervention, (2) transnational deregulation, and (3) international reregulation. The first pattern is characterized by
the demand for a high degree of intervention, but with a rather narrow spatial scope, and is combined with only minimum group activity. The second
pattern is more or less the exact opposite: on this approach groups favour a
wide spatial scope, a rather low degree of intervention and show a high level
of activity. The third pattern scores high on all three dimensions, but is
somewhat less common. The dominance of these three response patterns

indicates the potential for a new cleavage structure. Instead of a more or less binary structure, positioning the Left and Right in rigid opposition to each other, our studies reveal a gradual progression towards a triangular structure. The concrete manifestations of this new cleavage structure depend on the type of denationalization challenge and produce some unexpected bedfellows.

In explanatory terms, the type of denationalization challenge determines politics much more than differences between national political systems. To put it differently, it is policies, and not the traditions and path dependencies of national political systems, which determine the politics of denationalization.[40] Whereas in the migration cases there still is to some extent a central cleavage between Left and Right in both old and new politics, in the climate cases and content control in Internet traditional cleavages are for all practical purposes entirely absent. We argue that the more denationalized an issue, the more the politics of denationalization will differ from politics in the national constellation.

Moreover, the correlation between group types and response patterns is surprisingly weak. With the exception of the business umbrella organizations and the authoritarian new politics groups, there is little correlation between group type and response pattern. The unions (the Old Left), for example, exhibit all kinds of response patterns and have so far not developed a dominant response pattern to denationalization challenges. The New Left responds quite differently as well. Sometime they coalesce with specific groups from the Old Right in favour of transnational deregulation, sometimes they join the Old Left in a quest for international reregulation. In any case, the New Left appears to be the political spearhead of politics in the postnational constellation.

Nevertheless, the state remains the most important focal point for political action. Despite widespread demand for international or transnational cooperation, the state is still central to group activity, and the interest groups which form the major representational force in the societies under investigation are still to a large extent bound to the nation-state. If these groups do go beyond the national level, moreover, this does not necessarily translate into a lessening in domestic activity. Denationalization, therefore, apparently seems to multiply the channels of influence for societal actors rather than shifting them away from the nation state. Even in the context of the most extreme cases of denationalization, the nation-state is not simply withering away. Governance beyond the nation state will not be governance without the nation-state.

Generally speaking, societal denationalization has not been adequately matched by the political institutions that confront it, effectively leaving the nation-state in its position of central importance as a forum of political struggle. This struggle, however, itself looks quite different from what we are used to. Moreover, the state plays a different role in the overall arrangements. It is only when the politics of denationalization is more closely looked at that the larger process of denationalization can be more fully appreciated.

INSTEAD OF A CONCLUSION: TOWARDS GOVERNANCE IN A POSTNATIONAL POLITY?

What implications do these findings have for a postnational political order in general? What does a study with a focus on societal responses that tries to avoid the shackles of methodological nationalism tell us about the larger picture? While this section discusses some larger developments that are not completely covered by our empirical findings, they are clearly compatible with these findings.

In general, governance refers to the development and maintenance of purposive systems of norms and rules. It consists of both the formulation of policy goals and tools by translating the variety of societal interests into coordinated choices and the management of rule compliance. Governance beyond the nation-state extends the realm of the political beyond national borders and sovereign states. The emergence of political systems beyond the nation-state, however, cannot be seen as entirely substituting the structures of national politics (see Kohler-Koch 1999, 15). Governance beyond the nation-state still lacks a central authority equipped with a legitimate monopoly on the use of force.[41] Thus, governance beyond the nation-state cannot take the form of governance by government; rather, it is required to take the forms of either (a) governance with governments, such as can be seen today in the international institutions that exist, (b) governance without governments,[42] as is found in the context of transnational institutions, or (c) supranational governance, as exemplified by the first pillar of the EU.

Our findings emphasise the relative importance of postnational governance with national governments. At the same time, transnational self-regulation and supranational institutions obviously do play a role. It is the interplay of these different forms of governance beyond the nation-state that has led to new structures of governance that are entirely different from governance in the national sphere. Whereas the European Multi-Level Governance System already indicates such a new quality (see Marks, Hooghe and Blank 1996; Jachtenfuchs and Kohler-Koch 1996), those who speak of a global polity (Ougaard and Higgott 2001) point to governance built on even more remarkable foundations: the absence of constitutional treaties, the absence of centralized decision making bodies, and the absence of a fixed territory across a number of issue areas, making this notion even more difficult to grasp with traditional concepts than the EU polity (Mayntz 2001).

What are the features of this postnational polity in descriptive terms?[43] One chief characteristic of the postnational polity is that it operates at various levels. On the basis of our study, we conclude that it is the multilevel character that makes such a postnational polity special. Within the national sphere, the locus of policy formulation (i.e., national political institutions) is identical with the dominant locus of resources. Moreover, the authority that legitimizes these national political institutions, thus giving them the capacity to act, is also bound to the national level, first internally through a national society—that is, the nation—and then externally through other nation states. Within the national sphere, therefore, purposeful policy formulation, the resources of policy implementation and the authority that legitimizes this political structure are all united at the national level. In the postnational constellation, however, these three dimensions diverge. While resources remain at the national level, policy formulation is internationalized and recognition seems to be increasingly transnationalized (see Zürn 2002a).

The formulation of policies

As the number of (denationalized) problems increases, the site of policy formulation shifts into the sphere of prerogative of international institutions. International institutions comprise norms, rules, and decision making procedures that facilitate the harmonization and coordination of policies of different states. Without international institutions, the problems of governance in a denationalised world would be almost insuperable, and in fact, the number and significance of such international institutions has grown rapidly over the past two decades. In many issue areas, the growth of international institutions—that is, political denationalization—ran more or less parallel to societal denationalization, and where this has happened, nonstate actors and national interest groups have begun to act on this level as well. The growth in the number of international regimes has thus been accompanied by an explosion in the number of transnational nongovernmental organizations that are just beginning to play a significant role in the forums created by the new institutions. At the same time, nationally constituted interest groups are beginning to be active at this level as well. Nevertheless, the state still plays a decisive role in the decision making of these international institutions. States aggregate territorial interests and defend these interests in international institutions. And so far, territorial interest aggregation seems to be on the international level still more important than functional interest aggregation through transnationally organized interest groups.

Resources

There are more reasons why the rise in international institutions does not signify the end of the nation state, and. its importance is clearly recognised by national interest groups. There are, first of all, still issue areas in which societal denationalization has had no significant influence on the effectiveness of national policies. There is, moreover, no evidence that governance targets affected by denationalization can be better reached without the nation state. The nation-state, or territorial state, is absolutely indispensable for the implementation of policies formulated at the international level. Of the utmost significance here are its resources, which it appears to guard like gold. Without the monopoly of power and the financial resources provided by tax revenue the successful implementation of international policies would be almost unthinkable. National interest groups, which to some extent compete for these resources, know this very well and therefore keep a close eye on the national political forum, even when international institutions set the framework for national policy making.

Recognition
At the same time, there seems to be evidence that the criteria for state recognition are changing. Traditionally, once the right to self-determination was acknowledged, there was no further substantial monitoring of that state by other states. This is no longer so, as Thomas M. Franck (1992, 50) points out: "We are witnessing a sea change in international law, as a result of which the legitimacy of each government someday will be measured definitively by international rules and processes." Thus, the acknowledgement of individual civil liberty rights is increasingly becoming a requirement for the international recognition of a state. And there are further examples: there is an increase in the appointment of international observers at important national elections around the globe, suggesting a that critical elections are becoming regarded as a global event (Rosenau 1997, 259). The evaluation of national economic and environmental policies by international institutions has also become standard practice. Instead of achieving international recognition once and for all, therefore, there are signs that states are becoming subject to perpetual monitoring for legitimacy. What is more, the monitoring agencies that issue the stamp of legitimacy are no longer just other states, but increasingly also nonstate, transnational, and supranational institutions. These organizations are, for instance, NGOs such as Greenpeace on environmental issues, or Amnesty International with regard to human rights affairs, private credit rating agencies such as Moody's or Standard & Poor's and supranational institutions such as the IMF, the European Court of Justice, and so on. The judgements passed by such organizations have an authority states cannot ignore. Criticism by Greenpeace or Amnesty International, for example, can lead to consumer boycotts, and by Moody's or Standard & Poor's or the IMF to an exodus of investors. These organizations, therefore, have the power to affect the behaviour of transnationally active groups on whose approval states are becoming more and more dependent. In this way, nation-states are increasingly subject to external legitimacy controls by nonstate or supranational actors. While transnational NGOs and supranational organizations are vital for these processes of transnational

legitimacy, national interest groups that move beyond the nation state contribute to this development as well.

The age of denationalization, therefore, has seen the dimensions of statehood—dimensions that were hitherto closely interwoven within the framework of the nation state—gradually drift apart. While states are able to maintain and protect their resources, the formulation of policies has shifted to the international level. Furthermore, there have been changes in the process of international recognition. The conditions for authorization can be likened to an ongoing form of testing for states instead of eternal recognition.

There are other features of the postnational polity that further distinguish it from its national forebear. First, its members are corporate entities in highly organized and specialized subsystems rather than individual citizens. In all our cases, the role of individuals is of minor relevance. Political actors beyond the nation state are corporate actors, be they states, transnational NGOs or national interest groups. In this structure, states are—as already mentioned—a territorial form of interest organization and existing side by side with functionally segmented forms of interest organizations. States are in many respects still privileged in this structure as compared to NGOs and national interest groups.[44] Second, the motivation behind participation is primarily that of problem solving rather than the political organization of a common identity. Members share the notion of upgrading mutual interest rather than pursuing the common good. Nationally constituted interest groups discuss their interests quite candidly when they move beyond the nation state. Third, because there is no central authority, the organizing principle of this polity is negotiation, a mode of decision making more conducive to unanimity than the voting and majority rule mode, thus favouring bargaining and arguing over voting as a decision making mechanism.[45] National groups therefore use other instruments on the international level than on the national level. On the national level, the influence on the electorate is decisive for the large interest groups, on the transnational level expertise and bargaining power are more important.

This admittedly sketchy notion of the postnational polity includes the concept of functional differentiation and the conceptualization of world politics as a sphere in which not all actors, and not even all states, have similar functions (see e.g., Buzan, Jones, and Little 1993).[46] This concept recognises the fact that modern politics involves various forms of association located somewhere between hierarchy and anarchy, accepting some elements of authority in world politics (Rosenau 1997; Hurd 1999). This concept conceives of world politics less as a struggle for power than as a struggle over appropriate forms of governance (Reinicke 1998; Zürn 1998). Nation states and national interest groups will play a significant role in this process. To the extent that the three described dimensions of statehood diverge, this struggle takes place in a postnational constellation, and no longer in the national or

Westphalian constellation. National pressure groups have already—at least partially—adapted to the new constellation, addressing the international level if it helps them to pursue their interests.

NOTES

1. See especially the work of Goldmann (2001), Held et al. (1999), Rosenau (1990, 1997), Scholte (2000) and Zürn (1998) for broad accounts of the impacts of globalization on world politics. Beisheim and Walter (1997) and Held and McGrew (2002) offer a good introduction and survey.

2. See Bernauer (2000) for an excellent overview of this fast-growing body of literature. The most important empirical contributions are Bowles and Wagman (1997), Garrett (1998a), Pierson (1996), Leibfried and Rieger (2003), Rodrik (1997), Scharpf (1999, chap. 2–3), Scharpf and Schmidt (2000), Stephens, Huber, and Ray (1999), Vogel (1996), Weiss (1998). See also the contributions to Busch and Plümper (1999).

3. The term was introduced by Martins (1974, 273), who defined it as the "submission to national predefinitions of social realities. . . imposing itself in practice with national community as the terminal unit and boundary condition for the demarcation of problems and phenomena for social science." Smith (1979, 191) picked up the term to grasp the assumption which "views 'societies' as 'naturally' determined by the boundaries and properties of nation-states." In this sense, nationalism encompasses both the nation and the state, emphasising their interconnectedness. A more precise, yet much more awkward term, therefore, may be "methodological nation-statism."

4. The term "post-national constellation" was coined by Habermas (1998). Like Beck's (1996a) "second modernity" or the notion of "governance beyond the nation state", it implies that an adequate understanding of politics nowadays must be based on a toolkit that is dissociated from methodological nationalism, which is not an ontological given but a historical constellation (see Zürn 2001).

5. This is Keohane's (1993, 93) definition of autonomy on the basis of Waltz's (1979, 76) definition of sovereignty.

6. This figure includes only the most important coastal provinces of China as "threshold countries", but not the whole of China. If China as a whole were included, its share in world trade would increase marginally but its population ratio would increase by 15 per cent. See Reinicke (1998, 39–51) for additional economic indicators pointing to the OECD focus of the transnational economy.

7. In the remainder of this volume we mainly use the term denationalization, making use of the distinction between societal and political denationalization. When the term denationalization is used without an adjective, it refers to societal denationalization. The term "globalization" is used only in reference to debate or discourse on the phenomenon.

8. This, of course, depends on one's concept of a world society. The definition we adopt requires more than just transactions. On the question of a world society, see Luhmann (1971), the contributions in Beck (1998), World Society Research Group (2000) and Albert and Brock (2000).

9. The definition of societal denationalization adopted here is thus somewhat more narrow than that which might be conceived of by others. In our view, broad notions including the political sphere underestimate the extent to which politics is spatially bound. Politics tends to be more particularistic than, for example, economics, since, as Michael Walzer (1983, 50) writes, "communities must have boundaries" (see also Berking 1998).

10. Although societal denationalization also has political causes and origins, there is little agreement as to what these are. While some emphasize the role of technology, others highlight the role of political decision-making (see Helleiner 1994). Societal denationalization as an unintended and unanticipated side effect of the interplay of technological development and political decision-making is certainly a theoretically attractive, but little studied hypothesis. In that sense, Rosenau's (1986) critique of the lack of knowledge relating to the driving forces behind interdependence applies also to denationalization as well. This volume, however, is not the place to go into such issues; suffice it to say that the societal conceptualization of denationalization adopted here allows for further study in this direction.

11. See Deutsch and Eckstein (1961); Rosecrance and Stein (1973); Rosecrance et al. (1977); Katzenstein (1975); Hirst and Thompson (1996); Garrett (1998a); Reinicke (1998); Beisheim et al. (1999); Held et al. (1999).

12. The objection raised now and again by economists to this measurement approach is that by observing these transactions little can be said about real interdependence or, for that matter, globalization. For instance, changes in flow values may be due to market volatility, (i.e., changes in the attractiveness of economic locations), and perfectly integrated spaces could even be characterized by lower flow values (see Garrett 1998a, chap. 3). For this reason, economists often propose the use of transaction costs and convergent prices, which they claim more closely approximate the theoretical conception of integrated spaces (Frankel 1993, Garrett 1998a). For a number of reasons, however, we hold that the measurement of transactions is more appropriate than the measurement of transaction costs. First, it is by no means certain that low transaction costs are a more reliable indicator of integrated social spaces than the intensification of transactions. A reduction in the price of international phone calls, for instance, tells us much less about transboundary communication than an actual increase in phone calls. It is not the facilitation of communication, but communication itself that constitutes the relevant social action. Second, while the argument that perfectly integrated spaces do not necessarily show evidence of increased transactions is theoretically correct, it is of little practical significance. There are in effect no perfect, totally stable markets, there are rather only approximations to such. Yet real world approximations such as national markets are indeed characterized by extremely high transaction flows. Furthermore, if transaction flows are monitored over longer periods, temporary volatilities should be negligible as random noise created by periodic political events and spasmodic competitive shifts.

Third, the measurement of transaction costs is technically problematic, especially if specific national differences are taken into consideration. As a result, when it comes to operationalization, even researchers who for theoretical reasons opt for measuring transaction costs ultimately have to resort to measuring the transactions themselves (see Milner and Keohane 1996, 4).

13. Intensified integration not only manifests itself in the intensified exchange between partners in different countries, as in the international trade of finished products. It must also be considered that some goods are today no longer produced in one country and traded on the international market, but are manufactured in so-called transnational chains, and thus produced in transboundary production processes. With the exception of Japanese cars, no matter where a car is assembled, roughly fifty percent of its parts are always manufactured in other countries. The ensuing distinction between transborder exchange and transborder production can be applied in other issue areas as well. For example, ozone depletion is more characteristically a commonly produced form of environmental damage than the transboundary exchange of pollutants, as in the case of a river polluted by an upstream user shortly before it reaches the national border. Societal denationalization can thus be encountered both in the transborder exchange and the transborder production of goods and bads.

14. According to Elmar Altvater and Birgit Mahnkopf (1996, 26), globalization is, from a Marxist point of view, "a market-dictated trend toward economic standardisation." From a liberal perspective it is examined on the basis of "flows of goods, services and capital" (Milner and Keohane 1996, 4).

15. See that is, Robertson (1992); Waters (1995); Appadurai (1996).

16. In a research project funded by the German Research Association we developed seventy-two indicators to determine the extent of denationalization in different issue areas and across different OECD countries (see Beisheim et al. 1999). For article length summaries of the conceptualization and findings see Walter et al. (1999) and Zürn (1998, chap. 2). For a similar undertaking with similar results see Held et al. (1999). See now also A.T. Kearney (2003).

17. See Kobrin (2001) highlighting a similar point for the extreme case of cyberspace. The distinction between exchanged and commonly produced goods and bads and the emphasis on the latter in the most recent denationalization thrust also takes up Scholte's (2003, 7) point that the recent changes are more than just internalization and includes elements of supraterritirality.

18. Kahler (1995) has coined this term for another, yet structurally similar development: the change of issues in the international trade regime.

19. It is important to note that this applies only to a certain segment of the world. Here, Sørensen's (2001) apt distinction between states in pre-modern, modern and post-modern contexts that coexist currently on the globe is relevant.

20. On strategies see the excellent book by Palan and Abbott (1996).

21. In this respect we also want to overcome the "statism" that seems to be inherent in much international relations theory (see the criticisms of Strange 1982 and Scholte 1993).

22. See also Aldrich et al. (1999, 4), who question the convergence hypothesis for getting the micro-linkages wrong. "There are at least three specific steps that need to be established in order to substantiate the assumed micro-linkages between globalization and/or de-industrialization, the political preferences of the electorate, and policy outputs and institutions."

23. See that is, Beisheim and Zürn (1999), Princen and Finger (1994), Risse-Kappen (1995) and Risse, Rupp, and Sikkink (1999) for discussions of the rise and importance of NGOs.

24. The third, yet for our purposes least important, feature of FCoT concerns the direction of reasoning. StR is driven by the impulse to explain a certain outcome and thus follows the logic of backward reasoning. One implication of this research practice is that very often a single outcome (dependent variable) is linked to a multiplicity of explanatory factors (i.e., independent variables). By contrast, FCoT by its very nature does not work retroactively. Its starting point cannot be the dependent variable since the dependent variable is what is revealed as a result of the investigation. Rather, FCoT has to start out by focusing on the independent variable, that is, the ongoing transformation. Therefore, in contrast to StR, FCoT will very often look at one independent variable and link it to a multiplicity of consequences (i.e., changes in a number of dependent variables), thus utilizing forward reasoning.

25. Case, as used here is a loose term meaning sets of units of analysis. Units of analysis are the phenomena "for which we report and interpret only a single measure on any pertinent variable" (Eckstein 1975, 85)

26. This distinction goes back to Tinbergen (1965) who generally distinguished between positive and negative economic integration and Pinder (1968) who applied it to European integration. By contrast, we utilize this conceptual distinction in specific connection with regulations, maintaining that integration processes or even international regimes may contain positive and negative regulations in parallel. See Corbey (1995, 263) for a recent employment of this distinction that is very similar to our use. Distinctions like the ones between market-making and market-correction (used in the field of political economy), between enabling and restricting institutions used in the general theory of institutions, and between negative and positive rights of freedom rights (used in legal theory) are closely related and only marginally diverge .

27. See Zürn (1998, 17–20). For other distinctions see Garrett (1998b), Junne (1996) and Reinicke (1998).

28. These are essentially the G7 countries minus Japan and Italy, which were excluded mainly for pragmatic reasons.

29. This possibility of variance is conceptually part of our notion of denationalization. The type and degree of denationalization varies from country to country, dependent on, amongst other things, the starting position of the country.

30. For more on this standard definition of an interest group see Wilson (1990, 18).

31. The notion of abduction goes back to Pierce (1878). For a good general discussion see also Josephson (2000) and Schneider (2003).

32. In each of the three headings, we aim at combining explanatory variables taken from the broader fields of theories of international Institutions and collective

action (see Hasenclever, Mayer, and Rittberger 1997 for a succinct survey) and social movement research (see Hellmann 1999 for a survey). For the concept of problem structure in general see Rittberger and Zürn (1990) and Underdal (2002). For a critical discussion see Young (1999, chap. 4). For the notion of structural strains see McAdam (1982), Offe (1985a), Rucht (1994).

33. There are a number of somewhat different ways of categorising the different systems of interest mediation that are typical for advanced capitalist democracies. For a useful discussion of these different typologies, see Schmidt (2000).

34. See that is, Tarrow (1995, 11) for an application of this theory to the transnational level.

35. See Grande's (1994) excellent Habilitationsschrift (Professor's Thesis) on the paradoxes of weakness, in which he argues that international institutions gain autonomy from interest groups precisely because there is no clear-cut centre of decision-making power.

36. The mode of decision-making in a political system as developed by Arend Lijphart (1984, 1999) is among the most important in Comparative Politics. It distinguishes between consensus democracies and majoritarian democracies and can be operationalised by the number of veto points that have to be passed before a decision can be taken (see Tsebelis 1995; Schmidt 2000, 352).

37. Streeck (1995a, 60), (translation: MZ). See also Scharpf (1996a) and de Swaan (1994).

38. See that is, Cerny (1996), Gill (1993), Offe (1998), Streeck (1998). See however Zürn (2002) for an argument as to why positive regulation is difficult, yet by no means impossible to achieve, beyond the nation state.

39. See also Wolfgang Streeck's (1998) argument according to which business groups can remain passive on the international level when it comes to market-correcting policies. By not moving beyond the nation state, business groups can bring their interventionist counterparts on the Left in the predicament to be without the partner that is needed to develop policies.

40. This parallels Lowi's (1972) notion of policy determines politics.

41. See Young (1978) and Rittberger (2000) for arguments as to why a world state is neither possible nor desirable.

42. The meaning of the term here differs from Rosenau's (1992, 5) "governance without government," which refers to all politics without a central authority.

43. We do not discuss normative implications of such a new constellation.

44. For the limits of NGO influence see for instance Clark, Friedman, and Hochstatler (1998).

45. Referring to the EU as an example of network governance, Eising and Kohler-Koch (1999) and Kohler-Koch (1999) speak of consociation (see Lijphart 1977), as opposed to majority rule, as its organizing principle.

46. Note that the concept of functional differentiation does not appear in analyses of intergovernmental institutions.

Chapter 2

Conceptual Considerations

Analytical Framework, Design and Methodology

Gregor Walter, Marianne Beisheim, and Sabine Dreher

Conceptually speaking, a focus on the politics of denationalization has at least two obvious implications. First of all, what is meant by politics has to be clarified and, secondly, denationalization has to be transformed into a manageable unit of analysis. As has been outlined in the introduction, we have chosen to study the politics of denationalization by concentrating on political groups' responses to governance challenges caused by denationalization. The following chapter is geared towards explaining our conceptual considerations in greater detail than was possible in the introduction, and introduces analytical framework, structure, and methodology of the case studies that form the empirical core of the book. It provides further consideration of the unit of analysis and case studies as well as of the country and group selection procedures. Having thus identified the objects under investigation the chapter introduces the dependent variable and outlines the methodology and coding procedures that provide the basic framework of the study. Finally, we outline the pool of independent variables from which our efforts at explanation are drawn.

The basic structure of the methodology of this study may be briefly summarized as follows. A consideration of the unit of analysis leads us to three pairs of case studies marked by specific governance challenges resulting from denationalization processes in the issue areas of communications, environment, and migration. Our notion of politics is operationalized in the context of the study by examining seven aspects of group reactions to these specific governance challenges in four different countries. These group reactions are linked to a pool of five main independent variables from which we draw, both in the individual case studies and the concluding chapter, in order to contribute to the generation of hypotheses concerning the politics of denationalization.

UNIT OF ANALYSIS AND CASE SELECTION:
GOVERNANCE CHALLENGES

Any research into the consequences of a process that is assumed to be as fundamental and consequential as societal denationalization has to come to terms with the fact that (a) the independent variable is still unfolding and (b) the dependent variable (i.e., the consequences) cannot be directly observed. As mentioned in the introductory chapter, this type of concern can be labelled research on the future consequences of ongoing transformation (FCoT). Our essential response to the methodological challenges of such research lies in engaging a study design with a relatively high sensitivity to change. In an effort to adopt such a design we focus on particularly pronounced examples of denationalization posing specific governance challenges. Conceptually, denationalization is thus turned from an independent variable into the unit of analysis which, together with the sensitivity of the design, enables us to pick up tendencies in the present or the immediate past that may be relevant in the future.

What then are particularly pronounced examples of denationalization? The process itself is conceptualized as the expansion of areas of dense societal transactions beyond the borders of individual nation states. While there used to be many more transactions within nation states than across borders, it is precisely this ratio that is in the process of change. Back in 1969, Karl Deutsch defined a border as "the place where there is some critical reduction in the frequency of a certain type of transaction" (Deutsch 1969, 99). In our opinion, however, it is precisely the levelling of borders as thresholds of transactions that is at the core of the process under investigation. It is in this context that we prefer to use the term denationalization instead of globalization in order to signify the extension of societal transactions beyond the national level, no matter what scope these transactions actually reach. Despite the fact that the current debate on globalization mainly revolves around economic issues, we see no reason for limiting this conceptualization to economic transactions. Rather, in our understanding, different issue areas can be identified according to different objects of transaction. From this perspective, economy is just one issue area defined by transactions involving the exchange or joint production of goods, capital, and services. Signs and symbols, on the other hand, are the object of transactions in the field of communication and culture, while the exchange of pollutants and the joint production of environmental risks constitute the issue area environment. The transboundary movement of persons can be identified as the issue area of mobility while threats can be regarded as objects exchanged or jointly produced in the field of security.

In an effort to empirically evaluate the significance of denationalization processes using a set of more than forty indicators (see Beisheim et al. 1999), we came to the conclusion that significant denationalization tendencies are indeed visible for a large variety of issues. Even if it is taken into account that transnational transactions have to be compared against domestic transactions, denationalization processes can be clearly identified. This is particularly the case in relation to transboundary exchanges in telecommunications, and also in relation to the exchange of goods and capital, international travel, and migratory flows. At the same time, a number of important developments resemble what may be termed transboundary production as opposed to transboundary exchange. Objects can not only be exchanged between different countries, it is also possible that actors in different countries jointly bring about a phenomenon that is transnational in character and only loosely connected to any given territory. The evolution of the Internet and offshore financial markets, the rise of transnational corporations, the depletion of the ozone layer, global climate change, the transnationalization of societies, and the increasing prominence of international organised crime resemble transboundary production much closer than mere exchange. All these issues show a particularly intense dynamic of denationalization. The above phenomena therefore form the pool from which our case studies are drawn. In view of the fact that the current debate is so heavily dominated by economic issues, we deliberately opted for case studies from noneconomic fields; the latter, in our view, being even more indicative of the general process than the former.

On the basis of these considerations we selected the issue areas of communications, environment, and migration as settings for the case studies. The specific case studies within these issue areas (i.e., Internet, climate change, labour migration, and political asylum) are constructed in such a manner as to highlight particularly pronounced processes of denationalization while at the same time creating variance with regard to the type of denationalization challenge. In this regard the environment case studies offer relatively clear-cut examples of externality problems while the migration cases also feature aspects of competition problems. In the Internet cases, both types of problems are present.

The levelling of borders as thresholds of transactions potentially challenges the nation state and creates problems for effective governance. One central problem is the decreasing congruence between societal and state organization. Denationalization brings about a situation in which societal links, extending beyond the state, are out of the reach of the national government. In order for such a challenge to be consequential, however, it has to be perceived as such. What we call a governance challenge, therefore, is where there is the perception that, due to denationalization processes, a state is no longer able to govern effectively. Not being able to govern effectively means that a state can no longer reach specific goals set by public policies (cf. Kohler-Koch 1993, 116). This notion rests on a definition of governance as "control of activity by some means such that a range of desired outcomes is

Table 2.1. Case studies investigating the Politics of Denationalization

Chapter No.	Issue Area	Countries	Case Study	Case Study No.
3	Communications	Germany	Illegal contents on the Internet	1
		Canada	Internet and cryptography	2
4	Migration	Germany	Immigration and labor standards	3
		United States	Political asylum after the end of the Cold War	4
5	Environment	Germany	Climate change—CO_2- reduction targets for industrial countries	5
		Great Britain	Climate change —resource–transfers to developing countries	6

attained" (Hirst and Thompson 1996, 183f). A governance challenge, therefore, is a state in which either existing regulations are perceived as being
challenged by societal denationalization processes or in which new regulations are not seen as possible options or are not being implemented. In other
words, a governance challenge reveals a discrepancy between aspiration (to
govern effectively) and outcome (governance failure) which is recognised by
political groups engaged in public debate as problematic and attributed to
processes of denationalization.

It is thus the public perception of these kinds of governance challenges
in the above-mentioned issue areas that forms the point of reference for our
case studies. This perception is operationalized in the context of our study by
way of tracing complaints made by certain political groups—for example,
during an early deliberative phase of a policy cycle—that a special process of
societal denationalization represents a constraint on effective national policy
making or implementation. Following this conceptualization, the introduction of each case study outlines whether (1) relevant political actors point out
that (2) the state is no longer able to govern effectively because of (3) specific
societal denationalization processes and (4) whether, as a result, a policy
process is initiated. Each case study, therefore, begins with a discussion of
how the particular governance challenge was actually perceived and then
briefly outlines the ensuing policy cycle. This approach—having a clearly
defined common unit of analysis—ensures a comparability of cases across
otherwise widely divergent policy fields. In an effort to increase the scope of
our investigations we study two governance challenges for each of the three
issue areas by choosing two salient issues in each respective field. The following table provides an overview of the resulting three pairs of case studies.

COUNTRY SELECTION: GERMANY, CANADA, GREAT BRITAIN, AND THE UNITED STATES

To further increase variance and in order to take institutional factors into
account each case study analyses political groups from two different countries. In our above mentioned initial analysis of denationalization (Beisheim
et al. 1999) we focused on the six Western countries of the Group of Seven:
Italy, Germany, France, Great Britain, Canada, and the United States.[1] This
selection was originally driven by the assumption that—within the OECD-
world—these states, due to their size, constitute hard cases with regard to
denationalization. It is generally assumed that smaller states *ceteris paribus*
show higher levels of cross-border transactions. Hence, if even the larger
countries of the OECD are subject to denationalization, it is possible to conclude that the OECD-world as a whole is similarly affected. In the present
study we have returned to the same pool of countries on the assumption that

these states also constitute hard cases in terms of the politics of denationalization, specifically when it comes to governance challenges. The large Western industrial countries generally serve as role models of modern statehood and are assumed both to have the most fully developed state machineries and be highly effective in the practice of governance. We maintain that if even these countries were to experience governance challenges due to denationalization, other countries can be assumed to have at least as significant problems. Following this hard case design, we tried to cover states that (a) should be less affected by denationalization than others and (b) should be able to better deal with the ensuing problems than others. If we can demonstrate the specificity of the politics of denationalization in these countries, it appears likely that such conclusions would hold for a much broader group of states and evidence significant changes in the OECD-world as a whole.

Two main considerations drive the process of further narrowing down the country selection from the six Western countries of the Group of Seven. On the one hand, one country is to be held constant across all cases in order to differentiate between case and country specific effects on group responses. On the other hand, the country selection should lead to significant variance with regard to domestic structures in order to allow for conclusions about the role of these structures for group responses. The country selection thus simultaneously paves the way for the conceptualization of cases and countries as proxies for explanatory variables for group responses.

With regard to the first consideration we decided on a special focus on Germany, which constitutes one of the two countries in each case study. As table 2.1 illustrates, issue area and country selection are partly covariant. Holding one country constant across all case studies enables us to get a better understanding of the relative impact of issue area's specific and institutional effects. This makes it possible to cover and compare group responses with regard to different governance challenges in different issues areas within one country, that is, within a single institutional setting. Germany is a particularly interesting choice for this, as it allows for conclusions about the hypothesis that Germany has characteristics of the first postnational state, which would lead us to expect that German groups should develop particularly denationalized responses regardless of the case at hand (Sørensen 2001).

Because of the second consideration, each case study adds another country to the analysis in order to allow for conclusions about the effects of different domestic structures on group responses. The results for Germany are contrasted with those for Canada, Great Britain and the United States respectively. In this manner, we seek to create variance with regard to two (covariant) features of domestic structures: the system of interest mediation and the character of strategic interactions of societal actors. With regard to the first feature, Germany can be considered as being relatively corporatist whereas (in ascending order) Canada, Great Britain, and the United States can be assumed to be relatively closer to the pole of pluralism (Schmitter 1979). In addition, Germany is also considered as being different from the other countries in that its firms rely more heavily on nonmarket relationships in their strategic interactions with other actors. This allows Germany to be categorized as a coordinated market economy, whereas all three of the Anglo-Saxon countries are commonly classified as "liberal market economies" (Hall and Soskice 2001, 17).

Issue area specific considerations are used in order to determine which dyads from the remaining pool of four are included in which pair of case studies. For the Internet case studies, Canada is the preferred choice because in this country—not least because of its proximity to the United States—the effects of cross-border communications have reached a particularly prominent place within public awareness. In a similar manner the United States has the analytical advantage of being relatively severely affected by the transborder movement of people, which makes it a meaningful choice for the two case studies on migration. By the same token all countries in the above mentioned pool could be meaningfully selected for the climate cases as these problems are truly global. Comparing Great Britain with Germany in the climate cases is mainly driven by an intention to contrast two countries with a relatively different historical record in dealing with environmental problems, especially with regard to the preferred choice of regulatory instruments.

Overall, this framework enables us to evaluate to what degree group responses are determined by the specific nature of the governance challenge as against the constitution of a country's national institutions. In that respect, our research design transcends the line between two subdisciplines of political science: While the debate on globalization is generally situated within international relations, the design takes the concerns of comparative politics into account by allowing for conclusions about the relative importance of national institutional factors.

GROUP SELECTION: A MATRIX OF POLITICAL CLEAVAGES

Nationally constituted political groups are the central research object of the case studies. The focus on the responses of political groups rather than on actual policies implies an emphasis on the political process itself, increasing the sensitivity of our design in an attempt to counter some of the specific problems of FCoT. At the same time, analysing nationally constituted groups biases our results rather against discovering the possible effects of the politics of denationalization. All groups under investigation reached prominence and political relevance significantly before a governance challenge resulted from denationalization processes. They are relatively well integrated into national policy making and have a variety of established political procedures at their disposal. If the observation of even these groups yields specific results it is likely that the deviation of the politics of denationalization from traditional patterns of decision-making is a general trend. Considering our procedure of country selection this effectively leads to a double hard case design. Within these hard cases, however, the unit of analysis and the focus on political processes ensures a relatively high sensitivity.

We use three criteria to derive a representative set of nationally constituted political groups. First of all, groups have to be formally organised for the reason that we are not interested in studying statistical groupings such as workers or women. At the same time, the organization and/or orientation of the groups has to be national in the sense that either their organizational structure or their activities go beyond the local or regional level. This assures a certain minimum of political influence and relevance. Thus, the formal criteria all groups have to fulfil is that they are (at least) nationally oriented and/or organised. Secondly, in our understanding, the organizations have to be political in the sense that they attempt to influence decision-making procedures on public policies.[2] Political parties, however, are in most cases excluded from the scope of the study as they aspire to political power, that is, to be elected to government. With this conception of political groups we rely on the characterization of interest groups by Graham K. Wilson (1990, 12) as "organisations, separate from government though often in close partnership with government, which attempt to influence public policy."

Most important, the third criterion for group selection has to assure a certain representativeness for society and its concerns at large in order to maximize the potential reach of the conclusions we offer concerning the politics of denationalization. To ensure this kind of representativeness, we use the concept of cleavage lines that are assumed to structure the political system as a whole.[3] The underlying idea here is that modern societies are characterized by two central divisions: one stemming from the industrial age (old politics) and another which may be labelled postmaterialist (new politics).[4] The latter is all the more relevant given the we have selected not only highly industrialized but also highly modernized countries. It is assumed that not only the party system but also the general system of interest mediation fundamentally reflects both lines of social conflict. Both main cleavage lines are assumed to have two sides each, that is, Left and Right in the terms of the Old Politics and emancipatory and authoritarian orientation in relation to the New Politics. For the purposes of the present study, political groups have been selected to represent the two sides of both of these interest cleavages. Organized groups from old politics are capital and labour with employers' associations, industrial organizations, and trade unions as corresponding political groups. The postmaterial, or postindustrial cleavage (new politics) is represented by new social movement organizations. On the one side of this cleavage are groups with a focus on emancipatory issues such as civil rights.

There are, however, also new social movement organizations with a rather authoritarian emphasis on law and order, national identity, limits to immigration, etcetera.[5] The initial matrix for group selection thus consists of two groups from each of the two cleavages, that is, four political groups.

In addition to these particular divisions, we also distinguish between general groups and issue-specific groups in order to obtain a comprehensive account of the political spectrum along each division. While the general groups are assumed to represent the broader concerns of their respective side of the cleavage line, the issue-specific groups cover more narrow interests. Of course, for most case studies a number of issue-specific groups are available only one of which can be selected in order to keep the number of observations manageable. The selection of such a single issue-specific group is guided by the idea that the respective group should be specifically affected (negatively or positively) by the governance challenge of the case study at hand. If such a group cannot be identified, the issue-specific group has to be otherwise salient for the respective case study.[6] While issue-specific groups generally abound it is difficult to identify general groups amongst the new social movement organizations. Most of them tend to be single-issue oriented and, because the postindustrial cleavage is relatively new, it is sometimes difficult to find new social movement organizations that are nationally oriented and/or organized. In these cases we, by way of an exception to the rule, include political parties into the selection (from both the emancipatory and authoritarian spectrum) in order to be able to cover the concerns of the new social movements while maintaining a minimum of overall political relevance of the respective groups. The introduction of the differentiation between general and issue-specific groups doubled the number of groups under investigation as this classification was applied to the initial matrix as a whole. The following table illustrates the resulting general matrix for group selection.

Table 2.2. General Matrix of Group Selection

	General Group	Issue-specific Group
Old Politics—Left	Trade union umbrella organization	Sectoral trade union
Old Politics—Right	Business umbrella organization	Sectoral business employer association
New Politics—emancipatory	Civil rights oriented party movement	Issue-specific new social movement organization
New Politics—authoritarian	Right-wing Populist Party	Issue-specific right-wing organization

This general matrix for group selection is applied to each of the case studies. For each cell a specific group is identified for both countries under investigation. Thus, within a country eight groups are analyzed, within a case study 2 x 8 = 16 groups. With some minor exceptions the same group selection is used in each issue area. Thus, the same group selection applies to the two case studies on the Internet, migration, and climate change respectively. The general groups are almost invariant in any given country no matter what issue is analysed.[7] In addition, in most cases the selection criteria applying to the issue-specific groups (see above) did not suggest the analysis of different organizations within the same issue area. While the same groups were studied in each pair of case studies, the groups' responses were investigated separately and independently from each other. Considering all six cases this yields a theoretical maximum of 6 x 16 = 96 points of observation. Due to case specific problems of group selection this number is effectively reduced to 85.[8] While this figure is still relatively high, it has to be pointed out that using this selection procedure does not lead to an investigation of all groups that were relevant in any given policy cycle. It is important to keep in mind that our goal is not to reconstruct or explain policy output or outcome in any of the case studies. Rather, we focus on an analysis of policy preferences and activities of the most important political groups in general. The policy cycles in the case studies are not more than a means to this end. The main aim is to gain a deeper understanding of the different political responses of the most important political groups to various governance challenges and to develop and explore first tentative hypotheses about these responses.

DEPENDENT VARIABLE: GROUP RESPONSES TO GOVERNANCE CHALLENGES

The key question of this volume is how political groups react to governance challenges caused by denationalization processes. The central aim of the case studies is thus to map different group responses to a particular governance challenge. This is carried out by categorizing group responses, as the dependent variable, into three dimensions that we have labelled *spatiality, intervention*, and *activity*. The first two of these three dimensions look at the policy preferences of the groups, while the last one takes into account what activities were undertaken to articulate these political demands. First, the policy preferences of the groups in response to the problem at hand are analyzed under the perspective of their spatial and interventionary implications. In other words, we ask what policy scope, in terms of space, and what form of intervention, is preferred as a means of solving the problem at hand. Spatiality in this context refers to such issues as (1) the strength and powers of any envisioned international institutions vis-à-vis national institutions or (2) the geographic range of the regulatory demands. Intervention includes (3) the preferred depth or degree of intervention as well as (4) the mode of intervention, that is, which policy instruments are favoured. In addition, activity as the third dimension looks at the way in which the groups tried to further their political demands. This implies an analysis of (5) their initial response to the challenge, as well as (6) the intensity of their activities. Furthermore, we ask whether (7), groups operate on the national level only, or whether they also undertake actions in the international arena. These seven research questions constitute the basic analytical framework that is uniformly applied across all group responses to each of the governance challenges under review.

Spatiality

One of the central questions of our inquiry is whether and why groups demand denational policies[9] as a political answer to governance challenges posed by societal denationalization processes. For example, is there a demand for the extension of the territorial reach of a certain national regulation by means of international governmental negotiations? Questions like these—concerning the adequate spatial reach of rules and regulations—are of central concern within international relations as a discipline and in the globalization literature in particular. In our inquiry, we focus on the policy preferences of political groups in the context of these institutional questions. The spatiality dimension is composed of two factors: the degree of political denationalization and the territorial scope of demands.

Degree of Political Denationalization[10]
In order to evaluate the degree to which a group is supportive of political denationalization we look at three indicators. The first indicator is the argumentation strategy of the group, that is, the line of reasoning that lies behind its policy proposals. A so-called progressive strategy refers to arguments which reject unilateral national measures as inadequate and call for regulation at the international level in its place. A special version of this is the advance strategy, that is, the group advocates unilateral national measures with the intention of strategically promoting and strengthening the case for international regulation as the ultimate goal. These two strategies evidence the highest promotion of political denationalization. Next on the scale stand proposals which push for a national strategy as a compromise but still hope for an ultimately international solution—a strategy which we label the transition strategy. Further down on the scale is a strategy which could be called the resignation strategy. This refers to the argument that national solutions have to be accepted for the reason that international regulation may not be achievable. By contrast there is what we have termed the contra strategy, which promotes the impossibility of international regulation in order to push for national or for no regulation at all. And finally, at the lowest end of the scale, is the national strategy, a line of argument which does not even consider international strategies at all.

The second indicator is the degree of supranationality evident in the groups' policy preferences. Thus, if a political group encourages international regulation, their proposals are assessed in terms of the degree of power or authority allocated to the international level. The demand for powerful supranational organisations (in the sense of an authoritative power) is placed higher on a scale of support for political denationalization than the call for international treaties or conventions which merely harmonize national regulations but which do not establish new entities at the international level.

The third indicator of support for political denationalization is the degree of sophistication of the policy proposals put forward by the groups. Elaborate, specific and decisive concepts were considered to evidence a higher degree of denationalization than broad or superficial statements. Thus, if a group simply advocates some international solution this would *ceteris paribus* be considered lower on the scale than a proposition which describes the precise conditions and components of international cooperation. In sum, a policy proposal describing an international organization that would have the power to sanction states represents a high point of support for denationalization whereas a proposition which favours national regulation only would range at the low end of the scale. The suggestion that some kind of low intensity, largely declaratory international regime of harmonization be formed covers the middle ground.

Territorial Scope of Demands

A second concern within the dimension of spatiality is the territorial scope of the policy conceived by the political group. Here we ask whether political groups prefer regulation at the global, multinational, macroregional, bilateral, or national level. United Nations institutions and regimes associated with the UN-system are termed "global," as are other institutions that are global in reach. "Multinational" refers to political entities such as the OECD or the G7/G8 and macro-regional to regional integration projects such as NAFTA and the European Union. Other preferences in favour of foreign policy options are considered bilateral. Purely national policy preferences were evaluated accordingly.

Intervention

A second cluster of research questions focuses on the nature of the political intervention envisioned by the group, if any: To what degree should intervention in the free flow of transactions be permitted? and What steering mechanisms should be brought to bear?

Depth of Intervention

The depth of intervention is conceptualized as the extensiveness of regulatory interference in the type of transactions at hand. The question here is to what degree do the various groups suggest that the freedom to act be restrained by the state or other institutions? In the case of the Internet this refers to the free flow of information, in the migration cases to the free transit of people across borders, and in the climate cases to the freedom to emit climate relevant gases. In the latter case, for example, the call for a reduction of CO_2-emissions by 20 percent are *ceteris paribus* considered to evidence a demand for increased intervention as compared to the call for a 10 percent reduction. For each case study, specific guidelines were developed in order to allow a comparison of the group responses within the case.

Mode of Intervention

In addition, the groups are assessed in terms of their preferred steering mechanisms and the chosen mode of governance. As far as the steering mechanisms are concerned, the groups' preferred policy instruments are discussed according to the kind of intervention they invoke. Rather traditional are directly pre- or proscriptive regulative orders in contrast with market-conform measures which honour specific behaviours, for example by providing monetary incentives. Still different are educational efforts in relation to an issue, for example by providing information. All three steering mechanisms, however, allow the possibility of different modes of governance. The standard example of pre- or proscriptive regulation, for example, is state law which sanctions a specific behaviour and which is enforced by the courts. The mode of governance in this case is clearly hierarchical as it involves a hierarchical relationship between the author and addressee of the regulation. However, pre- or proscriptive regulations could also be incorporated into self-regulatory schemes such as Codes of Conduct. In this case, the steering mechanism may still be termed pre- or proscriptive though the relationship between author and addressee of the regulation is nonhierarchical. There is thus a systematic difference between the vertical and authoritative rule setting as against models of horizontal self-regulation (see Mayntz and Scharpf 1995).

In a similar manner, market-conform measures can take on a hierarchical or horizontal characterization. A state tax on mineral oil and its derivatives, used to provide an incentive to lower energy consumption, is an example of a hierarchical market-conform measure. Private rating agencies, on the other hand, constitute an example of a market-based steering mechanism based on a nonhierarchical mode of governance. In this latter example, rating provides an incentive to comply with certain standards as it can be a prerequisite for particular activities. It is, however, not state-administered and involves no hierarchical relationship between the author and addressee of the standard. Informative measures can also be used hierarchically (for example where the state provides information in educational campaigns) and nonhierarchically (for example where labels are used to mark the adherence of others to specific standards). The following table summarizes the different modes of intervention.

Table 2.3. Analytical Matrix for the mode of intervention based on steering mechanism and mode of governance with examples added.

	Pre- or proscriptive	Market-conform	Informative
Hierarchical	Standard Law	Tax	Education
	6	5	4
Nonhierarchical	Code of Conduct	Rating	Labelling
	3	2	1

A six-point ordinal scale in the above table is arrived at by setting standard law as the basic form of the traditional vertical and authoritative mode and labelling as the exemplar of low-interventionist, horizontal self-regulation. Furthermore, as the mode of governance, as opposed to the type of steering mechanism, is considered to constitute the more important difference between the various forms of intervention, the order of the scale is constructed such that it runs along the rows of the table.

Activity

A third cluster of research questions examines the actual activities of the political groups surveyed. Apart from their expressed policy preferences we are also interested in what the groups actually did in order to achieve recognition in the policy-making process. On the one hand, we look at the question when and with what motivation groups first started to act on the issue, an aspect we call the mode of activity. Next, the activities of the groups are considered according to their intensity. And last but not least, we ask whether the groups responded to the relevant societal denationalization challenges by becoming active at the transnational political level.

Mode of Activity

The first question is whether the group developed any activity at all in relation to the denationalization challenge—and if so, at what time of the policy cycle and because of what incentive. Passive groups displayed no reaction to the governance challenge at all. Some groups considered themselves temporarily passive in that they were considering the issues and were planning future action but had not yet explicitly responded to the challenge. Those organizations who merely responded to the issue as part of the ongoing policy process, for example in consultations, were termed re-active. In contrast, those groups which were active even before the official policy cycle got under way we labelled active. Such groups were prominent during the agenda-setting phase of the policy cycle. These considerations lead to a four point ordinal scale ranging from passive (1) to active (4). Where possible, we also explored the groups' motivation, that is whether groups developed their preferences in response to a government initiative, that is, their activities were government-induced, or whether they were acting of their own accord, that is, they were problem-induced.

Intensity of Activity

The intensity of activity refers to the amount of action undertaken and the vigour with which the group acted. If a group is passive with regard to the mode of activity the intensity of its activity is automatically considered zero. Beyond this mode of activity, however, the intensity of activity varies greatly. Examples range from such actions as lobbying, the issue of press releases, the publication of information material, and support or initiation of academic research to the staging of demonstrations etcetera. In this context, we also analyse whether the group undertook self-regulating activities in order to deal with the governance challenge on its own initiative or authority, that is, undertook activities in which they themselves are locus and object of governance as, for example, in the case of codes of conduct or voluntary initiatives.

Political Level of Activity

The final point of analysis concerns itself with the political arena in which the groups acted. The question here is whether the group was purely or mainly active at the national level or whether it had developed some degree of transnational activity. If the group had been active transnationally, we distinguish significant from insignificant transnational activities.[12] In addition, if the groups displayed significant international activity, their initiatives are differentiated according to their territorial scope, that is, whether the groups focus on the macroregional or the international level. Thus, each group's activities are evaluated according to the following ordinal four point scale: (1) activity at a purely national level, (2) activity at a mainly national level but with some insignificant international activity, (3) significant international activity at the macroregional level, (4) significant activity at the international level.

The following table provides an overview of the analytical framework developed for the dependent variable as a whole.

METHODOLOGY AND CODING: QUALITATIVE AND QUANTITATIVE APPROACHES

The design of the study in general, and the group selection procedure in particular, allows us to examine the findings from both a quantitative and qualitative perspective. Thus, on the one hand, the case studies, and the varying reactions of the different groups to the challenges presented in those case studies, provides, in itself, a great amount of information on the issue in focus.

Table 2.4. Analytical framework of group responses

Dimension	Element	Research question
Spatiality	Degree of Political denationalization	How far does the group go with its demands for international regulation?
	Territorial Scope of Demand	On which level should the issue be regulated (national, macroregional, global, etc.)?
Intervention	Depth of Intervention	To what degree should there be intervention into the free flow of transactions?
	Steering Mechanism and Mode of Governance	How should intervention occur?
Activity	Mode of Activity	Was the group active, reactive or passive?
	Intensity of Activity	How intensively did it pressure for its demands?
	Political Level of Activity	At what level was the group active?

On the other hand, the analytical framework of the study is sufficiently uniform to allow for a comparative evaluation across cases. In addition, the relatively high number of observation points makes it possible, at least partly, to use quantitative procedures for both descriptive and inferential purposes. As a result we are able to offer both an in-depth analysis of the cases under investigation as well as comparative results generalised across cases.

Accordingly, using qualitative methods, the first step of our research involves mapping the responses of the various groups to the governance challenges posed. These responses are collected from a wide range of primary sources and analysed according to the framework introduced above. Sources include all kinds of printed material authored by the groups, such as publications, brochures, policy papers, press releases, and statements given at hearings, as well as Internet presentations. This written material is supplemented by structured interviews with representatives from each group.[13] Both the interviews and the published material are then evaluated with regard to the dependent variable, that is, the groups' responses.

In an effort to supplement these qualitative insights we code the responses of the groups along ordinal scales for each element of the dependent variable using a test procedure to increase inter-coder-reliability.[14] Two types of procedure are used. In relation to some elements of the dependent variable the use of absolute scales provides meaningful results, that is, group responses are mapped directly to the scale. The mode of intervention, mode of activity and political level of activity dimensions suggest the use of this kind of measurement. In relation to the other response dimensions, however, it is not meaningful to construct scales with application across all cases. It is, for example, almost impossible to meaningfully construct a scale for depth of intervention that would be similarly applicable for, say the Internet and the climate cases. In these cases, rather than assigning group responses to one fixed category, they are ranked. For example, rather than assigning a high depth of intervention to the response of a German group, its response is evaluated relative to the responses of all other German groups in that dimension. Note that the ranking is not only case, but also country specific since the options discussed in any given national policy cycle may differ so greatly that the problems associated with absolute coding are just as large across countries as they are across cases. Where this kind of relative coding is used the number of scale points thus varies with the number of groups that are included in the given case and country. The following table 2.5, gives an overview of the scales and codings used:[15]

Table 2.5. Scales and coding for the elements of the dependent variable

Element of the dependent variable	Scale and coding
Degree of denationalization	Ordinal scale, coding relative to other groups
Territorial scope	Ordinal scale, coding relative to other groups
Depth of intervention	Ordinal scale, coding relative to other groups
Mode of intervention	Ordinal scale from 6 (hierarchical/pre- or proscriptive) to 1 (nonhierarchical/informative), absolute coding
Mode of activity	Ordinal scale from 4 (active) to 1 (passive), absolute coding
Intensity of activity	Ordinal scale, coding relative to other groups
Political level of activity	Ordinal scale from 4 (significant international activity) to 1 (purely national activity), absolute coding

In the case studies, the results for all groups are presented according to the elements of the dependent variable. Both qualitatively acquired findings and the results of the coding procedures are supplemental building blocks for the presentation of the conclusions at the end of the case study chapters. The final chapter builds on these qualitative results from the case studies but adds a quantitative perspective based on a simplification of the coding procedures and applies it across all cases.

INDEPENDENT VARIABLES: TOWARDS HYPOTHESES ON GROUP RESPONSES

The main emphasis of our study lies on descriptively analyzing group responses to governance challenges induced by denationalization. We thereby mainly aim at answering the question whether there is a specific politics of denationalization that is different from what we are used to from the national constellation. However, the analysis of group responses also begs the question why groups respond the way they do. The following section provides an overview of the five main independent variables that are used to probe and generate a number of inferential hypotheses on the politics of denationalization. Following an abductionist logic, these independent variables form a pool on which we draw in both case studies and the final concluding chapter and these variables are linked to separate results along the three dimensions of the dependent variable as well as complete response patterns.

Essentially, these independent variables are structured by the basic features of the research design introduced above. The design allows group responses to vary along its three fundamental elements: cases, countries, and groups. Thus, group responses may vary along with the specific governance challenges, the respective institutional characteristics of the countries, or the particular attributes of the groups. As such, however, case, country and group of course have little explanatory power. Rather, these three elements are seen as representing clusters summarising a number of underlying independent variables. The following table provides an overview of the these clusters and the associated five main independent variables used:

Table 2.6. Structure of independent variables

Variation of group responses	Variable cluster	Independent variable
Case	Problem structure and structural strains	(1) Strength of denationalization challenge
Country	Institutions and political opportunity structures	(2) Type of political system: (a) Pluralist vs. corporatist (b) CME vs. LME (c) "Postnational state" (3) Policy cycle
Group	Group specific properties and resource mobilization	(4) Financial and informational resources (5) Interests and ideas

Thus, if group responses vary along the cases, an explanation may lie in the problem structure or, more specifically, in (1) the strength of the denationalization challenge at hand. Possible variance across the countries may be linked to institutions and political opportunity structures. This can be translated into a number of explanatory factors, most prominently (2) a typology of political systems, three variations of which are considered (a to c). In addition, also specific to each country is (3) the policy cycle with regard to the problem at hand that also might have an influence on group responses. Finally, responses may vary on the group level, with different kinds of groups showing different reactions. Group-based explanations comprise independent variables such as (4) financial and information resources, and (5) ideas and interests.

Strength of Denationalization Challenge

The introduction outlined a typology of denationalization challenges that consists of three basic dimensions: the structure of the underlying transactions, the type of the ensuing challenge, and its spatial scope. The underlying transactions can either resemble the transborder exchange type or they can come closer to transborder production. The ensuing challenges can represent efficiency, competition or externality problems.[16] And these problems can be merely regional or truly global in scope. Taken together, these three dimensions can be seen as forming the elements of a single variable that might have an influence on group responses on the case level. Transborder production type transactions are more difficult to subject to regulations than transborder exchange ones. Similarly externality problems are more severe than efficiency or competition problems and the same holds for global as opposed to regional problems. Thus, it is plausible to assume that for each of the dimensions the strength of the challenge increases with variance along the respective dimension. Overall, the strength of the denationalization challenge can be expected to correlate with the significance of the politics of denationalization. The stronger the challenge, the more the ensuing political process might deviate from what we are used to from the national constellation.

In principle, the cases are analytically evaluated by the investigators with regard to the overall strength of the challenge at hand according to the above conceptualization. In addition, in order to increase the reliability of this evaluation, the groups' subjective perception of the denationalization challenge is taken into account. While this perception may vary among groups, it is still possible to arrive at a reasonable aggregate evaluation of the case with the regard to the typology introduced above. This is used to supplement and correct the objective classifications.

While all of our cases represent significant governance challenges (which defined the unit of analysis), the underlying challenges in the case studies on Illegal Content (1) and on Climate Change (5 and 6) can still be considered to be somewhat stronger than the challenges of migration (3 and 4) and cryptography (2). The transactions in cases 1, 5, and 6 closely resemble the transborder production type causing mainly externality problems on a truly global scale. In the migration cases, on the other hand, the problems arise out of transborder exchange (of human beings), which is largely regional, and national regulations are discussed strongly in terms of national competitiveness. Similarly, cryptography (2), while being linked to the global Internet, is also mainly framed as an issue of competitiveness in the OECD setting (i.e., in a regional context).

Type of Political System

Pluralism vs. Corporatism. Pluralism versus corporatism refers to the specifics of the domestic system of interest mediation. In a classical formulation, pluralism refers to a mode of interest mediation in which the constituent units are organised into an unspecified number of multiple, voluntary, competitive, non-hierarchically ordered, and self-determined (as to type or scope of interest) categories that are not specifically licensed, recognised, subsidised, created, or otherwise controlled in leadership election or interest articulation by the state and that do not exercise a monopoly of representational activity within their respective categories (Schmitter 1979, 12).

By contrast, corporatism is

"a system of interest mediation in which the constituent units are organised into a limited number of singular, compulsory, non-competitive, hierarchically ordered, and functionally differentiated categories, recognised or licensed (if not created) by the state and granted a deliberate representational monopoly within their respective categories in exchange for observing certain controls on their selection of leaders and articulation of demands and support" (Schmitter 1979, 13).

Corporatist systems of interest mediation are less open to outsiders and therefore, some groups might not respond (or they might not respond intensively) since they do not belong to the relevant policy network. Those groups, however, who are inside the relevant networks should have a strong inclination towards the nation state because of their close ties to it and their incorporation into national state institutions. Demands for political solutions over and above the nation state could thus be expected to be more common in pluralist systems of interest mediation. In addition, this effect might be enhanced by the fact that in pluralist systems political organizations participate in the implementation of policies to a lesser degree. Thus, their demands can be more extreme than in corporatist systems since they do not bear the consequences. Overall, we would then expect groups from pluralist systems to be more likely than groups from corporatist systems to show denationalized political demands. In classifying the countries under investigation according to pluralism and corporatism we rely largely on the established literature in the field (Schmitter 1974, Schmitter and Lehmbruch 1979, Lehmbruch and Schmitter 1982). As has been outlined above, this results in Germany being considered closest to the pole of corporatism and the United Kingdom and the United States coming closer to the ideal type of pluralism. In this roundup, Canada can be seen as covering the middle ground.

Coordinated vs. Liberal Market Economies. While by now the debate on corporatism has spanned almost twenty years, a more recent attempt to classify different political system highlights the role of firms as central actors in capitalist democracies. The varieties of capitalism approach (Kitschelt et al. 1999b; Soskice 1999; Hall and Soskice 2001) starts from the assumption that in capitalist democracies firms have to solve a number of coordination problems in their strategic interactions with other actors such as other firms, unions, state actors, and even their own employees. The way in which these coordination problems are solved serves as the defining characteristic of the associated typology. On the one hand, there are liberal market economies (LMEs) in which firms primarily address their coordination problems via market relations, that is, price signals and marginal calculations. In coordinated market economies (CMEs), on the other hand, non-market relationships such as information networks and collaborative connections play a much more important role.

Denationalization might change markets and prices but it hardly modifies the market system as such. Hence, we would expect political groups from LMEs to find it relatively easy to adapt to the postnational constellation with their preference for market-type solutions largely intact. Groups from CMEs, on the other hand, might find it relatively difficult to adapt non-market relationships and collaborative networks to the new situation. Overall, we would then expect groups from LMEs to be more likely than others to combine demands for denationalized policies with a preference for low levels of intervention and market-type steering mechanisms. Conversely, groups from CMEs can then be expected to prefer national solutions to a greater degree.

The classifications of the countries under consideration with regard to their variant of capitalism is more or less dichotomous. Germany is considered a prime example for a CME while Canada, the United Kingdom and the United States are generally assumed to be closer to the LME type of coordination mechanism (Hall and Soskice 2001, 17).

Germany as the "First Post-National State." Holding Germany constant across all cases allows some conclusions about an additional hypothesis specific to this country. It has been argued that Germany's postwar history has shaped the country's polity, economy, and nationhood in such a way that a strong bias towards international integration has been produced. Pointing to the complex interplay between the vertical division of power and the specific characteristics of the German *Länder* (federal) system, a system that is progressively being supplemented by the additional level of the European community, Katzenstein (1987) saw Germany as semi-sovereign. If one broadens this perspective to the—more or less—external (re-)construction of German sovereignty (from the Paris Agreements in 1954 to the 1990 Two-Plus-Four Treaty), the almost excentric outward orientation of its economy and its limited sense of national identity, one might even venture to call Germany the "first post-modern state" (Sørensen 2001). An empirical emphasis on Germany makes it possible to study whether or not nationally constituted political groups, at least in Germany, are particularly prone to or well-equipped for postnational politics and whether or not this holds true across each case study.

Policy Cycle

Another institutional factor that also varies with the country at hand is the policy cycle in the respective field. As an independent variable, a policy cycle consists of two separate dimensions: maturity and level. Maturity refers to the development and stage of the policy cycle (Windhoff-Héritier 1987) whereas level simply designates the political level (national vs. international) at which political processes converge. Conceptually, even an international policy cycle does not necessarily translate into the same value of this independent variable for all participating countries, as different countries may enter into international processes at different times, to different degrees, and parallel to national activities of varying intensity.

Both dimensions might influence group reactions, most prominently in the activity dimension of their responses. For example, a policy cycle which is still in its initial stage (agenda-setting) might lead to a low participation rate of groups whereas in a completed policy cycle chances are that many more groups will respond to the denationalization challenge. Similarly, the level of the policy cycle might have an influence on the level of group activities. While groups might find it rather difficult to initiate and maintain transnational activities on their own, the opportunity structure fundamentally changes once state actors put their weight behind the institutionalization of transborder political processes. The stage and level of the respective policy cycles as well as the connection to group responses are evaluated on the basis of various primary and secondary materials on the issues of the case studies. The results are briefly summarized in the introductions of the case study chapters.

Financial and Informational Resources

Of course, group responses might vary not only according to case and country, but also among the different groups. In other words, across cases and countries, different types of groups might exhibit different forms of responses. The first variable to be considered in this context are the financial and informational resources of a group. In general, we would especially expect group activities to be heavily dependent on the resources available. The better the resources of a group the easier it becomes for this group (a) to become active at all and at an early stage, (b) to undertake a high level of activities and (c) to step into the international arena. We would thus expect the resources of a group to be causally connected to all three of the elements of the activity dimension of group responses. In general, we assume the financial and informational resources to vary with all three dimensions of the typology we use for group selection. By and large, we expect groups from the Old Politics to have more resources at their disposal than groups from the New Politics. This is mainly due to the privileged role the class cleavage is assumed to play in the institutionalization of national politics. Within the Old Politics (but not within the New Politics) we expect the groups from the Right (i.e., business groups) to have access to resources superior to those of groups from the Left. By the same token, we expect general groups from the Old Politics to have more resources at their disposal than specific ones. This holds in particular for informational resources because the general groups of the Old Politics can be considered to be central information hubs for their whole side of the cleavage. Of course, these general assumptions are supplemented with group specific information on the financial and informational resources of the respective groups.

Ideas and Interests

Ideas and interests are assumed to form the fundamental motivational background of group activities. While in International Relations ideas and interests are sometimes seen as starting points of competing causal pathways, we consider them as being closely linked but set apart by the respective level of specificity. While interests are more specific, ideas are conceived of as general frames of reference, representing fundamental assumptions about political order and the appropriate resolution of political issues. As such, ideas influence the more specific interests and interests, in turn, help to stabilize normative ideas as "principled beliefs" (Goldstein and Keohane 1993). Conceptually, we are building on a distinction between material and nonmaterial interests with the former relating to the improvement of the economic situation of the respective group and the latter representing general normative concerns.

Initially, we again assume the dimensions of our group selection procedure to be relevant for the distribution of ideas and interests. While groups of the Old Politics are assumed to be driven mainly by material interests, groups from the postmaterialist New Politics are assumed to motivated mainly by nonmaterial factors. Within the Old Politics, on the Left, material interests correspond for example to such issues as employment, wages, and social security and generally correlate with a principled belief in the benefits of market correction and state intervention. Conversely, groups from the Old Right are assumed to be mainly motivated by opportunities to decrease costs and increase returns and the general idea that markets are efficient means of allocation that work best when left alone. Within the New Politics, nonmaterial interests of the emancipatory groups translate into libertarian concerns, the promotion of human rights, or the protection of the environment. The authoritarian groups, on the other hand, are assumed to be driven by nonmaterial factors such as national identity, the principle of law and order, etcetera The distinction between general and specific groups is assumed to be largely irrelevant for the respective motivations. If empirically, however, ideas, and interests in fact vary between general and specific groups, this can be seen as supporting the hypothesis that globalization leads to an increasing prominence of conflicts between economic sectors (Frieden 1991; Frieden and Rogowski 1996).

Similar to the evaluation of financial and informational resources we supplement these initial assumptions by empirical observations on the motivational background of the groups. Most prominent in this regard are the causal statements of the groups themselves in which they justify their demands by linking them to some specific interest or an overall idea. In addition to this outside evaluation, groups themselves were asked, wherever possible, to link their demands to what they considered their fundamental interests and ideas. As a result we arrived at an overall picture of the motivational background of the groups that served as an explanatory factor for their political demands.

NOTES

1. We thus limited our studies to the Atlantic economies in order to ensure a similar cultural background.

2. See Schmidt (1995, 435f, 2000) who in this context prefers the term interest association. Abromeit (1993) provides a succinct overview of conceptual matters. For a good overview see Richardson (1993).

3. The basic idea that party systems reflect societal conflicts was first developed by Lipset and Rokkan (1967).

4. A number of authors (see e.g., Betz 1993 or Kriesi 1999) have argued that the original Lipset and Rokkan (1967) classification of lines of political division has to be supplemented by a postmaterial cleavage resulting from a new modernization wave in the seventies. In this way the thesis of value change originally developed by Inglehart (1977) is transferred into the political realm (see also Beisheim et al. 1999: 507–515).

5. For a similar classification of the new social movements see Kriesi (1999).

6. Salience was only used as a fallback option for group selection in order to counter the problem that salience as a selection criterion implies a certain bias with regard to the observation of the groups' activities. In addition, some of the applied coding procedures worked with rankings rather than with an absolute evaluation thus limiting the effect of such a possible bias.

7. The exception is Germany with its two umbrella organizations of business interests which are active vis-à-vis government and vis-à-vis the unions respectively.

8. Specifically, in some cases it proved difficult to meaningfully identify authoritarian groups within the new politics sphere.

9. This question arises out of our understanding of political denationalization, a process in which the scope of political institutions changes and the dominance of political institutions at the national level diminishes (Beisheim et al. 1999, 322).

10. The term political denationalization is not to be confounded with societal denationalization or just denationalization. Whereas the latter is the societal process that triggers the challenges investigated in the case studies, the former describes a possible political reaction to this challenge. Societal denationalization concerns trans-actions, political denationalization rules to govern them.

11. Windhoff-Héritier (1987) provides a succinct overview of policy instru-ments.

12. Individual guidelines are developed within each case study for determining what significant activity amounts to. In most cases, the participation in international conferences is a major criterion.

13. For each pair of cases about twenty 60–90 minute interviews were con-ducted (including state agencies and other organizations connected to the case).

14. All material was coded twice. The first coding was carried out by the author responsible for that particular case study. In addition a neutral coder worked across all cases to ensure unified standards. Differences were broached in discussions involving all coders.

15. For a discussion of the consequences of this coding procedure for the quan-titative analysis see the technical appendix to chapter 6.

16. This typology of problems is also used in deriving the conceptualization of our unit of analysis—the governance challenge. In order to set this usage of the typol-ogy apart from its function here (i.e., as one of the elements of an independent vari-able), we prefer the term "denationalization challenge" for the independent variable whereas "governance challenge" refers to the unit of analysis.

Chapter 3

Internet Politics

Responses to Illegal Content and Cryptography in Germany and Canada

Gregor Walter

INTRODUCTION: THE INTERNET AND ITS GOVERNANCE CHALLENGES

It is slightly ironic that it was the US Department of Defence (DoD) that fathered a structure that is today a great challenge to national law and order, even national security, not only in the United States but in all countries around the world. In 1966, the Pentagon (or rather its Advanced Research Projects Agency, ARPA) began funding a project to link the computers of some of ARPA's contractors conducting defence related studies at various academic research institutions around the country.[1] The idea was to build a network that would enable scientists to share computing resources which were scarce and expensive at the time. According to the original plan, a maximum of twelve nodes were to be connected from locations scattered around the United States.

The first node was set up in September 1969 at the University of California in Los Angeles. By the end of that year, four other computers had been connected. It is this network, originally termed the Arpanet, that eventually became what is today known as the Internet. After the establishment of Arpanet's first nodes, an ever increasing dynamic set in, triggered by government funded network projects in a number of countries, and accelerated by decreasing computer hardware prices and an increase in the public availability of network software.[2] In 1991, a further boost was provided by the development of the graphics oriented World Wide Web, which constituted a quantum leap in user friendliness.

By the end of the 1990s, the Internet had spread throughout the world, connecting in January 2001 some 110 million so-called Internet hosts[3] representing an estimated minimum of 396 million users world-wide.[4] The truly denational scope of the network, combined with its extraordinary robust communications technology, makes transmissions extremely difficult to monitor, restrict or control, resulting in the fact that criminals and terrorists communicate largely undisturbed—certainly something the DoD never intended and probably never dreamt of. From a technical perspective, this robustness—and uncontrollability—derives from three design features of the Internet, namely packet switching, dynamic routing and the Internet's distributed design. Early experiments with computer networking demonstrate that the traditional technology of circuit switching used for long-distance telephone calls, was far too unreliable and slow for the purpose of connecting computers over long distances. In the early 1960s, and independently from each other, four researchers at MIT, the Rand Corporation, and the British National Physical Laboratory (NPL)[5] developed an alternative approach called packet switching (the term was coined by Donald Davies at the NPL), which was much faster and more reliable than circuit switching. This method involves disassembling a transmission into small packets, each with a header that includes all the information necessary for routing it through the network, and for reassembling the transmission once all the packets have reached their destination. The packets travel independently through the network, enabling each one to take the path that, at that point in time, is the fastest. This is called dynamic routing. From the perspective of bandwidth, a big advantage of this approach lies in the fact that different packets can simultaneously use the same line in the network. Following a 1967 conference organised by ARPA, at which these four researchers met and agreed to collaborate, the technology was further developed and ultimately implemented as the basic networking structure of the Arpanet. A result of this structure is that while en route it is almost impossible to monitor the progress of, or identify the content of a transmission; only some packets of any one transmission pass through the same particular node and even if these few packets could be identified, the entire transmission would still be very difficult to reconstruct.

The monitoring and control of these disassembled transmissions becomes all the more problematic once the distributed design of the Internet enters the picture. In the early 1960s, Paul Baran, of the Rand Corporation, started thinking about the vulnerability of US military communications network to a Soviet nuclear attack. He arrived at the conclusion that the capability of the United States to deliver a second strike was compromised by the fact that the command and control defense structure then in use relied on a centralized communications network that left the whole structure defunct once the centre was destroyed. His solution was not only to decentralize the network but also to distribute it, that is, create a network where each node was connected to a number of other nodes thereby increasing the level of redundancy of any one connection. Such a network would have no hierarchical center whatsoever, meaning that the hypothetical destruction of a number of nodes would leave the rest of the network largely unaffected.[6] When Baran's concept surfaced in the context of ARPA's 1967 conference, it became clear that, the more the connections between Arpanet's nodes were individually dispensable, the greater the reliability of the network, giving full potential to the concept of dynamic routing: the more connections, the more pathways to the final destination, making the network as a whole both faster and more reliable. Today, the Internet is not completely distributed in the sense that all connections are equal—there are backbones or aortas of Net traffic, which carry more transmission packets than others—but the level of redundancy of any one route is still relatively high: there are many ways for data packets to reach their destinations.

This distributive design, combined with packet switching and dynamic routing technology, creates a communication structure that is almost completely immune to any form of central control. As soon as any obstruction in the network is encountered, dynamic routing ensures that packets immediately search for and take other ways to their destination. Were the Internet located in only one country, control of communications would still be difficult. Some forms of one-to-many communications (for example, public World Wide Web pages) could be monitored by requiring authors or transmission senders to adhere to certain rules, just as publishers of books, magazines, and newspapers are. At the same time, one-to-one communications (such as e-mail) would still be extremely hard to control. The distributive design of the Internet, however, doesn't only involve a single country. The network extends to almost all the countries of the world. It is extremely difficult to track sender or recipient of a transmission and even if they could be identified it is clear which legal rules apply. This renders national rules and regulations for communication almost completely ineffective. In fact, given the structure of today's Internet, the very notion of territorial jurisdiction is virtually meaningless. Ultimately, on the Internet anyone can communicate anything to anyone else. The American Net activist John Gilmore is ascribed to have said: "The Internet treats censorship as damage, and routes around it."[7]

At first glance, this may not seem to pose a major problem, given that all OECD countries guarantee freedom of speech in some way, most of them even constitutionally.[8] There are, however, numerous restrictions on communication content, many flowing from guarantees attached to other rights. The case studies presented here focus on two aspects of content regulation. The first, termed here illegal content, deals with direct prohibitions on communication content such as the ban on (child) pornography and certain forms of political propaganda. The second case study looks at cryptography; it deals with legislation that allows the state to legally restrict the secrecy of post and telecommunications for the purpose of law enforcement or criminal prosecution. The Internet here serves as a perfect pathway for the distribution of strong cryptography methods, which make it almost impossible for the executive to exercise their interception rights.

Both case studies look at how nationally constituted political groups in Canada and Germany respond to the challenges posed by these issues. As will be seen, there is a fairly stable consensus among groups in both countries that an international approach provides the most appropriate means of dealing with the problem of illegal content. Here, nontraditional steering mechanisms, and relatively low levels of intervention are generally advocated as providing the solution. The dominant response to the cryptography problem, however, is the almost unanimous rejection of government intervention. International action, if it is considered, is regarded as appropriate only for the purpose of promoting cryptography rather than controlling it. Beyond this overall generalization, two basic response patterns can be identified. The first, a response adopted mainly by the authoritarian groups—but also some unions—is characterized by a high level of intervention, a strong emphasis on traditional national regulation, and a low level of activity. The second pattern, an approach taken by a trio made up from emancipatory new politics groups and the issue-specific business organizations, is characterized by a high level of activity both on the national and international level, and involves the promotion of new steering mechanisms and relatively low levels of intervention. These three groups are the only ones to show significant activities beyond the level of the nation-state. As these patterns make clear, the political divisions normally associated with national politics are partly suspended in the context of this denationalization challenge.

Group Selection

Group selection obviously depends first and foremost on the choice of countries to be studied. The first here is Germany, which, as mentioned in chapter 2, is selected throughout the volume to provide for a common denominator that can be compared across all cases. The United States would also have been an obvious choice given its great prominence in Internet affairs. The extremely large involvement of the United States in the overall network, however, results in the fact that Americans often treat the Internet as an almost internal affair. Its smaller neighbour, on the other hand, due to its geographic and linguistic proximity to the United States, has a much greater awareness of the problems associated with the transborder flow of information. Selecting Canada for the case studies here, therefore, ensures that the denationalized character of the Internet is as undisputed among the second lot of groups under investigation as it is in Germany.[9]

The selection of groups within these countries is the same for both case studies. It follows the criteria laid out in section 2.3, with one variation—the issue-specific groups. This is because the Internet is a fairly new topic and different groups have not yet formed on specific issues. A group was thus selected to represent Internet issue-specificity if its main activities are directly related to the Net, or at least, if a group could still not be found, the telecommunications sphere in general. Selection for Internet specificity was, even then however, slightly different in relation to the new politics authoritarian groups. Here, no group could be identified for which Internet or telecommunications politics was an end in itself; instead, the selection criterion was that the group used the Internet as its primary means of communication. The rationale behind this is that such groups are significantly affected by Internet politics and likely to develop a clear-cut position on the issues at hand. Based on these considerations the following groups were selected for observation:

In Germany, the *Deutscher Gewerkschaftsbund* (DGB) and *Bundesverband der Deutschen Industrie* (BDI) fulfill the requirements of general groups within the old politics sphere, as they are the peak organizations representing unions and business groups (respectively) throughout the country. The Green Party is a parliamentary party and, strictly speaking, outside of the chosen selection criteria, but they are nonetheless selected because they represent the tip of the new social movements iceberg, dealing with a wide array of typical new politics topics such as environmental protection, gender equality, and civil rights. Similarly, the right-wing Republikaner Party can be seen as the group advocating the broadest range of authoritarian new politics issues, such as traditional family values, patriotism, and limits to immigration. As opposed to smaller groups of their respective type, both the Greens and the Republikaner Party fulfill the selection requirements of being both nationally oriented and organised. As for an issue-specific leftist group within the old politics spectrum, the DPG was an obvious choice since it is the sectoral trade union under the umbrella of the DGB most closely linked to the telecommunications world.[10] On the business associations side, Eco-Forum is the premier group representing the German Internet industry; its more than thirty member companies handle roughly 80 per cent of all German Internet traffic.[11] Representing the new politics emancipatory approach is the Chaos Computer Club (CCC). Established at the beginning of the 1980s, the CCC considers itself "committed to the human right of at least world-wide unrestrained communication."[12] Explicitly demanding the freedom of information and communication, CCC represents core new politics values particularly prominent in Internet politics.

On the authoritarian side of new politics, an organization was chosen whose main concern is not the Internet as a political issue but which uses the Internet as its primary means of communication. Thule-Net is an Internet communication platform for right-wing groups. It provides an Internet site on which these groups display their points of view on various issues. While it is thus not fully accurate to talk of Thule-Net as having an opinion, statements

Table 3.1. Group Selection in Germany and Canada

	General	Issue area specific
Germany		
Old Politics—Left	Deutscher Gewerkschaftsbund (DGB)	Deutsche Postgewerkschaft (DPG)
Old Politics—Right	Bundesverband der Deutschen Industrie (BDI)	Electronic Commerce-Forum e.V. (Eco-Forum)
New Politics—Emancipatory	Bündnis 90/Die Grünen (The Green Party)	Chaos Computer Club (CCC)
New Politics—Authoritarian	The Republikaner Party	Thule-Netz (Thule-Net)
Canada		
Old Politics—Left	Canadian Labour Congress (CLC)	Telecommunication Workers Union (TWU)
Old Politics—Right	Business Council on National Issues (BCNI)	Canadian Association of Internet Providers
New Politics—Emancipatory	New Democratic Party (NDP)	Electronic Frontier Canada (EFC)
New Politics—Authoritarian	Reform Party of Canada (RPC)	Digital Freedom / Heritage Front (DF/HF)

attributed to Thule-Net in this study are more correctly those of right-wing individuals or groups transmitted via the service Thule-Net provides. The assumption behind selecting this organization was that the information on Thule-Net represents conclusions on policy preferences and activities of various groups in the right-wing political spectrum.

The Canadian Labour Congress (CLC) is the Canadian equivalent of the German DGB, and is the umbrella organization covering Canadian unions. And, taking the place of the general business organization, the Business Council on National Issues (BCNI) is the only central, overarching organization representing Canadian industry. It can not be directly compared to the German BDI, however, as the BCNI is a collective of CEOs from leading Canadian corporations rather than an umbrella organization as such. At the same time, it sees itself as the "senior voice of Canadian business on public policy issues in Canada and internationally."[13] At first glance selection of the New Democratic Party (NDP) as the equivalent of the German Green Party in its general representation of new politics may appear questionable. The NDP is rather old, with its roots in the Co-operative Commonwealth Federation (CCF) of 1932. At the same time, its constitution ascribes to it the values of democratic socialism[14] and the organization maintains close ties to the unions and is a member of Socialist International.

It should be noted in this context that the notion of new politics can hardly be assumed to be static across countries. In the context of Canada's political setting, the NDP can justifiably be identified as representing alternative politics. Thus, it has usually been the NDP that has taken on the typical issues of new politics, such as environmental protection, women's rights and the right of indigenous peoples, on the national level.[15] All other organizations that are close to the notion of a new social movement tend to be either single issue or grassroot oriented and thus fail to meet the requirements for group selection for other reasons. The Reform Party (RPC), on the other hand, can be easily identified as the most important organization in the pool of authoritarian movements that emerged in Canada at the end of the 1980s. The RPC emphasizes typical authoritarian topics such as limits to immigration, a tightening of criminal law, and a general emphasis on national politics.[16] In the early 1990s, the RPC gained approximately a fifth of the seats in the House of Commons and it retains its significance as a political force to this day.[17] As far as issue-specific groups are concerned, both the Telecommunication Workers Union (TWU) and the "Communication, Energy and Paperworkers Union" (CEP) could have been selected to represent the left of old politics. Ultimately, however, even though the CEP is significantly larger, the TWU was chosen because of its greater specialization in the area of telecommunications, thus increasing the likelihood of it having formed an opinion on such a relatively new and specialized matter as Internet politics. On the business side of the line, the Canadian Association of Internet Providers (CAIP) was chosen because it represents businesses that directly deal with (or rather, in) Internet affairs. It is the only nation-wide, and largest, association of Internet service providers (ISPs) in Canada and sees itself as "the principal spokesperson for the commercial Internet service industry" in that country.[18] Representing the emancipatory new politics point of view, the issue-specific Electronic Frontier Canada (EFC) was selected. The EFC was established in 1994 and defines its mission as being: "…to ensure that the principles embodied in the Canadian Charter of Rights and Freedoms remain protected as new computing, communications, and information technologies are introduced into Canadian society."[19]

While the general outlook of the EFC is rather similar to the German CCC, its focus on Internet affairs is even stronger. Representing the author-itarian side of new politics is Digital Freedom (DF); like the Thule-Net in Germany, DF is more a communication forum for right-wing groups than a clearly identifiable group. Founded in 1995 as a Bulletin-Board-System (BBS), DF established an equivalent on the Internet, called the Freedom Site, in 1996.[20] This site allows various right-wing groups to communicate and distribute information. A report of the Canadian Jewish Congress states in relation to DF that it "has provided a virtual library and town hall meeting place for Canadian white racists."[21] Information was gathered from the Freedom Site, therefore, in a manner similar to the Thule-Net. In addition (and more than was possible for Germany), a group active in the forum was found that was willing to cooperate in the study. Thus the views of the Heritage Front (HF), a group that, according to its own representation,[22] closely cooperates with DF on Internet politics was also taken into account.

ILLEGAL CONTENT ON THE INTERNET: GOVERNANCE CHALLENGE AND POLICY-CYCLES

The issue of illegal content on the Internet has probably received most public attention in relation to use of the medium for the distribution of pornogra-phy in general and child pornography in particular. Following a highly con-troversial 1995 *Time Magazine* article on Cyberporn,[23] a vibrant international debate on the topic began. Some called it the "Great Internet Sex Panic" (Godwin 1995), while others went as far as labelling the Internet as a whole a "smuggler's path for smut."[24] Generally speaking, pornography in most Western countries is not illegal. There are, however, usually restrictions of access to, and limitations in the creation of, certain types of depictions. For example, in terms of access, children are usually prohibited from viewing all forms of pornographic material. In Canada, this restriction is articulated in various provincial and municipal laws (Sansom 1995). In Germany it falls under such federal laws as the *Gesetz über die Verbreitung jugendgefährdender*

Schriften und Medieninhalte (GjS)[25] and *Gesetz zum Schutze der Jugend in der Öffentlichkeit (JÖSchG)*[26]. In terms of limitations in the creation of specific depictions, child pornography is a well-known example of a complete prohibition; child pornography is strictly outlawed by section 163.1 of the *Criminal Code of Canada* (CCC) and by art. 184 III of Germany's *Strafgesetzbuch (StGB)*.[27] In both countries, it is not only production and distribution of such material that is illegal, but also the mere possession of it.[28]

Publicly not quite as prominent but still a major area of concern is the distribution of certain forms of political propaganda. Germany has a number of detailed laws in this respect; for example, distribution of the propaganda and symbols of organizations deemed unconstitutional is prohibited.[29] Article 130 of the StGB, moreover, prohibits the incitement of racial, ethnics or religious hatreds as well as any public acceptance, denial, or belittlement of Nazi crimes. While not quite as detailed or far-reaching, Canada also has a number of similar provisions. Sections 318 to 320 of the CCC, for example, deal with hate propaganda such as the advocacy or promotion of genocide, defined as the physical destruction of identifiable groups. In a similar vein, sections 12 and 13 of the Canadian *Human Rights Act* prohibit publication of material that might contribute to the incitement of hatred, contempt, or discrimination.

Given the structure and technology of the Internet, it is clear these prohibitions are extremely difficult to enforce. Since anyone can communicate anything to anyone else, it is almost impossible to prevent minors, for example, from accessing material they ordinarily would not be allowed to see. Whereas traditionally it was the distributor of the relevant material (i.e., merchants, shopowners, broadcasters, etc.) who was held responsible for breaches of these laws, on the Internet the distributor is hard to identify and may live anywhere in the world. At the same time, the content is largely uncontrollable. During transmission, monitoring is almost impossible and the identification of sender and receiver is confronted with serious problems.

Aside from the very real practical issues involved in enforcement, this poses difficult legal problems. Thus, when all someone does is simply access a WWW page, it is far from obvious what exactly constitutes the criminal offense. More problematically, it is unclear which national legal system applies to exactly which action (see e.g., Tulmein 1999). The result is that national rules and regulations applying to communication content have come under serious challenge. To be sure, restrictions on communication content have never been perfectly implemented, but the Internet presents a new dimension to the challenge: the ease with which these rules can be circumvented has taken on unprecedented forms. It can fairly be said, therefore, that communication on the Internet as a denationalization phenomenon has effectively undermined states' ability to enforce their respective regimes on communication content. This constitutes a significant governance challenge.

This challenge is very well understood in both Germany and Canada. Reflecting on the issue of distribution of right-wing propaganda over the Internet, the German *Verfassungsschutz* (Office for the Protection of the Constitution) commented: "The fact that material can be put on-line and accessed world-wide means that for a long time to come criminally relevant texts will remain available in Germany."[30]

The *Verfassungsschutz* (which concerns itself mainly with the distribution of political propaganda) was not the only institution to note the problem. In 1996, following up on an initiative of the Chancellor's Council for Research, Technology, and Innovation,[31] the German government published its 1996 report entitled, "Info 2000: Germany's way into the Information Society." The report stated: "facilitated access to national and international networks like the Internet, raise the question of whether existing regulations for the protection of minors ... still suffice."[32]

One year later, a *Fortschrittsbericht* (progress report) on what had by then become known as the Info 2000 federal initiative was more explicit, noting (in the context of the protection of minors) that: "[t]here can be no doubt about the fact that worldwide developments such as growing data flows on global networks partly evade national influence... In the age of global information networks, national legislative regulations alone are not enough."[33]

The Federal Minister of Justice at the time, Schmidt-Jortzig, was probably the member of government most outspoken on the issue. Asked about his opinion in relation to child pornography on the Internet, he replied:

> The protection of minors is endangered ... and the state has to see to it that the law is enforced. This, however, is bound to fail if efforts are limited to one country. On the Internet there are no borders. What is outlawed in one state will be posted to the Net elsewhere. ... For better or worse, we will have to come to terms with the impossibility of implementing German law on the Internet. ... I think the Internet and its possibilities of border-less communication are one of the most interesting challenges the state is faced with today. The traditional nation state will prove to be outdated faster than we think. A legal system that ends at the border of a distinct territory will be harder and harder to maintain. A global medium can only be controlled globally or not at all.[34]

In Canada, the problem was raised relatively early in Parliament and resurfaced numerous times in the following years. As early as 1994, an MP noted:

> With this chunk of the electronic highway ... how can we prevent goods and services from crossing our borders electronically, when we know full well that we have legislation in place to prevent them from entering in material form?[35]

One year later another MP was led to comment: "Canada's current laws are apparently having little effect on the electronic highway"[36] and in 1998 yet another MP noted:

> ...an Internet provider...has become an electronic news-stand for publications fostering hate against aborigines, new Canadians, francophones, the Jewish community and other groups. Racist groups are flaunting the law by using the Internet.[37]

Similarly, a diversity of institutions came to recognize the scope of the problem. The Information Highway Advisory Council (IHAC), a committee initiated by Industry Canada in 1994 and comprising of a wide range of governmental, nongovernmental and industrial representatives commented as follows in its final report in 1995:

> Pornographic, obscene and hate materials distributed in digital form...are readily and widely accessible, using computer communications networks. Though easy to obtain, they are difficult to monitor and police....There are problems of enforcement related to jurisdictional boundaries. What might be considered illegal in one jurisdiction may be deemed acceptable in another.[38]

Law enforcement organizations also noted the problem. Thus, for example, the Canadian Association of Chiefs of Police noted in a resolution passed in 1995:

> ...use of the Internet System for unlawful purposes as a communications medium is expanding at an alarming rate...the dissemination of information; such as child pornography, the making of explosive devices...and hate propaganda have become a serious source of public concern and frustration...there are no effective laws currently in place to control the abuses of the Internet System.[39]

The issue also came under intense public discussion in the media,[40] often triggered by actions of law enforcement agencies and access providers (including universities).[41] Initially, these cases mainly revolved around the question of whether or not these actions constituted disproportionate cases of censorship. A well-known example involved legal proceedings launched by the German police force against CompuServe over Internet newsgroups on the ISP's server which contained the word sex. CompuServe was ultimately ordered to remove these newsgroups from its server thus making them unavailable to users worldwide.[42] The case gained a fair amount of international prominence, even leading to protests in several countries around the world.[43] Attempts such as these by law enforcement agencies to come to terms with illegal content on the Internet raised debate on the limits of free speech in general and in this way, the problem was publicly rather clearly defined. A complete policy cycle, however, did not really take place in Canada. There was a bill dealing with child pornography on the Internet introduced into the House of Commons in 1997 and—slightly modified—again in 1998, 1999, and 2001,[44] but the initiative never gained any relevant support and always died rather quickly. In Germany, on the other hand, discussion on the *Informations- und Kommunikationsdienstegesetz*[45] *(IuKDG)* passed by the *Bundestag* in 1997 (and coming into effect on January 1, 1998), represented for many groups the occasion to form a clear stand on the issue. The IuKDG itself however, contains little regulation with regard to illegal content. It extends the applicability of the Criminal Code to electronic media but explicitly limits the scope of liability of service providers to their own content.[46]

Responses of Political Groups to the Problem of Illegal Content

Results by dimension: Germany

Activity. When the German groups under investigation are compared in terms of activity three of the groups clearly stand out. The Eco-Forum, the Green Party, and the CCC show a rather high degree of activity, each of them having taken action on the issue of illegal content at a time significantly before the policy cycle came into full swing. Indeed, they themselves played a decisive role in defining the problem as well as in agenda-setting. In contrast, the DPG and the BDI only formed an opinion on the issue after having been called upon by the government to submit statements and/or attend hearings on the question. The DGB and the Republikaner Party were largely passive in their responses, providing only limited information relating to their political preferences and activities or forming opinions on a rather ad hoc basis, for example when asked about the issue in the context of this study. No systematic information could be obtained in relation to political activity from the Thule-Net.

The Greens, the CCC, and Eco-Forum also demonstrate the most advanced mode of activity, with Eco-Forum leading the pack. In addition to lobbying, this organization went as far as initiating significant self-regulatory activities. In 1996, it helped to establish the Internet Content Task Force (ICTF), which ultimately evolved into the *Freiwillige Selbstkontrolle Multimedia*[47] (Voluntary Selfcontrol Mutlimedia) one year later.[48] The Greens mainly tried to influence the legislative process in Parliament while the CCC concentrated on lobbying activities. The other groups clearly show a lower level of activity with the DGB and the Republikaner Party demonstrating least concern with the issue. As to the level of activity, only the Eco-Forum and the CCC have taken significant action beyond the immediate boundaries of the nation-state, with both organizations initiating action at the European Union level. Eco-Forum was heavily involved in the creation and activities of EuroISPA, an umbrella organization representing European Internet service providers and with a focus on influencing the various European Union institutions in Brussels. The CCC maintained contact with the European Parliament and took part in hearings held in that context. The other groups, such as the Green Party and the BDI, were either active only in the national sphere or involved themselves in an international sense to minor degree.

Spatiality. Spatiality in the context of this particular case study mainly translates into the question of what role international institutions or international cooperation could or should play with regard to a more effective implementation of norms on communication content. The various issues involved, therefore, mainly revolve around international rule setting (or harmonization) and international cooperation in law enforcement. With regard to the territorial scope of any kind of regulation there is a fairly stable consensus among the groups under consideration that in principle international cooperation would be the most meaningful way of solving the problem. Eco-Forum and CCC provide the clearest analysis in relation to the steps required for regulation on a worldwide scale. They both point to the fact that a single dissenter can effectively undermine any effort to solve the problem because the movement of data involves very little transaction cost. Hence they emphasise the need for an international effort on a scale as broad as possible. There is one major difference, however, between the two groups: whereas Eco-Forum sees a potential in, and a need for, interstate cooperation,[49] the CCC sets its hopes rather on a worldwide consensus among Internet users. They see a set of informal consensual rules emerging (referred to as Netiquette) that will lead to an effective ban of what is considered undue by the global community of users.[50] The Green Party and the BDI also point to the need for international cooperation but place an additional emphasis on the European Union as a meaningful forum for such efforts. Both unions (DGB and DPG) join the other groups in generally endorsing international efforts.[51] On a more concrete level, however, their policy suggestions deal with national institutions only.[52] The exception to this general consensus on international cooperation is the Republikaner Party. Although there is little evidence of any distinct opinion on Internet policy offered by this party,[53] this authoritarian group emphasises the sovereignty of the nation-state and strongly disapproves of any transfer of sovereignty to international institutions.[54] The various groups differ, however, in what precisely is meant by the term "international cooperation," and in particular, the degree of denationalization required for effective cooperation.

The Eco-Forum provides the most detailed plan of action and represents, perhaps, the most extreme point of view in relation to international cooperation. The Chairman of Eco-Forum argued: "...what is a necessary is the concerted action of all relevant forces, as far as possible beyond the borders of our legal system.[55]

A representative of Eco-Forum,[56] even suggested the establishment of some form of "Internet-NATO" or Internet-UNO on the basis of the G7. Such an institution would have the function of defining a normative consensus among its members, that is, some form of common denominator as to what is considered illegal (including, for example, child pornography). The institution would, internally (i.e., among its member states), improve cooperation in law enforcement, and externally use its power to persuade other countries to comply with such norms—using sanctions if necessary. The establishment of such an institution, however, is seen by the group as workable only in addition to self-regulatory action developed by the community of providers and users. The Green Party also strongly supports direct international regulation:

> ...the dissemination of indictable content or content morally harmful to youth can only be satisfactorily fought against in the context of international co-operation and supranational structures. Initiatives on the level of the G7, the EU, or other international organizations are therefore to be vigorously pursued.[57]

However, the Greens do not, go quite as far as advocating the establishment of an international Internet organization. The approach of the CCC, on the other hand, is to emphasize nongovernmental self-regulation on the level of individual Net users: "Something like a global consciousness will emerge about what is legal in the sense of respecting human dignity and what is not...this can only derive from a voluntary agreement amongst netizens."[58]

The CCC is strongly critical of any national attempt to regulate the Internet, calling instead exclusively on international efforts to deal with the problem.[59] The role of national regulation, however, is stressed by both the DPG and DGB. The DPG sees national regulation as necessary in a transitory sense, possibly serving as an example for other countries.[60] The DPG maintains that the difficulties of international cooperation should not be used as an excuse for national passivity. The DGB argues along similar lines, but its ideas are even less detailed than those of the DPG. This generality also holds for the BDI, which, at the same time, is opposed to creating any form of central European or even worldwide institution.[61] Nonetheless, the BDI stresses the negative impact of fragmented regional regulation[62] and argues in favor of a harmonization of national legislation rather than the establishment of any kind of centralized international institution. While information from Thule-Net with regard to the spatial implication of their position could not be found, the Republikaner display a comparatively low degree of tolerance for political denationalization. This is consistent with their typical approach to national media policy reform and their general distrust in international institutions.

Intervention. Although all groups, with the exception of the Republikaner, favour in one way or another an international approach to the problem, such an approach is not independent of their various notions of what should be considered illegal and what should and could be outlawed internationally, that is, the degree of intervention. Most of the groups, with the exception of the BDI, the Republikaner, and Thule-net, (especially in the interviews) pointed to the fact that international cooperation would only be possible to the extent that international consensus on acceptable norms for communication content can be reached. While most agree that child pornography is probably least problematic in this regard, they see an international normative consensus in general as emerging slowly, if at all. As a consequence, most groups see the actual chances of international cooperation as rather slim. The Green Party points out that even "...with regard to child pornography international harmonisation is necessary. For example, there is not yet any agreement on the age parameters of childhood, and hence the ages which require special protection.[63]

So, while there are those who are in principle against any intervention into the free flow of communication, others emphasize that a high of degree of intervention is simply unrealistic given the need for international consensus. Still, others emphasize the importance of banning various kinds of content. In this regard, the authoritarian Republikaner group—while coming out last on both aspects of spatiality—ranks first with regard to the question of how extensive intervention should be. They demand "a rigorous ban on depictions of violence, horror and pornography in all electronic media[64]—to give the struggle for the protection of our youth...against pornography...absolute priority.[65]

The DPG does not go as far, but still stresses the importance of extending the applicability of traditional content regulations to the new electronic media:[66]

> We welcome the attempt...to clarify whether transitory on-screen information can be considered a "publication" under the relevant penal regulations. Hitherto this uncertainty has significantly complicated the struggle against the dissemination of content disrespectful of human dignity or morally harmful to youth...[67]

Rather than extending traditional content regulation to the Net, Eco-Forum, and the Green Party both argue that the regulatory effect should work precisely the other way around. In the interview, the representative of the Forum[68] presented the view that the traditional wisdom of Internet politics held that what is illegal offline can not be legal online. Rather, he maintained, the rule has to be what cannot be implemented online can not be illegal offline. In other words, communication content legislation currently in force would have to be reviewed from the perspective of what can reasonably be assumed to be enforceable on the Internet against the background of the need for international consensus. In particular, the representative of Eco-Forum saw little chance for the control of right-wing political propaganda in Germany to be tenable internationally. The representative of the Green Party expressed a similar thought by pointing out that one should not try to *apply* German laws to the world but to *adapt* German laws to the world.[69] A weeding out, therefore, of German laws was considered unavoidable. The Greens, however, went even further than the Eco-Forum in emphasizing that any attempt to make the Internet suitable for family viewing would be unenforceable and that it was of great importance, for constitutional reasons, not to infringe the freedom of speech. While the BDI only emphasised the need for a "consistent, liberal design of multimedia regulation"[70] in a very general sense, the DGB maintained that any attempt of the state to control Internet content would be ill-fated. According to the DGB,[71] any attempts at enforcement would always lag behind, in a technical sense, the possibilities available to Net users. In a similar vein, the CCC maintained that an effective 100 per cent ban is co-operatively and internationally not possible.[72] In addition, the CCC stressed the importance of free speech, arguing that it was high time that society finally accepted that language and thoughts are free. In their view, the suppression of opinion not only amounts to an infringement of constitutional rights but is also futile, because illegal content has its origins in societal problems: "The prevention of abuse in a technical medium is as impossible as a solution to the societal problems that form the causes for this abuse."[73]

Instead of the outright prohibition of right-wing propaganda, for example, the view of the CCC is that the protagonists of such propaganda should be engaged in political discussion. This corresponds with the CCC's notion of nongovernmental self-regulation by way of societal debate. Finally, the right-wing Thule-Net is fully opposed to any type of content regulation. Any form of intervention is labelled censorship suggesting an undue infringement of rights: "Childporn and NaziNazi were of course only excuses for the authorities to get a 'foot in the door' under the cover of moral hypocrisy. Now, the FRG shows its true intentions."[74]

Those groups who favor a comparatively high degree of intervention also prefer a rather traditional mode of intervention. The rigorous ban on pornography argued for by the Republikaner no doubt implies state adminis-tered regulatory measures. The comments of the DPG on an extension of existing laws to the new media also suggest usage of the traditional hierarchi-cal form of statutory ordinance. By contrast, although both business organi-zations (BDI and Eco-Forum) call for the implementation of a regulatory regime controlling what is acceptable and what is not, they want such a regime to be administered nonhierarchically by means of self-regulation. Thus, the BDI maintains that "only self-control promises meaningful protection",[75] whereas Eco-Forum has already initiated a variety of self-regulatory activities. The Forum points out:

> The leading Internet service providers...will contribute to a channelling of the dissemination of illegal information. This has to happen in such a manner as to assure that no inappropriate or undifferentiated censorship occurs—this would be unavoidable if the state were to intervene.[76]

The other groups prefer a mix of policy instruments. The view of the DGB, for example, is that the state must continue to play a significant role, both with regard to hierarchical regulation and the dissemination of information, for example, through introducing media competence education in schools.[77] According to the Greens and the CCC, the role of the state in the policymix is mainly limited to the dissemination of information and the mobilization of public debate on what should be considered acceptable and what not.[78] More emphasis is put on the role of self-regulation. In the words of the Green Party: "Special attention is to be given to the culture of voluntary self-control which is currently still functioning on the Internet, the so-called 'netiquette.'"[79]

Or as the CCC put it: "Considering that those who use the Internet (in all countries) are potential information providers, it is meaningful to promote Netiquette."[80]

In addition, both the Greens and the CCC favour self-regulation in the form of the private use of software filters to block unwanted information. Thule-Net, being strictly opposed to any form of intervention, presents of course no view on any particular mode of intervention.

Results by dimension: Canada

Activity. The level of activity of the Canadian groups is generally lower than those of the German groups studied in this investigation. In relation to mode of activity three of the four old politics groups were largely passive including both unions and the BCNI. While only a limited amount of information could be gathered from CLC and TWU, the BCNI admitted to not having formed an opinion on the issue at all.[81] The Reform Party was also mostly passive in its response—with the exception perhaps of individual MPs who spoke out on the issue. A representative of the Party made mention of the fact, however, that there had been a number of internal task forces on Internet issues and that it would undertake public activity in the future,[82] suggesting that the process of opinion formation is somewhat further developed within the RPC as compared to the aforementioned old politics groups. The NDP and the right-wing Digital Front/Heritage Front (DF/HF) were reactive, the former to police demands[83] and the latter to a series of events that made the groups themselves the victims of what they considered censorship.[84] The issue-specific business organization (CAIP) and the issue-specific emancipatory group (EFC), like their German equivalents, reacted not only comparatively early but also played an important role in shaping the way discussion on the issue proceeded. Commenting on its self-regulatory activities, CAIP explicitly made mention of the fact that it became active early on in the debate in order to prevent state intervention: "CAIP's approach to the Internet is to evolve rules of conduct that will obviate the need for governmental regulation, and that will keep the many transactions on the net as self-regulating as possible."[85]

As to intensity of activity, CAIP and EFC also rank first, with CAIP taking the lead over the EFC due to a greater variety of activities undertaken by the group. In addition to lobbying, CAIP developed a voluntary Code of Conduct for its members as early as 1996[86] and instituted various programmes in cooperation with the police.[87] The NDP was involved mainly in parliamentary initiatives via one of its MPs, while DF/HF limited their activity to press contacts and lobbying. The BCNI, CLC and TWU were the least active amongst the groups. CAIP was not only the most active Canadian group, but also the only group to go beyond a merely national level of activity. Its international activities were significant; according to its own account the group engaged in international lobbying (in the context of OECD conferences)[88] and participated in: "an international working group of ISP representatives, Justice department officials and police forces delegates from the G8 countries."[89]

The EFC maintains some ties to organizations abroad that are similar to its own, like the US-based EFF[90] or the Australian EFA[91] and also took part in the international Global Information Liberty Campaign (GILC);[92] most of its activities, however, are geared towards the national sphere.[93] The rest of the groups were only active (if indeed they were active at all) on the national level.

Spatiality. Among the three most active groups (CAIP, EFC, NDP) there is a consensus that the territorial scope of any regulation of the problem should be international. These groups agree that this need for international regulation, derives from the transnational scope of the Internet itself. As CAIP puts it: "Since the Internet is international in scope and transnational in its applications, the development of guiding legal and policy frameworks cannot stop at our domestic borders."[94]

The NDP also emphasizes that international cooperation is the right approach to the problem[95] as does the EFC.[96] The CLC—given its rather limited activity in relation to the issue—is not quite as outspoken, referring to the international approach as not a bad idea.[97] The RPC similarly acknowledges the usefulness of such an approach, but is fairly limited in the scope of cooperation it sees as appropriate. Its most concrete suggestion only provides for a bilateral agreement with the United States and was a reaction to a US initiative along these lines.[98] Both the TWU and DF/HF are against any form of Internet regulation no matter what scope it would actually attain, and therefore are as opposed to international as to national regulation.[99]

The attitudes of the groups in terms of degree of denationalization follow a similar pattern, but there are some significant differences. CAIP reveals a comparatively high degree of denationalization while taking a differentiated approach. The group maintains the necessity of a regulatory framework of internationally defined guidelines but also argues that these guidelines be supplemented by self-regulation on a transnational scale.[100] While EFC's position is not quite as detailed, the group still emphasizes the need for an international approach, arguing for a more extensive role to be taken on by international law, multilateral treaties, and international governing bodies; its comments, however, do not go beyond that level of generality.[101] NDP MPs introduced the bill mentioned above regulating child pornography on the Internet.[102] Although this bill was oriented at the national sphere, its different versions always explicitly provided for the Minister of Industry to enter into international agreements: "... to prevent or minimize the use of the Internet for the publication or proliferation of child pornography or to facilitate the commission of an offence under the Criminal Code or this Act or a similar law of the ... foreign state."[103]

The introduction of this bill was apparently mainly geared towards stimulating national discussion on the topic, which was seen by the group as a necessary prerequisite for international action.[104] The NDP, therefore, while in principle favouring an international approach to the problem, nevertheless regards national regulation as the necessary precursor of any such attempt. The Reform Party, while in basic agreement that "regulation of the Internet ... require[s] international cooperation,"[105] remains, however, rather critical of the effectiveness of such an effort—reflecting the Party's general lack of faith in the merits of international cooperation.[106] They point out that national regulation still has an important role to play:

> Hate literature and hate propaganda on the Internet are like pollution washing up on a seashore. Although we may never get rid of all the pollution, we must always keep cleaning the sand on our portion of the beach or else eventually we will be buried in the pollution.[107]

The CLC's comments on international regulation indicate a somewhat lacklustre support—it sees such an approach as merely an attempt to solve the problem.[108] The TWU is opposed to any form of intervention, considering debate with and engagement of, for example, those who disseminate, for example, hate propaganda, as the only solution to the problem. Examples given by the group in the interview, however, suggest that this debate could take the form of a transnational discussion.[109] DF / HF, however, does not make any such concession; they flatly reject the idea of any form of joint international censorship.[110]

Intervention. The question of degree of intervention was largely influenced by the attitude taken by groups to the realities of achieving international cooperation. As with the German groups, almost all groups highlight the fact that any international cooperation has to be based on a consensus as to what is considered illegal and that this consensus is not going to be easily to come by. Only the NDP is of the view that basic international standards are not really that difficult to reach. This group maintains that a problem would only arise in the unlikely scenario of a state or group of states actually advocating child pornography or hate speech.[111] In the main, however, there is widespread pessimism amongst groups as to the international compatibility of certain norms covering communication content, at least at any level above the most basic ban on child pornography. The RPC, for example, commented that even if a number of countries would agree on a ban of child pornography, there would always be a dissenting state which would then become the safe harbor for this kind of material.[112] CAIP pointed to the additional problem that not only would vastly different states have to agree on common content norms (such as Canada and Saudi Arabia), but that there also might be various communities within states that would favor different standards. For example, Canadian Moslems might actually agree with Saudi Arabia on certain notions of illegal content while a majority of Canadians might not.[113] As the EFC put it: "international agreement" on the subject is likely to be "very difficult to achieve."[114]

It is remarkable then, that despite this widespread pessimism, many groups still emphasise the need to apply existing communication content regulations to the Internet just as they apply to all other media. Rather than advocating the weeding out of national norms in order to establish a workable international basis of content restriction (a position, as we saw above, which was adopted by some German groups), most groups take existing national laws as their starting point. Thus the same five groups which put forward an international approach (RPC, NDP, CLC, CAIP, and EFC) also comment (in more or less the same words as the following of the CAIP) that: "...the Internet is subject to the normal laws of the land regarding speech: which is to say that speech is free within broad limits established by law for all media of communication."[115]

Despite this commonality, however, there are significant differences amongst these groups as to the degree of intervention considered appropriate. In particular, the groups differ both in terms of the specificity with which they advance their respective positions and in relation to the sanctions for infringement considered necessary. The RPC, for example, mentioned on a number of occasions that stiffer penalties[116] for child pornography would make an important contribution towards solving the problem:

> Recent cases involving importation, possession and distribution of child pornography on the Internet demonstrate the need to crack down and crack down hard....A Reform government will: ...Introduce tougher sentences for anyone convicted of producing, peddling or promoting child pornography."[117]

This emphasis on enforcement and penalties reflects The RPC's preference for a relatively high degree of intervention. The NDP also supports a relatively high degree of intervention, and, as mentioned above, is the only group to have actually identified the need for specific Internet legislation.[118] This proposal would have—if the Bill were to have been passed—established a specific set of rules for the Internet, including various Internet specific criminal offenses, as well as procedures to deal with these rules. The CLC was generally silent on the issue, emphasizing only the applicability of ordinary media content legislation to the Internet. CAIP, however, was strictly opposed to the NDP's proposed bill, or any special Internet legislation for that matter. The group argues that: "...[e]xisting Canadian laws are adequate to conduct search and seizure of evidence and to charge and convict distributors of child porn or paedophiles."[119]

As for the EFC, it went as far as calling the proposed piece of legislation a cynical ploy and an anti-Internet bill.[120] The group calls into question any form of intervention: "EFC believes the expression of controversial opinions, no matter how erroneous or repugnant, should be protected from government censorship by the Charter of Rights and Freedoms."[121]

The attitude of the group is that international cooperation should not take on the form of international efforts to restrict free speech, but rather international efforts to stop the abuse of children.[122] At the same time, the group does support the continuing relevance of the existing legislation: "This is not to say that existing laws don't apply to the Internet—they do. Expression over the Internet is no different from any form of expression: there are legal limits."[123]

It seems fair to assume, therefore, that overall, the degree of intervention preferred by EFC is comparatively low. Even lower on the scale, however, is the TWU and DF/HF, who are strictly opposed to any kind of intervention.

The Canadian groups under consideration are on the whole unambiguous with respect to mode of intervention. CLC and NDP, for example, are very clear about the need for state intervention. The CLC, commenting that the whole information highway debate had "been colored by the ideology of the free market"[124] was specific in its rejection of self-regulation. In its view, illegal content has to be seen as a criminal prosecution issue and therefore entirely within the prerogative of the state. It regards self-regulation as serving the interests of the industry to the exclusion of all other legitimate interests.[125] The NDP also came out in favour of the traditional mode of hierarchical state intervention. Its proposed law attempted to institute a registration system whereby ISPs were to be licensed by the Canadian Radio-Television and Telecommunications Commission (CRTC). The granting of a licence was to be dependant on the ISP taking on certain responsibilities for content communicated via their facilities, with failure to comply resulting in loss of license and criminal prosecution. In addition, special powers were to be granted to the Industrial Minister to determine the parameters of child pornography, issue search warrants and regulate the details of enforcement.[126] Traditional hierarchical state intervention also plays an important role in RPC's policy preferences. There are some indications, however, that the group regards this form of intervention as requiring some form of supplementation by other means: "...the most effective action the government could take is not legislative. Government could get the best bang for its buck by supporting the development of a set of Internet conventions or broadly based rules. Call them operating rules, call them a public code of conduct or electronic ethics."[127]

It appears then, that rather than relying on state intervention alone the group prefers a mix of penal and criminal law as well as state supported self-regulation. The position of CAIP is almost exactly opposite that of the CLC, with a clear focus on the development of a code of conduct as the most appropriate means of regulation. In its opinion international cooperation is only meaningful with self-regulation as a basic foundation. On this view, the role of the state is to develop general outlines according to which both ISPs and content providers can institute their own regulatory measures.[128] As was mentioned above, the TWU puts its emphasis on public debate as the most appropriate method of tackling the dissemination of illegal content, thus indicating its preference for a nonhierarchical information driven approach. DF/HF also adopts an information driven approach, although in a somewhat different sense. They point to the fact that users should be able to freely choose what they wanted to read and see.[129] EFC also relies heavily on public debate, but emphasizes the role of both state and nonstate institutions in providing a minimum of necessary information on the relevant issues.[130] Specific attention is in this context given to the role of schools: "Parents and teachers should provide students with background, perspective, and context that allows them to make wise choices. The proper way to combat bad speech on the Internet is with good speech, not with censorship."[131]

Patterns across countries and across dimensions: Cross country comparisons along dimensions

Activity. In general, the correlation between the different activity elements is quite high. This means that groups who were active early (mode of activity) tend to display a relatively high intensity of activity and are also more likely than others to have been active beyond the national level (level of activity). What is also interesting is that the distribution of groups along this correlated activity spectrum is rather similar in both Germany and Canada. In Germany, one prominent result is a trio, made up of Eco-Forum, CCC, and the Green Party. These groups became active very early and show the highest levels of intensity, with at least two of them (Eco-Forum and CCC) also ranking first in terms of international activity. An analysis of the corresponding Canadian groups reveals a similar pattern: the issue-specific business organization (CAIP), and the emancipatory new politics groups (EFC and NDP respectively) also rank highest on activity. The NDP, in comparison to the German Green Party, however, ranks as slightly less active, due to the fact that the group was reactive (instead of active) and didn't involve itself internationally while the Greens were more proactive and had at least minor involvement beyond the national level. In both countries, most of the old politics groups, that is, both unions and the peak business organizations, rank rather low. The authoritarian groups are also less active although this is more pronounced in Germany than in Canada. In both countries, therefore, the main dividing line with regard to activity is between the emancipatory groups and the issue-specific business organizations on the one hand, and the unions, the general business organizations, and the authoritarian groups on the other.

Spatiality. Most of the groups studied, in both Canada and Germany, agree that an international approach is in principle the appropriate solution to the problem of illegal content on the Internet. Only the authoritarian groups, and those opposed to any form of intervention at all, consider international cooperation undesirable. The general authoritarian groups are noteworthy in this context; both the German Republikaner and the Canadian RPC show great distrust in international institutions in general. When the results are broken down according to the individual spatiality elements, such as, territorial scope and degree of denationalization, the correlation is not, however, as clear as we saw above. Still, by and large, it is possible to say that those groups who favour a relatively high territorial scope also have a tendency to opt for a relatively high degree of denationalization and vice versa. A significant exception is the German BDI, which ranks relatively highly with regard to territorial scope, but rather low in degree of denationalization. This is mainly due to the fact that, while emphasizing an international approach as a whole, its preference is for international harmonization and is opposed to the involvement of any international institution. Most remarkable, however, is that again, in both countries, a trio emerges, made up of the issue-specific business organization and the two emancipatory groups. These three groups (in both Germany and Canada) rank highest on both elements of spatiality. Of the six groups formed by these two trios, Eco-Forum and CAIP (i.e., both of the issue-specific business organizations) stand out in their advocacy of a combination of inter and transnational efforts.

Intervention. While it is widely accepted amongst groups that international cooperation is both important and desirable, most are not too optimistic about the chances of such cooperation actually being achieved. In both Germany and Canada, most of the groups make the point that cooperation would have to be based on international consensus and that such a consensus is far from likely to occur. One view that emerged (but only in Germany) was that a consequence of this is that existing national regulations be called into question; thus, according to Eco-Forum and the Green Party, existing rules must be reviewed from the perspective of what can reasonably be expected to be acceptable in an international sense. The difficulty of enforcing rules on the Internet thus becomes an argument for a reconsideration of the rules themselves (i.e., in relation to all media). Once again, comparing the individual elements of this dimension (i.e., degree and mode of intervention), reveals a specific pattern, although the correlation is not quite as high as was seen in the activity dimension. Thus, in both countries, groups that favour a relatively high degree of intervention also show a tendency towards the traditional hierarchical mode of intervention. The less interested a group is in strong intervention the more likely it is to opt for a nonhierarchical forms of self-regulation. An interesting similarity across countries involves the general authoritarian groups (the Republikaner Party in Germany, and the RPC in Canada) and the issue-specific authoritarian groups (Thule-Net in Germany and DF/HF in Canada). While the former maintained the necessity for traditional means of intervention, and specifically called for tighter bans on specific content and more severe penalties for infringement, the latter—having themselves been the targets of censorship—were adamant in their stance of nonintervention. The German issue-specific union, the DPG, and the Canadian NDP (the general emancipatory group) were alike in their preference for state intervention taking its more traditional hierarchical form. This implies that the trio identified above, consisting of the issue-specific business organization and the two emancipatory groups, is not quite as clear-cut in this response dimension. It is still possible to say, however, that (with the exception of the NDP) the two national trios favor a low to middle degree of intervention and have a tendency to emphasize the role of self-regulation and Netiquette. Also common between the countries is the fact that within their respective trios, the issue-specific emancipatory groups opt for the lowest levels of intervention. Having said that, the major line of division in this dimension, for both countries, is that between the general authoritarian groups on the one hand, and the rest of groups on the other.

Overall patterns

Despite differences in their respective policy cycles, a comparison between Germany and Canada shows a surprising degree of convergence in group reactions. Looking at a combination of spatiality and intervention across all groups yields similar results in both countries. By and large, a majority of groups in both Canada and Germany see international cooperation in principle as the appropriate approach to the issue, but also agree that self-regulatory measures should at least serve a supplementary function.[132] Another feature common to both countries is the lack of international activity. Only three of the sixteen groups under investigation were significant in this regard. Domestic politics remains the focus of group activity despite the fact that all groups agree on the desirability of international cooperation. At the same time, there is a uniform tendency in both countries for the old politics groups (with the exception of the issue-specific business organizations) to be rather passive. It is also possible to discern response patterns that are group specific and constant across both countries. Thus, as has been seen, in both countries a combination of three groups stands out. The division between these groups and the rest can be clearly identified in both the activity and spatiality dimensions, while in relation to intervention the grouping still holds albeit with a minor variation. The pattern is marked by high rankings on activity (an early, intensive reaction together with international efforts), high rankings on spatiality (a concern for international integration) and a preference for comparatively low levels of intervention coupled with an emphasis on self-regulation. The pattern is most pronounced for the issue-specific business organizations (Eco-Forum and CAIP) and the issue-specific emancipatory groups (CCC and EFC). This pattern also characterizes the response of the German general emancipatory group (The Greens), but its Canadian counterpart, the NDP, forms an exception ranking relatively high on all three dimensions. It is worthwhile to note that this trio, as a whole, cuts across traditional political cleavages.

Interestingly, an almost exact reversal of this pattern can also be identified in both countries, this time in relation to the general authoritarian groups. These groups combine low levels of activity with a preference for national regulation and a general mistrust in international institutions. At the same time, they evidence the highest levels of intervention in comparison to the other groups and combine this with a predisposition towards the traditional hierarchical approach to regulation. This pattern is marked therefore by low rankings on activity and spatiality with comparatively high levels of intervention. Traces of the pattern can also be found among some of the unions in both countries. The issue-specific DPG and CLC in particular display tendencies in this regard. It should be noted, however, that their spatiality levels are generally higher than those of the authoritarian groups. By way of summary, therefore, the most significant result emerging from this case study is that the two trio groupings and the general authoritarian groups exhibit clearly visible and opposing response patterns in both countries. In relation to the two trios, they represent alliances that cut across traditional political cleavages in their support of denationalized politics.

CRYPTOGRAPHY: DENATIONALIZATION CHALLENGE AND POLICY CYCLES

Derived from the Greek *"cryptos graphein,"* the term cryptography refers to the art of secret writing. It encompasses all techniques by which information is encoded such that it is impossible for anybody but sender and receiver to access its content. Technically, cryptography relies on some form of code or key that is used to transform a message into cipher. Using a mathematical algorithm, this key is usually applied to a text to transform it into the coded text. In order to decode the text the same key has to be applied to the ciphertext—usually involving a reversal of the original algorithm. This implies that key and algorithm must be known to both, sender and receiver of a message. Cryptography has for a very long time been the domain of the military and secret services, who used it to transmit strategic information, orders, or intelligence reports.[133] Of course, as old as cryptography itself, are attempts to break it. There are essentially two ways to break an encryption. One option is to attack the key, that is, by making assumptions as to what its algorithm is and testing whether the decrypted text makes any sense. The other method is to try to gather information on the key—ideally by intercepting or capturing it whole. From the perspective of the coders, therefore, the more advanced and safer the code, the more important it is to safely and secretly transmit the key between sender and receiver. In fact, the establishment of a secure channel for exchange of the key has been one of the most vexing problems of cryptography for most of its history. How is it possible to safely communicate a key whose very function it is to make communications secret?

In 1976, a seminal article was published by two American scientists, Whitfield Diffie, and Martin Hellman (Diffie and Hellmann 1976) dealing with this very question. The solution proposed by Diffie and Hellman was a type of cryptography called public key encryption. The basic idea behind this concept is the use of two keys instead of one with the two keys being mathematically linked to each other. Every potential receiver of a coded message has to have such a pair of keys. One of the keys is public in the sense that it is not kept secret and freely transmitted, while the other is private, and permanently remains with its owner. In order to establish safe communication, the receiver of a message first transmits his public key to the sender. The sender then uses this public key to encode the message. However, there is a special algorithm used for the encoding that can not be reversed, in other words, the message can not be decoded with the public key. Instead, it can only be decoded using the private key that remained with the receiver. The system thus has two special features: (1) coding can be done with the public key while decoding has to be done with the private key and (2) it is safe to openly transmit the public key because it is virtually impossible to infer the private key from the public one.[134] This makes it possible to establish safe communication without having established any safe contact beforehand in order to transmit the key.

The development of encryption has occurred side by side with developments in information technology. In fact, the relationship between the two has always been something of a head chasing tail phenomenon. On the one hand, attempts in code breaking have significantly spurred developments in information technology thus literally multiplying computing power in the hands of those attempting to break encryption codes. On the other hand, the rise of information technology and computing has simultaneously led to totally new opportunities in the development of stronger codes. Today, extremely complex algorithms based on elaborate keys can be applied to any information in a fraction of a second. In this context, the idea of a one way algorithm necessarily implies that on equal levels of technology coders will always have the edge over code breakers, this because any attempt at breaking a key will mathematically always be a much more formidable task than the effort necessary to encode the original information. It is thus no overstatement to say that the advent of public key cryptography together with the advancement of computer technology has lead to virtually unbreakable code.[135]

The rise of information technology, however, has not only been responsible for the creation of stronger codes. Today's communication technologies have fundamentally changed the role of cryptography as a whole. No longer an arcane art managed by specialized mathematicians and used by members of national security administrations or spies, cryptography is today the concern of anyone using or involved with network computing. In an electronic environment, communication can very easily be intercepted, modified, manipulated, forged, copied, or simply read without leaving any trace of the interference on the original text and without any noticeable influence on the communication process. The very strengths of digitized information—the ease and speed with which text can be duplicated, transformed, and transmitted—are severe problems from the perspective of privacy and security. This is all the more problematic in the context of computer networks—the greater the network the greater the risk of unauthorized access.

Communication over open networks (such as the Internet) with theoretically unlimited access are thus particularly at risk. Most of the data on the Net is plain text, making even sensitive information such as private or corporate e-mail, credit card numbers, or banking information entirely available to the person who knows how to access it. Maintaining the secrecy of post and telecommunications has thus become a serious problem.[136] Public key cryptography was developed roughly fifteen years before use of the Internet surged at the beginning of the 1990s. Nonetheless, its design is almost perfect for communications occurring in open international networks such as the Internet, where communication is often established between complete strangers over large distances and where it is almost impossible to establish any alternative secure (i.e., offline) channel for exchange of a key before the actual communication takes place. Indeed, it is widely believed that cryptography in general, and public key cryptography in particular, has the potential to solve the problem of security in Internet communications. This, however, creates another problem—one which forms the basis of this case study: today's cryptographic schemes may just be a bit too safe—and the Internet is not only a perfect place to use them but also a perfect tool to distribute them.

Most Western countries provide for lawful exceptions to the general rule of postal and telecommunications secrecy for the purpose of national security and criminal prosecution. In Canada, for example, a public officer or peace officer can legally access otherwise private communications if "there are reasonable grounds to believe that an offence against this or any other Act of Parliament has been or will be committed" and the appropriate judicial authorization declaring such is obtained.[137] In a similar manner, articles 100(a) and 100(b) of the German *Strafprozeßordnung* (Code of Criminal Procedure) provide for a judicial order to be made authorizing surveillance and wire-tapping for the purposes of criminal prosecution. A further piece of legislation, the *Gesetz zur Beschränkung des Brief-, Post- und Fernmeldegeheimnisses* (i.e., Law on the Restriction of Postal and Telecommunications Secrecy) extends the right to intercept communications to the *Verfassungsschutzbehörden* (Offices for the Protection of the Constitution) and the secret service where the security of the state is in jeopardy or where the liberal democratic order is threatened.[138] The fact that code is available today which is more or less unbreakable has the result that these exceptions to postal and telecommunications secrecy are basically ineffective. While state authorities may obtain the necessary authorization to tap into communications their ability to actually do so is frustrated by some of the encryption technology available today. This is particularly the case in relation to computer mediated communications where the advantages of advanced mathematical algorithms can be fully brought to bear. The Internet is not only the perfect place for using state of the art cryptography methods, it is also the perfect tool for their distribution. In 1991, a hitherto largely unknown American software engineer by the name of Philip Zimmermann developed a program called PGP (Pretty Good Privacy) which applied public key cryptography to Internet communications. PGP could easily be used to code e-mails or file transfers. Rather than selling the program, Zimmermann—motivated by his concern for civil liberties—published the program as freeware and it ended up on the Net:

> 'Like thousands of dandelion seeds blowing in the wind,' he wrote, PGP spread throughout cyberspace. Within hours, people were downloading it all over the country and beyond. 'It was overseas the day after the release,' he said. 'I've gotten mail from just about every country on Earth' (Levy 1993).

Within hours a fully functional and usable version of strong public key cryptography had spread throughout the world. On that day the ability of the state to intervene in communications experienced a serious blow. The crypto genie was out of its bottle.[139] By posting his public key cryptography program on the Net, Zimmermann provided Internet users worldwide with a tool that allowed them to immunize their communication against virtually any form of wire-tapping.

The problems associated with cryptography on the Internet have been acknowledged in various contexts both in Germany and Canada. A typical statement, dating from 1996, by the German Inter-Ministerial Council for Research, Technology and Innovation[140] mentions both the need for cryptography and the necessity of upholding the state's right to investigate matters of public security:

> The use of cryptographic methods is one of the means of guaranteeing technical security and privacy in the transmission of information. The application of such methods is, therefore, of increasing importance. On the other hand, state authorities—for example in connection with police activities or criminal prosecution—have to have to be able to acquire unencrypted data."[141]

The approach of the German government to the issue, however, was far from consistent. Officials from the Ministry of Economics typically put forward the view that lack of security on the Internet is one of the most severe obstacles to unlocking the potential of electronic commerce. Thus, the then Economic Minister, Günther Rexroth remarked in 1996:

> The security of communication in open networks such as the Internet is of central importance for the development of the information society as a whole....A central question here is how we could support the employment of efficient cryptographic methods....[142]

The Ministry of the Interior, however, gave quite a different response; great emphasis was put on the undermining effects of cryptography:

> If in a few years all data flows on the Internet and other networks, as well as perhaps even ordinary phone calls, will—if effective regulations are not put in place—be encrypted, this will render the powers of prosecuting and security authorities...to tap into telephone and data communications totally ineffective.[143]

The Ministry of Justice, in turn, clearly saw the conflicting issues involved in regulating cryptography on the Internet. The then Minister of Justice, Eberhard Schmidt-Jortzig, asked in 1996: "Do you want to prohibit encryption?...Even if I wanted to I couldn't implement such a ban. Encryption programs can be freely downloaded from the Internet to your computer."[144]

In Canada, the Information Highway Advisory Council (IHAC) commented as follows in its final report in 1995: "It is in the interest of all Information Highway users and providers that an appropriate balance be found between privacy, civil and human rights, law enforcement and national security on the Information Highway."[145]

Three years later, Industry Canada's "Task Force on Electronic Commerce" saw the trade-off involved in the widespread application of strong cryptographic methods in the following terms:

> Cryptography is important to the growth of electronic commerce because it allows users to authenticate and safeguard sensitive data...the very elements that make cryptography attractive...can also conceal activities which pose a threat to the public safety of Canadians.... The inability to access or to decrypt information could well have a significant impact on the prevention, detection, investigation and prosecution of crime, as well as Canada's ability to monitor security threats to Canadians."[146]

As these quotes illustrate the denationalization challenge was clearly seen in both Germany and Canada by a variety of governmental institutions.

The issue of governmental control of cryptography was widely debated in both countries. The discussion mainly revolved around methods of regulation, ranging from an outright ban on the use of encryption to control of the export and import of cryptographic products. Two cryptography control schemes in particular gained some public prominence, namely, key escrow and key recovery. Key escrow involves the depositing of all keys with some form of agency which keeps the keys in secret but which can reveal them to state officials provided that the standard legal infringement conditions are met. Key recovery, on the other hand, involves limiting the length (i.e., the strength) of the keys in public use in order to allow governmental agencies some sort of back door access, such as, the ability to break the code.

When the German Inter-Ministerial Council for Research, Technology and Innovation in 1996 released its balanced statement quoted above, discussion on the possible regulation of cryptography had apparently been going on behind closed doors for quite some time. As early as 1993 the Minister of the Interior had come up with plans to license the use of cryptography and this possibility remained on the agenda in that agency for some years,[147] with apparent support from the Federal Office for the Protection of the Constitution (*Verfassungsschutz*),[148] the military and civil secret service, and the Federal Office of Criminal Investigation (*Bundeskriminalamt*).

Key recovery and key escrow were regarded as some form of middle way between a total ban and no regulation whatsoever.[149] It was clear at the time, however, that there was considerable tension between the different ministries on the issue, and especially between the Ministry of the Interior on the one hand and the Economics Ministry, the Ministry of Research and Technology, and the Ministry of Justice on the other hand.[150] In 1996 the Ministry of Economics set up the "*Task Force Kryptopolitik*" (i.e., "Task Force on Cryptopolicy") with the purpose of establishing a forum for interministerial discussion.[151] In a 1997 speech, and for the first time in public, the then Minister of the Interior, Manfred Kanther, advocated the regulation of cryptography with the result of further intensifying public debate.[152] Discussion on the issue spread to Parliament and its committees, and was taken up by an *Enquete-Kommission* on the "Future of Media."[153] Subsequently, rumours intensified that the government was going to introduce some form of control of cryptography,[154] but these claims were officially denied.[155] After the 1998 change of government, however, the rumours subsided and in 1999, the federal cabinet came out with the statement that "cryptographic methods and cryptographic products will continue to be allowed to be developed, produced, marketed, and used without any restriction."[156] As to possible abuses of the technology, the relevant ministries were requested to observe further developments and to submit a report due in 2001. Although there was little official government activity on the issue, the rumours that the government was going to intervene, and the public debate sparked by those rumours, provided the incentive for (some of) the groups under investigation to form a stand on the subject.

In Canada, the issue came up relatively early and was addressed by the Information Highway Advisory Council in its final report in 1995 (see above). At around the same time, institutions such as the Canadian Association of Chiefs of Police (CACP), the Royal Canadian Mounted Police (RCMP), and the Canadian Security and Intelligence Service (CSIS) began to express concern about losing the ability to intercept email or voice communications when conducting investigations.[157] It took another two years, however, for further governmental action. In 1997, Industry Canada—in the context of its "Task Force on Electronic Commerce"—formed a committee to investigate cryptography on the Internet.[158] In early 1998, this committee released a consultation paper[159] outlining the general problems and challenges associated with cryptography and calling for submissions by the public. Roughly two hundred submissions were received including contributions from private individuals, companies and industry associations, law enforcement agencies, and human rights organizations. This process provided the opportunity for a number of the groups under investigation to develop their position on the issue. Later that year, the Minister of Industry publicly announced an outline of "Canadian cryptography policy"[160] according to which cryptography would remain largely unregulated. The government explicitly decided against mandatory key recovery with the assurance that "Canadians are free to develop, import and use whatever cryptography products they wish."[161]

In addition to these national political debates, international discussion on cryptography policy also took place, most notably in the European Union and OECD. The European Commission took up the issue in the context of its investigations into a unified European regulatory framework for the information society, and in 1996, published a green paper on cryptography.[162] While the Green Paper led to some policy debate, as yet no regulatory intervention has occurred at the European level with the Commission consistently advocating freedom of trade in cryptographic products within the common market and a generally liberal approach to the issue.[163] In March 1997, OECD members also agreed on rather liberal cryptography guidelines.[164] This agreement was reached despite strong opposition from the USA which tried to negotiate, but unsuccessfully, international implementation of a key escrow scheme.[165] These international discussions, however, were relevant only for a small number of the groups under investigation.

Responses of Political Organizations

Results by dimension: Germany

Activity. Overall, the level of activity for all groups was rather low. As to the mode of activity, the CCC was the only group to have been active on the issue before any governmental statement on the matter was released.[166] The rest of the groups either only reacted to the rumours that the government was going to restrict cryptography in some way (these groups were the DPG, BDI, and the Greens) or remained passive throughout the debate (the DGB and Eco-Forum). No information at all could be gathered on the activities of the Republikaner Party or Thule-Net, suggesting that these groups were also passive in the debate. [167] Not surprisingly then, CCC also ranks highest on intensity of activity. The group engaged in lobbying activities, took part in

hearings and maintained contact with politicians, media, and industry representatives on the issue. The Green Party was active chiefly in Parliament
where it questioned the government on its plans to regulate cryptography.[168]
Despite the lack of information on their mode of activity, Eco-Forum ranks
equally with the Green Party on intensity of activity. The group took part in
conferences and hearings and kept in contact with the media on the issue.
BDI and DPG were very much limited their activity, with the BDI at least
engaging in internal discussions with government officials on the issue. As to
level of activity, it is not surprising that the sparse activity undertaken by
BDI, DPG, and DGB took place on the national level only. The Green
Party similarly limited its involvement to the national level, restricting its
activity to the national Parliament. Eco-Forum and CCC, however, went a
little further. On top of their national activities, these groups also engaged in
significant international activity, both of them chiefly at the European level.
Eco-Forum closely cooperated with EuroISPA, its European counterpart,
while CCC maintained ties to the European Parliament.

Intervention. There is an almost unanimous rejection by groups of governmental control of cryptography in any way. The degree of intervention
advocated by groups is thus generally very low with little difference among
the groups. Only two groups, namely, both general old politics groups
(DGB and BDI) acknowledge the legitimacy of some form of control of
communication by the state. Thus, the BDI maintains that the interest of
the state in criminal prosecution is legitimate in principle and has to be
weighed up against the also legitimate interest of citizens in safeguarding
the privacy of their communications.[169] Still, the group emphasises:
"...encryption has to be possible, to prevent unauthorized access to sensitive information and damage to business transactions....We reject an outright ban of cryptography."[170]

It should be noted, however, that this statement leaves room for intervention by other means below that of an outright ban. Similarly, the DGB,
while stressing the importance of ensuring the continued effectiveness of
state investigative agencies, at the same time does not want cryptography
restrictions to be too strong: "State authorities...have to be able to fulfil
their new tasks defined by the changed architecture of electronic networks
without creating a legal framework that allows them easier access to
encrypted messages."[171]

The other five groups (Thule-Net, Eco-From, CCC, the Green Party,
and the DPG)[172] are opposed, in principle, to any form of regulation of cryptography. Consider the example of the DPG which put its opposition in the
following terms: "In telecommunications services, the public interest in the
protection of privacy outweighs the state's interest in the control of communications for the purpose of protection against abuse and criminal activities."[173]

Or, in the slightly more polemic words of the CCC: "...the necessity of safe and confidential communications (essential in business communications in particular) has to be given priority over the demands of the so-called security authorities."[174]

Essentially three arguments are put forward to support this opposition: regulation of cryptography is seen as (1) ineffective for crime prevention, (2) dubious from the perspective of basic rights and freedoms, and (3) economically harmful (in particular to electronic commerce). While all three arguments are not made by all of the five groups, most of them at least point to a combination of two. The most common argument, mentioned in some form or another by all five groups, is the first: the ineffectiveness of attempts to control cryptography. According to this argument, there will always be ways to circumvent any regulation, making all attempts at regulation futile. The Green Party put this the following way:

> The idea of reducing crime on the Internet by a ban on cryptography is absurd considering the possibilities of hiding the encryption itself, for example by steganography.[175]—"People who have a disposition to commit crimes will not adhere to the rules and use cryptographic methods anyway. It would mainly hurt ordinary citizens."[176]

A text posted to the Thule-Net site argues along very similar lines:

> Organized crime won't be bothered by the crypto ban....The only consequence of the proposed law would be that respectable citizens would lose the secrecy of post for E-Mail and would be helpless in the face of spying by the authorities.[177]

Both of these quotes refer indirectly to the second argument, that ordinary or respectable citizens would be hurt most affected by regulation. The emancipatory groups in particular emphasize this point. Both CCC and the Green Party highlight the relevance of privacy and a basic right of "informational self-determination,"[178] regarded as of paramount importance in the age of the information society: "...the increasing relevance of the secrecy of telecommunications in the information society is used to legitimize its dismantling. The exact opposite is necessary."[179]

While the third argument (i.e., the harmful consequences of cryptographic regulation for e-commerce) is also mentioned by other groups (such as the CCC), the Eco-Forum is most pronounced on the point. The Forum sees crypto regulation as both weakening the competitiveness of the German cryptography industry and significantly increasing the vulnerability of e-commerce in general to industrial espionage.[180] Given this large consensus on nonintervention, it is apparent that most groups can not be meaningfully classified with regard to mode of intervention. DGB and BDI, however, who do approve of some form of cryptography control, can be assumed to favour the traditional mode of top-down regulation.

Spatiality. The widespread opposition amongst groups to governmental control of cryptography also means that most are also against any form of international cooperation in crypto regulation. Thus the US efforts, mentioned above, to establish international key escrow infrastructure in the OECD were heavily criticized. The Green Party had the following to say: "Those who think the dissemination of cryptography would be made easier by a sufficient number of OECD countries uniformly regulating key escrow couldn't be more wrong."[181]

A number of groups, however, went further by not only objecting to international crypto control, but by also calling for international efforts to foster cryptography. In this context, the Green Party and the CCC were most outspoken, both groups arguing that if international cooperation were to exist, it should serve the goal of encouraging the application of cryptographic methods to protect personal privacy rather than its control. In the words of the Green Party: "What would be an improvement is if the impediments to the international standardisation of cryptographic methods find an end."[182]

Crypto standardization, furthermore, is seen as something that can only be meaningfully achieved at the international level:

> [T]he question of international coordination has to be considered
> if application of and trade with cryptographic products should not
> be subjected to artificial barriers.[183] The federal government will try
> foster the application of cryptographic methods for the protection
> of the right to privacy....In coming international directives it will
> work to ensure the implementation of this norm.[184]

The DGB was not quite as vocal on the issue as CCC and the Green Party, but it did indicate that there should be no single-handed efforts in cryptography policy. It maintained that any such policy should be coordinated at the international level. The group was against the US scheme for the reason that it saw the proposal as an attempt by the United States to expand its regulatory ideas beyond its borders.[185] The Eco-Forum limited its statements on the issue to pointing out that any crypto ban in a single country would be totally ineffective.[186] The only activity of Thule-Net on the matter was in publishing endorsements of the OECD guidelines on its Web-site.[187] No information on spatiality could be gathered from the DPG, BDI, or Republikaner Party.

Canada

Activity. Activity in Canada was even lower than in Germany. The only group that took up the issue in a meaningfull, active sense was EFC. This group, following up on American debates on the feasibility of governmental cryptography control, was the only group to address the issue publically before the Canadian discussion came into full swing.[188] CAIP was at least reactive to governmental initiatives while the Reform Party claimed it would become more active on the issue in due course.[189] The other old politics groups (i.e., CLC, TWU, and BCNI) as well as the NDP were largely passive. No information relating to mode of activity could be gathered from DF / HF. In terms of intensity of activity, the distribution of the groups is more or less the same, with EFC clearly ranking first. In addition to making contact with various government representatives on the issue, EFC initiated several conferences on the subject and launched a golden key campaign to spur public debate.[190] CAIP became quite active later on in the debate, picking up its lobbying activities in particular in relation to Industry Canada. RPC set up internal task forces to deal with various aspects of Internet politics including cryptography, thus although publicly largely imperceptible, RPC thus can at least be said to have been more active than the rest of the groups. CLC, TWU, BCNI, and NDP barely dealt with the issue at all. The few activities RPC carried out took place on the national level only, while CAIP and EFC took their efforts to the international level as well. As it did in relation to the illegal content debate, EFC cooperated with partner organizations in the US and Australia and took part in a transnational campaign on the issue;[191] the focus of its activities, however, were clearly still national in scope. The international activities of CAIP were somewhat more significant as the group engaged itself in discussions held in the context of the aforementioned OECD negotiations.

Intervention. While there is still a considerable amount of opposition amongst the Canadian groups to governmental control of cryptography, the consensus is not quite as unanimous as it is in Germany. The NDP, for example, maintains that some form of restriction of cryptographic methods is necessary for crime control.[192] Although the group does note the importance of respecting privacy, in its view the state's responsibility for criminal prosecution prevails. The CLC presents a similar view, although it does not go quite so far. While insisting that "privacy on the information highway must be protected,"[193] it argues that some kind of state control over cryptography is desirable for the purposes of criminal prosecution and that compared to industry control (e.g., via market power) regulation by the state would be relatively harmless.[194]

One thing to be noted, however, is that both CLC and NDP were largely passive while the policy debate was actually occurring, with the views presented here really only being made clear in the context of the interviews held for this study. The issue-specific union, TWU, is opposed to both key escrow and key recovery. In its view the state's ability to monitor communications ought not be expanded,[195] with, however, one significant exception: the group maintains that, in order to obstruct attempts to evade taxation, financial information, especially that of transnational corporations, should not be allowed to be encrypted. In general, CAIP is also opposed to intervention. The group recognizes, however, the necessity of complying with international agreements that require export controls on cryptography products:[196] "We recommend that Canada take the most progressive position possible while maintaining its International obligations."[197]

The EFC is somewhat more pronounced in its opposition to crypto control—whether it be through licensing, banning, key recovery or key escrow:

> Electronic Frontier Canada would be opposed to any law that prevents Canadians from manufacturing, selling, or using any form of encryption within Canada. Electronic Frontier Canada is strongly opposed to mandatory key escrow and key recovery[198]...
> "Canadians should be able to keep secrets from the government, but not the other way around."[199]

The EFC's golden key campaign was designed to advance precisely this argument, the group's motto in the campaign being "Canadian Crypto: True, Strong, Free."[200] When a representative of EFC was interviewed for this study the point was made, however, that a situation of legitimate restriction could arise in export cases where security interests are directly affected (e.g., exports to Iraq or Libya).[201] The other groups were even more extreme in their opposition to cryptography control; BCNI, RPC, and the authoritarian DF / HF admit of no legitimate restriction at all. CATA (Canadian Advanced Technologies Association),[202] an affiliate of BCNI summarizes the point as follows:

> Canada should not limit the use, export or import of cryptographic products, there should be no government-mandated key recovery obliging parties to place their cryptography keys in the hands of government agencies or other entities.[203]

The arguments put forward against intervention are essentially the same as those advanced by the German groups. First, it is argued that crypto control would be ineffective because criminals would find a way to use the outlawed methods anyway. Indeed, what is sought to be controlled is already widely disseminated (in the words of the representative of CAIP, "the cat is out of the bag").[204] The second point made is that any regulation of cryptography would unduly infringe the privacy rights of citizens; and the third point is that it would be harmful to the e-commerce industry and drive Canadian crypto businesses out of the country. The first argument is common to almost all groups; the second is emphasized by the RPC and strongly supported by EFC; and the third advanced mainly by CAIP[205] and—although to a lesser degree –by DF / HF. There is, however, one additional argument that is specific to the Canadian groups. EFC and CAIP, and to a certain extend also RPC and DF / HF, maintain that existing laws already provide adequate possibilities for gaining access to encrypted information—once there is sufficient reason to believe that a crime will be or has been committed. Thus EFC comments: "... there are already adequate laws against... aiding, hindering, or concealing. There is no need for specific anti-cryptography provisions."[206]

Similarly, the CAIP argues: "The owner of the data in question should be required to provide such data in plain-text under appropriate lawful warrant provisions available today."[207]

In terms of mode of intervention, and as with the German groups, because most groups oppose intervention altogether, the question doesn't really come to the fore. NDP and CLC, who exhibit the clearest preference for some form of regulation of cryptography, refer to traditional state intervention as their preferred mode. CLC made the comment[208] that contrary to common consensus on Internet affairs the group does not want to prohibit all state involvement in the information highway. Among other things, the group sees surveillance and control of abuse as still being the role of the state– both on and off the Internet.

Spatiality. The degree of denationalization considered appropriate by groups in dealing with the problem of cryptography control is linked to their approach to intervention in general. The CLC and NDP—both consider some form of intervention desirable—do not directly comment on the issue of national versus international regulation. Given the background of the debate on the issue, however, it is safe to assume that the references of both groups to state control points to regulation at the level of the nation-state. The TWU, BCNI, and DF / HF do not comment on the international implications of their approach; they restrict themselves to comments in which intervention is opposed in a general sense. The EFC, RPC, and CAIP, however, do make mention of the international side of the issue. The EFC comments[209] that international coordination would be desirable if its purpose was the promotion, and not the limitation, of cryptographic methods. The RPC made a similar point, going on to say that international crypto control would not work anyway because of the possibility of conflict between states; thus, according to a representative of the group, it would hardly be imaginable that both Americans and Russians deposit cryptographic keys with the same agency.[210] CAIP went a little further. The group sees transnational industry cooperation as the appropriate way to further develop and distribute crypto technology.[211] CAIP went on to say: "Since the Internet is international in scope and transnational in its applications, the development of guiding legal and policy frameworks cannot stop at our domestic borders."[212]

Patterns across countries and across dimensions: Cross-country comparisons along dimensions

Activity. As in the illegal content case study, correlation along the different activity elements is quite high. It should be noted, however, that the overall level of activity in both Germany and Canada in relation to crypto policy is rather low. In both countries, half the groups either record no identifiable level of activity or can positively be regarded as having remained passive throughout the debate. Not surprisingly, these passive groups also display a low intensity level and limit their activity to the national sphere. The early movers, on the other hand, show a comparatively high level of intensity and are also more likely to act beyond the national level. As in the illegal content study, in this case study a trio consisting of the two emancipatory groups and the issue-specific business organization stands out in a number of respects. In Germany, the CCC, the Green Party and Eco-Forum demonstrate the highest level of activity intensity, with Eco-Forum and the CCC as the only ones to have been active internationally and the CCC as the first one to respond to the issue. In Canada, the EFC and CAIP (corresponding to the CCC and Eco-Forum) were most active, were the first to get involved in the debate and moved beyond the national level. The NDP (the equivalent to the Greens in Germany), however, clearly lags behind. Thus, in both countries, the issue-specific emancipatory groups and the issue-specific business organizations play a leading role. The old politics groups, in both Germany and Canada, occupy the other end of the scale (with the exception of the issue-specific business organization). Thus, the unions and the umbrella business organization join each other in recording a late, low intensity, and purely national (if there was any reaction at all). Given that there was hardly any information available on the activity of the authoritarian groups, they can be assumed to have remained largely passive. Once again, therefore, and for both countries, the central cleavage with respect to activity seems to have been formed between the unions, umbrella business organizations and authoritarian groups on the one hand and the trio groups on the other.

Intervention. The most striking feature of the reactions in this case study is probably the broad consensus across the vast majority of groups that regulatory intervention is to be avoided. Overall, the Canadian groups tend to be more accepting of regulation than the German groups. Canada's CLC and NDP were the only groups to approve of some form of control on cryptography, although these groups were largely passive during the debate and did not take a public stand on the matter. Still, in Germany, not even the passive groups go as far as the CLC or NDP. The only groups to acknowledge a certain trade-off between the private and public interests in privacy and its limits are the DGB and BDI. It is largely from the ranks of the old politics groups, in both countries, that these moderate interventionists come. Interestingly, the groups that do take a stand against control of cryptography do so in both countries for remarkably similar reasons. The argument that any form of crypto control is bound to be largely ineffective is common to most groups in both countries. Emancipatory groups such as the CCC, the Green Party in Germany, and the EFC in Canada make the point that any infringement of privacy is illegitimate (the Canadian NDP once again forms a notable exception here), while the issue-specific business organizations Eco-Forum and CAIP bring economic damage into the debate. One argument brought up by only some Canadian groups is that current search and seizure laws are strong enough to meet the needs of investigative agencies to not require special Internet controls. In relation to those groups that do favour some kind of control of cryptography, however, it can be assumed that the traditional top-down mode of intervention is what they have in mind.

Spatiality. As most groups are against any form of control, the spatial aspects of regulation simply do not come into the picture. Those groups that do propose some kind of intervention (such as CLC and NDP), moreover, do not comment on the possibility of joint international efforts despite the fact that the abovementioned US initiative for the OECD could have provided a reference point for such. Instead, a number of groups in both Germany and Canada look to the international sphere for support in promoting cryptography methods. Strictly speaking, this call for international cooperation does not constitute an attempt to address the problem of weakened governmental power in the face of a denationalization challenge. In fact, such efforts represent the very opposite; namely, an appeal to international institutions to lock in this weakening of governmental power. These responses suggest a relatively high level of denationalization on an extremely low level of intervention, such as, a joint effort of international nonintervention. Structurally, this resembles negative as opposed to positive integration[213] and can thus still be meaningfully tied back to the notion of denationalization. In Germany, the CCC and Green Party once again play a leading role in this respect; in Canada the CAIP, EFC and RPC are the main proponents of this view. Interestingly, four out of five of these denationalization-conscious groups are trio groups.

Overall Patterns
As with the illegal content results, the convergence between Germany and Canada in this case study is fairly significant. Although opposition by groups

to control of cryptography is slightly greater in Germany than in Canada, it is still fair to say that in both countries nonintervention is the dominant approach. A large majority of groups feel that the concerns of communication privacy outweigh any claim that the state might have in seeking to empower criminal investigation agencies. Intervention is generally seen as ineffective, economically harmful, and contrary to basic rights and freedoms. As a result, international coordination is seen as beneficial (if at all) only for the purpose of encouraging and facilitating the use of cryptographic methods and not for their restriction. Despite this strong opposition to intervention, however, the general level of activity among groups is rather low and international action on the matter rare. In both countries such international activity is limited to the issue-specific groups, and in particular the issue-specific business organizations and emancipatory groups.

Interestingly enough, the response patterns that emerged in the illegal content case study were largely present again here. On the one hand, there are those groups who actively press for low levels of intervention backed by international action to both ensure nonintervention and promote the advance of cryptography. These groups are, in both countries, the issue-specific business organizations (Eco-Forum and CAIP) and the issue-specific emancipatory groups (CCC and EFC). In Germany, the above two groups, Eco-Forum and CCC, are joined by the Green Party, thus exactly reconstituting the trio that the illegal content case study revealed. On the other hand, there are other groups who favour national intervention, but who are not very active on the issue. This is the same pattern that emerged in the content case, even though the groups that it relates to in this study are somewhat different. In the illegal content study the pattern applied to the authoritarian groups and some of the unions. Here, only the unions are the constant factor—with both the DGB and CLC evidencing this kind of approach. Interestingly, the Canadian NDP also falls into this pattern here, while the position of the authoritarian RPC comes much closer to the EFC or CAIP, thus representing a kind of "trio turnaround" between the NDP and RPC. As for the other authoritarian groups, little information on their stance in the debate was available.

CASES, PATTERNS, AND THEIR EXPLANATION: SOME HYPOTHESES

Both case studies reflect on problems associated with the Internet as a denationalization phenomenon. The two cases, however, reveal different approaches to the respective denationalization challenges. In the first case, the groups see international cooperation as an appropriate solution, but are pessimistic about the possibility of the necessary international consensus actually coming to fruition. They regard (transnational) self-regulation as an appropriate supplement or alternative. In the second case, most groups, are opposed to any regulation, and if they are looking to the international sphere, they call for international cooperation for the purpose of the promotion of cryptography rather than for its control. In effect, groups are more willing to accept the undermining of governance represented by the denationalization challenge in the second case than they are in the first—with some groups in the second case even appearing to welcome this loss of governance effectiveness. This result could be seen in the following manner: in the first case, groups are in favour of positive integration while in the second case, they are not only opposed to positive integration, but in favor of negative integration (in the sense of collective abstention from government intervention).

One way to explain this discrepancy is that the type of rule affected by the denationalization challenge is different between the two cases; it would thus appear to be an issue of national political institutions. In the first case study, the laws affected by the denationalization challenge protect community standards that are widely accepted in both Canada and Germany.

Thus, societal consensus requires a limitation in what members of society can say (i.e., the laws represent a limit to the right of freedom of expression) and the function of the state is merely in the formulation and implementation of this consensus. In the second case study, however, the relevant laws are of a different type. Long before the advent of the Internet, intense debates took place in numerous countries concerning whether or not, and to what extent, the state should be allowed to intercept and monitor communications. Thus, while the second case study involves the limitation of a basic right (i.e., that of privacy), the purpose of the regulation at hand is to empower the state to infringe upon that right. As a consequence it commands much less support than, for example, a ban on child pornography. The governance challenge at hand (i.e., the distribution of strong cryptography) thus undermines privileges that were reluctantly conferred upon the state (i.e., limits to privacy). From this perspective—in a specific institutional context—denationalization provides the opportunity for citizens to reclaim a limitation of their rights that was conceded to the state.

This argument adds an interesting aspect to a point often made in the globalization literature that welfare regulations are necessarily bound to the nation state. Scholars such as Streeck (1998), Cerny (1995), and Offe (1998), for example, maintain that the national constellation provides a unique opportunity for the conferral of welfare rights, and that these rights are not likely to find recognition at the international level. The cryptography case study presents this point the other way round: It is not only rights conceded by the state to the individual that are unlikely to find correspondence on the international level, it is also where society in general concedes rights to the state that international regulation of such rights is unlikely. A more general way to articulate the argument (by Streeck and others) is that there appears to be an important difference between a situation when the "winners" and "losers" of the denationalization process find themselves on the same side of the state / society cleavage, and when they find themselves on different sides of that cleavage. When they are on the same side, international regulation is more likely. When they are on different sides, the losers (vis-à-vis the state), are likely to be unwilling or unable (i.e., when international business interests stand in the way) to seek international regulation. However, if society obtains relative gains, it may attempt to block any such effort. One qualification is in order: Most striking about the second case study is the unanimity of the opposition against government intervention into cryptography. The motives of the different groups, however, may vary.

It is more or less obvious that emancipatory groups are driven by libertarian concerns (i.e., nonmaterial interests) in their objection to limitations of privacy. But the opposition of the old politics groups, in relation to cryptography regulation, seems to derive from their material interests, that is, concern for the economic consequences of (international) reregulation (i.e., obstacles to the further development if e-commerce). This has two implications: (1) The above argument is all the more plausible if the societal actors are united in their demands vis-à-vis government (albeit for different reasons), and (2) the responses of the old politics groups suggest that, in general, we can expect the promotion of international re-regulation to increase as the economic cost of such regulation decreases. The higher its potential economic cost, the greater the likelihood of resistance against it. Here the cleavage within old politics (i.e., that between capital and labor) is of little importance, as regulation is seen as impacting on the electronic economic sector as a whole. This explanation sits well with the proposition that, in the context of denationalization, the conflict between capital and labor loses importance when juxtaposed to conflicts between economic sectors. The new conflict lines depend on the position of the various sectors in the denationalization process (Frieden 1991; Frieden and Rogowski 1996).

One aspect particular to the first case study is also worth mentioning. Interestingly, groups in Germany, as a whole, favored lower levels of content regulation than groups in Canada, despite the fact that the intensity of regulation currently in force in Germany is significantly higher than in Canada. Germany has more, and stricter, rules on communication content (especially as regards right-wing political propaganda) than Canada and yet the level of intervention called for by the German groups is lower than the level favored by their Canadian counterparts.

The familiar path dependency argument is thus turned on its head. The higher the level of current intervention, the less there is argument for regulation of the new challenge. This somewhat surprising result is, however, compatible with the notion that denationalization drives states to a (low) common denominator of regulatory intervention (Scharpf 1996a; Cerny 1996). As Germany starts at a higher baseline of intervention, groups recognize that the adaptation necessary to reach this common level is more extreme. Indeed, the point is explicitly made by some of the German groups that there are laws currently in force in Germany that in a global environment are simply untenable. This reinforces the notion that the denationalization challenge—as an element of problem structure—translates into unifying pressures independent of the institutional environment. The fact that the degree of convergence in group demands is relatively high across both countries lends support to this hypothesis.

Another general result worth pointing out is that the overall level of activity varies with both case and country. It is higher in relation to illegal content than cryptography and higher for Germany than Canada. This is likely to be a factor of the respective policy cycles of both countries. The further developed a policy cycle is, the more likely it is that groups form clear-cut positions on the issues. This illustrates the close relationship between group activity and the institutional context in which a group is located. This relationship goes both ways: the institutional environment affects group activity and group activity affects the institutional environment. In the present case studies, both directions of this relationship are evident. Thus, while some of the groups—most notably the issue-specific emancipatory groups and the issue-specific business organizations—decisively influenced the way public debate progressed, state initiated discussion (itself often a reaction to public debate) was the trigger for a majority of groups to become involved (if they did so at all). This implies that overall, the nation-state remains the focal point of politics. This result is supported by two additional considerations. These are (1) activity on the international level was exceptional in both cases (the groups once again most prominent in this regard being the issue-specific emancipatory groups and issue-specific business organizations); and (2) international activity (where it did occur) did not replace national activity. In other words, the groups that did go beyond the national political system did so on top of activity at the national level.

The nation-state appears to retain its central role for politics. However, some groups actively influence the shaping of the issues and become active on a level above the nation-state. Below the level of these overall generalizations, a significant finding in both cases studies is that the different elements of each response dimension correlate rather strongly. That is to say, groups who rank high on one element of a dimension also tend to rank high on the other elements. In both cases, groups who are active early display a higher intensity of activity and are more likely than others to engage in activities beyond the national level and vice versa. Similarly, groups who favour stronger international institutions adopt a rather broad territorial scope, and vice versa. Furthermore, a highly interventionist approach goes hand in hand with a preference for classical top-down steering mechanisms while a low intervention approach correlates with self-regulation as the chosen means. Moreover, based on these correlations, two basic patterns emerge. The first pattern combines high rankings on spatiality and activity with a low ranking on intervention; in other words, groups adopting this pattern actively press for international regulation but with a low degree of intervention. The second pattern is a reverse of the first; groups within this pattern prefer national action which is highly interventionist but are largely passive. These groups thus exhibit low rankings on spatiality and activity but a high ranking on intervention.

One interesting aspect of the relationship between these two patterns is that spatiality and intervention are inversely correlated. In other words, the higher the territorial scope of a group's position, the more likely the group is to favor lower levels of intervention together with alternative steering mechanisms. Groups tend to see traditional steering mechanisms as relating to the nation-state and look to new regulatory approaches where an international focus comes into the picture. This finding is consistent with the theory that there is a functional connection between the nation-state and certain degrees and types of regulatory intervention. Denationalization, on the other hand, forces a rethinking of regulation and intervention in terms of new "public private partnerships" (Reinicke 1998). The low level of activity of groups who favour a high degree of intervention suggests that this inverse correlation is linked to group expertise. It seems that more active groups are much clearer on the denationalized character of the issue and know much more about both the problem and the implications of possible solutions. Common to these active groups is the viewpoint that an international approach is essential, but the low feasibility of international cooperation requires lower levels of intervention and alternative steering mechanisms as the only alternatives. The lower the expertise of the relevant group, the more likely it is to resort to standard politics (i.e., a focus on the nation-state and top-down interventionist measures). The inverse correlation between spatiality and intervention can be explained, therefore, as being a direct consequence of the denationalized character of the challenge. If groups are well-informed about the issue, they realize the challenge suggests a high level of spatiality, but a low level of intervention. If their level of expertise is low, they will stick to their demands standard politics—which also represents an inverse correlation.

Interestingly, the distribution of groups making up these response patterns is similar both between the two countries and across the two cases. In the illegal content case study the first pattern is linked, in both countries, to a trio of the two emancipatory groups (Green Party / CCC and NDP / EFC respectively) and the issue-specific business organization (Eco-Forum and CAIP respectively), forming a coalition that cuts across the traditional cleavage between old and new politics. The second pattern is linked to the authoritarian groups and some unions, notably the German issue-specific DPG and the Canadian umbrella organization CLC. In the cryptography case study, this trio coalition emerged again in relation to the German groups, and was partly represented in relation to the Canadian groups, with only the NDP standing apart. The second pattern was taken up again by a number of union groups, namely, both umbrella organizations, CLC and DGB. It was also adopted by the NDP.

In order to explain the distribution of these patterns, it seems plausible to turn again to the specific interests and in addition to the regulatory ideas of the different groups. It can be argued that if the interests of a group are strongly affected by an issue, it is likely that that group will become active on the issue and acquire the appropriate expertise necessary to respond in accordance with those interests. That expertise, in turn, can be hypothesized to drive the groups in the direction of the first pattern—even if the underlying interests are of a disparate nature. As has been argued above, the emancipatory groups appear to be mainly motivated by nonmaterialistic interests, while the issue-specific business organizations seem to be driven mainly by material interests. Indeed, in the reasoning accompanying their respective positions, the emancipatory groups specifically highlight the issues of free speech and privacy while the business organizations point to the economic side effects of regulation. This explains the rather unintuitive combination of groups within the trio. At the same time, it is not very surprising that the general emancipatory groups constitute the weakest elements of the trio as their interests are not as strongly affected as those of issue-specific groups On the other hand, those groups whose primary interests are not specifically engaged by the relevant issue can be assumed to be less concerned with acquiring the necessary expertise to deal with it. On the above hypothesis this leads these groups into the second response pattern, assuming however that the regulatory mode of this pattern is consistent with their principled ideas. In other words, groups (1) whose interests are not directly affected and (2) who traditionally favour strong national intervention (which both unions and authoritarian groups do—albeit for very different reasons) react with a kind of regulatory default that translates into the second pattern.

Considering the different types of groups, the (issue-specific) emancipatory groups and issue-specific business organizations stand out in almost all respects. Despite diverging interests they are united in their preference for international approaches to the Internet challenges on lower levels of intervention and/or alternative steering mechanisms. At the same time, they took note of the changing role of the state and the additional channels of influence available to them. Leaving behind the traditional cleavages between Left and Right and old and new politics, this combination of groups appear to be best prepared to use the opportunities denationalization provides and to meet the ensuing challenges.

NOTES

1. For the history of the Internet, see Hafner and Lyon 1998.

2. Most notable in this regard is the TCP/IP communication protocol that provides the lingua franca of inter-computer communications.

3. An Internet-host is a computer that is communicating via the use of one or more languages (i.e., protocols) that are specific to the Internet (in particular the TCP/IP protocol). For Internet statistics, see Network Wizards, "Internet Domain Survey," January 2001 @ http://www. nw.com.

4. The number of users is much higher than the number of hosts because multiple users can access the Net via a single host. The estimate presented here uses the rather conservative multiplier of 3.6 (see Computer Industry Almanac Inc. 1999, "U.S. Tops 100 Million Internet Users — November 1999," Press Release, 4. November 1999 @ http://www.c-i-a.com/199911iu.htm).

5. Leonard Kleinrock (MIT), Paul Baran (Rand Corporation), Donald Davies (NPL), and Roger Scantlebury (NPL).

6. See Baran, Paul 1964, "On Distributed Communications," Rand Corporation Technical report (Memorandum RM-3420-PR, 1964). Document accessible @ http://www.rand.org/publications/RM/ RM3420/.

7. See John Gilmore's own comment @ http://www.cygnus.com/~gnu/.

8. For Germany, see Art. 5, I *Grundgesetz* (Basic Law); for Canada see Sec. 2 (b), *Canadian Charter of Rights and Freedoms*.

9. As will be shown, this does not determine how groups will react to the issues at hand.

10. An alternative might have been the IG Medien (The media industry union). Initial investigations, however, showed that the IG Medien had not yet dealt with Internet issues.

11. See Eco-Forum 1998, "*Hohe Nachfrage nach elektronischen Geschäften*," press release, January 1998.

12. CCC 1998, "Frequently Asked Questions V1.1a," as at 10 June 1998 @ https://www.ccc.de/faq.html.

13. BCNI, "About BCNI: Business Leadership"; document accessible @ http://www.bcni.com/ aboutBusiness.html.

14. See NDP, Constitution of the New Democratic Party As amended by the Federal Convention, Ottawa 1999.

15. See NDP 1983, "Statement of Principles," adopted by the 12th Federal NDP Convention, Regina, 1 July, 1983. In addition, it should be noted that the

NDP's positions put the party into permanent opposition within the Canadian political arena.

16. On the Reform Party in general, see Harrison 1995.

17. In January 2000 the Reform Party regrouped as the "Canadian Reform Conservative Alliance." In the 2000 general election, the Conservative Alliance again won slightly more than a fifth of the seats in the House of Commons (66 of 301).

18. CAIP 1998, "A Cryptography Policy Framework for Electronic Commerce: Building Canada's Information Economy and Society," Comments by the Canadian Association of Internet Providers; document accessible @ http://www.caip.ca/ecomm/caipcryp.htm.

19. Electronic Frontier Canada, homepage accessible @ http://insight.mcmaster.ca/org/efc/efc.html.

20. See the site itself @ http://www.freedomsite.org/.

21. Dunphy, Bill, and Lemire, Marc 1997 in Farber, Bernie M. (ed.), *From Marches to Modems: A Report on Organised Hate In Metro Toronto*, Canadian Jewish Congress, Ontario; document accessible @ http://www.cjc.ca/marchestomodems002-05.htm.

22. Interview with a representative of the Heritage Front, 21 April 1998.

23. Elmer-Dewitt, Philip 1995, "On a Screen Near You: Cyberporn", *Time Magazine*, 3 July 1995.

24. "Schmuggelpfad für Schmuddelkram," *Süddeutsche Zeitung*, 10 February 1996.

25. In other words, "Law Concerning the Distribution of Media Content Harmful to Minors."

26. In other words, "Law Concerning the Protection of Minors in Public."

27. In other words, "Criminal Code."

28. In Canada, this is stipulated in sec. 163.1. (4) of the CCC, in Germany in art.184 V of the StGB. The depiction of children, however, is only one form of illegal pornography. In Canada that is, sec. 163 of the CCC deals with obscene materials. In a similar manner art. 131 and 184 III of the StGB prohibits certain sexual depictions.

29. See, for example, arts. 86 and 86a of the StGB. Article 86a of the StGB specifically prohibits the import and export of the symbols of these organizations. While not specified in the StGB, the organizations to which these regulations are generally applied are those of the radical right and left which are under scrutiny by the *Verfassungsschutz* (Federal Office for the Protection of the Constitution).

30. Bundesamt für Verfassungsschutz 1998, *Extremistische Bestrebungen im INTERNET*, Bundesamt für Verfasssungsschutz: Köln, 28; (translation: GW).

31. *Interministerieller Rat für Forschung, Technologie und Innovation beim Bundeskanzler*.

32. BMWi 1996, *Info 2000: Deutschlands Weg in die Informationsgesellschaft*, Bericht der Bundesregierung, Bonn, BMWi; (translation: GW).

33. BMWi 1997, *Info 2000: Deutschlands Weg in die Informationsgesellschaft*, Fortschrittsbericht der Bundesregierung, Bonn: BMWi, "Vorwort" and p. 15; (translation: GW)

34. "'Der Nationalstaat ist überholt.' Spiegel-Gespräch mit Justizminister Edzard Schmidt-Jortzig über die Kontrolle des Internets", *Der Spiegel,* 11/1996, p. 104; (translation: GW).

35. de Savoye, Pierre, MP, of the Bloc Québecois Party, Edited Hansard, No. 145, Tuesday, December 15, 1994 (Debates of the House of Commons in Canada).

36. Phinney, Beth, MP, of the Liberal Party, Edited Hansard, No. 198, Wednesday, May 10, 1995 (Debates of the House of Commons in Canada).

37. Riis, Nelson, MP, of the NDP, Edited Hansard, No. 77, Thursday, March 19, 1998 (Debates of the House of Commons in Canada).

38. Industry Canada 1995, "Connection, Community, Content: The Challenge of the Information Highway," Final Report of the Information Highway Advisory Council, Ottawa, 48–49.

39. Resolution passed at the 90th Annual Conference of the Canadian Association of Chiefs of Police, Resolutions, Regina, Saskatchewan, 24 August, 1995.

40. Consider for example the following examples of newspaper headlines from the German daily *Süddeutsche Zeitung* (SZ) from a single year (1996): "Underworld in the Internet" (*"Unterwelt im Internet"*), 2 January 1996; "25-year-old spreads child porn on the Internet" (*"25 jähriger verbreitet Kinderpornos im Internet"*), 11 May 1996; "Murder pictures on the Internet" (*"Mordbilder im Internet"*), 14 August 1996; "The Internet—neither clean nor safe" (*"Internet—weder sauber noch sicher"*), 29 August 1996.

41. On the use of university Internet systems in Canada, see Shade (1996).

42. See for example, Borchers, Detlef 1996, "Ein Elefant im Sauladen," *Die Zeit,* 12 January 1996. For a timeline of the events, see Möller, Ulf 1997, "Zensur?" @ http://www.fitug.de/ulf/zensur/96.html

43. See, for example, Global Internet Liberty Campaign, Electronic Frontier Canada 1997, "Letter to Chancellor Kohl urges investigation of CompuServe prosecution", Joint Press Release, 23 April 1997 @ http://insight. mcmaster.ca/org/ efc/pages/pr/gilc-pr.23apr97.html).

44. The "Internet Child Pornography Restriction Act" was first introduced on 8 April 1997 as Bill C-396 in the 35th Parliament but because of the June 1997 parliamentary elections it was reintroduced in the following year in the 36th Parliament as Bill C-424 (First Reading 11 June 1998). See also Campbell, K.K. 1998, "Porn Prevention", *The Toronto Star,* 16 July 1998. The bill surfaced again in the 36th Parliament as Bill C-231 (First Reading 18 October 1999) and most recently as Bill C-212 in the 37th Parliament, first read 05 February 2001.

45. Act on Information and Communication Services

46. See art. 4 and art. 1, §5 of the IuKDG.

47. Voluntary Self-Control Multimedia

48. See the homepage of the FSM @ http://www.fsm.de.

49. Eco-Forum 1998, "Appell an die Vernunft", press release, 13 May 1998.

50. CCC 1996, "Stellungnahme zur Anhörung 'Jugendschutz und neue Medien' des Ausschusses für Familie, Senioren, Frauen und Jugend vom 09.10.1996", press release, 9 October 1996. See also the intervention section below.

51. See for example, "If we want to avoid this development leading to a state of lawlessness in Cyberspace and a feeling of defencelessness of the people we have to strive for solutions beyond the scope of national activities"; Source: van Haaren, Kurt 1997, *Diskussionbeitrag zur Konferenz "Global Information Networks,"* Bonn, 6–8 July 1997; [(translation: GW)]. (Kurt von Haaren is chairman of the DPG).

52. Both groups demand the establishment of a unified institution for regulating multimedia, bringing together the competencies hitherto lying with the different German *Länder*. See e.g. DGB 1998, *Die Informationsgesellschaft sozial gestalten,* Antrag an den 16. Ordentlichen Bundeskongreß des DGB, 8-12 June 1998, Düsseldorf or DPG 1995, *Stellungnahme der Deutschen Postgewerkschaft für die öffentliche Anhörung zum Thema "Multimediale Kommunikation"* am 20. September 1995 beim Ausschuß für Post und Telekommunikation des Deutschen Bundestages.

53. The only available evidence shows that they demand—like the unions, see above—a review of the division of competencies between the federal and *Länder* governments with regard to media policy in the face "global technical developments." See Die Republikaner, "Medienpolitik," in *Wahlplattform '98,* document accessible @ http://www.republikaner.org/wahl98/17medi98.htm.

54. See Die Republikaner, "Außenpolitik," in *Wahlplattform '98*, document accessible @ http://www.republikaner. org/wahl98/25auss98.htm.

55. Eco-Forum 1996, "Zensur im Internet—Internet Service Provider ergreifen die Initiative," press release, 1 March 1996; (translation: GW).

56. Interview with a representative of Eco-Forum, 11 May1998.

57. *Ausschuß für Bildung, Wissenschaft, Forschung, Technologie und Technikfolgenabschätzung: Beschlußempfehlung und Bericht,* Bundestags-Drucksache 13/5163, 19 June 1996. MdB Manuel Kiper (of the Green Party) was rapporteur of this committee and consensus on the report was reached in Parliament (see Bundestags-Drucksache 13/5163); (translation: GW).

58. Statement by CCC's press spokesman Andy Müller-Maguhn in the public hearing on the "protection of minors and new media" (*"Jugendschutz und Neue Medien"*) of parliament's "Committee on Family, Senior Citizens, Women and Youth" *("Ausschuß für Familie, Senioren, Frauen und Jugend"),* 09 October 1996; (translation: GW).

59. CCC 1996, "Internet-Zensurgesetz in den USA beschränkt Freiheit der Meinungsäußerung auch in Deutschland", press release 12 February 1996; (translation: GW).

60. Interview with a representative of the board of management of the DPG, 14 April 1998.

61. Interview with three representatives from BDI, 19 March 1998.

62. BDI 1997, *Stellungnahme zum Entwurf des Informations- und Kommunikationsdienste-Gesetzes* (IuKDG) Bundestags-Drucksache 13/7385, BDI, Abteilung Rechung und Versicherung, Köln, 30 April 1997; (translation: GW).

63. Fraktion Bündnis 90/Die Grünen, *Elektronische Netze—Rechtsfreier Raum? Raum für freie Meinung!*, kompakt & griffig, 13/23; (translation: GW).

64. Die Republikaner: "Medienpolitik," in *Wahlplattform '98*; (translation: GW), document document accessible @ http://www.republikaner. org/wahl98/17medi98.htm.

65. Die Republikaner: "Jugend," in *Wahlplattform '98*; (translation: GW), document document accessible @ http://www.republikaner.org/wahl98/22jugd98.htm.

66. This was emphasized in the interview with a representative of the board of management of the DPG, 14 April 1998.

67. DPG Hauptvorstand 1996, *Stellungnahme zum Referentenentwurf für ein Gesetz des Bundes zur Regelung der Rahmenbedingungen für Informations-und Kommunikationsdienste*, Frankfurt, 17 December 1996; (translation: GW).

68. Interview with a representative of Eco-Forum, 11 May 1998.

69. Interview with a representative of the Green Party, 18 March 1998.

70. BDI 1997, *Antworten des Bundesverbandes der Deutschen Industrie (BDI) auf die Fragen der Fraktionen im Ausschuß für Bildung, Wissenschaft, Forschung, Technologie und Technikfolgenabschätzung des Deutschen Bundestages für den Teil der Anhörung zum Informations-und Kommunikationsdienstegesetz (IuKDG) am 14. Mai 1997*, BDI, Köln, 30 April 1997, 2; (translation: GW).

71. Interview with a representative of the IG-Metall (i.e., the steelworkers union), 29 July 1998. The representative was nominated as the cooperating expert by the DGB.

72. CCC 1997, "Stellungnahme zum Entwurf eines Gesetzes zur Regelung der Rahmenbedingungen für Informations- und Kommunikationsdienste (IUKDG) zur öffentlichen Anhörung am 14. Mai 1997 in Bonn beim Auschuß für Bildung, Wissenschaft, Forschung und Technologie und Technologiefolgenabschätzung", press release 15 May 1997; (translation: GW).

73. CCC 1996, "Stellungnahme zur Anhörung "Jugendschutz und neue Medien" des Ausschusses für Familie, Senioren, Frauen und Jugend vom 09.10.1996", press release 09 October 1996; (translation: GW).

74. Text published on the Thule-Net—public board briefs (i.e., *"Kurzmeldungen"*) @ http://www.thulenet. com/texte/orgpol/text0001.htm; "FRG" = Federal Republic of Germany; [translation GW].

75. BDI 1997: Antworten des Bundesverbandes der Deutschen Industrie (BDI) auf die Fragen der Fraktionen im Ausschuß für Bildung, Wissenschaft, Forschung, Technologie und Technikfolgenabschätzung des Deutschen Bundestages für den Teil

der Anhörung zum Informations-und Kommunikationsdienstegesetz (IuKDG) am 14. Mai 1997, BDI, Köln, 04/30/1997, 12; (translation: GW).

76. Eco-Forum 1996, "Zensur im Internet—Internet Service Provider ergreifen die Initiative," press release 01 March 1996.

77. See DGB Bundesvorstand 1996, *Multimedia und Informationsgesellschaft: Chancen nutzen, Risiken bewältigen,* Düsseldorf.

78. For the Greens see for example, Fraktion Bündnis 90/Die Grünen, *Entschließungsantrag,* Bundestags-Drucksache 13/7937 vom 11.06.1997; for the CCC see for example, "Stellungnahme zur Anhörung "Jugendschutz und neue Medien" des Ausschusses für Familie, Senioren, Frauen und Jugend vom 09.10.1996," press release 09 October 1996.

79. Fraktion Bündnis 90/Die Grünen, *Elektronische Netze—Rechtsfreier Raum? Raum für freie Meinung!,* kompakt & griffig, 13/23.

80. CCC 1997, "Stellungnahme zum Entwurf eines Gesetzes zur Regelung der Rahmenbedingungen für Informations-und Kommunikationsdienste (IUKDG) zur öffentlichen Anhörung am 14. Mai 1997 in Bonn beim Auschuß für Bildung, Wissenschaft, Forschung und Technologie und Technologiefolgenabschätzung," press release 15 May 1997.

81. Interview with a representative of the Business Council on National Issues, 29 April 1998.

82. Interview with a representative of the Reform Party of Canada, 24 April 1998.

83. Interview with an MP of the New Democratic Party, 23 April 1998.

84. Interview with a representative of the Heritage Front, 21 April 1998.

85. CAIP 1997, *Report on Political and Regulatory Activities for 1996-1997,* document accessible @ http://www.caip.ca/agmrepor.htm.

86. The Code of Conduct enables complaints to be made about offensive or illegal content. See CAIP 1996, "CAIP Responses to Questions from the IHAC Steering Committee on the Internet," document accessible @ http://www.caip.ca/hacan.htm.

87. This included the training of police officers and the maintenance of dialogue with the Association of Police Chiefs, the Royal Canadian Mounted Police (RCMP), and the Child Pornography Unit (other wise known as "Project P") of the Ontario Provincial Police (OPP). See Langford, Margo 1998, "Internet Licensing Bill—CAIP Comments," document accessible @ http://www.caip.ca/c-424.htm. Margo Langford is chairman of CAIP.

88. Interview with a representative of the Canadian Association of Internet Providers, 04/20/1998.

89. Langford, Margo 1998 (see note 87).

90. Electronic Frontier Foundation.

91. Electronic Frontier Australia.

92. See the homepage of the GILC @ http://www.gilc.org/

93. This was outlined in an interview with a representative of Electronic Frontier Canada, 21 April 1998.

94. CAIP 1996, "CAIP Responses to Questions from the IHAC Steering Committee on the Internet," document accessible @ http:// www.caip.ca/ihacan.htm.

95. Interview with an MP of the New Democratic Party, 23 April 1998.

96. See Shallit, Jeffrey 1997, "Regulating the Internet: National Necessity or Global Folly?," paper presented at a conference on *Global Markets, Global Morals?* at Wilfrid Laurier University, 24 October 1997; document accessible @ http://math.uwaterloo.ca/~shallit/talks.html. Jeffrey Shallit is vice-president of EFC.

97. Interview with two representatives of the Canadian Labor Congress, 23 April 1998.

98. See, Martin, Keith, MP, Edited Hansard, No. 181, Friday, March 31, 1995 (Debates of the Canadian House of Commons).

99. Interview with a representative of the Telecommunication Workers Union, 29 April 1998; interview with a representative of the Heritage Front, 21 April 1998.

100. Interview with a representative of the Canadian Association of Internet Providers, 04/20/1998.

101. Shallit, Jeffrey 1997; see note 96.

102. See sec. 3.1.1, and note 44.

103. Sec. 8 in the original bill C-396 and sec. 9 in the reintroduced bills C-424, C-231, and C-212; see note 44.

104. Interview with an MP of the New Democratic Party, 23 April 1998.

105. Strahl, Chuck, MP, Edited Hansard, No. 198, Wednesday, May 10, 1995 (Debates of the House of Commons in Canada).

106. Interview with a representative of the Reform Party of Canada, 24 April 1998.

107. Strahl, Chuck, see note 105.

108. Interview with two representatives of the Canadian Labor Congress, 23 April 1998.

109. One example given was the "Nizkor Project" which publishes all kinds of information on Nazi crimes on the Internet and receives suggestions and comments from a global audience. See the home page of the Nizkor Project @ http://www. nizkor.net/; Interview with a representative of the Telecommunication Workers Union, 29 April 1998.

110. Interview with a representative of the Heritage Front, 21 April 1998.

111. In the interview, it was said that even Saddam Hussein would probably not publicly support hate speech; interview with a representative of the New Democratic Party, 23 April 1998.

112. Interview with a representative of the Reform Party of Canada, 24 April 1998.

113. Interview with a representative of the Canadian Association of Internet Providers, 20 April 1998.

114. Shallit, Jeffrey 1997, see note 96.

115. CAIP 1997, *Report on Political and Regulatory Activities for 1996-1997*,. document accessible @ http://www.caip.ca/agmrepor.htm

116. Forseth, Paul, MP, RPC, Edited Hansard, No. 75, Tuesday, March 17, 1998 (Debates of the House of Commons in Canada). This comment was made in the context of a discussion of Bill C-245, introduced by Mr. John Finlay MB of the Liberal Party and aimed at amending the Criminal Code of Canada for the purpose of strengthening various provisions, including those relating to child pornography.

117. Breitkreuz, Garry, MP, RPC, Edited Hansard, No. 155, Monday, April 14, 1997 (Debates of the House of Commons in Canada). See also Forseth, Paul, MP, RPC, see note 116.

118. See note 102 and surrounding text, as well as note 44 and surrounding text.

119. Langford, Margo 1998, "Internet Licensing Bill—CAIP Comments," document accessible @ http://www. caip.ca/c-424.htm. Margo Langford was chairman of CAIP.

120. EFC 1997, "Anti-Internet Bill a Cynical Ploy," press release 23 April 1997.

121. EFC 1997, "Electronic Frontier Canada says the Canadian Human Rights Commission should not attempt to control Internet content," press release 16 October 1997.

122. Interview with a representative of the Electronic Frontier Foundation, 21 April 1998.

123. Shallit, Jeffrey 1997: Should governments try to censor the Internet?—No. in: The Costco Connection, May/June 1997, p. 14f. Jeffrey Shallit was vice-president of EFC.

124. CLC 1995, "Info Highway to Serve Big Business: IHAC Member Parrot," press release 27 August 1995.

125. Interview with two representatives of the Canadian Labour Congress, 23 April 1998.

126. See secs. 4, 10, and 11 of the Bill C-424 (see note 44).

127. Strahl, Chuck, MP, RPC, Edited Hansard, No. 198, Wednesday, May 10, 1995 (Debates of the House of Commons in Canada).

128. Whereas an ISP provides access to the Internet (and access only), content providers are responsible for designing Web-pages and other types of content services. Interview with a representative of the Canadian Association of Internet Providers, 20 April 1998.

129. Interview with a representative of the Heritage Front, 21 April 1998.

130. Interview with a representative of Electronic Frontier Canada, 21 April 1998.

131. Jones, David 1997, "Re: Internet in the classroom," Letter to The Honorable Mr. John Snobelen Minister of Education & Training, 10 February 1997; document accessible @ http://www.efc.ca/pages/pr/efc-snobelen-letter.10feb97.html. David Jones was president of EFC.

132. Some features of the groups' responses, of course, are particular to their national setting. For example, in Canada, the general old politics groups tend to be more detached from the issue than in Germany, a result that is probably due to their stronger focus on the semantic core of old politics issues (i.e., business interests and industrial relations).

133. For the history of cryptography, see Kahn 1969.

134. The special algorithms used for this purpose are called one way algorithms. They are distinguished by the fact that they are easy to apply, but difficult to reverse. A classic example of this is multiplication as against factoring.

135. Today, keys longer than 40 bits are generally considered to represent strong cryptography, while keys longer than 128 bit are considered virtually unbreakable. See CAIP 1998, "A Cryptography Policy Framework for Electronic Commerce: Building Canada's Information Economy and Society," Comments by the Canadian Association of Internet Providers; document accessible @ http://www.caip.ca/ecomm/caipcryp.htm.

136. The secrecy of post and telecommunications is constitutionally guaranteed in most OECD countries. In Germany this provision is in art. 10 (1) of the *Grundgesetz* (Basic Law); in Canada it can be found in sec. 8 of the *Canadian Charter of Rights and Freedoms*. Both countries also explicitly outlaw the unlawful infringement of this right to secrecy. In relation to Germany, see §§ 201–203 of the *StGB*; in relation to Canada, see subsec. 184 (1) of the *Criminal Code of Canada*.

137. See sec. 184.2 (3) of the *Criminal Code of Canada*. According to the *Criminal Code*, peace officers include—among others—police officers or constables, sheriffs, justices of the peace, mayors, and wardens, etcetera (see sec. 2).

138. See art. 1 (1) No. 1, G10-Gesetz. Art. 2 (1) of the said law specifically enumerates the criminal offences for which the law applies. Relevant in this context is also art. 39 of the Law on Foreign Trade and Payment (*Außenwirtschaftsgesetz, AWG*).

139. Following the international dissemination of PGP, Zimmermann became the target of a three-year criminal investigation by the US Customs Service, due to an alleged violation of US export restrictions. See Sussman, Vic 1995, "Lost in Kafka Territory: The Feds go after a man who hoped to protect privacy rights," *U.S. News & World Report*, 3 April 1995; accessible @ http://www.eff.org/pub/ Legal/Cases/ PGP_Zimmermann/sussman.article. See also Zimmermann's homepage @ http://www. pgp.com/phil/.

140. See note 31.

141. BMWi 1996, *Info 2000. Deutschlands Weg in die Informationsgesellschaft. Bericht der Bundesregierung*, Bonn, BMWi; (translation: GW).

142. BMWi, Rexrodt: 'Task Force Kryptopolitik' für mehr Sicherheit im Bereich Informationstechnologie, press release 07 October 1996; (translation: GW).

143. Kanther, Manfred 1997, "Mit Sicherheit in die Informationsgesellschaft," Speech by Federal Minister of the Interior Manfred Kanther on the occasion of the 5. IT-Security Congress, 28 April 1997, Bonn (Transcript quoted from homepage of "crypto.de" @ http://www.crypto.de/kanther1.html); (translation: GW).

144. "'Der Nationalstaat ist überholt.' Spiegel-Gespräch mit Justizminister Edzard Schmidt-Jortzig über die Kontrolle des Internets," *Der Spiegel* 11/1996, p. 104; (translation: GW).

145. Industry Canada 1995: Connection, Community, Content. The Challenge of the Information Highway. Final Report of the Information Highway Advisory Council, Ottawa: Industry Canada, 143.

146. Industry Canada. Task Force on Electronic Commerce 1998: A Cryptography Policy Framework for Electronic Commerce, Ottawa: Industry Canada, 2.

147. Gast, Wolfgang 1995, "Kanther will mitlesen," *Die Tageszeitung*, 28 December 1995.

148. See interview with the president of the Federal Office for the Protection of the Constitution, *Hannoversche Allgemeine Zeitung*, 18 December 1996.

149. See Gast, Wolfgang 1998, "Polizeispitzel in jeder Datenleitung," *Die Tageszeitung*, 23 July 1998; Lorenz-Meyer, Lorenz 1997, "Das Kreuz mit der Kryptographie," *Spiegel-Online* 03/1997.

150. See "Lauschangriff im Internet," *Die Wirtschaftswoche*, 08 May 1997.

151. BMWi 1996, Rexrodt, "'Task Force Kryptopolitik' für mehr Sicherheit im Bereich Informationstechnologie," press release, 07 October 1996.

152. See note 143 above and Wiegold, Thomas 1997, "Hintertür für Behörden," *Frankfurter Rundschau*, 06 May 1997.

153. An "*Enquete Commission*" is a special parliamentary committee. In it's final report, the commission urged that: "Above all agreement has to be reached on the... acceptability of cryptographic systems;" Deutscher Bundestag 1998, *Schlußbericht der Enquete-Kommission Zukunft der Medien in Wirtschaft und Gesellschaft—Deutschlands Weg in die Informationsgesellschaft*, Bundestags Drucksache 13/11004, 22 May 1998.

154. See, for example, "Innenministerium plant deutschen 'Clipper'-Chip," *Der Spiegel*, 22 October 1997; and "Kanther feilt weiter am Polizeischlüssel," *Die Tageszeitung*, 5 February 1998.

155. See, for example, "Kanther kippt Krypto-Verbot," *Chip* July 1997, p. 106 and "Verwirrung um Kanthers Kryptopläne," *VDI Nachrichten*, 20 February 1998, p. 22.

156. BMWi 1999, "Eckpunkte der deutschen Kryptopolitik," press release, 02 June 1999; (translation: GW).

157. The CACP, for example, specifically demanded the facilitation of the "lawful interception of communications" in the face of "sophisticated new communications technology... (See Resolution passed at the 90th Annual Conference of the Canadian Association of Chiefs of Police, Resolutions, Regina, Saskatchewan, 24 August, 1995).

158. Enman, Charles 1997, "It's the law vs. privacy in high-tech debate: Secret codes are contentious issue as study begins," *The Ottawa Citizen*, 06 August 1997.

159. Industry Canada, Task Force on Electronic Commerce 1997, *Setting a Cryptography Policy Framework for Electronic Commerce: Building Canada's Information Economy and Society*, Notice No. IPPB-003-98.

160. Accessible @ http://www.e-com.ic.gc.ca/english/releases/41d6.html.

161. Only some minor amendments to the *Criminal Code* were proposed including provisions to "deter the use of cryptography to conceal evidence" and to "apply existing interception, search and seizure and assistance procedures to cryptographic situations and circumstances." See Industry Canada 1998, *Summary of Canada's Cryptography Policy: Backgrounder*, Industry Canada, Ottawa; document accessible @ http:// www.e-com.ic.gc.ca/english/fastfacts/43d7.html.

162. European Commission (DG XIII) 1996, *Legal protection for encrypted services in the internal market Consultation on the need for community action*, Commission Green Paper, COM (96) 76.

163. See, for example, European Commission (DG XIII) 1997, *Ensuring security and trust in electronic communication. Towards a European Framework for Digital Signatures and Encryption*, Communication from the Commission to the European Parliament, the Council, The Economic and Social Committee and the Committee of the Regions ensuring Security and Trust in Electronic Communication, COM (97) 503.

164. OECD 1997, *Cryptography Policy: The Guidelines and the Issues*, OECD, Paris; document accessible @ http://www.oecd.org/dsti/sti/it/secur/prod/e-crypto.htm.

165. Schulzki-Haddouti, Christiane 1997, "OECD-Krypto-Richtlinien: Internationales Signal für eine liberale Kryptopolitik," *Telepolis: Magazin der Netzkultur*, 9 April 1997; document accessible @ http://www.heise.de /tp/.

166. Interview with a representative of the Chaos Computer Club, 27 March 1998.

167. This general lack of information on Republikaner and Thule-Net unfortunately limits the conclusions that can be drawn about the other dimensions of these groups' reactions.

168. See, for example, "Überlegungen der Bundesregierung zur Verschlüsselung von Daten in der Telekommunikation," Kleine Anfrage, 12 June 1995, Bundestags Drucksache 13/1676; and "Sicherheit der Informationstechnik und Kryptierung," Kleine Anfrage, 13 February 1996, Bundestags Drucksache 13/3932.

169. Interview with three representatives from the BDI, 19 March 1998.

170. BDI 1997, *Stellungnahme zum Entwurf des Informations-und Kommuni-kationsdienste-Gesetzes (IuKDG)*, Bundestags-Drucksache 13/7385, BDI, Abteilung Rechung und Versicherung, Köln, 30 April 1997; (translation: GW).

171. DGB 1998, *Die Informationsgesellschaft sozial gestalten, einstimmig angenommener Antrag der Deutsche Postgewerkschaft, der IG Medien Druck und Papier, Publizistik und Kunst und der Gewerkschaft Handel, Banken und Versicherungen an den 16. Ordentlichen Bundeskongreß des DGB*, 8–12 June 1998, Düsseldorf; (translation: GW).

172. No information in this respect could be found for the Republikaner Party.

173. DPG 1995, *Stellungnahme der Deutschen Postgewerkschaft für die öffentliche Anhörung zum Thema "Multimediale Kommunikation" an 20. September 1995 beim Ausschuß für Post und Telekommunikation des Deutschen Bundestages.*

174. CCC 1997, "Stellungnahme zur Öffentlichen Anhörung am 12. Mai 1997 "Datensicherheit" der Enquete-Kommission "Informationsgesellschaft" des Deutschen Bundestages," press release 2 May 1997; (translation: GW).

175. Steganography is a method by which information is hidden within other pieces of information (a text in a picture, for example).

176. "Es trifft den braven Bürger," Interview with Manuel Kiper, *PC-Online*, July 1996, p. 44; (translation: GW). Manuel Kiper was an MP of the Green Party.

177. Text posted to Thule-Net—public area "Kurzmeldungen" @ http://www. thulenet.com/texte/ rechallg/text0009.htm.

178. For the Green Party see: Fraktion Bündnis 90/Die Grünen 1995, *Antrag*, Bundestags-Drucksache 13/3010, 10 November 1995; for the CCC see: CCC 1997, "Stellungnahme zum Entwurf eines Gesetzes zur Regelung der Rahmenbedingungen für Informations-und Kommunikationsdienste (IUKDG) zur öffentlichen Anhörung am 14. Mai 1997 in Bonn beim Auschuß für Bildung, Wissenschaft, Forschung und Technologie und Technologiefolgenabschätzung," press release 15 May 1997.

179. Kiper, Manuel, and Ingo Ruhmann 1998: Abgesang auf ein strategisches Grundrecht. Lauschangriff auf die Informationsgesellschaft, in: Kommune. Forum für Politik, Ökonomie, Kultur, 3/1998, 49; (translation: GW), see note 176; Ingo Ruhman was an assisstant to Mr. Kiper.

180. Interview with a representative of Eco-Forum, 11 May 1998.

181. Schulzki-Haddouti, Christiane 1997, "EMail-Interview mit dem Bundestagsabgeordneten von Bündnis 90/Die Grünen, Dr. Manuel Kiper," *Telepolis: Magazin der Netzkultur*, 14 April 1997; document accessible @ http://www.heise.de/ tp/; (translation: GW), see also note 176 above.

182. Ibid.

183. Fraktion Bündnis 90/Die Grünen 1996; Kleine Anfrage, Bundestags-Drucksache 13/3932, 13 February 1996; (translation: GW).

184. Fraktion Bündnis 90/Die Grünen: Antrag, Bundestags-Drucksache 13/5777, 11 October 1996; (translation: GW).

185. Interview with a representative of the IG-Metall (i.e., the steelworkers union), 29 July 1998. The representative was nominated as the cooperating expert by the DGB.

186. Interview with a representative of Eco-Forum, 11 May 1998.

187. "Die Empfehlungen der OECD," Text published on the Thule-Net @ http://www.thulenet.com/texte /rechallg/text0010.htm.

188. Interview with a representative of Electronic Frontier Canada, 21 April 1998.

189. Interview with a representative of the Reform Party of Canada, 24 April 1998.

190. One of its conferences was entitled "Free Speech and Privacy in the Information Age," held at the University of Waterloo on 26 November 1994; See the homepage of the conference @ http://insight. mcmaster.ca/org/efc/pages/symposium-94–11–26-overview.html. For information on the golden key campaign, see EFC's homepage @ http://insight.mcmaster.ca/org/efc/pages/crypto/golden-key.html.

191. See footnotes 90–92 above and surrounding text.

192. Interview with an MP of the New Democratic Party, 23 April 1998.

193. Parrot, Jean-Claude 1995, "Labour's View," Presentation at a Conference on "Community Access to the Information Highway," 7–9 September 1995, Ottawa. (Jean-Claude Parrot was executive vice-president of the Canadian Labor Congress.)

194. Interview with two representatives of the Canadian Labor Congress, 23 April 1998.

195. Interview with a representative of the Telecommunication Workers Union, 29 April 1998.

196. Most notable in this context is the Wassenaar Arrangement of 1996, which is essentially the successor of the CoCom Regime. See the hompage of the Arrangement at www.wassenaar.org.

197. CAIP 1998, "A Cryptography Policy Framework for Electronic Commerce: Building Canada's Information Economy and Society," Comments by the Canadian Association of Internet Providers; document accessible @ http://www.caip.ca/ecomm/ caipcryp.htm.

198. EFC 1997, Statement on Canadian Cryptography Policy, August 14, 1997; document accessible @ http://www.efc.ca/pages/ crypto/policy.html.

199. Jones, David 1997, "Can you keep a Secret? Canadian Crypto: True, Strong, Free," *The Convergence*, 8 February 1997 @ http://www.theconvergence.com/columns/djones/08021997/. David Jones was president of the EFC.

200. See EFC's homepage @ http://insight.mcmaster.ca/org/efc/pages/crypto/golden-key.html.

201. Interview with a representative of the Electronic Frontier Foundation, 21 April 1998.

202. According to information from the interview with the representative of the Business Council on National Issues (04/29/1998), BCNI had not yet form an official position on the issue. However, due to the close ties between BCNI and CATA the future position of BCNI can be expected to by very close to CATA's views.

203. CATA 1998, New CATA Alliance Sets High-Tech Priorities, press release 03 Juni 1998.

204. Interview with a representative of the Canadian Association of Internet Providers, 20 April 1998.

205. CAIP emphasises that key escrow or key recovery would "only increase costs for the vast majority of legitimate businesses." See CAIP 1998, "A Cryptography Policy Framework for Electronic Commerce: Building Canada s Information Economy and Society," Comments by the Canadian Association of Internet Providers; document accessible @ http://www.caip.ca/ecomm/caipcryp.htm.

206. EFC 1997, Statement on Canadian Cryptography Policy, August 14, 1997; document accessible @ http://www.efc.ca/pages/ crypto/policy.html.

207. CAIP 1998, "A Cryptography Policy Framework for Electronic Commerce: Building Canada s Information Economy and Society," Comments by the Canadian Association of Internet Providers; document accessible @ http:// www.caip.ca/ecomm/ caipcryp.htm.

208. Interview with two representatives of the Canadian Labor Congress, 23 April 1998.

209. Interview with a representative of Electronic Frontier Canada, 21 April 1998.

210. Interview with a representative of the Reform Party of Canada, 24 April 1998.

211. Interview with a representative of the Canadian Association of Internet Providers, 20 April 1998.

212. CAIP 1996, "CAIP Responses to Questions from the IHAC Steering Committee on the Internet," document accessible @ http:// www.caip.ca/ihacan.htm.

213. For the theoretical distinction between positive and negative integration, see Scharpf (1996b).

Chapter 4

Citizenship and Migration in Germany and the United States

Sabine Dreher

International migration can be defined as a person's "transfer from the juris-diction of one sovereign to another" (Zolberg 1994, 153), whether temporary or permanent. In contrast to the internet and the problems of climate change, migration is not a new phenomenon. History is replete with the movements of large numbers of people from rural communities to both cities and faraway countries (Rosenberg 1994, 163ff). The presence of borders and territorial states in modern times, however, distinguishes migration flows in recent history from the migration of peoples in prehistoric times (Zolberg 1994). Furthermore, migration processes always have been limited to specific regional spaces, they have been restricted to specific periods (e.g., the settler migration from Europe to the United States in the nineteenth century), and to a limited number of people (Sassen 1996, 149). For these reasons it is pos-sible to differentiate migration processes. The focus of this chapter will be on the renewed increase in migration flows in the eighties and nineties that have turned migration into one of the more important determinants of social change (see Castles and Miller 1998, 4). In this context, Germany and the United States stand out because they have experienced impressive immigra-tion flows in comparison with other countries in their respective regions,[1] giving rise to an intense public debate on immigration. This chapter will dis-cuss, therefore, how interest organizations have responded to the renewed increase in migration in Germany and the United States, and what factors have shaped their responses.

Special to the migration case studies is social inclusivity as an element of group responses. It refers to the scope of citizenship rights honoured by a state. Following Marshall (1992, 40), three dimensions of citizenship may be distin-guished: civil, political, and social. Civil rights refer to individual freedom, political rights are linked to the participation in the exertion of political power, and social rights focus on the material preconditions underlying both civil and political rights. It is generally accepted that the provision of some form of social citizenship is crucial to the stability of modern society (see

Faist 1995, 14). Migrants challenge many of the assumptions on which citizenship rights are based. Does a democratic state have the right to limit these (human) rights to its citizens only? For example, does an undocumented immigrant have the right to organise or strike (Frost 1998, 873)? Political groups that push for some form of migrant access and the granting of full social, political, and civil citizenship rights are termed socially inclusive. At the other extreme of the spectrum, we expect groups to favor the closing of borders and the removal of aliens from the territory of the respective state.

INTRODUCTION TO THE CASE STUDIES AND GROUP SELECTION

Scholarship on migration distinguishes between politically and economically induced migration flows, with the former referring to those who flee from life threatening political persecution, and the latter to those who want to change their individual or familial circumstances by emigrating to a country offering more opportunities.[2] Following this distinction, the first case study investigates a new form of labor migration in which the migrants—owing to the fact their stay is supposed to be temporary (Germany) or because they are undocumented (United States)—do not have extensive social citizenship rights. As a result, they undermine social citizenship rights of the host countries because they displace domestic workers who are integrated into this regime. The second case study explores the discussion, on the future of political asylum, that was initiated by the surge of refugees in the 1990s. In both cases, the central problem was whether or how the nationally oriented regime of social, political, and civil citizenship rights should be adjusted.

The main findings arising out of the case studies are, first, that out of all the groups studied, trade unions display the most innovative, intensive, and internationally-oriented response, and second, that groups in Germany are more oriented towards solutions at the European level and use influence mechanisms beyond the nation-state more intensively than political organizations in the United States. This leads to the conclusion that an explanation of group responses has to take into account both institutional or structural and actor-centered factors.

Group Selection

Governance challenges posed by denationalization that have been publicly discussed constitute the point of reference for the case studies. These publicly discussed issues influenced the selection of the more specialized organizations. This is visible most clearly in the labor migration case, where the public debate on wage and labor standards in Germany and the United States focused on different industries.

In Germany, the issue of immigrant labor under substandard conditions arose, at the end of 1994, in the context of the use of temporary workers, from other EU member countries, in the construction industry that were posted to German construction sites, mostly from Portugal. In the United States, the existence of migrant sweatshops operating in the clothing industry was revealed in the media in the 1990s and intensive public debate followed.

With regard to the umbrella organizations in Germany, the DGB, the Bündnis 90/Die Grünen (The Green Party), and the Republikaner Party were chosen for the same reasons as in the other two cases. The central organization for employers in Germany that deals with wage and labor standards and matters of collective bargaining is the Bundesvereinigung der deutschen Arbeitgeberverbände (BDA). Sectorally, the trade union in the construction industry, IG-Bauen-Agrar-Umwelt (IG BAU), and the Hauptverband der deutschen Bauindustrie (HDB), one of the three employers' organizations that is representative of the industry as a whole (in this case), were selected. The HDB comprises employers of the main trades and the larger construction companies, but all three organizations cooperated closely and followed a similar argumentation in this case.

The rationale behind including both umbrella and sectoral organizations for research was that sectoral groups are specifically affected by a governance dilemma, in the sense that the dilemma directly concerns their interests, and are likely to respond differently to the dilemma than an umbrella group, which comprises divergent interests. The asylum case study is, in this sense, peculiar, because no sectoral organization representing old politics is specifically affected by asylum as an interest group. Trade unions and employer organizations referred to their respective peak organizations, and were largely inactive on the issue. Their inactivity was therefore not coded as a nonresponse.

As regards the groups active within the new politics sphere, selection was based on whether the organization was concerned with welfare rights issues and immigration in general, as it was assumed that such organizations would deal with more specific concerns related to refugees and the labor market as well. These issues have been taken up in Germany by major welfare organizations such as *Caritas*, the *Paritätischer Wohlfahrtsverband*, the *Diakonisches Werk* and the *AWO*. The *AWO* was opted for because its origins are in the labor movement and because its work is concentrated on Turkish immigrants, the largest immigrant group in Germany. An issue specific authoritarian organization focusing solely on immigration could not be identified.

Table 4.1. Group Selection in Germany and the United States

	General	Issue area specific
Germany		
Old Politics—Left	Deutscher Gewerkschaftsbund (DGB)	IG-Bauen Agrar Umwelt (IG-BAU)
Old Politics—Right	Bundesvereinigung der deutschen Arbeitgeberverbände (BDA)	Hauptverband der deutschen Bauindustrie (HDB)
New Politics—Emancipatory	Bündnis 90/Die Grünen (Greens)	Arbeiterwohlfahrt (AWO)
New Politics—Authoritarian	Die Republikaner	—
USA		
Old Politics—Left	American Federation of Labor—Congress of Industrial Organizations (AFL-CIO)	Union of Needlestrades Industrial and Textile Employees (UNITE)
Old Politics—Right	National Association of Manufacturers (NAM)	American Apparel Manufacturers Association (AAMA)
New Politics—Emancipatory	American Civil Liberties Union (ACLU)	National Immigration Forum (NIF)
New Politics—Authoritarian	Reform Party (Reform)	Federation for American Immigration Reform (FAIR)

The general groups within the old politics sphere are the American Federation of Labor/Congress of Industrial Organizations (AFL-CIO), and the National Association of Manufacturers (NAM). The AFL-CIO is a federation of trade unions representing the trade union movement both nationally, and in international organizations such as the ILO in Geneva. The NAM comprises small and middle-size firms focused on the US domestic market, and which, theoretically, are negatively affected by import competition (Lösche 1992, 423). As to the new politics sphere, the American Civil Liberties Union (ACLU) aggregates many concerns of the new social movements in the field of civil rights, including immigrant's rights while the Reform Party was selected as a representative of the new authoritarian angle. Its leader, Ross Perot, had dominated populist politics in the United States throughout much of the period under investigation.

The issue specific organizations under investigation for he old politics sphere are as follows: The Union of Needlestrades Industrial and Textile Employees (UNITE) was formed in 1995 by way of a merger between the Amalgamated Clothing and Textile Workers Union and the International Ladies Garment Workers Union. UNITE is a major union covering a range of industries but with an emphasis on the clothing production and domestic goods industries. The union was chosen because it is negatively affected by the hollowing out of wage and labor standards. The American Apparel Manufacturers Association (AAMA) which is a central trade association for companies in the clothing industry was picked out as a representative of the Old Right.

As regards issue specific organizations within the new politics sphere, the focus was again on groups dealing with immigration in general. For these reasons, the National Immigration Forum (NIF) representing emancipatory politics and the Federation for American Immigration Reform (FAIR) representing the authoritarian approach were selected. The NIF is an umbrella organization uniting groups concerned about the growing anti-immigration sentiment in the United States in the mid-nineties it comprises trade unions and corporate representatives. FAIR is at the center of anti-immigration politics at the national level in the United States and was established in 1979 by demographers concerned with the negative impact of immigration on population growth. From there it has evolved into a more right wing populist anti-immigrant organization.[3]

LABOR MIGRATION AND SOCIAL STANDARDS IN GERMANY AND THE UNITED STATES

Governance Challenge: the Issue of Low Wage Migrant Labor

The literature on migration cites various factors determining labor migration flows (for an overview see Massey et al. 1993) of which employer demand is one of the more important ones (Piore 1979, 19–24). The reason for this is that migrant labor has a specific function in the labor market which domestic labor cannot fulfill. Understanding migration flows between richer and poorer countries, therefore, is a matter of understanding the structure of job opportunities in the host country, and the motivation of migrant workers to take up these jobs (Piore 1986, 24). According to Piore, labor markets are characterized by a fundamental duality: core (primary) jobs with employment and income security, and peripheral (secondary) jobs characterized by flexibility and precariousness of employment. Most workers are not interested in the latter type of job because they do not provide the income and security necessary to build and lead a socially accepted life, raise a family, or pursue other life goals. Employers rely on specific groups to fill these positions. For example, young people in between school and university, housewives, and farmers in the off season. These groups are target earners, working to finance specific projects, and do not define themselves through these jobs. Migrant workers are target earners too, defining themselves through what they can achieve with earnings in their home countries. Their stay in the host country is seen as temporary (Piore 1986, 24–25; 1979, 54).[4] The distribution of secondary and primary jobs changes over time, with an increase in secondary jobs generally occurring at a time of economic crisis and/or tight competition. It is this context that forms the background for the issue at hand because it is widely believed that the rigidity and inflexibility of European labor markets is the central impediment for a revival of stable economic growth, and much effort has been put into transforming the majority of jobs into more flexible arrangements (OECD 1994). One central element of labor market flexibility is that there is a greater dispersion of wage levels. The contribution of migration to flexibility, in this sense in the United States is not generally acknowledged, even though officials are generally aware of the problem. The central fear of trade unions in Germany is that the new labor migration contributes to the creation of a similar low wage sector. At issue is whether Germany will follow the US model (as the OECD recommends) or whether, within the European Union, an alternative solution to regaining competitiveness can be found.

The governance challenge in this case, then, is created by firms which, in order to cut costs and hence increase competitiveness, use migrant labor under substandard working conditions. This practice constitutes a challenge for the governance capacity of the state because national wage levels and labor standards are undermined and industry collective agreements placed under pressure. Often, even basic human rights are not adhered to at the working place. The employment of migrants under substandard conditions thus contributes to the creation of a low wage and low standards sector.

The two country sections are organized along similar lines. First, the specific nature of the governance challenge within the particular industry is introduced. Next, is a discussion of the way members of the public perceived the challenge, and of the policy cycles that the challenge created. They are concluded with a presentation of the various responses of the political organizations to the governance challenge structured according to the three dimensions introduced in chapter 2: activity, spatiality, and intervention.

Germany

Compared to other industries, the construction industry is characterized by three somewhat unique features. The first is that while the industry has played an integral role in the functioning of industrial society, the actual labor process, which makes up the construction industry, can only be termed industrial to a limited extent. Whereas the typical industrial labor process is characterized by the employment of unskilled workers, construction still relies on artisan work, on skills associated with the individual (Voswinkel et al. 1996, 31). Second, the industry presents a difficult economy of scale, for the reason that continually changing production locations mean that transport and organization costs are always high. Even in the context of a market dominated by the increasing liberalization of services, economics of scale remain limited (Koch 1991, 265). A third specificity of the construction industry is the seasonal character of work—concentrated mainly in the summer and more or less coming to a standstill in the winter months. Employment in the industry is thus somewhat different from the industrial norm.

The problem of low wage temporary migrant workers has to be seen in the context of the changes in the production process in the industry. Whereas, in the past, the success of a firm was based on its construction expertise and the quality of its actual work, today it is efficiency in organization and mediation processes such as marketing, logistics, and financial knowledge that dictate who succeeds and who does not. Tied up with this trend has been the increasing systematic differentiation of firms into general building contractors (*Generalunternehmer*) and subcontractors (Voswinkel et al. 1996, 121). This differentiation has had two direct consequences. The first is a fragmentation of the organization of production, a process which, since the 1980s, has been gaining ground. The second is an increase in the centralization of planning and control taken on by large firms, namely, the general construction companies. Instead of having many single and independent firms for each step of the production process, which have to be coordinated by the builder, the builder hires a general construction company who organizes and coordinates the production process, and who employs subcontractors for the specific steps. As a result, the core personnel of firms is reduced, with workers acquired on a task-specific basis. At the same time, competition is increasingly determined by price, and decreasingly determined by quality, reliability, and the formation of long-term relationships

(Steinmann and Haardt 1996, 7). The liberalization of services under the single European market in 1993 has also played its part in this trend, as firms increasingly make use of differential wage levels across Europe when subcontracting tasks. The employment of migrant labor thus has to be seen as an expression of the changes in the organization of the production process.

The impact of denationalization, in this case the employment of temporary migrant labor, undermines a highly developed set of social standards that considerably mitigate problems stemming from the irregular employment patterns in the industry. Collective agreements concerning working time, holidays, hire-and-fire policies, wage scales, and workplace safety are negotiated between the trade union, the *Industriegewerkschaft Bauen Agrar Umwelt* (IG BAU), and the two employer associations: *Zentralverband des deutschen Baugewerbes* (ZDB), and *Hauptverband der deutschen Bauindustrie* (HDB) (Voswinkel et al 1996, 107).

Besides collective agreements covering wage levels, there is another set of agreements setting up an industry-wide insurance scheme, the aim of which is to compensate workers for the various disadvantages they suffer in comparison to workers in other industries. There are four such insurance schemes covering holiday, pay, training, and additional benefits. By way of example, the holiday fund, organized on an intra-firm basis, allows worker to change an employer without losing holiday entitlements (Voswinkel et al. 1996, 110). One problem arising from foreign service provision is that foreign companies do not contribute to these additional funds. The concern within the industry, therefore, is that as more and more services are provided by foreign firms, this system of additional social funding is becoming less viable.

Perception of the Governance Challenge and the Policy Cycle
In the 1990s, the German construction industry was faced, according to one analysis (Sahl and Stang 1996), its biggest crisis since 1945. Indicative of this crisis is increased unemployment, extreme price competition, the withdrawal of employers from collective agreements, massive violations of work time regulations, and the near collapse of the industry's system of collective financing for training. In addition, since 1993, large contractors have increasingly relied on the use of posted contract workers, resulting in a further increase in domestic unemployment.

At the center of the issue is the fact that a part of the labor migration inflow currently facing Germany does not lie within its own sphere of jurisdiction. The posting of workers constitutes an integral part of the services aspect of the Common Market as set out by the Single Market Initiative 1992. This freedom is guaranteed under Articles. 3, 18 and 49–66 of the Treaty of Amsterdam. Since 1993, therefore, it has been possible for firms from all European member states to offer their services Europe-wide. It was the construction industry that made use of this freedom to the greatest extent, and, in the early 1990s, Germany experienced a rapid increase of service providers from Portugal who used posted workers to carry out their services.[5] These workers were employed under Portuguese employment conditions and paid according to Portuguese wage levels, with the only exception being that German employment protection laws (i.e., termination of employment issues) applied to them. The workers were not even covered by German accident prevention regulations. The result of this was that German wage and working conditions were increasingly hollowed out. According to Eichhorst (1998, 189–190), in 1994–1995 there were between approximately one hundred fifty thousand and two hundred thousand posted workers in Germany, with the same number of domestic construction workers unemployed at the same time. According to one "guestimate," approximately 20 per cent of workers in the major construction sectors were posted workers. In other words, and according to these numbers between 1990 (when the number of posted workers was zero) and 1995, about 25 to 30 percent of the labor market had been claimed by posted workers (Faist et al. 1998; 106–121). The impact of posting on the German construction labor market was thus quite substantial.

While political efforts to add a social welfare dimension to the Common Market had already begun in December 1989, the European Posted Worker's Directive came into effect in December 1996. The national policy process in Germany was triggered off only in December 1994, when a renewed attempt to pass a European directive on posted workers failed. Complaints were raised that there was an increase in service provisions by foreign subcontractors in member states of the European Union, who employed posted workers covered by the lower wage and labor standards of the sending country. In draft legislation, the federal government pointed out that the increase in the number of unemployed construction workers seemed to be related to the competitive advantage enjoyed by firms relying on such workers.[6] Dr. Christine Bergmann, Senator for Labor and Women in the city of Berlin, pointed out the urgency of national legislation during a hearing in the Bundesrat in November 1995, providing Berlin as an example of the seriousness of the problem. According to Dr. Bergmann, in 1994, the total volume of investment in Berlin and its surrounding area amounted to thirty-six billion DM, while at the same time there were about thirty thousand unemployed construction workers in the same area—a figure that was increasing. In addition, there were an increasing number of bankruptcies in the industry. She also pointed out that at the level of the city-state of Berlin, every possible measure had already been undertaken to remedy the situation. Berlin had introduced a law that only firms that paid wages according to collective agreements would be considered for public works projects. If the idea of Europe as a single market was not to suffer long-term damage, she argued, a solution to the problem had to be found.[7] The call for national regulation was also sounded by the Bavarian Ministerpräsident, Edmund Stoiber, in 1995. He argued:

> It is no longer acceptable that in Germany, the biggest construction site in Europe, small and medium size firms are being driven out of business by firms taking advantage of standards inequalities. ...It is therefore completely justified to demand the compliance of these firms with national wage and labor standards.[8]

Lobbying by political groups for a national law dealing with posted workers began at the end of 1994, spearheaded by both the construction industry's trade unions and employer associations. On September 1, 1995, the government introduced legislation regulating the use of posted workers into Parliament; this law came into effect on March 1, 1996 (the European directive came into effect in December of the same year). The passing of a national law was only the first step in the process. The law only extends collective agreements that had been declared universally binding to posted workers. However, in order for it to be effective, such a declaration of general binding had to be achieved in the first place. A declaration of general binding is negotiated in a committee consisting of three unions and three employer associations, all of which were opposed to minimum standards for the construction industry. The main employer organization, the BDA, only agreed after the wage level had been considerably lowered. For this case study, the group reactions have been analysed during 1995 before the passing of the national posted workers law.

Responses of Political Organizations in Germany to the Governance Challenge

Activity. National public discourse on the issue of posted workers started in December 1994. Taking this date as a yardstick for establishing response time, three groups can be regarded as having been actively involved in the demand for a national posted workers law in Germany from the very beginning, namely, the DGB, IG BAU, and HDB. They called for a national regulation immediately after the negotiations for a regulation on the European level failed. All other groups only responded to these initiatives (BDA, the Greens, and Republikaner), or were passive (AWO).

In terms of the degree of activity, most active were the two trade unions (IG BAU more than the DGB). Both participated in the parliamentary hearings, coordinated their initiatives with other European trade unions, and lobbied at the European Union level. Most impressive is the record of IG BAU who organized several academic conferences on the issue, bringing together scholars and trade union activists from several European countries.[9] The trade union further organized various seminars involving regional monitoring agencies with the purpose of bringing together all parties involved in the implementation of the legislation.[10] In addition, the organization was involved in both national and Europe-wide lobbying activities during the various meetings of the Council of Ministers. It set up an office for posted workers in Berlin, and concluded a bilateral agreement with the Portuguese construction trade union recognizing each other's memberships. In fact, IG BAU had already recognized the challenges stemming from liberalization and the Single Market when it was first being discussed in the 1980s and had started to prepare from then on.

As to the level of activity of the seven groups, three actively used Europe-wide institutional links, namely, the DGB, IG BAU and BDA while one group (HDB) was only insignificantly involved at the European level. The extent of European activities of both the IG BAU and the DGB is quite impressive in this context, given that they are nationally organized interest groups. The Green party and the Republikaner party were only active at the national level.

Spatiality. Since it was the exploitation of a comparative advantage that was made possible through the Common Market, it is not surprising that the degree of political denationalization of group responses is rather high. Most groups called for a Europe-wide directive, the sole exception being the authoritarian Republikaner party. The central focus of debate was, however, between those groups which favored public intervention as the means of solving the problem (all other groups) and the BDA, who was initially against any legislation. This led to a division between those groups which called for national legislation in the interim in 1994—as soon as it was clear that no majority could be found for a Europe-wide directive (IG-BAU, HDB, the Greens, the DGB) and the BDA, who persisted in its demand for international regulation. The DGB, for example, argued that a national regulation in Germany would represent a second-best solution while a European directive would be the best option.[11] The IG BAU concurred that the national posted worker legislation is needed in the interim as long as it remained impossible to achieve consensus at the European level. The IG BAU pointed out that this does not contradict a later European directive since the latter depended on a national implementation in any case.[12] The BDA, in contrast continued to insist on the need for a European directive because it perceived all national attempts at regulation as protectionist.[13]

Intervention. The central point of contention among the groups revolved around the question as to whether or not there should be prescriptive government intervention into market forces at all (and if so, to what extent), as most groups wanted, or whether there should be no intervention—a position maintained by the main employer association, the BDA. In other words, the

main point at issue was whether social citizenship rights should be extended
to posted workers. Social citizenship rights, in this context, mainly refer to
the system of social rights developed within the construction industry itself
and laid down in collective agreements. These comprize first, an agreement
on wage levels, fixing eight main wage levels in the industry corresponding to
eight degrees of qualification (Eichhorst 1998, 208–209). Second, separate
agreements establish a system of additional social funds (Sozialkassen) in
order to mitigate the difficulties associated with the irregularity of employment (see above).

The policy process in this case occurred at two levels: the public level
concerning the posted workers law, and the private level, the declaration of
general binding of collective agreements covering wage levels through a specific committee in which the state does not have a vote, but in which three
employer associations and three trade unions are represented. As regards the
public law, one central question was whether the law should apply only to the
construction industry (both main and ancillary trades) or to the labor market
as such. A further point of contention was whether the law should apply
from day one of the posting, or only be applicable after a specific period.
Last, there was the issue of control and sanction mechanisms (which agency
was to be responsible for monitoring the system and whether a general liability of the general contractor should be introduced). The main point of contention regarding the declaration of general binding was whether the whole
differentiated wage scale or merely the lowest one should be extended to
posted workers. However, the question of the additional social funds was
discussed intensively as well.

One central finding of this case is that a high degree of intervention
does not translate into social inclusivity: the extension social citizenship right
to migrants. The stance of the HDB, the Green Party, and trade unions may
be considered socially inclusive because it seeks to extend social citizenship
rights to posted workers without blaming the posted workers themselves for
the problem. The position of the trade unions was simply that they considered posted workers eligible for the same rights as were applicable under the
system of guest worker employment, when temporary migrants were allowed
into the country and employed under the same conditions as German workers.[14] The position of the BDA may be considered less socially inclusive, as it
advocates the maintenance of the status quo; the Republikaner party, on the
other hand, must be considered outright exclusive, with its insistence on a
"political rule ordaining that the German labor market is limited to Germans
only."[15] In summary, while the highest degree of intervention was displayed
by the Republikaner party, the focal point of the debate was between the
proregulation camp, consisting of the trade unions and the Green Party
joined by the construction industry employer association on the one hand,
and the anti-regulation stance of the BDA on the other hand.

The proregulation camp (trade unions, HDB and the Greens) was characterized by a high degree of intervention. They wanted to entirely eradicate the problem by extending all national standards to posted workers, including provisions for paid holidays, full accident prevention coverage and wage level equality from day one of the posting. The central slogan of this camp was *Gleicher Lohn für gleiche Arbeit am gleichen Ort* (Equal pay for equal work at the same place). The Green party had the least problem in recognizing the validity of such a claim: as they pointed out, it was the same claim put forward by the women's movement.[16] The main argument of the DGB was that "low wages should not be the foundation for competition" in the Common Market.[17] According to the DGB:

> The current practice of posting challenges a core feature of our welfare state and of our system of industrial autonomy. No state should be a bystander where national legislative regulations and collective agreements are denigrated in this manner. Since the non-discrimination of migrant workers is anchored in European law pertaining to the freedom of movement, it has to be made applicable to posted workers as well.[18]

The DGB argued that the employment of posted workers constituted a case of social dumping and resulted in the creation of an unfair competitive advantage because foreign service providers possessed advantages which firms working under domestic conditions did not. This, they argued, had the effect of undermining the levelling function of the industry's collective agreements. The DGB further pointed out that this also created a situation in which foreign firms were using German infrastructure without paying taxes for it.[19] The same argument was put forward by the Green party.[20] Similarly, the IG BAU argued that:

> The employment of up to 200,000 workers under the conditions of the sending country creates "islands of foreign rights" in Germany. The posted workers are competing with 500,000 workers in the main trades for whom German collective agreements are valid. The total wage and social wage costs of these employers are up to 50 per cent below that of German wage costs. In addition, these employees are not covered by German accident prevention laws. Because of this social dumping the right to free collective bargaining in the construction industry is undermined leading to unemployment among those workers covered by German collective agreements. If this continues, trade unions will lose the ability to manage labor relations in the industry via collective agreements.[21]

The IG BAU thus argued that not only the construction industry, but other industries as well, should be covered by the law (and in particular the trades ancillary to construction),[22] and that the complete wage scale should be extended to posted workers. The DGB also called for the general liability of the general contractor.[23] It was further argued by these organizations that all construction firms providing services in Germany ought to contribute to the insurance funds, especially to the paid holiday schemes. In addition, it was argued that a federal agency be appointed to take on responsibility for monitoring compliance with the law. The most detailed suggestion concerning the monitoring of the labor market was put forward by the IG-BAU, who distinguishes three levels of compliance enforcement. First, is the registration of foreign employees and their employees. Second, is the inclusion of foreign employers within the insurance fund system. Third, is the empowering of trade unions to enforce the rights of foreign employees.

The sectoral employer association of the construction industry agreed with the general thrust of these arguments. For the HDB, the core feature of the problem consisted in the fact that foreign competition had reached an intensity which endangered the existence of both small firms and jobs in the industry.[24] It claimed that domestic firms were not able to offer services at prices comparable to foreign competitors who were 25 per cent cheaper than domestic producers. It was also concerned that industry training programs would be threatened and that the segmented labor market might cause social unrest on construction sites. In the long run, it was argued that this would increase scepticism towards European integration in general.[25] Consequently, the HDB supported calls for a European directive on posted workers and for national action, which would secure a level playing field in the industry. The main differences in approach between the above groups and the HDB were that the HDB wanted the imposition of a transition period, and advocated the extension of only the lowest wage level as opposed to the whole wage scale. The latter was seen as unfeasible given that the wage scale reflects the German training system and would be too difficult to monitor.

The main employer association, the BDA, was explicitly opposed to extending equal social citizenship rights to posted workers, arguing that this would be contrary to the spirit of the Common Market Project and would be understood in other member states as an example of protectionism.[26] According to the BDA, foreign service provision through posted workers could not be considered a case of social dumping because the foreign service providers used legally available competitive advantages:

> The supposed practice of social dumping or unfair low wage competition does not exist. Social dumping creating unfair distortions in competition only exists if a competitor acquires a special advantage which is not based upon effort or on natural or general economic production and location conditions, but on illegal practices which are unlawful under national or European law. The competi-

tive advantages which location provides—because of more favorable wage and non-wage costs—is a legitimate part of competition among nations, they do not create unlawful advantages.[27]

As a result, the BDA advocated the maintenance of the status quo: a liberalized common market for services with more or less no intervention. The organization pointed out that as a part of the single market initiative the freedom of services had been agreed upon; they further pointed out that the service provision of firms, via posting, is in full accordance with both German and European law and is an expression of the logic of the Common Market. One effect of the Common Market is the levelling of wages and working standards. The BDA thus assumed that differences in wage levels between Portugal and Germany would disappear within due course, just as had occurred in Spain, and claimed that "[t]hose who disagree with this, do not accept the logic of the common market."[28] According to the BDA, the real problem of the construction industry was not a result of the process of European integration, but in domestic distortions of competition. A European directive would be of no help at all. The BDA regarded such a directive as a protectionist measure, liable to create more problems than it solved. For example, it would diminish the export opportunities of German firms.[29] Furthermore, the proposed national legislation would not be in conformity with either German constitutional law or with European law.[30]

At the same time, as mentioned above, the BDA did accept that the construction industry had a particular problem that needed to be solved by some form of intervention. Its grudging acceptance was, however, coupled with a host of conditions. The organization insisted that any such regulation should be limited in terms of time and only cover the main trades within the industry. The BDA was adamant, moreover, that such measures of protectionism be considered the exception rather than the rule.[31] The group rejected outright the claim that the same wages should be paid at the same place for the reason that domestic postings, for example, from the Bavarian forest to Stuttgart, did not operate according to such a standard.[32] The BDA was furthermore pessimistic about the possibility of controlling such regulation, and it feared that the control system would suffocate entrepreneurs with unnecessary paperwork.

Most problematic in the debate, however, was the question of the steering mechanism through which wage levels were to be determined. Here, the problem was that Germany did not have minimum wage legislation. There is a law on minimum labor standards, which theoretically enables the state to fix a minimum wage. But, thus far, the state has not made use of this ability. Instead, wages are settled by collective agreements, a process guaranteed by Germany's Basic Law (Art. 9 III 1 GG). For this reason, the government proposed to regulate the problem of wage levels applying to posted workers in a highly problematic way: by leaving it to the industry to negotiate and conclude, just as usual, a collective agreement covering wage levels in general. The idea was that the government would do two things: first, declare that this wage agreement was binding for the industry as a whole, and second, pass legislation extending this agreement to posted workers.

Even though it is traditionally uncommon for a collective agreement to be declared generally binding on a whole industry, this solution was favored by the government because it ensured that wage levels in the industry would continue to be set by the industry itself (collective bargaining autonomy), while leaving the social welfare question of extension to the government. This declaration was to be issued by the federal labor minister after a mandatory consultation process involving a special committee consisting of three employer association representatives (among them the BDA), and three trade union representatives (among them the DGB).

The umbrella employer association, the BDA, was in favor of this procedure, not only because it guaranteed the autonomy of the industry, but also because the BDA retained the power to veto the declaration by virtue of its involvement in the committee responsible for the declaration process (*Tarifausschuß*). In fact, the BDA actually blocked the declaration several times. It took the view that declaring the general application of a collective agreement constituted a break with the traditions of German labor law. They saw it as the first step in a process that could lead to an undermining of the autonomy of the collective bargaining process.

The umbrella trade union organization, the DGB, only reluctantly agreed to the extension by law of a generally applicable collective agreement to posted workers, regarding this method as one, albeit not the best, solution to the problem.[33] Instead, it favored a legislative guarantee that existent wage levels be applied to posted workers since this would preserve the autonomy of the industrial partners.[34] The IG BAU was equally hesitant in relation to the legal extension of a collective agreement, which had been declared generally binding. Ultimately, they accepted this approach because they did not want to delay the problem much longer and considered the proposal beneficial for the negotiating autonomy in the long run.[35]

The sectoral employer association, the HDB, went one step further and suggested that if a declaration of general binding was politically impossible, minimum wage legislation should be introduced.[36] The Republikaner Party was in favor of minimum wage legislation from the outset. The Green Party also seemed to take this view (but without making explicit reference to minimum wage legislation).[37] In the end, therefore, four out of seven groups (namely, the DGB, IG BAU, BDA, and the HDB) were in favor of posted worker legislation complemented by a declaration of general binding.

The main results can be briefly summarized. Most groups favored a European directive and were active at a European level. But whether there should be public intervention to secure German wage and labor standards was the central point of contention. Despite a majority of groups from across the spectrum (trade unions, sectoral employer associations, and the Green Party) this proved to be difficult because of the two levels involved in this process. The federal posted worker's law only extends collective agreements to posted workers that have been declared generally binding. However, a declaration of general binding proved difficult to achieve because of the veto position of the BDA in the committee negotiating the declaration of general binding. Only after the trade unions agreed to a separate wage level that was below the lowest wage in the construction industry was an agreement possible and the posted worker's law applied to posted workers from European countries.

The United States

The specific governance challenge that confronted the apparel industry in the United States has to be seen in the context of the structure of that particular industry, and in view of the changing nature of competition in and immigration into the United States. Similar to the construction industry, the production process of a garment is splintered between apparel production organizers or distributors such as Wal-Mart and textile and apparel producers. Especially in the latter group, subcontracting is prevalent (Glasmeier, Thompson, and Kays 1993, 23). On closer inspection, however, different commodity chains have to be differentiated: first, there is the standardized mass production chain where apparel manufacturers undertake the design, preparation, manufacture, and finishing of the garment, which is then distributed to retail outlets. Second, there are the fashion oriented chains with fast changing product lines, where the apparel manufacturer is a design firm that outsources the actual production of the garment to domestic producers, or to firms typically located in free trade zones (Taplin 1994, 207).

Unlike the construction industry in Germany, the restructuring of the apparel industry in the United States has taken place over a long period of time, beginning in the 1960s and with increasing imports from Japan and developing countries (Aggarwal 1985, 6). Initially, this import competition was dealt with through voluntary export restraints, first on a bilateral, and then on a multilateral basis.[38] This did not, however, prevent further import penetration because technological adjustments that increase productivity are limited.

Two methods of coping with import competition developed. One response was to relocate some aspect of production abroad, a process actively supported by regional trade initiatives such as Caribbean Basin Initiative (CBI), and NAFTA, as well as clauses in the United States Tariff Schedule (807 now 9802) giving tariff concessions (Dickerson 1991, 264). Another reaction was to tap into the pool of recently arrived immigrant labor, or the even larger pool of undocumented migrants from the Americas (Sassen 1988, 22). Accordingly, sweatshop working conditions are to be found only in peripheral firms that "operate on short term contracts and produce garments of low to medium grade quality" (Glasmeier et al. 1993, 24). Such firms only survive because they are able to exploit (undocumented) immigrants. According to Piore (1997, 136), the phenomenon of the sweatshop involves the violation of a host of legal provisions that developed out of campaigns to eliminate the use of sweatshop labor in the late nineteenth and early twentieth century campaigns, which finally came to fruition in the New Deal legislation of the thirties, especially the Fair Labor Standards Act of 1938. The act included the prohibition of child labor, the regulation and prohibition of work carried out from home, the regulation of piecework and overtime, the development of codes regulating health, safety, fire and building arrangements, and, crucially, the introduction of a minimum wage. This legislation served as a baseline for the development of a primary job structure in the garment industry, a structure which carried through until the 1970s, when violations of these rules became more frequent, and sweatshop operators returned on a larger scale in the late eighties and nineties (Taplin 1994, 211–212).

There is no agreed upon official definition of sweatshops. The United States General Accounting Office (GAO) defines a sweatshop operator as "an employer that violates more than one federal or state labor law governing minimum wage and overtime, child labor, industrial homework, occupational safety and health, workers' compensation, or industry registration" (GAO 1994, 1). According to a report published in 1988 by the GAO, federal labor law was, at that time, contained in three distinct Acts: the Fair Labor Standards Act (1938) (FLSA); the Occupational Safety and Health Act (OSHA) (1970), which set standards for working conditions; and the Immigration Reform and Control Act (IRCA) (1986), which introduced sanctions against employing workers who lacked documents authorizing them to work in the United States (GAO 1988, 36; Zolberg 1991, 317).

There are no reliable figures on the extent of the sweatshop problem. As the GAO (1988, 19) states: "we are not aware of an acceptable methodology for empirically measuring what is by its nature a hidden problem."[39] The main message of GAO's 1988 report is that sweatshops exist, had even increased in number, and that the groups suffering most are Hispanics and Asians. "Immigrants often provide the labor for sweatshops" (GAO 1988, 34). The report indicated that the restaurant, apparel, and meat processing industries were the most seriously affected, but, as Fernández Kelly (1989) has shown, multiple labor law violations can also be found in the electronics industry. Typical violations include:

> ...failure to keep required records of wages, hours worked, and injuries; incorrect wages, both below the minimum wage and with-

out overtime compensation; illegal work by minors; fire hazards created by combustible materials and blocked exits; and work procedures that cause crippling illnesses (GAO 1988, 21).

Physical abuse of workers, especially of female workers, unclean bathrooms, and lack of drinking water are also cited in the report. Through various campaigns, these issues came to public attention with the El Monte case in 1995.

The challenge this situation creates, therefore, is that undocumented immigrants, who come mostly from Third World countries to the United States, are being employed in the United States under substandard conditions. The question now is what was the response of political groups to this hollowing out of labor standards in the garment industry? Before this question can be answered, however, the policy process and discussion in the 1990s will be outlined.

Perception of the Governance Dilemma and Policy Cycle
The political struggle to end sweatshops has a long history in the United States. As has been indicated, the "Great Immigration Wave" at the turn of the century had already created situations conducive to sweatshop operators and the International Ladies' Garment Workers Union, one of the two founding unions of UNITE, was formed at that time to fight for better working conditions and higher wages. While wage and labor conditions were largely neglected during the Reagan and Bush years, the Clinton Administration made wage and labor standards one of its central concerns (Krupat 1997, 73). The Clinton Administration implemented a two-way strategy in order to deal with the issue: reducing the extent of undocumented immigration and improving the enforcement of existing standards at the workplace. As far as the latter is concerned, the Clinton administration largely relied on public-private partnership establishing codes of conduct and on selective enforcement of wage and labor standards. As regards the immigration side of the strategy, the administration focused on border control and worksite enforcement because it saw both as related (Clinton 1994, 35).

In February 1995, the President of the United States, Bill Clinton, published a Memorandum entitled "Deterring Illegal Immigration" which was to provide "a blueprint of policies and priorities for this Administration's continuing work to curtail illegal immigration." This document outlined the Administration's two-pronged approach to the problem.

> Our strategy, which targets enforcement efforts at employers and industries that historically have relied upon employment of illegal immigrants, will not only strengthen deterrence of illegal immigration, but better protect American workers and businesses that do not hire illegal immigrants.[40]

In the same vein Labor Department Secretary, Robert Reich pointed out:

> One reason that employers in the United States are willing to risk employer sanctions right now and hire illegal immigrants is because they can get those illegal immigrants at less than the minimum wage, put them in squalid working conditions, subject them to subminimal working conditions and they know that those illegal immigrants are unlikely to complain. And therefore, part of our strategy is focusing not only on those areas, but also those industries that are likely to have those kinds of problems....It's no secret why illegal immigrants come to the United States. They want a job, and there are unscrupulous employers who know it. ...The goal is very simple: Get rid of the working conditions that attract illegal immigrants in targeted areas and in targeted industries where we find substantial abuses....This administration is not going to tolerate sweatshops or working conditions that are like sweatshops. We are going after employers just as we are making sure that illegal immigrants are not coming across the border.[41]

The nationwide public debate on sweatshops was triggered in August 1995 with the discovery of a sweatshop operation in El Monte, California. Public reaction to this discovery was one of shock. Robert Reich, the Labor Department Secretary was quoted as saying: "We were appalled at the sight of the slave labor sweatshop. Many of us continue to shake our heads in disbelief that this could happen in this country in the 1990s."[42]

In 1996, the anti-immigrant wave, which had started in California in 1994 with Proposition 187, bore fruit at the federal level with the passing of the Illegal Immigration Reform and Immigrant Responsibility Act 1996.[43] This Act, among other things, amended various, existing regulations pertaining to worksite enforcement. For example, the reduction of acceptable documents that are required in order to give proof for employment legibility (Fragomen 1997, 442). In August 1996, President Clinton invited some of the major textile operators, human rights organizations and trade unions to the White House to discuss the issue and inaugurated the so-called White House Apparel Industry Partnership (AIP). No public law was passed, instead, the focus of the debate was on this voluntary public-private partnership. In 1997, it established the Workplace Code of Conduct and in 1998, the Fair Labor Association. The task of the Fair Labor Association was to oversee compliance of the Code and ensure that factories were monitored. The present case study focuses on group responses between August 1995 (El Monte) and the end of 1998, when the Fair Labor Association was inaugurated.

Responses of Political Organizations in the United States

Activity. Of the groups here under review, only the trade unions are part of the Apparel Industry Partnership (AIP).[44] The apparel manufacturer association (AAMA) participated in some aspects of the White House Apparel Industry Partnership Process, but is not a member of the AIP. The organization did cooperate, however, with the Department of Labor in organizing Compliance Monitoring Workshops, and participated in the Fashion Industry Forum in July 1996 that brought together the major players for discussion. From September 1997, it developed its own program of workplace monitoring. The Reform Party was not involved actively in any of the political processes discussed here but it did ultimately develop explicit policy preferences concerning the issue; Ross Perot was one of the central figures during the NAFTA debate.

Since the NIF, NAM and ACLU did not develop an explicit position on the eradication of the sweatshop they may be considered as nonresponsive, but in a rather specific sense. That is to say, their failure to respond was intentional. The main reason for their inaction was that they did not perceive the sweatshop issue as a problem about which something had to be done. All three groups view immigration as beneficial to the United States and they are not overly concerned with wage and labor standards. The NAM was mostly interested in skilled immigration. In this context it sponsored a study by Stuart Anderson[45] which took the view that the employment of high-skilled immigrants does neither displace American workers nor lower wage levels. The NAM argued that "[l]egal immigrants play a critical role in filling key positions for which there are not enough qualified US applicants."[46] This support for more immigration and the demand for more trade liberalization at the international level[47] made NAM an active supporter of the status quo. The ACLU focused more on the overall benefits of immigration to the national economy and society in general and, as regards the impact of immigration on the labor market, argued that "immigrants create more jobs than they fill."[48] The ACLU also advocated the maintenance of the immigration status quo. The following quote from NIF highlights the general approach of all three groups:

> Immigrant labor allows many goods and services to be produced more cheaply and provides the workforce with some businesses that would not otherwise exist. For example, immigration has helped build and maintain America's textile and agricultural industries. Other businesses that employ many immigrants—such as restaurants and domestic household services—would not exist on the same scale without immigrant workers. Immigrants may have

contributed to a decline in wages of native-born high-school dropouts, though the overall effects are quite minor.[49]

While the NIF has paid lipservice to the problems associated with immigration, the organization accepted that "[i]llegal immigration is a different matter. As a sovereign nation, the United States has a right and a duty to regulate entry and to curb illegal immigration." The NIF did not undertake any concrete action in relation to the issue. One the one hand it asserted that "[r]eceiving countries must ... protect both legal and illegal immigrants from exploitation and discrimination,"[50] while on the other hand, it proudly stated it was successful in defeating one of the policy initiatives facilitating worksite enforcement: a national identity card.[51] For these three nonresponsive organizations, the most salient aspect of the immigration debate from 1994 onwards was an increase in nativism and their efforts were accordingly focused towards fighting this development. In the remainder of this section, therefore, only the reactions of those groups which developed concrete policies in relation to the governance challenge (both trade unions, AAMA, Reform and FAIR) are presented. These intentional nonresponses will, however, be taken into account later when more general patterns of reactions are discussed.

Of the five organizations considered responsive, three—the AFL-CIO, UNITE, and FAIR—were engaged with the issue fairly early on, and can be termed active. Of the remaining two organizations, the AAMA merely responded to the problem, becoming active only when it was already a national issue as a result of growing media and governmental pressure, while the Reform Party only became involved in the context of the NAFTA debate. With the possible exception of AAMA, none of these responses was government induced. As to the intensity of response, UNITE and AFL-CIO were the most active on the issue of sweatshops (UNITE more so than the AFL-CIO), while FAIR dealt with the sweatshop problem as part of its general campaign to stop immigration. The AAMA's response was the least intensive: it participated in official fora and was responsible for a rather unconvincing code of conduct, but carried out no lobbying activities. The trade unions groups also responded by strengthening their own capacity to act. Both trade unions developed information campaigns for members and new membership, and were instrumental in the establishing of various nongovernmental organizations or carrying out of campaigns such as Sweatshop Watch, the Stop Sweatshop campaign, the National Labor Committee, and Union Label. As regards the territorial scope of action, only the trade unions and the sectoral employer association responded to the denationalization challenge by enlarging their scope of action to the macroregional and global level (with respect to the latter, only the trade unions took the issue this far); the Reform Party and FAIR only campaigned at the national level.

UNITE, the sectoral trade union, clearly stands out when compared to the other organizations under review. Its campaign, Partnership for Responsibility, can be considered the most differentiated and innovative of all the responses: it brings into the discussion consumers, workers, retailers, manufacturers, and contractors as well as government and takes into account both the global and national level, and both immigration law and international trade.[52] UNITE undertook efforts to build coalitions with students, churches, and synagogues, civil rights leaders, and government and industry leaders.[53] One such example is the Stop Sweatshops campaign, carried out in 1996 in cooperation with the National Consumers League that alerted consumers about the problem of clothes produced in sweatshops.[54] Another is its support for the National Labor Committee, the organization at the center of a campaign pressing for human rights for workers (Krupat 1997). In cooperation with the International Textile, Garment, and Leather Workers Federation, UNITE took active steps in assisting apparel workers in Central America and the Caribbean to organize themselves (Mazur 2000, 90). UNITE thus developed an extremely diversified response, complementing its actions at the national level with involvement at the international level, and building support across both social lines and borders (more on UNITE's Partnership for Responsibility is set out in the discussion of intervention).

Spatiality. In terms of the degree of denationalization and territorial scope of demand, three groups—the two trade unions and the sectoral employer association AAMA—argued that international action was needed to prevent downward competitive pressures resulting in the operation of sweatshops in the United States. The AFL-CIO saw its position as a way to promote fair instead of free trade:

> At present, our corporations are doing business in a global marketplace that is virtually free of regulation or protection for workers. . . . For its opposition to "fast track" and to bailouts with no strings attached, the AFL-CIO has been unfairly labeled "protectionist." We're not against fair trade and we're not opposed to international financial interdependence, but we definitely against trading with or lending money to countries that would refuse to abide by accepted and reasonable standards of conduct that have already been established by the International Labor Organization.[55]

UNITE also defended itself against the charge of protectionism; as the President of UNITE pointed out: "the demand for enforceable labor rights . . . is not an effort to build walls against the global economy. It is an effort to build rules into it, and a floor under it, to lift wages and conditions up rather than drive them down" (Mazur 2000, 92). And:

...[t]he problem of sweatshops in the new global village must be solved globally. International trade must be linked to workers' rights, both in international agreements and our own national laws. Countries and corporations that systematically violate those rights are competing unfairly and must be penalized.[56]

UNITE and the AFL-CIO also called for effective corporate codes of conduct whose enforcement would be monitored.[57] The strategy of the two trade unions, therefore, was to attempt to achieve a levelling of the playing field at the international level.

AAMA, the sectoral employer association, was in favor of more international economic integration. The organization argued that labor and environmental issues should not be mixed with trade issues, because doing so would undermine trade agreements.[58] However, in relation to sweatshops in September 1998, the organization introduced the Responsible Apparel Production Principles (RAPP), a code of conduct which is macroregional in scope but which does not involve governmental organizations.[59] AAMA also made specific demands for the improvement of national labor law enforcement.

The above represents the more internationalist responses. The Reform Party and FAIR went in a completely different direction. The Reform Party centered its proposals on national and international measures geared solely towards dealing with undocumented immigration to the United States. At the international level, it argued that NAFTA should be restructured to "provide labor standards, [and improve] environmental and living conditions in the Border area [of] Maquiladoras...[to enable] Mexican workers to make a decent living in Mexico."[60] Such a stance is fairly within the sphere of foreign policy. There is no clear cut advocacy of international norms to ensure a level playing field. The party called for the establishment of a "constitutional protectionist trade policy to create trade surpluses for the United States of America", the repeal of NAFTA, and the withdrawal of the United States from the WTO. A further demand was for the imposition of a social tariff that would equalize wages between importing and exporting countries.[61] These remarks suggest a disapproval of strong international institutions in general because such institutions operate to weaken the unilateral exertion of foreign policy measures. FAIR presented a national response to the problem, arguing that a moratorium on immigration would vastly improve working and living conditions in the United States: "The age of mass migration is over, and nearly all people must 'bloom where they're planted.'"[62]

In summary, therefore, the territorial scope and degree of denationalization considered necessary in dealing with the issue of undocumented migrant sweatshop labor is contested among the five political organizations under review. Revealing the most internationalist approach are the unions, for whom international action was essential. They are followed by the sectoral employer association who argued in favor of a mutual recognition of standards. Both the unions and the employer association developed policies for action at the national level as well. In contrast to these approaches, FAIR and the Reform Party only called for action at the national level.

Intervention. Intervention in this case has several dimensions. The first is to what degree the freedom of employers to make use of undocumented migrant labor should be interfered with (depth of intervention). Four methods of intervention were suggested during the debate:

(1) the strengthening of border controls,
(2) the strengthening of immigration controls within the country,[63]
(3) the strengthening of worksite enforcement in general (without regard to immigration enforcement), and
(4) raising the minimum wage.

These methods are not neutral concerning social inclusivity. The first two target immigrants and can be considered socially exclusive, the latter two extend wage and labor standards to all employees, regardless of immigration status. A further issue was which steering mechanism should be used to deal with wage and labor standard questions: public enforcement or voluntary codes of conducts.

The highest degree of intervention was displayed by the sectoral authoritarian organization FAIR. It called for (amongst other things) both tougher border controls and tighter immigration restrictions. It also developed a detailed inventory on how border control and immigration law enforcement could be made more effective.[64] Somewhat less interventionist was the Reform Party, who advocated the extension of social citizenship rights to workers in other countries in order to reduce import competition from countries with lower standards. At the national level, the organization was in favor of restricting immigration and fighting illegal immigration through stricter laws (for example, employer sanctions). The Party claimed that increased illegal immigration was a result of economic crises abroad and the availability of employment in the United States. According to the Reform Party:

> The employment of these workers has led directly to a reduction in real wages and the displacement of native U.S. workers in some fields. Therefore we resolve that in order to control the rapidly increasing population of U.S. residents who are undocumented immigrants, the U.S. shall: A. Adopt laws which are practical, enforceable and provide strong penalties for companies employing

illegal workers in the U.S. Guest worker programs which do not displace U.S. workers and which pay compensating taxes to local communities and bonded worker return provisions shall be created to supply critical labor shortfalls. B. Restructure the NAFTA to provide labor standards, environmental and living conditions in the Border area Maquiladoras which will allow Mexican workers to make a decent living in Mexico.[65]

Next in line in terms of depth of intervention is the AFL-CIO, followed by UNITE. Both emphasize border control to a lesser extent but favored better worksite enforcement and a raise in the minimum wage. At times the position of the AFL-CIO appeared quite close to that of the Reform Party. But, while the AFL-CIO supported tighter border and internal controls and called for more rigorous worksite enforcement, it cautioned against nativism and warned that immigrants were not the cause of the problem, a sentiment that was nowhere be found in the platform of either the Reform Party or FAIR.[66] The AFL-CIO, moreover, in contrast to UNITE (but in line with the Reform Party) supported (at least in 1998) employer sanctions "as the most effective way to deter employers from hiring illegal aliens."[67] They did point out, however, that care should be taken so that these sanctions did not lead to a new form of discrimination.[68] A further difference in the stance of AFL-CIO and the Reform Party was that the former was against a temporary worker program and in favor of a higher minimum wage. In addition, the AFL-CIO developed national measures and initiatives against sweatshops, and, with UNITE, conceived the problem of migrant labor as being not restricted to merely an issue of immigration, but rather one which took in the concerns of both social welfare and economic policy.

Both, AFL-CIO and UNITE pressed explicitly for higher wages; in fact, both groups regarded low wages as one of the biggest problem in the United States.[69] The AFL-CIO supported the campaign for a living wage, a concern it sought to turn into a national movement.[70] It demanded that: "city contractors [be required] to pay wages that are higher than the federally required minimum. These ordinances ensure that government won't be a party to poverty and that workers can better support their families."[71]

UNITE did not deal as deeply with immigration issues because it did not see immigration as the problem, but rather nonenforcement of wage and labor standards. UNITE's response to the lowering of wage and labor standards has to be considered as the most comprehensive of all the groups under review. Its campaign, Partnership for Responsibility addressed all levels of the commodity chain: it called on consumers not to buy goods made in sweatshops; it pressed for retailer and manufacturer liability for the working conditions under which goods were produced (corporate responsibility); it called for tighter enforcement of labor law; it argued for both the introduction of global standards within trade agreements and for codes of conducts for multinational corporations (it regarded purely national standards as inadequate because they could be easily undermined by companies producing goods in countries with lower wage and labor standards); and last, it argued that the position of sweatshop workers had to be strengthened by doing away with employer sanctions.[72] According to UNITE:

> The employer sanctions law must be repealed so as to eliminate the special advantage it grants unscrupulous employers. Whatever position one takes on illegal immigration, it is imperative that U.S. labor laws and effective remedies apply to all workers—without regard to their immigration status. If they don't we are simply providing additional incentive for employers to continue to hire undocumented workers.[73]

UNITE supported the Stop Sweatshops Act which had been introduced by Senator Edward Kennedy and Congressman Bill Clay into Congress. The aim of this legislation was to introduce garment the liability of garment industry manufacturers and retailers when they act as manufacturers for their contractors' labor law violations.[74] UNITE insisted that manufacturers and retailers had to take responsibility for the conditions under which the goods they sold were produced, arguing that "[w]e must change fundamentally the ruthless system of contracting and sub-contracting in which those at the top of the pyramid claim no responsibility for the abuse, exploitation and impoverishment of those at the base." [75]

However, as regards the steering mechanisms to be used to implement better wage and labor standards, the trade unions were sceptical of codes of conduct as, for example, advocated by the Apparel Industry Partnership and the sectoral employer association, the AAMA. As the AFL-CIO argued:

> America's unions insist that such codes be mandatory and monitored by acceptable third parties. This disagreement illustrates a long-standing disagreement between labor and management over how our country should be run. America's unions do not believe, for instance, that free markets are necessarily fair, or that the government that governs least necessarily governs best—and both of those viewpoints have been historically opposed by America's corporations. If we are to solve the problem of "sweatshop labor", business leaders are going to have to join union and consumer leaders in insisting on mandatory standards of worker rights and human rights, as well as mandatory consumer and environmental protections.[76]

UNITE made a similar point:

> Corporate codes of conduct, which are applied primarily to off-shore production, are useful in articulating ethical business standards. In practice, however, they have not significantly improved conditions in the industry due to a lack of uniformity and weak monitoring provisions. Independent monitoring, involving credible human rights groups, other non-governmental organizations and even official international organizations could dramatically increase the effectiveness of these codes.... While voluntary measures and self-policing by corporations are essential, reforms in the system must be codified in law and the department of Labor must be given the resources and powers to enforce the law. Workers must be empowered to exercise their lawful rights to speak freely, to organize and to engage in collective bargaining with representatives of their choice.[77]

By contrast, the sectoral employer association (AAMA) was the least interventionist among the various groups studied. Nowhere in its documentation does the organization explicitly refer to the problems undocumented immigrants experience at the workplace. The AAMA strongly opposed the concept of a living wage which was so central to the platform of the trade unions. The organization put out the Responsible Apparel Production Principles (RAPP), a series of guidelines in the form of a code of conduct purporting to ensure responsible clothing production processes, but the effectiveness of these principles was highly contested during the debate. One reason for this was that the Principles were entirely voluntaristic in nature and did not involve any process of independent monitoring. The standards contained in the RAPP are far less comprehensive than those developed in the White House Apparel Industry Partnership process. The RAPP only prescribe that apparel firms should "pay at least the minimum total compensation required by local law, including all mandated wages, allowances and benefits."[78] In fact, the actual substance of the organization's overall response to the issue throws doubt on the sincerity with which it acted, suggesting that it wanted to appear to be doing something about the problem rather than being seriously concerned with it.

As was the case in the German part of this case study, a high degree of intervention does not necessarily correspond with a high degree of social inclusivity favored by the particular group. Thus, if one assesses the various group responses in terms of the scope of citizenship rights they want to extend, a different picture emerges. The trade unions and AAMA indicated more of a leaning towards social inclusivity because they did not blame undocumented immigrants for the problem, which was the strategy of FAIR. The trade unions in fact approved of the extension of (some) citizenship rights to undocumented immigrants. Both unions were strongly supportive of America's tradition as a country of immigration, and rejected the argument that immigration was the problem. As the AFL-CIO commented:

> The facts are these: immigrants are not the cause of America's declining wages and the export of good jobs overseas. Immigrants are not responsible for the "downsizing" that is sweeping through many U.S. industries and throwing millions of Americans out of work. And immigrants cannot be blamed for the fraying of the country's social fabric that so many Americans perceive with uneasiness and alarm.[79]

UNITE presented the following view:

> The best way to help America's low-wage workers is to stick to the basics: improved wages, improved health care and reform of our labor laws so that all workers—immigrants and native born—can freely join unions and protect their rights....When layoffs and depressed wages face America's working poor, many politicians and demagogues are tempted to scapegoat immigrants. The theory that immigrants are responsible for the deteriorating living standards of America's low-wage workers must be clearly rejected....Low wage workers are suffering because inflation has outpaced minimum wage and because union membership has declined.[80]

As to the AAMA, it did not present a policy on immigration because it did not see immigration as an issue it should concern itself with.[81] The AAMA is placed fairly low on the social inclusivity scale for the reason that it does not take a stand on the minimum wage, and its voluntary code of conduct reveals something of a lack of concern for the problems migrants face. The AAMA cannot be placed, however, in the same category as FAIR. The latter organization targeted immigrants themselves, considering them to be the source of the problem.[82] As a consequence, FAIR pressed for a complete moratorium on immigration, taking the view that immigration induced population growth was unsustainable.[83]

The Reform Party defies any classification on this scale. Its views on the issue were quite clearly not as anti-immigrant as those of FAIR and it did not attribute the causes of declining wage and labor standards to the immigrants but rather to other factors such as weak law enforcement. However, its aim was to put an end to undocumented immigration, and to tighten the standards of legal immigration. There was no clear advocacy in the Reform Party for an overall strengthening of wage and labor standards in the United States and it made no reference to a raise of the minimum wage as such. By way of a classification, therefore, the Reform Party is placed below the trade unions in terms of inclusivity, but not on the same level of exclusivity as FAIR.[84]

Comparing the groups along this dimension of social inclusivity places them more or less directly in opposition to where they were in respect of depth of intervention. While FAIR could be regarded as highly interventionist, here it is classified as exclusive. In turn, while the AAMA evidenced the least interventionist stance, it cannot be labelled exclusive because it did not scapegoat immigrants or display xenophobic tendencies. Nevertheless, the AAMA was still much less inclusive than the unions as it did not consider immigrants' rights in the country at all. This example demonstrates how immigration affects the typical cleavages that are formed in relation to questions of social justice. If one were to view the issue purely along the lines of the typical cleavage, the response of both the AAMA and the trade unions would have been sufficient to come to the conclusion that the AAMA was socially exclusive (as it was against the extension of social rights to workers) and the trade unions socially inclusive. The fact that a more in depth take on social inclusivity reveals a far more complex pattern indicates just how much immigration complicates the nature of politics, especially in relation to the concept of citizenship rights.

A similarly complicated cleavage pattern surfaces when questions relating to mode of intervention are assessed. The problem that concerns us here is what role various entities in society have when it comes to rule enforcement (subject of governance) and how these rules should be enforced (steering mechanisms). In more concrete terms, the issue addresses the question of whether groups are in favor of public legislation or prefer private and voluntary codes of conduct as the most appropriate means of regulation. In this regard, all groups advocated some form of effective intervention by the state or by international institutions, even if in relation to different issues. One dispute that did emerge was between the employers and the trade unions: while the trade unions insisted on the regulation of wage and labor standards by public means, the AAMA referred to public law only with respect to worksite enforcement and health issues while relying on a voluntary code of conduct to regulate wage and labor standards. Another division was between the trade unions and employers on the one hand, and the right wing populist organizations on the other. The latter preferred to deal with the problem of migrant labor in terms of immigration regulation whereas the former saw the central issue as lying in the sphere of wage and health reform.

POLITICAL ASYLUM IN GERMANY AND THE UNITED STATES AFTER THE COLD WAR: GOVERNANCE CHALLENGE

At the end of the 1980s, the number of refugees seeking asylum in Western industrial states increased dramatically. In 1987, approximately

58,000 asylum applications were filed in Germany; in 1988 that number was 100,000 and in 1992 it had risen to 438,000. In the United States, 26,000 asylum applications were filed in 1987, a number that increased to 100,000 in 1989 and 150,000 in 1993 and 1994 (Beisheim et al. 1999, 125). This boost in asylum applications exerted pressure on both the decision makers and communities in both countries and led to a questioning of the asylum system in general in both international and domestic discussions.

At the international level, the problem of refugees comes under the mandate of the United Nations High Commissioner for Refugees, applying the Geneva Convention 1951 as supplemented by the 1967 Protocol. According to the Convention and Protocol, a refugee is a person who "owing to a well-founded fear of being persecuted for reasons of race, religion, nationality, membership of a particular social group or political opinion, is outside the country of his nationality and is unable or, owing to such fear, is unwilling to avail himself of the protection of that country...."[85] The institution of territorial asylum is the cornerstone of refugee protection (Mills 1998, 105); in granting political asylum states fulfill their obligations under the Convention. The refugee regime, however, does not give every individual the right to asylum. It is still up to the nation-state or specific community of states (e.g., Europe) to determine who counts as a refugee and who does not. During the Cold War, and in Germany in particular, as a reaction to its own history, the institution of political asylum became part of the identity of Western states, with a system of asylum provision entrenched in national legislation. Thus, foreign citizens, as asylum seekers, had a guaranteed right of entry into a country that could be defended in court. Within recent years, however, the main debate in asylum policy has centered precisely on this guarantee: whether and to what extent entry should be regarded a right of the foreign citizen, as opposed to a privilege.

Two divergent trends within asylum policy can be noted as having occurred within the last fifteen years. On the one hand, the scope of the refugee regime has broadened. Thus, in 1992, a secretary-general for Internally Displaced Persons was established within the UNHCR (Mills 1998, 175) and, at the national level, new grounds for asylum have been recognized by many states, for example, victims of female genital mutilation are now regarded as falling within the definition of political persecution. On the other hand, states have undertaken concerted efforts at the national, and especially at the international, level to alter the system of refugee protection. At the national level, most Western states have modified their asylum laws to restrict access to the application process, for example, by excluding applications from refugees arriving via a safe third country (see Beisheim et al. 1999, 416–423). At the international level, states have established various cooperation mechanisms in both the regional and global spheres to cope with the influx of refugees. At the global level, the "Intergovernmental Consultations on Asylum, Refugee and Migration Policies in Europe, North America and Australia" (IGC) was established to provide states with a forum within which to discuss immigration control (see Weiner 1995, 159–164).[86] The main approach adopted by the Forum has been to seek to reduce immigration, either by agreeing on efforts to improve living conditions in sending countries, or by making border controls in receiving countries more efficient. It is clear, however, that even though the IGC Forum discusses both questions, its emphasis is on border control. At the macroregional level, there is the European cooperation process which culminated in the Schengen and Dublin Conventions (see Overbeek 1995, 30–32; Weiner 1995, 160). These two conventions arose in the context of the creation of the Common Market, in 1992, when the internal liberalization of movement within Europe required a common policy on controlling external borders. The Schengen Agreement of 1985, and the Execution Agreement of 1990 articulate, among other things, which state is to be responsible for the examination of asylum requests within the Schengen countries. The purpose of the Dublin Convention is to avoid multiple asylum applications across European states. Overall, countries within Europe have reached agreement on a number of related issues including common definitions of a refugee, safe third countries, secure countries of origin, unfounded asylum claims, minimal guarantees in asylum procedures, and the distribution of costs arising out of the temporary protection of refugees (Tomei 1997, 71). Thus, there is a broadly perceived crisis in territorial asylum to which Western states have responded in such a manner as to lead one scholar to argue that the principle of nonrefoulement has been replaced by a principle of nonentrée (Mills 1998, 105). The challenge to asylum created by the growing number of refugees, however, took on a very individual character in both Germany and the United States.

Perception of the Governance Dilemma and Policy Cycle: Germany

The provisions to protect refugees were transferred into Germany's domestic legal system even before the Geneva Convention existed. Article 16 of Germany's Basic Law stated simply: *Politisch Verfolgte genießen Asylrecht.*[87] This article was interpreted as providing a guarantee of access to German territory to every person who submitted an asylum application, for the duration of the examination of that application. According to one scholar, this implies an effective limitation on state sovereignty because the German state could not deny access to its territory and its judiciary system to individuals applying for asylum (Joppke 1998, 122).

Political asylum had already been a topic of some discussion in the early 1980s, but as more and more refugees arrived in Germany by the end of the 1980s, the issue resurfaced on the political agenda. In 1989, the Ministry of the Interior decided to put and end to the preferential treatment refugees of

Eastern countries had until then enjoyed. In the same year, legislation dealing with asylum seekers was drawn up—legislation which came into force in 1991 and which was supposed to deal with the backlog of asylum applications.

One sticking point in the debate was disagreement about numbers. The opponents of asylum alleged that because only ten per cent of applications for political asylum were accepted, that meant that 90 per cent of applications were not genuine. Those taking the side of asylum seekers, however, accused such statistics of misleading the issue, pointing out that 10 per cent of rejected applications are reversed in the court process, and that a significant number of rejected applicants (34 per cent in 1989) nonetheless retain a right to stay under the provisions of the Geneva Convention. In addition, about 17 per cent of applicants are not expelled because of civil war in their home country. This adds up to about 60 per cent of the asylum applications which genuinely represent the attempt of persons to escape from violence (Schönwälder 1999, 80).

In the election campaigns of the early 1990s, asylum and immigrant policy was a major feature of the platforms of the different parties. In 1991, for example, Edmund Stoiber (of the CSU), then the interior minister of Bavaria, pointed to the fact that every third administrative judge was occupied with asylum cases, and asked: "How do I get more judges?"[88] He demanded that application hearings be limited in time and that special courts be created for asylum applicants. He quipped that there were simply not enough applicants for the number of open positions as administrative judges.[89] Volker Rühe, at that time general secretary of the CDU, complained about the social tension that would result if the empty barracks earmarked for students and the elderly had to be used to house asylum applicants.[90] The president of IG-Chemie, Hermann Rappe, called for an amendment to Germany's Basic Law in order to cut down on massive abuses of the asylum system.[91] Also figuring prominently in the debate were mayors of large cities such as Georg Kronawitter from Munich. In an open letter to his party (the SPD), Kronawitter deviated from the official party line and called for the asylum application process to be changed in order to ensure that only genuine refugees could apply. In his words, "[t]he protests of the people of Munich are on the increase. There is no longer any place in the city where resistance to residences for asylum applicants does not exist."[92] At the same time, the right-wing populist Republikaner Party gained ground in local and state elections, and violence against foreigners increased. In the discussion surrounding the amendment of Article 16, in 1992, each of the main political parties (CDU / CSU, SPD, and FDP) argued that the low recognition rate of asylum applications demonstrated that most refugees were not "really" politically persecuted but only "abused" the system in order to immigrate to Germany. Therefore, they called for the law to be changed to guarantee that those who were actually politically persecuted be guaranteed protection, but also to ensure that unfounded asylum applications could be rejected more easily.[93] All this demonstrates that relevant political groups in Germany perceived an external challenge to the capacity of the German state to effectively regulate the inflow of asylum seekers. Their response was either to press for an increase in the amount of resources dedicated to dealing with the crisis, or for a modification, or abolishment, of the right of access to the asylum procedure.

In 1992, legislation was passed to increase the speed and effectiveness of the asylum procedure. Its purpose was to prevent amendment of Art. 16 of the Basic Law. The act was supposed to come into effect in 1993, but before the law could be tested, the SPD caved into pressure from the CDU to amend Art. 16. The central principles as to how the article would be modified were agreed upon in December 1992. In July 1993, a new article, Art. 16a was inserted into the Basic Law. This new article still states that *"Politisch Verfolgte genießen Asylrecht,"* but now it is accompanied by three exceptions: refugees from a member state of the European Union, refugees from a third country in which the Geneva Convention is applied, and refugees from a list of countries which have been considered safe cannot apply for asylum. The article was also amended to facilitate the deportation of aliens by limiting the possibility of challenging a deportation order in the courts, and it made the precise content of the regulation of political asylum dependent on developments in the European Union. The focus of the present case study is on the political responses of nationally organized lobby groups to the asylum crisis in the period between December 1992, and July 1993, during which most groups were active.

Responses of Political Organizations

Activity. The sectoral associations (IG BAU and HDB), representing the old politics, were inactive on the issue, deferring to their respective peak organizations which carry responsibility for general political topics. As regards the mode of activity, the DGB, the Green Party, the AWO, and the Republikaner Party were actively involved in the debate, while the BDA was rather more responsive to it. All other organizations, while they did respond to and deal with proposals put forward by the Christian Democratic Party (in power) or by the Social Democratic Party, intervened in the debate on their own initiative.

As to the question of intensity, the activities of the BDA and AWO were comparatively low key[94] while the Republikaner Party was comparatively more active. Most intense were the initiatives undertaken by the DBG and the Green Party. The scope of activity engaged in by the DGB was indeed remarkable, the most interesting aspect being its cooperation with PRO ASYL, a lobby organization founded in the mid-1980s to deal with the growing anti-asylum movement in Germany.[95] Together with PRO ASYL, the DGB collected signatures, gave several statements in public hearings against the proposed changes, prepared information and supported the call for a public demonstration in July 1992.[96] Such activity reflects the fact that the self-understanding of trade unions is in the process of change: away from a mere concern with economic interests, and towards a focus on human rights in general.[97] While the debate on political asylum in Germany cannot be separated from the accelerating process of European integration taking place at the same time (i.e., the Single Market Initiative 1992 and the Schengen and Dublin Conventions), none of the organizations under review were active in the international (or European) sphere.

Spatiality. At the same time, the responses of the groups evidenced a rather high degree of political denationalization; with the exception of the Republikaner Party, all groups saw the solution to the problem as taking on a European dimension (territorial scope). Differences between the groups with an international focus did emerge, however, in terms of the degree of supranationality that was considered appropriate. Thus, while the BDA advocated intergovernmental cooperation amongst European states in order to restrict access to the asylum process, the AWO, the Greens and the DGB, revealing a higher degree of political denationalization, called for the introduction of a Europe-wide individual right to asylum. The DGB, for instance, lobbied the German government to press for a European asylum law which took into account Germany's own experience of dictatorship[98] In a joint declaration with PRO ASYL this point was repeated:

> Development of the Basic Law into a common constitution for the whole of Germany as well as the further development of the European Community into a European Union must be bound up with a maintenance and extension of the democratic and social standards already guaranteed in the Basic Law. There is no reason for changing tried and tested constitutional provisions such as autonomy of the industrial partners to negotiate collective agreements (*Tarifautonomie*) and the right to asylum.... The process of further European Integration requires a European asylum law. This harmonisation must not lead, however, to the abolishment of national standards. Individual claims to asylum and a guaranteed due process of law are indispensable components of any European solution.[99]

The DGB further endorsed an orientation of development policy which focuses on basic needs in developing countries and champions initiatives and solutions for a just world economic order in order to fight the root causes of refugee flows.[100] The DGB was also highly critical of the current state of European integration with regard to the asylum problematique:

> It can be seen that only responsibilities, controlling procedures and sanctions are regulated. No substantive harmonisation of asylum law is taking place. The harmonisation is limited to the deterrence of refugee without regard to whether they are politically perse-cuted. All the same, the insistence is on the acceleration of the asylum application process, on a definition of "evidently unfounded asylum applications" and the "secure safe-third country." There are no guarantees for the processes developed. In the light of these harmonisation efforts, it is even more important to defend the existing right to asylum and here especially Article 16.[101]

On this point the DGB found agreement with the Green Party. In fact, the Greens brought a resolution before Parliament arguing that to change the Basic Law would be tantamount to an abandonment of intensive national regulation in favor of a harmonized European standard which fell well below those contained in German law.[102]

The response of the AWO reflected the fact that the asylum crisis was regarded by many as bringing into question how Germany dealt with immigration in general. Thus, the AWO treated the asylum debate as evi-dencing Germany's need for a law on immigration that takes into account European developments, arguing that new immigration legislation was necessary to ensure a more rational management of the immigration process as a whole.[103]

The BDA also pressed for European harmonization but for quite differ-ent reasons. According to the BDA, migration pressures represented one more example of the burden that Eastern Europe and Third World countries already placed on industrialized states. It argued, therefore, for international coordination of East-West migration and of refugee and asylum flows in order to reduce immigration in general. In this context, the BDA explicitly welcomed the second Schengen Agreement and Dublin Convention and pointed out:

> Legally speaking, the Federal Republic of Germany cannot partici-pate fully in these agreements because Art. 16 of the Basic Law guarantees to whoever applies for asylum the right to a processing of the claim. There is therefore a need to adjust German asylum law such that it squares with the Geneva Convention and other European standards."[104]

The sole exception to this chorus for Europeanization was the Republikaner Party. They took the view that the Geneva Convention left room to maneuver in terms of reducing the number of asylum applicants that Germany was obliged to accept. They argued that, as it was impossible to wait for a coordinated European policy on the issue, national measures had to be taken.[105] One such measure which the Republikaner Party suggested was to focus development aid on reducing the number of immigrants entering the country—but the Republikaner Party did not seem to expect that this measure would be entirely effective.[106] Some years later, the Republikaner Party commented that the government's Europe-focused immigration policy had failed and that a cancellation of the Schengen Agreement was necessary in order to "maintain our welfare state and our country as the home (*Heimat*) of the German people."[107]

Intervention. Here again, the Left-leaning pro-asylum coalition, consisting of the DGB, AWO and Green Party, developed a similar approach—an approach opposed by the Republikaner Party and the BDA. Thus, the Left groups argued for an extension of the scope of the definition of refugee (social inclusiveness). The DGB pointed out that the Geneva Convention needed to be modified as it did not take into account several bases of persecution, such as civil war, sexual discrimination, and torture.[108] According to the organization, the refugee problem is a world order problem (*Weltordnungsproblem*) "which can only be solved by the international community. Therefore what we need is a comprehensive set of instruments to deal with the causes of refugee flows."[109] The Greens also advocated an extension of the definition of a refugee and the inclusion of, for example, sexual discrimination as a basis for asylum. Both the DGB and the Green Party emphasized the need for improving the regulation of immigration, such as an easier naturalization processes which took account of conditions in the labor market.[110] While the AWO wanted to see better treatment of refugees fleeing from civil war (such as those from the former Yugoslavia), it did not push for an extension of the definition of refugee, favoring the definition as it was.[111]

As to regulatory intensity, which in this context, refers to how far groups supported interference with the right of free entry, the left groups called for maintenance of the asylum right and stressed that a more rational treatment of the whole problem was necessary. These groups rejected the proposed changes to Art. 16 and opposed, in particular, the introduction of the concept of safe third countries or lists of secure countries, claiming that such provisions were in contravention of the Geneva Convention.[112] The DGB, for example, argued that "[a]sylum applicants must have access to an individual hearing and to the due process of law."[113] The DGB disagreed with the claim that most applicants merely came to Germany for economic reasons, and pointed to the fact that many applicants who were not granted asylum nevertheless could not return to their country of origin because of the political situation there. This right of nonrefoulement, they argued, is guaranteed by the Geneva Convention, and thus—as the Convention has been ratified by Germany—by German law as well. Thus, they continued, 50 per cent of rejected asylum applicants had a right to stay in the country. The DGB further pointed out that many refugees from the former Yugoslavia had been pressed into the asylum application process even though they did not stand a chance of success. They therefore called for the institutionalization of a specific guarantee for refugees fleeing from civil war, claiming that this would ease pressure off the asylum process. The DGB highlighted the irony that in 1990, Germany spent 3.5 billion DM on refugees, but spent only 161 million DM in fighting the root causes of refugee flows.

In a similar vein, the AWO opposed the amendment of Art. 16, pushed for the introduction of a separate category for refugees from countries torn by civil war, demanded the inclusion of the problem of the *Aussiedler* (ethnic Germans) in the debate, and called for immigration in general to be brought into the discussion. But, unlike the other Left-oriented groups, the AWO also emphasized that those who exploited the asylum procedure in a criminal manner should be prosecuted.[114] It seems, however, that the issue of asylum brought out some division within the organization, with the group's final position representing something of a minimal compromise.[115]

All three organizations (namely, the DGB, the Greens and the AWO) accused the government and main political parties of instrumentalizing the asylum issue, of quoting misleading figures, and of ignoring basic facts in the debate, such as that the number of asylum applicants was lower than the number of ethnic immigrants from the Soviet Union. The three organizations also charged that by constantly rehashing the metaphor of the unbearable inflow of asylum applicants, the government was responsible for a strengthening of right-wing groups and affiliated organizations.[116] The AWO, for instance, warned against "political propaganda tricks promising a quick solution" and commented that what was really needed was an:

> Active foreign policy and a new dimension of development aid combined with a more active social policy within the country itself, dealing with unemployment, housing shortage, the problems of young people and the social questions arising out of German unification.[117]

Unsurprisingly, political organizations on the right were opposed to all such considerations. The employer organization, the BDA maintained its policy of reducing immigration in general, pointing out that, in 1989, Germany's intake of immigrants as a proportion of its population was six times higher than that of the United States. It is argued that the institution of political asylum was being abused, and it called for a tightening of access to the procedure. Thus, the BDA sought to exclude from the process: applicants from countries where there was no obvious political persecution; applicants who had arrived in Germany from a safe third country; those whose application had already been denied in another European state; and those whose claim to persecution was unfounded. It argued that the amendment of Art. 16 was a necessary precondition for the development of a coherent and acceptable refugee and asylum policy, both at the national and especially at the international level.[118] Such amendment was important, it argued, because it enabled deportation of applicants whose claims to asylum were without basis. The Republikaner Party went one step further in calling for the abolishment of the constitutional right to asylum, arguing that there were too many asylum applicants already and taking care of them was too costly. They presented the view that accepting more foreigners from alien cultures was not appropriate in a country which was already densely populated. The party pressed for general acceptance of the fact that Germany was not a country of immigration.[119]

In terms of steering mechanisms, all political organizations were in favor of public regulation of the issue. It should be noted, however, that the argument of the Green Party, AWO and DGB was that the real heart of the issue was a lack of accurate information on refugees and the causes of refugee flight. Thus, instead of an amendment of the Basic Law, the organizations called for a more sophisticated information policy on the causes of refugee flows and the reasons why low recognition rates did not mean that rejected asylum seekers were abusing the system. By contrast, the BDA and the Republikaner Party called on public intervention to reduce immigration.[120]

Perception of the Governance Dilemma and Policy Cycle: the United States

In the United States, the provisions for territorial asylum were effectively transferred into law in 1980, with the passing of the Refugee Act, which separated refugee policy from immigration policy. The Act established a corps of professional asylum officers trained in international relations and human rights law.[121] But it was only in 1990, with the issue of administrative provisions specifically dealing with asylum seekers, that granting asylum was separated from foreign policy considerations (Joppke 1998, 114–199, see also Copeland 1997, 14). As Joppke notes: "Just when western Europe erected its fabled 'fortress' against the turmoils of the post-communist East, America's doors for refugees... swung wide open" (Joppke 1998, 120). In 1993, however, criticism arose as to the effectiveness of the institution of political asylum, criticism which was fuelled by heavy media attention on the issue in the wake of the bombing of the World Trade Center on February 26, 1993, following revelations that one of the suspects in the bombing had entered the country as an asylum applicant. This led to a wide-ranging discussion on the system of political asylum which was eventually taken up in Congress. As R. L. Mazzoli (Chairman of the House of Representatives Committee on the Judiciary, Subcommittee on International Law, Immigration, and Refugees) argued in 1993:

> The asylum system is sick. The asylum system needs attention in the very worst way. Roughly one hundred thousand new asylum cases are filed each year. Depending on whose view you use anywhere from 200,000 to perhaps even 300,000 cases are pending at this point, at the end of the fiscal year 1992. Facing this torrent, this giant cascade of cases, are 150 trained asylum officers. I have not done the mathematics, but I think it could be easily said that if these men and women heard cases steadily through, 24 hours a day, we are probably talking about never, ever diminishing that mountain, and probably not doing so, at least until the next century.... So we have a great body of these people who come in seeking asylum, who do not really wind up achieving that status."[122]

Political pressure groups also complained about the inefficiency and leniency of the asylum system. According to Dan Stein, from the Federation of American Immigration Reform (FAIR), a group very influential during the debate:

> Every single person on the planet Earth, if he gets into this country, can stay indefinitely by saying two magic words: political asylum. You say "political asylum" you get a work card and you get an indefinite right to stay until the immigration service gets around to hearing your claims.[123]

After the attack on the World Trade Center in 1993, three pieces of legislation were introduced into Congress to reform the administration of political asylum, although it took until 1995 for these laws to take effect.[124] Also in 1995, President Clinton announced that his administration would seek international cooperation to address the issue of illegal immigration. Amongst the measures suggested were the negotiation of readmission agreements for persons who could have sought asylum in the last country from which they arrived, the negotiation of expanded arrangements with foreign countries for the return of criminal and deportable aliens, and the undertaking of international efforts to counter alien smuggling.[125] Some of these proposals were taken up in the Illegal Immigration Reform and Immigrant Responsibility Act of 1996 (IIRAIRA), an Act which according to Fragomen (1997, 443), "wiped out asylum as we know it, replacing it with a much stricter process." The Act brought in striking changes to the asylum process. Three new bars to asylum were institutionalized including the provision that individuals who could be returned to a safe third country (where that third country was one with which the United States had reached agreement on the issue) were to be barred from making an asylum application in the United States. The Act further required asylum applications to be filed within one year of arrival, with rejected asylum applicants barred from reapplication unless there was a substantial change in the conditions of that person's home country. Removal procedures were also strengthened, with immigration inspectors given the power to order summary exclusion without the right to a hearing before an immigration judge—a clause with, according to Austin Fragomen, a dramatic impact on asylum claims at the border. On the other hand, the Act broadened the definition of refugee to include people subject to forced birth control measures and victims of female genital mutilation.

In the following section, responses of political organizations to the asylum issue are taken mainly from the 1995–1996 legislation process, during which time the Illegal Immigrant and Immigrant Responsibility Act was being discussed. In cases where information on responses to the 1993 debate was available it is also included.

Responses of Political Organizations

Activity. Of the eight groups under review, four did not become engaged at all in the political asylum debate—UNITE, NAM, AAMA, and the Reform Party—while two of the groups (NIF and AFL-CIO) adopted a very low-key approach. They referred to their peak organizations to respond. Their nonresponse, therefore, is not taken into account. However, of those four, only two, namely, the ACLU and FAIR, actually developed a serious approach to the matter; these two organizations can therefore be considered most active on the issue. FAIR, which has continually been involved in the push to reduce immigration since its inception in 1978, was actively involved in radio programs and in congressional hearings and produced a booklet on illegal immigration containing a detailed catalogue of measures pertaining to political asylum.[126] The ACLU established an Immigrant's Rights Project in 1985, with the purpose of advocating the rights of "immigrants, refugees, and non-citizens" and more generally dealing with anti-immigration sentiment in the United States.[127] The ACLU also participated in congressional hearings and as a public law firm has even taken certain exemplary cases to court. None of the organizations was active at the international level, all focusing their lobbying activities in Washington and towards the national public sphere.

Spatiality. In terms of the spatial aspect of the groups' positions (degree of denationalization and territorial scope of demand), all four groups active on the issue (AFL-CIO, NIF (National Immigration Forum), ACLU, and

FAIR) developed policies concerning only the national sphere. None of them argued that asylum should be coordinated at the international level. For all groups the granting of political asylum, and the basis on which this grant is made, was still a national prerogative rooted in national traditions: America as the harbour of the wretched and the persecuted.[128] FAIR's response is of interest because it explicitly rejects the use of international human rights instruments in dealing with immigration issues.[129] The organization has repeatedly sought to narrow the application of international law by the courts, accusing the courts of broadening the definition of asylum to include cases never contemplated by the law. Only by curtailing such judicial practice, a representative of FAIR commented, will asylum law come to embody "not just international standards for the protection of individuals, but also standards that will be supported by the American public over the long run."[130]

Intervention. In terms of degree of intervention, central to the US debate, as in Germany, was the question of access to the asylum application procedure, and whether certain categories of people should be summarily excluded from making an application. In contrast to Germany, however, the question of how broadly the definition of what counts as political persecution (social inclusivity) was to be drawn did not really figure in the debate.

The extent of AFL-CIO and NIF's involvement in the debate was to make some broad statements indicating their general support for the principle of asylum. Thus the only comment by AFL-CIO in the debate, was the following: "[w]e welcome and support diversity in this nation's policies of admitting legal immigrants including those seeking political asylum."[131] The NIF was similarly general in its approach.[132] When interviewed, the organization's representative made the point that, in 1996 (the period the interviews focused on), no new measures were considered necessary since the organization was content with the earlier reforms of the asylum procedure that had taken place.[133]

By contrast, FAIR and the ACLU were specific and extensive in their respective responses. While FAIR opted for a restrictive course, it did not press for the outright abolishment of the institution of political asylum. It argued:

> America's obligation to provide refuge for those truly persecuted does not require us to lose control over our borders or establish a program wide open to fraud and abuse.... FAIR emphatically supports the principle of asylum and the humanitarian principle of providing refuge for those truly facing imminent death or torture at the hands of persecutors.[134]

FAIR maintained that there was a need to regain control of the asylum process in order put an end to the abuses which the status quo supported.

FAIR pressed, therefore, for an abolishment of due process for every single individual and called for summary denial in certain circumstances, such as, for example, when the applicant had not asked for asylum within fifteen days of arrival, when the applicant had destroyed documents, or when the person had been refused political asylum in another country.[135] This narrowing of the scope of asylum was, according to FAIR, necessary to end the advantage asylum applicants had over refugees: "[w]e do not accept refugees seeking protection from societal practices or prejudices, so we should not accept these claims from asylum applicants."[136] In a statement commenting on a draft of IIRAIRA, the organization moreover urged that "asylum grants be only temporary and of limited duration. Asylum grants should also be set off against refugee admissions for the following year."[137] In sum, FAIR's aim was to exclude more people from the asylum application process (social exclusion) and to strengthen the capacity of the state to act against abuse.

The ACLU, on the other hand, approached the issue in an inclusive manner. It, for example, advocated an enlargement of the concept of political asylum, arguing that asylum should be available not only to those who had a well-founded fear of persecution by their government, but also to those who feared persecution by persons their government was unable or unwilling to control.[138] The organization criticized the 1996 reform proposals on the grounds that they reflected the intent not to safeguard the right to asylum but to discourage asylum applications altogether: "[a]s a result, most current proposals represent a deliberate attempt to deter valid and invalid asylum claims alike, a policy which the ACLU must strongly oppose."[139] The group further opposed moves to reduce due process within the law by measures geared, for example, at the acceleration of the application procedure, commenting that this could be fatal to a true asylum process since the "totality of the circumstances faced by the asylum applicant" could not thereby be taken into account.[140] In the words of the ACLU:

> While the ACLU does not oppose expedited asylum procedures per se, current proposals to limit administrative review of INS [the Immigration and Naturalization Service] asylum determinations seriously undermine the due process rights of asylum seekers.... The ACLU strongly opposes any attempts to streamline INS procedures that sacrifice asylum applicants' right to due process, which requires a meaningful opportunity for appeal and the ability to pursue habeas relief.[141]

The ACLU vehemently resisted a strengthening of the administrative capacity of the INS if this led to a curtailing of the judicial review process:

> The idea of immunizing a government agency from being called to account in the courts goes against what most Americans have

thought was the theme of our system: government under Law.... To do it for one of the most troubled of all Federal agencies, the INS, is a step so extreme that it is hard to believe that it is happening.[142]

The ACLU was also opposed to the proposed amendment of the Equal Access to Justice Act, (EAJA), a proposal that would have removed the right of asylum applicants to funding for legal representation. According to this Act, fees for an attorney are provided if an individual's rights have been violated by the government, thus enabling asylum seekers and others whose constitutional rights had been violated through unreasonable INS action to bring an action against the organization. In an open letter, the ACLU argued "[i]f EAJA were amended, none of these individuals would be allowed attorneys' fees no matter how egregious is the INS's illegal conduct toward them. The EAJA amendment is unnecessary."[143] In addition, the organization entreated both the public and the lawmakers not to exaggerate the problem by focusing on the one asylum applicant supposedly responsible for the 1993 World Trade Center bombing. A complete overhaul of the system was not necessary, it argued, just because of one case: "[l]aw professors and judges are fond of saying that hard cases make bad law. If there is a legislative version of that adage perhaps it is that dramatic events make bad law."[144] Overall, therefore, the organization called for an improvement in the asylum process, favoring administrative over legislative change, and opposed efforts to speed up or streamline the process if such changes violated the rights of the applicant. It opposed the reform proposals of 1996 precisely for the reason that the reforms went against this more inclusive approach.

As the above demonstrates, yet again in this case study does a difference emerge between the depth of intervention advocated by the groups in response to the relevant government challenge and the degree of social inclusivity. Thus, the approach of FAIR was to seek a reduction in political asylum applications by all means (highly interventionist but highly exclusive), while the ACLU aimed at maintaining and extending the institution of political asylum (less interventionist but highly inclusive). FAIR revealed, in fact, a rather racist slant at times during the debate.

If the responses of the two organizations are assessed in terms of steering mechanisms and the subject of governance, the same difference in approach can be seen. Thus, on the one hand, FAIR relied on state intervention to secure the reduction of immigration via the asylum system, coupled with a strengthening of the administrative capacity of the state. In this context, the organization called for a total overhaul of the asylum system for example to require that asylum applications have to be filed within thirty days, that asylum applicants without documents are excluded from the process and third country transit applicants rejected from the very beginning.[145] The ACLU, on the other hand, called upon the government to ensure and enhance the due process of law guaranteed to asylum applicants. Thus, while FAIR wanted to strengthen the executive apparatus of the state and enable it to act more unilaterally, the ACLU, wanted to remove the asylum process from political and executive control and bring it completely under the auspices of the judiciary. In both cases, the intervention is one of public action but by very different means.

TOWARDS AN EXPLANATION OF SOCIETAL RESPONSES

To recapitulate, the governance challenge in the labor migration case was caused by the employment of migrant labor under substandard conditions, with the result that national labor standards were being undermined. The governance challenge in the asylum case was caused by an increasing number of asylum applications putting existing regulatory mechanisms and institutions under immense stress. What both cases have in common is the question whether national regimes of citizenship rights should be extended to migrants. To put the matter in concrete terms: Should every asylum applicant have the same guarantee of a due process of law as a national citizen? Should the labor migrant be integrated into national social citizenship regimes thus making it impossible for employers to create a competitive advantage based on the hollowing out of national standards?

Studying the answers of the political organizations at the center of the case studies reveals that there is no overall agreement as to how these issues should be resolved, and that a variety of approaches can be distinguished. A second result is that groups in the United States respond differently from groups in Germany, and lastly, the most impressive and innovative response was presented by the trade unions.

Dealing with the Governance Dilemma: Extending, Reducing or Expanding Citizenship Rights

The question for the labor migration case study was how the national regime of social citizenship rights should be adapted to changing circumstances: in both countries, the employment of migrant labor outside the national social citizenship rights regimes had become more prevalent because of growing import competition from developing countries or increasing competitive pressure stemming from the Common Market in Europe. There are basically three solutions to this problem. One solution is to do nothing about this situation since the situation creates specific advantages (politics of the status quo). A second solution is to include all the workers in the same social citizenship rights regime either by extending national standards (this can also be done as a part of a European wide regulation), or by creating international standards (international civil and social rights). A third solution is to target the immigrants and to demand their removal (renationalization). All three solutions were pushed by the groups under discussion.

The politics of the status quo that favored the maintenance of the deregulation brought about by the employment of migrant labor under substandard conditions were advocated the peak employer associations in both countries (BDA, NAM) and, surprisingly, by the emancipatory organizations of the new politics, the ACLU and the NIF in the United States, whereas the emancipatory organization in Germany (the Green party) favored an extension of social citizenship to all workers preferably through a European wide regulation that fixed specific minimum standards. A solution involving international standards was also advocated by all trade unions in both countries. Immigrants were targeted by organizations of the new authoritarian populism: the Republikaner Party, Ross Perot's Reform Party, and FAIR. It has to be noted however, the Reform Party is more complicated, and partially includes rather progressive solutions and insights on the problem. Its classification under the heading of immigrant targeting or as a re-nationalization strategy therefore have to be taken with a grain of salt. The responses of the sectoral employer associations in both states, the HDB and the AAMA proved difficult to classify. They are somewhere in the middle between a politics of the status quo, and the pro-regulation camp. On the one hand, they recognized that a politics of the status quo was clearly not tenable, on the other hand, they had to bear most of the costs of a regulation, and were rather cautious as to precisely how far citizenship rights should be extended.

In the asylum case study political organizations were confronted by the problem that the increase in asylum applications put the institutions of asylum under immense stress especially in times of a financial crisis of the state, domestic unemployment, elections, and the impression that there are asylum applicants who use the asylum process to immigrate rather than to seek protection from political persecution. The question was whether the system of individual asylum—that is the guarantee that every individual asylum application had to be scrutinized—could be maintained (or even extended to new problems such as female genital mutilation), or whether access restrictions had to be imposed. In contrast to the labor migration case, the solutions presented by political organizations were simple: on the one hand there were those who wanted to reduce the number of asylum applications no matter how, and on the other hand there were those whose main aim was to maintain and even to extend asylum procedures to adjust to the new realities of political persecution after the end of the Cold War. The first solution was advocated by the political organizations of the right, the political organizations from the left in contrast, wanted to maintain or extend the institution of political asylum.

The question is whether there is any correlation between specific group characteristics and response patterns. Are socially inclusive policies pushed only by political organizations from the left or can socially inclusive solutions also be expected by political organizations from the right? In the asylum case, the picture is clear cut: ideological orientation of the group not material interests determine the main thrust of the policies advocated. This can be seen in the fact that the trade unions who are similarly affected by immigration as voters for right wing populist parties advocated completely different policies. In the labor migration case the picture is rather complicated. Socially inclusive policies are pushed for by organizations from the left (trade unions in both countries, the Green Party). A politics of the status quo is advocated by emancipatory groups in the United States (NIF and ACLU), and by the peak employer associations in both countries.

This can be explained by the fact that the employer associations and the two emancipatory political organizations are both in favor of reduced state intervention as regards labor market regulation. The main drive seems to be antigovernment rhetoric whereas the trade unions (in both countries), and the Green Party in Germany do not share this idea about the need to reduce the intervention of the government. Instead, while these groups also pushed for supplementary private actions such as union certificates or codes of conducts for firms, they mainly argued that there is a need for state regulation of labor markets. The central argument in favor of state intervention was that otherwise labor rights cannot be guaranteed as nobody enforces voluntary standards made by firms. Ideas about social order, not necessarily material interests alone seem to be the central driving factor that explains whether groups would extend citizenship rights to migrants or not.

Material interest calculations are of course not absent. It is easier for emancipatory groups such as the NIF or the ACLU to play down the social consequences of denationalization because their membership comprises mostly occupational groups that are not negatively affected by denationalization processes. They are supported mainly by highly skilled professionals who can easily move from one job to another, and who easily can adjust to a denationalized world. It is more difficult for voters of the Reform Party who are confronted by the relocation of factories and who experience a decline of living standards as the new jobs they find do in most cases not provide the same income.

Mainly material interests in contrast explain the response of the two sectoral employer associations, the apparel association (AAMA) and the construction association in Germany (HDB). They recognized that there was indeed a problem if employers undermine rules of competition by employing labor under substandard conditions, and that this would create a downwards spiral damaging to all parties but on the other hand they were mostly implicated in bearing the costs of any regulations. Thus, in contrast to the regulatory coalition they were less enthusiastic about the depths of any regulation, and as regards the American association about state involvement. The actions of the AAMA can be interpreted as face-saving measures to pre-empt stricter public regulation. This response thus has as much to do with ideas about government intervention as with an interest in reducing costs that a public regulation would imply.

While the response of the trade unions in the United States is influenced by ideas about human rights in general, their support for social citizenship rights to migrants is a new feature (Haus 1995) and can also be explained in material terms by the fact that immigrants make up an increasingly larger proportion of the membership. This makes the unequivocal support of the German trade union movement for the maintenance of the asylum regulation all the more interesting because one would assume that the union would at least show some concern for the costs involved. Instead the union contrasted the costs of providing military aid with the costs of protecting refugees that come from countries to which military aid was provided. This again shows how ideas (in this case a respect for human rights) can influence a policy response even if this policy response is expensive for the community as a whole. The membership of the Green Party, in contrast, is usually among the more affluent and more secure middle class who is less concerned with the fiscal crisis of the state. Its support for the institution of asylum can be traced back to absent material interests in terms of costs such as lack of adequate housing.

In conclusion, it can be said that the reasons why political organizations push for the extension of citizenship rights, why they favor the deregulated status quo, or why they even resort to immigrant targeting appear to have as much to do with material interests to avoid the costs of regulation, or to reduce the costs of the unregulated status quo, as with ideas about human rights and government intervention in markets.

Complex Governance?

One central concern in the debate about denationalization is how the newly created space that reaches beyond the regulatory power of any individual nation state should be regulated. There are several approaches to this problem (besides imperialism or colonialism).[146] One solution is to create government beyond the state: effective and binding regulations that have to be adhered to by all parties concerned, and where there is a guarantee that non-compliance is punished effectively and promptly. Another solution is to establish governance beyond the state that involves private and public actors in a joint effort at regulation. Governance beyond the state also involves a division of labor between international regimes or organizations, and the nation states in the sense that the internationalized state structure complements rather than supplements the nation-state. A further solution is to resort only to private initiatives. The question is whether the above discussed approaches to the governance challenges in both cases also contain elements that point towards a more denationalized form of government or governance.

In the labor migration case, only the groups interested in internationally guaranteed political, civil, and social human rights presented ideas as to political denationalization (trade unions, Green Party in Germany). The trade unions were most explicit with regard to their ideas about political denationalization. They argued that effective, internationally guaranteed labor standards are needed. While codes of conduct that contain such standards may be a step in this direction, they were highly sceptical as to the effective implementation of such codes since such codes essentially are private declarations by firms. In their opinion only if these were backed up by public power could they be seen as a viable option that would lead to an improvement of worker's rights in the global economy. At the same time, the trade unions also pushed for more effective enforcement of national labor laws. Both unions in the United States now argue that undocumented immigrants should not be criminalized by strengthening the enforcement of immigration laws but that in effect a stricter enforcement of labor laws within the country provides a level playing field for all workers whether undocumented or documented. In contrast to Streeck's (1999, 53) and Panitch's (1994) insistence that the main bulwark against globalization is still the nation state, since only states thus far have the power to effectively regulate conflicts between capital and labor, trade unions do take the international level into account both by insisting on structures beyond the nation-state, and by becoming actively involved at the international level. However, at the same time, they do not rely solely on such global governance structures. Rather, political denationalization has led to a diversification of channels of lobbying activities and regulatory activities.

The reasons why trade unions and the Green Party demanded transnationally guaranteed worker's rights can be explained by the structure of the problem created by denationalization. The commodity chain in both the construction and the clothing industry reaches across borders in several ways. On the one hand firms can relocate part of the production process abroad or they hire migrant labor within the country that are not covered by domestic wage and labor standards because they are undocumented or because they are service providers. This transnational commodity chain requires that the enforcement of workers' rights be therefore transnationally as well, otherwise firms can play off workers in one location against workers in other locations.

However, and this is important, the structure of the problem does not necessarily lead to a demand for public enforcement of workers' rights. This can be seen in the response pattern of the apparel association in the United States, the AAMA. The association presented its own program of worker's rights certification but at the same time it opposed the Fair Labor

Association created under the leadership of the President of the United States. Furthermore it strictly opposed all demands for creating a public enforcement of labor laws through international organizations such as the International Labor Organization. At the same time, the association however demanded that international trade agreements that guarantee the freedom of investment and trade be extended. This again has to do with the structure of the problem since the import competition stemming from developing countries pushes firms in the United States to at least relocate part of their production process abroad too. Thus, the specific form of public power beyond the nation state depends on the interests and ideas of the actors involved. Complex governance or government beyond the nation state is therefore possible and actively pushed for if it furthers the interests or if it is in conformity with ideas of the actors involved, and if it is an adequate solution to the problem created by denationalization.

A further result is that overall, the demand for political denationalization is higher in Germany than in the United States. In Germany, most groups argued that the question of asylum has to be regulated at the European level while in the United States none of the groups mentioned international norms. A similar degree of uneven denationalization has been obtained in the labor migration case where the groups in Germany on average were more in favor of regulations beyond the nation-state than in the United States. As to the level of political acitivity, the result was similar. In the labor migration case there was a higher degree of activity beyond the nation-state in Germany than in the United States. In the asylum case in contrast, none of the groups displayed international activities. These observations support the argument that the maturity of the international policy cycle influences whether groups develop demands for political denationalization, and whether they develop activities beyond the nation-state. The German policy debate in both cases developed as a part of the process of European integration which is characterized by a high degree of institutionalization beyond the level of the nation-state whereas as regards political asylum and questions of worker's rights in the United States similar international fora simply do not exist.

It is interesting to note the insistence of the peak German employer association, the BDA for a strengthening of the European level in order to hollow out the more liberal German asylum regulation. This demand for a more effective (i.e., less liberal) asylum regulation is puzzling since one associates liberalism in general with less rather than more government intervention. It can only be explained if one accepts the argument that economic liberals restrict their liberalism to the economic sphere, and display more conservative postures in other spheres (see e.g., Overbeek and van der Pijl 1993, 14; Zürn 1998, 296–299). The response pattern of the BDA seems to confirm this selective liberalism displayed by employer associations in Germany and the United States (see also Dreher 2001).

Adapting to Changing Times: Trade Unions and Migration
The activities of the trade unions in both cases (in Germany more than in the United States) clearly stand out in terms of their internationality, inclusivity, and intensity of activity. While one would expect that emancipatory movements are at the forefront when it comes to innovative and denationalized responses to globalization because of their progressive ideas and their nonembeddedness in national systems of interest representation (especially by transnationally organized NGOs), this expectation was not confirmed for the migration case.

Only in Germany did the peak organization of the progressive movements, the Green Party take an active interest in the issue. Instead trade unions, rather traditional, and thus far rather nationally oriented organizations have taken on the lead towards complex, socially inclusive form of global governance, and global government. Other observers have also noted that the new left in general seems to be more interested in multiculturalism and civil rights, and less inclined to deal with such mundane matters as ensuring that workers get paid at least the minimum wage (North 1994, 64–65). This result seems to be due to the fact that social citizenship rights are at the core of trade union activities whereas other issues such as illegal content on the Internet or cryptography clearly are not.

Two questions were at the center of this chapter. How do political organizations respond to challenges posed by labor and refugee migration, and secondly, which factors determine these responses? In answer to the first question the main result is that there are different responses, a fact that needs to be kept in mind during a time when the tendency in the globalization debate seems to be that there is only one solution to globalization. As regards the determining factors, we are on the one hand back to politics as usual: material and non-material interests are centrally important for any explanation. However, on the other hand, the nature of the problem, and the maturity of the policy cycle cannot be neglected as intervening factors. Especially the latter points to the central importance of the state in shaping globalization. In areas where states have created a framework of complex governance beyond the nation-state (as in Europe), societal interest groups have followed.

NOTES

1. See Beisheim et al. (1999, 106–168).

2. This differentiation is not undisputed, for a critical discussion see Zolberg et al. (1989, 30–33).

3. Quoted in Tucker Carlson "The Intellectual Roots of Nativism," *Wall Street Journal*, New York, Oct 2, 1997.

4. This situation changes as soon as migration is transformed into permanent settlement (Piore 1986, 25; Piore 1979, 52).

5. The influx of guest workers entering Germany from Portugal was a result of several factors. One important (push) factor was that in 1992 Portuguese citizens acquired full free movement rights which had not been granted to them with their entry into the European Union (Butt Philip 1994, 169). Furthermore, the Portuguese construction industry was in a recession while German unification had created a construction boom (see Faist et al. 1998).

6. Gesetzentwurf der Bundesregierung. Entwurf eines Gesetzes über zwingende Arbeitsbedingungen bei grenzüberschreitenden Dienstleistungen. Drucksache 13/2414, 25.09.1995.

7. Probleme im Baugewerbe umfassend lösen, in: Die Woche im Bundestag (wib), No. 21, 29. November 1995 (online edition, July 1998).

8. Frankfurter Rundschau, 18. January .1995

9. In March 1995 the IG BAU organized a conference on the "European Labor Market and Unlimited Mobility" documented in Köbele and Leuschner (1995). Another conference dealt with insurance funds and is documented in Köbele and Sahl (1993). The DGB organized a conference in October 1995 on "Short Term Migrant Workers in the European Union" where the Portuguese construction union supported the DGB's demand for a posted workers law (DGB (1995), Kurzfristig Beschäftigte Wanderarbeitnehmer in der Europäischen Union, 13–19).

10. IG BAU press release, 19 February 1997.

11. DGB, press release, 22 December 1994.

12. IG BAU Schriftliche Stellungnahme zur öffentlichen Anhörung am 28 Juni 1995, Deutscher Bundestag, Ausschuß für Arbeit und Sozialordnung, Ausschußdrucksache 13/0168, 8 (translation: SD).

13. BDA Schriftliche Stellungnahme zur öffentlichen Anhörung am 25. Oktober 1995, Deutscher Bundestag, Ausschuß für Arbeit und Sozialordnung, Ausschußdrucksache 13/0292, 10.

14. Köbele and Sahl (1993, 11). (Köbele was president of the IG BAU). Similarly, the DGB at the anniversary of the bilateral treaty for guest worker employment between Portugal and Germany pointed to fact that guest workers were treated like domestic workers on the labor market and that this equal treatment had been the precondition for their employment. See DGB, press declaration 20th March 1995.

15. Die Republikaner: IG-Metall-Chef Zwickel bestätigt REP-Position. Endlich Zusammenhang zwischen Einwanderung und Arbeitsplatzmangel zugegeben, Press Release 06/97, 29.01.1997, summarizing a statement of the Party Chairman (Schlierer).

16. Bündnis 90/Die Grünen (1997): Hoffentlich sozialversichert!? Zum Regulierungsbedarf bei Geringfügiger Beschäftigung, Scheinselbständigkeit, Telearbeit. Anhörung der Bundestagsfraktion, Bonn, 113.

17. DGB, press release 20 March 1995. A similar Angst was expressed by the IG BAU: "The construction sector has become a test case for the introduction of a low wage sector in Germany. Large firms especially have left the concept of a highly qualified work force behind." (Bruno Köbele, president of the IG-BAU in Handelsblatt, 14.10.1994).

18. DGB press release 29 June 1995 (translation: SD).

19. DGB, Stellungnahme zur europäischen Entsenderichtlinie, Deutscher Bundestag, Ausschuß für Arbeit und Sozialordnung, Ausschußdrucksache 13/0160, 20.

20. Bündnis 90/Die Grünen: Antrag, Bundestags-Drucksache 13/786 vom 15.03.1995.

21. IG BAU Schriftliche Stellungnahme zur öffentlichen Anhörung am 28 Juni 1995, Deutscher Bundestag, Ausschuß für Arbeit und Sozialordnung, Ausschußdrucksache 13/0168, 7 (translation: SD).

22. These are covered by a different union (the IG Metall). The approach of the trade unions was coordinated by a working group within the DGB in which both IG Metall and the IG BAU participated.

23. DGB, Stellungnahme zur europäischen Entsenderichtlinie, Deutscher Bundestag, Ausschuß für Arbeit und Sozialordnung, Ausschußdrucksache 13/0160, 20.

24. Hauptverband der Deutschen Bauindustrie, Stellungahme zum nationalen Entsendegesetz, Deutscher Bundestag, Ausschuß für Arbeit und Sozialordnung, Ausschußdrucksache 13/0292 vom 25. Oktober 1995 (Folge 2), 36.

25. Hauptverband der Deutschen Bauindustrie, Stellungnahme zur europäischen Entsenderichtlinie, Deutscher Bundestag, Ausschuß für Arbeit und Sozialordnung, Ausschußdrucksache 13/1068 vom 28. Juni 1995 (Folge 2), 13.

26. BDA, Stellungnahme—September 1992—zum Vorschlag für eine Richtlinie des Rates über die Entsendung von Arbeitnehmern im Rahmen der Erbringung von Dienstleistungen (ABL C 225 vom 30.08.1991). This was updated in 1994.

27. BDA, Stellungnahme vom 25.10.1995 zur Anhörung vor dem Ausschuß für Arbeit und Sozialordnung des Deutschen Bundestages, 2–3.

28. Mündliche Stellungnahme der BDA, Deutscher Bundestag, Ausschuß für Arbeit-und Sozialordnung, 13. Wahlperiode, Wortprotokoll der 18. Sitzung vom 28.06.1995, 58.

29. BDA, Stellungnahme—September 1992—zum Vorschlag für eine Richtlinie des Rates über die Entsendung von Arbeitnehmern im Rahmen der Erbringung von Dienstleistungen (ABL C 225 vom 30.08.1991), 7.

30. Their argument was that such legislation would interfere with the tariff autonomy and freedom of coalition provisions found in Art. 9, par. 3 of the German Basic Law, as well as fall foul of the freedom of movement of workers provisions in European law and freedom of services guarantees. BDA, Stellungnahme vom

25.10.1995 zur Anhörung vor dem Ausschuß für Arbeit und Sozialordnung des Deutschen Bundestages am 25.10.1995, 10–13.

31. BDA, Aktualisierte Stellungnahme—Juli 1994—zum Vorschlag für eine Richtlinie des Rates über die Entsendung von Arbeitnehmern im Rahmen der Erbringung von Dienstleistungen (Kommissionsvorschlag vom 30. August 1991; geänderter Kommissionsvorschlag vom 16. Juni 1993—Kom (93) 225 endg.—Syn. 346); BDA, Stellungnahme vom 25.10.1995 zur Anhörung vor dem Ausschuß für Arbeit und Sozialordnung des Deutschen Bundestages am 25.10.1995.

32. Mündliche Stellungnahme der BDA, Deutscher Bundestag, Ausschuß für Arbeit-und Sozialordnung, 13. Wahlperiode, Wortprotokoll der 18. Sitzung vom 28.06.1995, 61.

33. DGB, Stellungnahme zum Entwurf eines Gesetzes über zwingende Arbeitsbedingungen bei grenzüber-schreitenden Dienstleistungen vom 13. Juli 1995.

34. Mündliche Stellungnahme des DGB, Deutscher Bundestag, Ausschuß für Arbeit und Sozialordnung, 13. Wahlperiode, Wortprotokoll der 18. Sitzung vom 28.06.1995, 33.

35. IG-BAU, Stellungnahme zur europäischen Entsenderichtlinie, Deutscher Bundestag, Ausschuß für Arbeit und Sozialordnung, Ausschußdrucksache 13/1068 vom 28. Juni 1995 Folge 2, 9.

36. Hauptverband der Deutschen Bauindustrie, Stellungnahme zur europäischen Entsenderichtlinie, Deutscher Bundestag, Ausschuß für Arbeit und Sozialordnung, Ausschußdrucksache 13/1068 vom 28. Juni 1995 (Folge 2), 15.

37. The Greens in the European Parliament support the introduction of a minimum wage, see http://www.europeangreens.org/policy.

38. This story is told in detail by Aggarwal (1985).

39. The GAO bases its findings on interviews with over one hundred federal and state government officials from departments monitoring the labor market (namely, the Immigration and Naturalization Service, Wage and Hour Division and the Occupational Safety and Health Administration).

40. The President, Federal Register: February 10, 1995, Vol 60, No 28, p. 7886 (from the Federal Register Online via GPO Access: http://www.wais.access.gpo.gov.

41. The White House, Office of the Press Secretary, Remarks on Illegal Immigration by Attorney General Reno; INS Commissioner Meissner, Secretary of Labor Reich, El Paso Chief Border Patrol Agent Reyes, and INS Western Region Director Urs de la Vina, February 7, 1995 @ http://www. pubwhitehou...ov. us/1995/2/7/6.txt.1

42. Muriel H. Cooper, "Thai Sweatshop Tip of Iceberg", AFL-CIO News, 25 August 1995 @ http://www.aflcio.org/ newsonline/; July 1998).

43. This Act was first introduced in 1995 as the *Immigration in the National Interest Act* and, in its original form, was supposed to completely overhaul immigration policy by reducing the level of legal immigration and introducing measures to

stop illegal immigration. The proimmigrant lobbying groups, however, were success-full in removing the passages pertaining to legal immigration completely and, in the end, the Act focused only on illegal immigration.

44. Other participants are Liz Clairborne, Inc., Nicole Miller, Inc., the National Consumers League, NIKE, Inc., Reebok International, Ltd., Duke Universit,; Retail Wholesale Department Store Union, AFL-CIO, Kathie Lee Gifford, Tweeds Inc., LL. Bean, Inc., among many others.

45. "Employment-based Immigration and High Technology," NAM: Washington, 1996.

46. NAM Briefing, 105th Congress, First Session, Special Issue.

47. NAM @ http://www.nam.org/Programs/history.html.

48. ACLU, "The Rights of Immigrants." Briefing Paper No. 20 (Autumn 1997 update).

49. NIF, 1998 @ http://www.immigrationforum.org/national.htm.

50. NIF, "Finding Common Ground. A Primer for Environment and Population Advocates Concerned About Immigration," Washington, DC, 1996, p. 11–12.

51. NIF 1997: Annual Report 1996, Washington DC: 3–4.

52. UNITE "The Sweatshop Campaign" @ http://www.uniteunion.org/sweat-shops.

53. UNITE @ http://www.uniteunion.org/.

54. Linda Golodner, National Consumers League, "Apparel Industry Code of Conduct: A Consumer Perspective on Social Responsibility," paper presented to Notre Dame Center for Ethics and Religious Values in Business, 6 October, 1997.

55. Remarks by John J. Sweeney, President of the AFL-CIO at the Symposium on Corporate Social Responsibility, Mount St. Mary's College, 24 March, 1998 @ http://www.aflcio.org/publ/speech98/sp0324.htm.

56. UNITE, press release, 16 September 1996.

57. UNITE (no year) "The Face of Change"(brochure); see also Remarks by John J. Sweeney, President of the AFL-CIO, Symposium on Corporate Social Responsibility, Mount St. Mary's College, 24 March, 1998 @ http://www.aflcio.org/publ/speech98/sp0324.html.

58. AAMA, Statement Submitted to the Chairman, Free Trade Area of the Americas, Committee of Government Representatives On Civil Society, 31 March 1999 @ http://www.americanapparel.org/ AAMA_ Industry_News. html.

59. AAMA, "Monitoring and Compliance Activities by the U.S. Apparel Industry," Testimony by Larry K. Martin, President of AAMA, before Oversight and

Investigations Subcommittee of the House Education and Workforce Committee, 25 September, 1998. Available @ http://www.americanapparel.org/ AAMA_Industy_ News.html.

60. Platform of the Reform Party of the United States of America, Adopted in Kansas City, Missouri National Founding Convention 2 November 1997 @ http://www.reformparty.org/headquarters/platform.htm.

61. Ross Perot and Pat Choate, "Save Your Job, Save Our Country: Why NAFTA Must Be Stopped—Now!" New York: Hyperion, 1993, p. 106.

62. Statement of a representative of FAIR, United States House of Representatives, Committee on the Judiciary, Subcommittee on Immigration and Claims, 1995. "*Immigration in the National Interest Act of 1995*," Hearing, 29 June, 1995, p. 302. See also FAIR, "How to win the Immigration Debate," Washington, DC, 1997.

63. This could be achieved by establishing a secure identity card, by combining worksite enforcement with immigration enforcement or by introducing sanctions against employers who hire undocumented aliens. This latter measure was adopted by the US in 1986.

64. FAIR, "Ten Steps to Ending Illegal Immigration," Washington, DC, 1995. These suggestions are part of step two, "Inspections." The other nine steps concern: legislation, asylum reform, intelligence gathering improvements (databases), border patrol, eligibility (for welfare benefits), improving the investigations program, reducing the power of the judiciary, improving detention facilities and deportation procedures, and last, improving funding for immigration law enforcement agencies.

65. Platform of the Reform Party of the United States of America, Adopted in Kansas City, Missouri National Founding Convention 2 November, 1997 @ http://www.reformparty.org/headquarters/ platform.htm.

66. Statement of a represenative of the AFL-CIO, United States House of Representatives, Committee on the Judiciary, Subcommittee on Immigration and Claims, 1995. "Legal Immigration Reform Proposals," Hearing, 17 May, 1995.

67. Ibid. The AFL-CIO has, however, more recently changed its position on employer sanctions and today stands with UNITE for their repeal, see AFL-CIO, "Immigration," Executive Council Actions, Adopted Policy Statement, New Orleans, 15 February 2000.

68. Statement by the AFL-CIO Executive Council on Immigration and the American Dream, Bal Harbour, 23 February, 1995.

69. John J. Sweeney, President of the AFL-CIO, "The Labor Movement in '96—The New Activism," The New School for Social Research, 03 June 1996 (downloaded in 1998) @ http://www.aflcio.org/publ/speech96/ sp06032.html; for UNITE see press release from 20 August 1996 (Miami Workers Join Clinton in Signing Minimum Wage Bill). Please note: UNITE's web page has been redesigned since these press releases were downloaded in 1998.

70. AFL-CIO Resolution, "Economic and Social Justice", in AFL-CIO, "Resolutions and Constitutional Amendements Adopted at the Twenty-Second AFL-CIO Convention", AFL-CIO, Washington, DC, 1997.

71. Ibid.

72. UNITE: "The Sweatshop Campaign" 1998 @ http://www.uniteunion.org/sweatshops.

73. Jay Mazur, President of UNITE, "Labor's New Langugage," *The Dissident,* May 1997, Vol 8–9, p. 30.

74. UNITE (1996) Kennedy, Clay introduces Stop Sweatshops Act of 1996, at the sweatshop newspaper archive of UNITE @ http://www.niteunion.org/ sweatshops/sweatshopsarchive.

75. UNITE, press release, 16 July 1996.

76. Remarks by John J. Sweeney, President of the AFL-CIO, at the Symposium on Corporate Social Responsibility, Mount St. Mary's College, 24 March, 1998 @ http://www.aflcio.org/publ/speech98/sp0324.htm.

77. UNITE, press release, 16 July 1996.

78. AAMA, "Responsible Apparel Production Program. an Initative Aimed at Improving Apparel Industry Working Conditions Worldwide", December 1998 (downloaded in 1999) @ http://www.americanapparel. org/RAPP_Principles. html.

79. Statement by the AFL-CIO, Executive Council on Immigration and the American Dream, Bal Harbour, 23 February, 1995.

80. Jay Mazur, President of UNITE, "Labor's New Language", *The Dissident,* May 1997, Vol 8–9, p. 30.

81. Interview with a represenative of the organization, April 1998.

82. Dan Stein, "Making Immigration Great Again" FAIR, Speech to the Commonwealth Club, San Francisco, 28 July 28 1997 (downloaded in 1998) @ http://www.fairus.org

83. Ibid.

84. Reform Party, "Proposed Platform Text of New Section 13," October 1998, at http://www.reformparty. org/convention1998/; see also Reform Party, The Immigration Sub-Committee of the Issues/Platform Committee, "The Abuse of Immigration in the Agricultural Industry," October 1998 @ http://issues.reform-party.org/iss_immindex.htm.

85. Convention Relating to the Status of Refugees of 28 July 1951 (Art. 1, A, 2.) and Protocol Relating to the Status of Refugees of 31 January 1967 Art. 1 para 2; in the Protocol, a temporal limitation in the original definition of refugee was dropped.

86. The participating states are: Australia, Austria, Belgium, Canada, Denmark, Finland, France, Germany, Italy, the Netherlands, Norway, Spain, Sweden, Switzerland, the United Kingdom, and the United States. See also the web page http://www.igc.ch/.

87. Asylum is granted to persons who are politically persecuted.

88. *Der Spiegel*, 42/1991: 27.

89. *Süddeutsche Zeitung*, 10 April, 1992.

90. *Süddeutsche Zeitung*, 1 February, 1992.

91. *Hamburger Abendblatt*, 13 April, 1992.

92. *Süddeutsche Zeitung*, 25 April 25, 1992.

93. Deutscher Bundestag; 12 Wahlperiode/Drucksache 12/4152: Gesetzentwurf der Fraktionen der CDU/CSU, SPD und F. D. P. Entwurf eines Gesetzes zur Änderung des Grundgesetzes, 19.01.1993.

94. It has to be noted, however, that in the context of the history of the BDA itself, its activities were quite remarkable. It signed a declaration against xenophobia in Germany (see BDA, KND Kurz-Nachrichten-Dienst Nr. 93, December. 1991), it printed an anti-racism pamphlet (Faltblatt "Deutsche Wirtschaft gegen Ausländerfeindlichkeit" in: BDA January 1993: KND Kurznachrichten, Nr. 1.) which was distributed amongst member organizations and it joined in a declaration condemning xenophobia, together with other peak employer organizations (BDA, KND Kurz-Nachrichten-Dienst Nr. 81, November 1992). According to the BDA, these activities were intended as an explicit signal that racism had to be countered in an active manner (Interview with a representative of BDA, March 1998). See also the common declaration of the peak organizations of the old politics on the issue of xenophobic tendencies: DGB und BDA: Gemeinsamer Aufruf von DGB und Arbeitgebern gegen Ausländerfeindlichkeit, 11 January 1993.

95. Interview with PRO ASYL, 16 February 1998.

96. PRO ASYL-Unterschriftenliste: Keine Änderung des Grundrechts auf Asyl; (1)DGB, Bundesvorstand 21.7.1992: Gemeinsame Erklärung zur aktuellen Asyldiskussion von Pfarrer Herbert Leuninger (Sprecher von PRO ASYL) und Jochen Richert (Mitglied des DGB-Bundesvorstandes); (2) DGB-Bundesvorstand / PRO ASYL (Hrsg.): Keine Änderung des Grundrechts auf Asyl (Faltblatt). (3) DGB: Gemeinsames Argumentationsblatt der Abteilung Ausländische Arbeitnehmer und PRO ASYL, 30.10.1992; (3) Flugblatt: 14.11.1992 in Bonn. Grundrechte verteidigen. Flüchtinge schützen Rassismus bekämpfen. Verteidigt Art. 16; (4) DGB-Bundesvorstand/PRO ASYL (Hrsg.): Argumente zur Asyldiskussion (Faltblatt) 1992; (5) DGB-Bundesvorstand/PRO ASYL (Hrsg.): Flüchtlinge schützen! Nein zum Bonner Asylkompromiß. (6)Dez. 1992; PRO ASYL/DGB: An die Abgeordneten des Deutschen Bundestages. Gemeinsame Stellungnahme des DGB-Bundesvorstandes, Abteilung ausländische Arbeitnehmer und der Arbeitsgemeinschaft PRO ASYL, DGB und PRO ASYL: Grundrecht auf Asyl erhalten, 01.03.1993.

97. This attitude also emerged in the interview held with a representative of the DGB for the purposes of this study. The representative stressed that the DGB no longer regards a focus on the rights of workers in the narrow sense as sufficient, and that it now concerns itself with a wider sphere of social rights. See also Leo Monz: "Interessenverband und Menschenrechtsorganisation," in: Die Mitbestimmung 8/92.

98. Franz Steinkühler (DGB) 1992: Rückfragen zur Asyldebatte in: Neue Gesellschaft Frankfurter Hefte 39:6, 500–502.

99. DGB 1996: Von der Ausländerbeschäftigung zur Einwanderungspolitik.Beschlüsse, Stellungnahmen und Forderungen des DGB 1990–1993. S. 18/19. Februar 1992.

100. DGB 1986: Stellungnahme des Deutschen Gewerkschaftsbundes zum Asylrecht und zum Asylverfahren in der Bundesrepublik Deutschland, press declaration 16/09/1986; DGB 1991: Gemeinsam mit Ausländern leben und arbeiten. Beschluß des DGB Bundesvorstandes vom Oktober 1991. For a similar response see: Arbeiterwohlfahrt Bundesverband e.V. 1991: Aufnahme und Integration von Zuwanderern als politische Aufgabe-Denkschrift. Bonn: Arbeiterwohlfahrt Bundesverband e.V., Abteilung Migration: 16.

101. DGB-Bundesvorstand, Abteilung ausländische Arbeitnehmer / PROASYL, Bundesweite Arbeitsgemeinschaft für Flüchtlinge 1992: Keine Änderung des Grundrechts auf Asyl (Faltblatt vom Oktober 1992).

102. Bündnis 90/Ddie Grünen 1992: Antrag: Das Asylrecht ist unverzichtbar, Deutscher Bundestag, 12. Wahlperiode, Drucksacher 12/3235.

103. AWO Bundeskonferenz (1992). Antrags-Nr. 02.03.03.

104. BDA 1992: Ausländerbeschäftigung in Deutschland. Grundsätze und Empfehlungen der Arbeitgeber. Köln, Oktober 1992: 19.

105. Abgeordneter Schlierer 1992: Landtag von Baden-Württemberg-11. Wahlperiode-5. Sitzung-Dienstag, 30. Juni 1992.

106. Abgeordneter König 1992: Landtag von Baden-Württemberg-11. Wahlperiode-9. Sitzung-Donnerstag, 22. Oktober 1992.

107. Die Republikaner 1997 press release, 7 January 1998.

108. Bündnis'90/Die Grünen: Unantastbares Grundrecht auf Asyl und die jüngsten ausländerfeindlichen Ausschreitungen (Antrag an den Deutschen Bundestag), Bundestags-Drucksache 12/1216 vom 27.09.1991; DGB 1992: Es geht doch nichts über deutsche Sauberkeit. Argumente gegen Ausländerfeindlichkeit, Faltblatt.

109. DGB 1992: Es geht doch nichts über deutsche Sauberkeit. Argumente gegen Ausländerfeindlichkeit, Faltblatt.

110. Weiß, Konrad, 1992: Rede im Deutschen Bundestag zur 1. Lesung des Einwanderungs-und des Flüchtlingsgesetzes von Bündnis'90/Die Grünen. In: Bündnis '90/Die Grünen, Bundestagsgruppe (Hrsg.); DGB 1992: DGB-Position zur aktuellen Asyldiskussion (24.9.1992).

111. Arbeiterwohlfahrt Bundeskonferenz 1992: Antrags-Nr. 02.03.03.

112. Bündnis'90/Die Grünen: Unantastbares Grundrecht auf Asyl und die jüngsten ausländerfeindlichen Ausschreitungen (Antrag an den Deutschen Bundestag), Bundestags-Drucksache 12/1216 vom 27.09.1991; DGB 1992: Es geht doch nichts über deutsche Sauberkeit. Argumente gegen Ausländerfeindlichkeit, Faltblatt.

113. DGB 1992: Es geht doch nichts über deutsche Sauberkeit. Argumente gegen Ausländerfeindlichkeit, Faltblatt.

114. AWO Bundeskonferenz 1992: Antrags-Nr. 02.03.03.

115. Interview with a representative of AWO, March 1998.

116. Franz Steinkühler 1992: Rückfragen zur Asyldebatte in: Neue Gesellschaft Frankfurter Hefte 39: 6, 500–502.

117. AWO Bundeskonferenz 1992: Antrags-Nr. 02.03.03.

118. BDA 1992: Ausländerbeschäftigung in Deutschland. Grundsätze und Empfehlungen der Arbeitgeber. Köln, Oktober 1992, 17–19.

119. Die Republikaner (o.J.): Parteiprogramm. Wir machen uns stark für deutsche Interessen, 22–24.

120. Die Grünen, Bundespartei (Hrsg.), 1990: Das Programm zur 1. gesamtdeutschen Wahl 1990; DGB, Arbeitsausschuß, Grundsatz des Ausschusses für ausländische Arbeitnehmer vom Januar 1992: Thesen zur Problematik eines Einwanderungsgesetzes in: DGB Dokumentation 1992: Asyl-und Zuwanderungspolitik. Gewerkschaftliche Positionsbestimmung. Dokumentation 1989–1992: 47–49; Arbeiterwohlfahrt Bundeskonferenz 1992: Antrags-Nr. 02.03.03.

121. In the United States, refugees have to be distinguished from asylum seekers. The former are persons screened abroad by United States refugee organizations while the latter refers to persons who arrive at the border of the United States on their own efforts seeking asylum. This case study only deals with the issue of territorial asylum and not with the refugee programs and policies of the United States. The term refugee is, in this part of the chapter, however, at times also used to refer to asylum seekers.

122. United States House of Representatives, Committee on the Judiciary Subcommittee on International Law, Immigration and Refugees, 1993: "Asylum and Inspections Reform," Hearing, 27 April, 1993, p. 1,3.

123. CBS, Profile "How did he get here? Asking for political asylum gains easy entrance to United States," 14 March 1993. According to Mazzoli, this sixty minute program triggered the discussion on asylum in Congress (United States House of Representatives, Committee on the Judiciary, Subcommittee on International Law, Immigration and Refugees, 1993: "Asylum and Inspections Reform," Hearing, 27 April, 1993, p. 50–51).

124. These three Acts were the following: *The Exclusion and Asylum Reform Amendment of 1993*, HR 1355; *The Asylum Reform Act of 1993*, H.R. 1679; and *The Immigration Pre-Inspection Act of 1993*, H.R. 1153. Included in the reforms was a doubling of the number of asylum officers from 150 to 325 and an increase in the number of judges from 112 to 179. Other changes were also aimed at an acceleration of the procedure with the aspiration of reducing the duration of the application process to 60 days. Another change introduced by the reforms was that a work permit would be granted only after a stay of over 180 days (Copeland 1997, 17).

125. The President, Federal Register, 10 February, 1995, Vol. 60, No. 28, p. 7886 (from the Federal Register Online via GPO Access: http://www. wais. access.gpo.gov).

126. FAIR, "Ten Steps to Ending Illegal Immigration," Federation for American Immigration Reform, Washington, DC, 1995, p. 3–6.

127. ACLU, "The Rights of Immigrants," Briefing Paper No. 20, Autumn 1997 update (downloaded in 1998).

128. A sole exception to this could be construed from a comment made by FAIR, that "[t]here is also a need for international applications tracking, so a claim denied in, say Switzerland or Belgium, also operates as a denial in the United States." But, since FAIR nowhere actively pressed for international cooperation on the issue, the response of the organization is still classified as national. See Response of a Representative of FAIR, United States House of Representatives, Committee on the Judiciary, Subcommittee on International Law, Immigration and Refugees. 1993. Asylum and Inspections Reform: Hearing, April 27, 1993.

129. While the United States has not ratified many international human rights treaties (Jacobson 1996: 95), the courts are nonetheless increasingly turning to these instruments for guidance in their decision making. The Universal Declaration of Human Rights, for example, has been referred to in seventy-six federal cases (59 of these cases occurring after 1980). The interesting point is that 54 per cent of these cases involved immigration or refugee issues (Jacobson 1996, 97).

130. FAIR, "The Need for Asylum Reform", Submitted to the Commission on Immigration Reform, 12 June, 1996.

131. AFL-CIO, United States House of Representatives, Committee on the Judiciary, Subcommittee on Immigration and Claims, 1995: "Legal Immigration Reform Proposals," Hearing, 17 May, 1995.

132. NIF, "Finding Common Ground: A Primer for Environment and Population Advocates Concerned About Immigration," Washington, DC, 1996, p. 11.

133. Interview with a representative of the National Immigration Forum, April 1998.

134. FAIR, United States House of Representatives, Committee on the Judiciary, Subcommittee on International Law, Immigration and Refugees, 1993: "Asylum and Inspections Reform," Hearing, 27 April, 1993.

135. Ibid. More detailed proposals can be found in FAIR, "Ten Steps to Ending Illegal Immigration", Federation for American Immigration Reform, Washington, D.C., 1995, p. 3–6.

136. John L. Martin, Special Projects Director, FAIR, "The Need for Asylum Reform," submitted to the Commission on Immigration Reform, 12 June 1996.

137. FAIR, United States House of Representatives, Committee on the Judiciary, Subcommittee on Immigration and Claims, 1995: "Immigration in the National Interest Act of 1995," Hearing, 29 June, 1995, p. 321.

138. ACLU, "Policy Guide of ACLU", Policy No. 325: "Admission of Immigrants," 1994, p. 420; Board Minutes, 25–26 January 1986; 21–22. June 1986.

139. ACLU; United States Senate, Committee on the Judiciary, Subcommittee on Immigration and Refugee Affairs: "Terrorism, Asylum Issues, and U.S. Immigration Policy," Hearing, 28 May, 1993.

140. ACLU, United States Senate, Committee on the Judiciary, Subcommittee on Immigration and Refugee Affairs, 1994: "Terrorism, Asylum Issues, and U.S. Immigration Policy," Hearing, 28 May, 1993. AFL-CIO, United States House of Representatives, Committee on the Judiciary, Subcommittee on Immigration and Claims, 1995: "Legal Immigration Reform Proposals," Hearing, 17 May, 1995.

141. ACLU, United States Senate, Committee on the Judiciary, Subcommittee on Immigration and Refugee Affairs, 1994: "Terrorism, Asylum Issues, and U.S. Immigration Policy," Hearing, 28 May, 1993. United States House of Representatives, Committee on the Judiciary, Subcommittee on Immigration and Claims, 1995: "Legal Immigration Reform Proposals," Hearing, 17 May, 1995.

142. ACLU, "Immigration Measure Moves Towards Passage," Press declaration 24 September 1996.

143. ACLU, letter to a Senator, 24 April 1996 (downloaded in 1998) @ http://www.aclu.org/congress/discuss.html. The ACLU is wary of the INS. In the letter the ACLU continues: "The INS is notorious for making mistakes, subjecting individuals to unfair treatment and violating its own statute and regulations. Recently, it admitted to having lost sixty-thousand political asylum applications. Judicial oversight is critical to protecting individuals against abuses."

144. ACLU, United States. House of Representatives, Committee on the Judiciary, Subcommittee on International Law, Immigration and Refugees, 1993: "Asylum and Inspections Reform," Hearing, 27 April, 1993.

145. FAIR, "Ten Steps to Ending Illegal Immigration," Washington, DC, 1995. These suggestions are found under "Step 3 asylum reform." The brochure is full of such detailed suggestions for policy reform.

146. See Lacher (2004, 213) for a discussion of what he calls spatialization strategies of states, classes, and firms which aim to deal with the fundamental tensions that are created by the territorial noncoincidence of the state and the world economy.

Chapter 5

Politics From Above or Below? Climate Politics in Germany and Great Britain

Marianne Beisheim

INTRODUCTION: GOVERNANCE CHALLENGE, POLICY CYCLES, AND GROUP SELECTION

It is now commonly accepted that mankind is changing the climate of the world, resulting in serious consequences for the environment. This fact has confronted the international community with a major challenge, to globally determine sustainable ways to produce and consume. With negotiations over the Framework Convention on Climate Change (FCCC) still under way, it is clear that the issue is yet to be resolved on a political level. Since climate change is global in both its causes and consequences, no single country is able to effectively deal with the problem unilaterally. This fact poses a major challenge to the very concept of the nation state and its responsibilities: it is no longer feasible to regard any single state as responsible for the kind of guarantee that the European Charter on Environment and Health regards as a basic right:

> Every individual is entitled to an environment conducive to the highest attainable level of health and well-being; information and consultation on the state of the environment and on plans, decisions and activities likely to affect both the environment and health; participation in the decision-making process.[1]

All those groups under investigation in this chapter—even if they themselves are not very active—agree on one point: the problem has to be dealt with effectively. Not surprisingly, however, considerable differences exist between the groups' beliefs of how this is to be best achieved: it is easy to see that a problem of this magnitude brings in its wake serious conflicts between the diverse number of groups involved with an attempt to find a solution to climate change. As this chapter aims to show, it is only once these conflicting positions are taken into account that an understanding of the cleavages in national and international climate politics can occur. This chapter, thus, presents two case studies with the purpose of investigating the responses of pressure groups in Germany and Great Britain to the governance challenges brought about by the problem of anthropogenic climate change.

Governance Challenges: CO_2-Targets and Resource-Transfers

The first case study presented in this chapter examines the specific governance challenge of implementing an effective system of carbon dioxide (CO_2) emissions control by industrial countries, represented here by Germany and Great Britain. The subject of this case study reflects the fact that the international climate debate has focused on CO_2 emissions, among other greenhouse gases (GHG), as representing the main human cause of global warming. Remedial policies at the purely national level appear ineffective for two reasons. Firstly, as already indicated above, the reduction of CO_2 emissions by one country alone will not be able to stop global climate change. Hence, a congruence problem exists. Secondly, the implementation of policies aimed at climate protection come at a considerable cost, and—where other industrial countries do not take equivalent measures—such policies operate to reduce the international competitiveness of that country.[2] The emphasis has thus been on a global approach in order to prevent countries gaining a competitive advantage as a result of their disregard for the environment. It is for these reasons that binding international CO_2 emissions targets and timetables and efficient measures for their national implementation (such as an EU-wide energy or carbon tax) have, in particular among industrialized countries, dominated the international climate change agenda. The second case study deals with the challenges arising out of the further industrialization of developing and newly industrialized countries. This case study looks at the necessity of resource transfers to those countries and how the idea is debated in Germany and Great Britain.[3]

Developed countries account for by far the largest part of both historical and current greenhouse gas emissions (their share in 1994 was about 75 per cent of the global total). However, while per-capita emissions in developed countries are likely to stabilize (well above the world average), the emissions of developing countries continue to grow and are expected to represent some 50 per cent of the global total before the year 2025. If these countries continue to develop as they have done up to now, their CO_2 emissions will more than outweigh the reductions currently contemplated by industrial countries and thus further advance climate change. Again there is a congruence problem. And then again, even if developing countries should decide to agree on a future limitation on their CO_2 emissions, there is still the danger of an involuntary defection: many developing countries are simply not able to finance the path of sustainable development. In this second case study, therefore, the problem is less one of competitiveness than one of distribution which translates into an external challenge for the industrialized countries' attempts to stabilize the global climate: "The problem is not that poor countries are driving rich country standards downward [i.e., a competition problem, MB]; it is rather that rich countries lack adequate ability to drive poor country standard upward" (Vogel 1997, 556–571). Hence, one aspect of climate politics is the discussion of how international financial mechanisms and resource transfers can help developing and threshold countries achieve the means of environmentally responsible development,[4] a discussion which is, in the context of a general greening of development politics, largely focused on transfer mechanisms for sustainable technologies. In sum, the governance challenge in the second case study is that of securing sustainable development in developing and threshold countries.

International and National Policy Cycles

At the international level, scientific discussion about the possibility of anthropogenic climate change began in the 1950s. This discussion intensified in the 1970s,[5] culminating in the First World Climate Conference in 1979. In 1987, the Brundtland-Report suggested the staging of a second environmental conference under the auspices of the United Nations. In 1988, the Intergovernmental Panel on Climate Change (IPCC) began its work and ultimately published a series of scientific reports which have become considered leading authorities on the issue. Public interest in the topic grew drastically during the 1980s and in December 1990, the General Assembly of the United Nations passed a resolution initiating preparations for the United Nations Conference on Environment and Development (UNCED). In the following two years, national delegations as well as representatives of UN bodies, other international organizations, and various nongovernmental organizations (NGOs) worked together in so-called Preparatory Committees (PrepComs) and in the "Intergovernmental Negotiating Committee" (INC) in order to prepare for the Conference. At UNCED 1992 in Rio de Janeiro, the Framework Convention on Climate Change (FCCC) was signed. Agreement on the final design of the Convention's implementation measures, however, has not yet been reached, with continued negotiations being held at the international level through various Conferences of the Parties(COPs).[6]

The setting of targets to reduce emissions of CO_2 is a central feature of the FCCC, one of its central aims being the "stabilization of greenhouse gas concentrations in the atmosphere at a level that...prevent[s] dangerous anthropogenic interference with the climate system."[7] Already the wording of the Convention is aspirational, encouraging industrial countries to return CO_2 and other greenhouse gas emissions to their 1990 levels by the year 2000.[8] It was not before COP 3 in Kyoto 1997, however, that a protocol was

passed enabling the setting of legally binding targets and timetables for cut-
ting emissions in developed countries. The Protocol commits participating
countries to a reduction of collective emissions by at least 5 per cent, with
1990 as the base of comparison.[9] Each country's emissions level is calculated
by taking an average of emissions levels during the years 2008–2012. In the
first commitment period, that is, by the year 2005, governments must make
demonstrable progress towards achievement of their respective goals. The
transfer of resources to developing and threshold countries has also been a
central aspect of the debate and, consequently, of the FCCC.[10] For many
years a climate fund was discussed as a possible mechanism through which
financial resources could be directed to developing countries. These discussions culminated in the setting up of the Global Environmental Facility
(GEF), a multibillion dollar fund established in 1990 by the World Bank,
the UN Development Program, and the UN Environment Program. This
fund operates as the Convention's financial mechanism and is used to support developing country projects that are beneficial for the environment; for
example, it provides the funding to cover the added cost of introducing cli-
mate-friendly technology in the place of more traditional technologies.

The establishment of a climate fund is, however, only one among a
number of possible resource transfer techniques. Another strategy, geared at
enabling the transfer of low-emission technologies to developing countries, is
that of joint implementation (or JI) projects. This concept starts with the
assumption that it makes no difference in which part of the world a reduction of greenhouse gases actually occurs. The reasoning behind JI, then, is
that it may be cheaper to reduce a given quantity of emissions in many developing and transition countries than in some developed countries. JI projects
operate as follows: a partnership is set up between a company in a developed
country and a counterpart in a host country (which could be developed,
developing, or in transition to a market economy); the investing partner then
provides most of the capital and technology required for establishing, in the
host country, emissions reduction measures, and in exchange, the investing
country receives the credits for the emissions it helps to reduce. This strategy
recognizes that some of the greatest benefits of climate policies may be
realised in developing countries that are experiencing rapid economic growth
and in countries with economies in transition to a market economy. It both
helps developing countries achieve sustainable development and contributes
to the overall emissions reduction goals of the Convention.[11] The details of
how this mechanism will work in practice, however, is still to be developed.[12]
A further means for the transfer of resources is in international trade of emissions certificates (ET). This mechanism derives from the 1997 Kyoto
Protocol which contains provisions enabling the trading of permits for
greenhouse gas emissions amongst developed countries; the details of this
scheme, however, have not yet been fully clarified.[13] In both cases—the

reduction of emissions and the transfer of resources—the preferences and activities of the groups under investigation relate to the above mentioned subjects of negotiation. As we are interested in the group's fundamental position vis-à-vis the governance challenge, our focus is on the early stage of the policy process. This follows our assumption that, in the agenda-setting phase of the policy cycle, the groups' positions are less driven by the process itself and more by their actual attitudes.

In Germany, the protection of the environment is a responsibility of the federal government and has been expressed as such in the constitution. Impending climate change, therefore, forms a real challenge to the state—as the BMU (the German Federal Ministry of the Environment) has emphasized:

> In 1994, the state's responsibility to future generations in protecting the natural environment was laid out in the constitution. Today, more than ever, global demographic and ecological trends confront the community of states with a serious challenge.[14]

In the early 1980s, the BMFT (the former German Federal Ministry of Research and Technology) initiated a federal government program with the purpose of supporting climate research. In 1985, a report of the German Physical Society, entitled "Beware of a Threatening Climate Catastrophy," was published and stimulated quite a considerable amount of public discussion; since that time the media has increasingly taken up the issue.[15] In 1987, the German Parliament established an Enquete Commission[16] on "Preventive Measures to Protect the Earth's Atmosphere" which published three reports between 1988 and 1990. Relying on the recommendations in these reports, the federal government passed two resolutions, the first identifying the challenge of climate change and the second announcing corresponding measures to reduce CO_2 emissions (case 1):

> The federal government regards the greenhouse effect and climate change as a global challenge that cannot be dealt with by national measures alone but which needs international cooperation.[17]

> As an important step ... the federal government aspires to a clear decrease in energy-related emissions of Carbon dioxide (CO_2).[18]

A second Enquete Commission entitled "Protection of the Atmosphere" was appointed by the federal Parliament in 1991. Their report emphasized the global dimensions of the problem:

> The looming climate catastrophe has a global character. Impending environmental damage is no longer limited regionally or locally but is a danger to the whole of mankind.... The menacing problem of climate change represents a global problem that cannot be solved but by combined international efforts.[19]

In 1990, the German Government established an Inter-Ministerial Working Group (*Interministerielle Arbeitsgruppe*, IMA) chaired by the German Federal Ministry of the Environment. The title of the 1991 IMA report, CO_2 Reduction, refers to climate change as a global challenge and stresses the limited effectiveness of purely national CO_2 reduction measures. Because of this, and because of the pressures of international competition, it concluded that coordinated international action was a necessity.[20] Accordingly, commenting on one of the IMA's reports, the federal government emphasized:

> ...the necessity for other industrialized countries to also significantly reduce their greenhouse gas emissions, in the interest of global climate protection, and in the light of competition criteria....In the light of the global dimensions of the greenhouse effect, the Federal Government reaffirms the position it has repeatedly expressed in previous decisions: that the global climate problem cannot be solved by countries acting alone.[21]

In relation to the issue of resource transfers (case #2), the Enquete Commission "Protection of Atmosphere" formulated, in 1992, the need for financial and technological support in the following terms:

> Although climate politics at first is a task of the industrial countries as the side that mainly cause climate problems, the further development of those countries which are not yet industrialized must not escalate the crisis....Developing countries will not be able to make their contribution without the support of industrial countries; that is why they need technological and financial support.[22]

Based on the recommendations of the Commission, the federal government passed several resolutions—even prior to UNCED—recognizing the challenge that developing and threshold countries present to the worldwide reduction of CO_2 emissions:

> In the fields of bilateral development politics as well as in international organizations and financial institutions, the federal government will make efforts to help Third World countries with their part in coping with climate change.[23]

At the beginning of May 1991, a National Committee, with the Federal Minister of the Environment at the head, was appointed with the mandate of preparing for UNCED. During UNCED, Germany strongly supported the Convention on Climate Change and ultimately ratified it in 1993. The German delegation also made a stand for the GEF mechanism and, in particular, the instrument of Joint Implementation. The German government's national policy goal is to reduce CO_2 emissions by 25 per cent by the year 2005 as compared to 1990 levels.

In Great Britain it has also been widely recognized that climate change presents a important challenge to the nation. The Climate Change Impacts Review Group (CCIRG), set up by the former "Department of the Environment" (DOE), for example, put the danger in the following terms: "Climate change has potential risks for the UK....If such impacts are to be avoided, not just the UK but the rest of the world must react to the threat of global warming."[24]

Prior to UNCED, the need for CO_2 reduction targets (case 1) had been formulated by both the British government and by the scientific community, (for example, by the Global Climate Change Information Program, GCCIP, established in 1991). In a white paper on the issue, entitled "This Common Inheritance," and published in 1990, the government not only emphasized the necessity for international coordination but also presented it as a prerequisite for domestic action: "The Government believes that countries must act together to respond to this challenge....If other countries take similar action, Britain is prepared to set itself the demanding target of reversing the upward trend of CO_2 emissions."[25]

The government also identified the problem of greenhouse-gas emissions in developing and threshold countries (case 2) and announced its willingness to take appropriate measures:

> International action is essential to tackle the threat of climate change. No single country or group of countries can tackle the problem alone.... Given the rates of economic and population growth in many developing countries, the Convention's objectives can only be realised if they play a full and active part in it. Under the Convention, the UK, along with other developed countries, will provide support for developing countries to help them to prepare inventories of greenhouse gas emissions and to put in place programs to ensure that future economic development has the lowest possible impact on the environment.[26]

Decisions on climate policy take place within the interministerial Cabinet Committee on the Environment chaired by the Deputy Prime Minister, who also heads up the new Department of the Environment, Transport and the Regions (DETR). Great Britain ratified the FCCC in 1993 and since then has published several reports on its national climate program. Greenhouse gas emissions are currently on the decrease in the UK. This is largely the result of changes in the energy sector, where deregulation and liberalization of the energy markets in the 1990s resulted in a move away from carbon intensive fuels such as coal towards gas and nuclear energy.

Originally, the intention of the British government was to stabilize emissions of the most important greenhouse gases at 1990 levels by 2000. In Kyoto in 1997, however, the UK agreed to the target of a 12.5 per cent cut in a basket of six greenhouse gases. Domestically, the government has gone further, setting a national goal of a 20 per cent reduction in emissions by 2010 (based on 1990 levels). In addition, Great Britain is, in principle, very much in favor of market instruments such as joint implementation (JI) and emissions trading (ET).

Group Selection

According to the selection criteria of the study as a whole, the following political groups were selected for Germany and Great Britain.

As the umbrella organizations of German employee and employer groups, the DGB (German Trade Union Federation) and BDI (Federation of German Industries), respectively, are taken as representing general organizations within the old politics sphere. Although Bündnis 90 / Die Grünen (The Green Party) are a governmental party as opposed to merely an interest group, they can be seen as the organized top of a diversity of New Social Movements dealing with progressive new politics issues such as, for example, environmental protection, equal rights, and citizen participation.[27] Similarly, the Republikaner Party has been selected to represent the authoritarian angle of new politics, with concerns such as, for example, the limitation of immigration, the preservation of traditional family values, and patriotism. These issues are also taken on by less well-organized groups within the progressive or authoritarian spectrum, but in contrast to many of these single issue groups, both parties selected fulfil the added criteria of being fairly strong in both nationwide organization and orientation.

Almost 90 per cent of energy consumed in Germany derives from fossil sources (coal, oil and natural gas). It is mainly by changing these patterns of energy consumption, therefore, that the targeted CO_2 reductions will be achieved. For this reason, IG BCE and VDEW have been selected as the trade union and business association (respectively) most important within the energy sector. IG BCE emerged from an amalgamation in 1997 of IG Bergbau-Energie (Union of Mining and Energy, IG BE) and IG Chemie-Papier-Keramik (Union of Chemistry, Paper, and Ceramics, IG CPK). Because the two former unions had supported opposing views in relation to climate protection, both the positions of the original associations until 1997 as well as the present position of the amalgamated IG BCE are taken into consideration. VDEW represents German electricity suppliers and, together with other associations like the Association of Industrial Energy and Power Economy (*Verband der industriellen Energie und Kraftwirtschaft*, VIK) and the Association of Communal Enterprises (*Verband kommunaler Unternehmen*, VKU)—can be taken as representing the energy industry in general.

The DNR (German League for Nature Conservation and Environmental Protection) is an umbrella organization representing German nature

Table 5.1. Group selection in Germany and Great Britain

	General	Issue-area specific
Germany		
Old Politics—Left	Deutscher Gewerkschaftsbund (DGB)	Industriegewerkschaft Bergbau, Chemie und Energie (IG BCE)
Old Politics—Right	Bundesverband der Deutschen Industrie (BDI)	Vereinigung Deutscher Elektrizitätswerke e.V. (VDEW)
New Politics—Emancipatory	Bündnis 90/ Die Grünen (Green Party)	Deutscher Naturschutzring (DNR)/ Forum Umwelt und Entwicklung (Forum U & E)
New Politics—Authoritarian	Die Republikaner	–
Great Britain		
Old Politics—Left	Trades Union Congress (TUC)	Amalgamated Engineering and Electrical Union (AEEU)
Old Politics—Right	Confederation of British Industry (CBI)	Electricity Association (EA)
New Politics—Emancipatory	Green Party	Friends of the Earth (FOE) UK
	Global Commons Institute (GCI)	Climate Action Network (CAN) UK
New Politics—Authoritarian		

conservation and environment NGOs. Established in 1950, DNR today counts 108 member organizations. Its position, therefore, serves as a good approximation of the views of many national environmental groups on climate change. Since December 1992, moreover, the Forum Umwelt & Entwicklung (a German NGO Forum on Environment and Development, Forum U & E) has been based at the DNR premises. This forum, bringing together a network of thirty-five associations in the field of environmental protection and development politics, was founded with the express purpose of following up the UNCED process.[28]

TUC and CBI are the largest umbrella groups covering employee and employer organizations (respectively) in Great Britain and thus represent the most general grouping of left and right in the old politics sphere. The AEEU emerged in 1992 from the merger of the Amalgamated Engineering Union (AEU), the Electrical, Electronic, Telecommunication, and Plumbing Union (EETPU), and the Electrical and Engineering Staff Association (EESA). It focuses on manufacturing, public utilities, construction, and energy supply and is, therefore, a relevant union in the energy sector. The EA is the collective voice of the major electricity companies in the UK and thus a good choice in terms of a political group representing the energy sector.

Within the British two-party system, the Green Party is not nearly as important as its counterpart in Germany (see Rootes 1995, 66–90). Although it may be seen as representing the most general grouping of new politics issues, the Green Party's resources are extremely limited. With respect to climate change, the Green Party's program is based on the work of the Global Commons Institute (GCI), a British NGO founded after the Second World Climate Conference in 1990 and dedicated to international climactic matters. For this reason, the analysis below is also based on selected materials of the GCI that were made available, for the purposes of this study, by a representative of the Green Party.

Next to the Royal Society for the Protection of Birds, and Greenpeace, Friends of the Earth UK (FOE UK) forms one of the largest and most important general environmental groups in Great Britain and claims to be the first NGO in Great Britain that took up the issue of climate change. FOE has started its own climate campaign and is a member of the Climate Action Network UK (CAN UK), to which the climate issue in part has been commissioned. CAN UK, as a regional member of the global Climate Action Network (CAN), is an association of thirteen British environmental groups focused on the subject of climate change.[29] It is the only NGO in Great Britain that has exclusively been handling the subject of climate change since 1989. British groups representing the "new politics-authoritarian" part of the spectrum could not be identified. Parties like the British National Party, the National Democrats, and the UK Independence Party do not really fall into the new politics delineation they pursue either old-fashioned fascist, ultra-libertarian, or single issue anti-European programs.[30]

A nationally organized issue-area specific group representing the authoritarian new social movements could not be identified for either Germany or Britain. There is a circle of so-called climate skeptics, but this grouping was not considered appropriate for the purposes of this study. This is for two reasons; first, although some of these climate skeptics are said to be in contact not only with the fossil fuel industry but also with right-wing groups, these connections cannot be proved except by assertions of third parties. Second, this loose transnational assembly of individuals is not an organized group and therefore does not really match our selection criteria.

Responses of Political Groups to Climate Change: Germany

As mentioned above, in December 1990, the General Assembly of the United Nations called on member countries to form national committees in order to prepare for UNCED, to be held in 1992. In Germany such a committee was established in May 1991 under the auspices of the Federal Ministry of the Environment. A total of thirty-five delegates from a variety of nongovernmental organizations, covering the fields of environment and development, scientific research, industry and workers' interest were invited to join the committee.[31] They were asked to give their opinions on the issues to be raised at the conference in order to assist the government in developing its negotiating position. It was at this point that most major German interest groups first elaborated their position on climate change in the public domain. It is interesting to note, therefore, that most groups—with the exception of the environmental NGOs—only took up the issue in reaction to this (intergovernmental initiative). Also notable is the fact that the intensity of the groups' responses differed as between the two climate change issues here under investigation. In relation to the issue of domestic carbon dioxide emission reductions, all groups, though differing among themselves in both degree of involvement and proposal content, nevertheless detailed the measures they preferred to achieve emissions reductions. In relation to the issue of international transfer mechanisms, however, even though all groups emphasized the importance of such mechanisms for effective climate protection, there were hardly any groups that actually developed a specific concept of how the transfer of resources to developing and newly industrialized countries could be put into practice.[32] Here again the environmental NGOs stand out as the exception, being more agile in their involvement in the climate concerns of developing countries.

Activity. Most organizations in Germany began their activities in relation to CO_2 emissions reductions (case 1) in the context of a series of events in the political arena: the proceedings of the two parliamentary Enquete commissions, the 1990 federal elections, which included campaigning on a CO_2/energy tax, and the run-up to UNCED in 1992. The mode of activity for most groups, therefore, was that of government inducement, i.e., in reaction to governmental initiatives. The intensity of each group's activity, however, was widely different between the groups; the following section will sketch each organization's most important activities—ranging from the most active to the least active group.

Although compared to the environmental NGOs the German umbrella organization DNR does not stand out as the forerunner of climate politics, it was one of the first to jump in on the climate issue—at the latest in 1988, in the context of the first Enquete Commission. The DNR's first activities were focused on providing information on the issue to the public, but it has also engaged in more directly political activities. In fact, at UNCED, the president of the DNR was an observing member of the German delegation. Since 1993, the DNR has hosted the "Projektstelle Umwelt & Entwicklung," a committee sponsored by BMU and BMZ and originally set up to both prepare for and evaluate the results of UNCED. Since December 1992, it coordinates and organizes the "Forum Umwelt & Entwicklung" (the German NGO Forum on Environment & Development or "Forum U & E", which has already been introduced above in section 5.1.3). The nine working groups of Forum U & E develop joint NGO position papers on various issues, one group being devoted to the issue of climate change. These position papers take on different functions depending on the issue at hand, serving the purposes of information provision, lobbying and monitoring, as the case may be. One of the tasks of the Forum, for example, is to monitor the implementation of Germany's commitments under the FCCC, and to this end, they publish an analysis of the National Reports prepared by the German government in accordance with their obligations under the convention. The Forum also holds regular informational meetings with the German FCCC negotiations delegation, through which the Forum intends to influence the positions that the government adopts in the negotiation process. A high point of DNR's activities was COP 1, in Berlin, in 1995. Together with a local member organization, the DNR hosted and sponsored Klimaforum '95, a working group in Berlin that coordinated the activities of all the environmental NGOs present at COP 1. For instance, Klimaforum '95 prepared, together with CAN, a conference entitled "Rio Is Not Enough" that took place one day before the beginning of the official negotiations. It also organized the NGO Service Centre at the official conference and participated in the production of the well-known ECO-

Newsletter. Subsequent to COP 1, in addition to being involved in later FCCC negotiations, DNR has largely focused especially on the promotion of eco-tax reform.

At the beginning of the climate change debate the Green Party was somewhat reluctant to take up the issue, with many in the party fearing that the discussion would benefit the nuclear industry who argued that CO_2-free nuclear energy could provide a solution to the problem. Ultimately, however, this concern gave way in the face of the growing seriousness of global warming. In the early years, the group focused its attention on the Enquete Commission's work and other parliamentary initiatives. In 1989, however, its Energy working group got more fully behind the issue, and in 1990 published a policy study entitled "Energiewendeszenarios" covering CO_2 mitigation strategies. The 1990 federal election was a significant milestone: in campaigning for that election, the Green Party lobbied for the introduction of an environmental tax to be placed on gasoline and fossil fuel consumption; this brought the climate issue right into the heart of mainstream politics, and was the first strong political signal of the seriousness of the issue for the Greens. It was not before 1994, however, that a climate working group was set up within the Green Party, marking the beginning of intense inner-parliamentary work by the Party on climate change. Much of that work was centred around international events, such as the annual FCCC-COPs (and especially COP 1 in Berlin in 1995) and the 1997 UN General Assembly Special Session on Sustainable Development ("Earth Summit II").[33] These parliamentary activities have, of course, also been combined with public information campaigns and press work. In 1998, the Greens again made climate change an election issue with further proposals for an environmental tax; today, climate change remains an integral part of the parties environmental and economic election program.

The umbrella organization of German industry, the BDI, first developed a position on climate change in 1989. In 1990, taking up the reports of the Enquete Commission, BDI initiated a forum with the title "*Vorsorge zum Schutz der Erdatmosphäre—Eine internationale Herausforderung*" (Preventive measures to protect the earth's atmosphere—an international challenge), where both scientific findings and political responses could be discussed. Subsequently, the BDI continued an intense information program—directed both internally at its own member industries and externally at the political sphere and public. As regards the political sphere, the BDI enjoyed good access to various government authorities, and in particular the Interministerial Working Group. One of the most important activities of the BDI was the *Initiativpapier* that the BDI drafted in cooperation with other business associations and presented to both the German government and EC-Commission in 1991. This initiative lead to the development of a voluntary agreement

(*Selbstverpflichtungserklärung*) for German industry, coming into effect in the lead up to COP 1 in Berlin in 1995.[34]

The business association of German electricity providers, *VDEW*, has been involved with the issue of climate change and CO_2 emissions since the mid-1980s. At that time, VDEW initiated an internal expert committee (*Fachgremium*) and working group with the purpose of assembling the expertise of member industries and developing a common position on the issue. The VDEW conveys somehow the impression of being a no-fuss decision-taker and has emphasized its constant willingness to constructively help the government with its special expertise. Perhaps unsurprisingly, then, the German government, interested in the CO_2 reduction potential within the electricity sector, involved VDEW very early in its own deliberations. The VDEW has also launched various public relations activities such as, for example, the so-called "Eta–Initiative" in 1990. Within that framework, the VDEW organized several information campaigns largely geared towards publicizing energy saving measures. The organization has also been actively involved in providing information on energy saving to member businesses. Of a somewhat different character, but nevertheless of importance are projects which VDEW has organized in the context of the Activities Implemented Jointly initiative.[35] It has long been the view of VDEW that involving industry in the political process is essential since in the end it is businesses that have to implement the relevant decisions. VDEW also took part in the voluntary agreement set up for German industry by the BDI in 1995.

The German trade union umbrella organization, the *DGB*, drafted its first resolution on climate change in 1990 as a direct response to a proposal of the German government and EC Commission to introduce a CO_2 tax. The DGB's standpoint on climate change in these early years was not very detailed and somewhat repetitious. Later, however, the DGB formulated a precise trade union specific position on the issue, focusing on the social and employment aspects of the problem. Like the other groups, the DGB centred its activities around prominent international events, in particular COP 1 in Berlin, where it organized an international trade union conference on the issue. One of the themes of the conference was how employees could help in implementing climate change measures. As with the industry organizations, the trade unions also argue that in the end it is their members that have to deal with the consequences of climate mitigation policies.

The energy sector union, IG CPK delivered an early and, at the time, relatively strong response, with representatives taking a role in the preparatory committees leading up to the Rio conference. By contrast, the more conservative IG BE was reluctant to get involved in the matter. After the two unions merged, there were (and still are) serious problems in formulating a common position on the issue, and as a consequence, the current approach of the IG BCE on climate change is somewhat restrained. Still in existence, however, is the Foundation *Arbeit und Umwelt* (Foundation for Employment and Environment), that had been established by the IG CPK as a forum for its environmental work.

In contrast to the other groups, the Republikaner Party did not take up the issue before being confronted with it during discussions on implementation policies in the regional parliaments where it had a presence at that time. Even then, its statements were not very substantial. The issue does not seen to be of great importance to them.

As has already been mentioned, most groups display a considerably lower intensity of activity in relation to the issue of resource transfers (case 2). Although the topic is addressed in most policy papers or press briefings, there are hardly any proposals or activities devoted specifically to the issue. This is especially true for the trade unions and business associations, as well as the authoritarian Republikaner Party. In fact, there were only a few groups that really directed themselves to the matter. The DGB addressed the subject by concentrating on education as a means of providing information on global sustainable development.[36] Similarly, the BDI also focuses on information on, and discussion of, the issue.[37] The BDI and IG BCE are both supporting partners of the *Internationales Transferzentrum für Umwelttechnik* (ITUT, Center for the International Transfer of Environmental Technology) an institute with a focus on strategies for international environmental technology transfer and management. ITUT was involved in the Activities Implemented Jointly initiative, having taken part in assessing the pilot phase of the project. VDEW is also involved in the AIJ projects, providing support for member companies taking part in the pilot phase. The Green Party has been more active in relation to the issue, indeed, the necessity for resource transfers forms part of its standard parliamentary platform. Demonstrating its concern for enviro-developmental issues, the Green Party invited representatives from green parties and NGOs from Kenya, Togo, and Senegal, as well as Russia, Poland, and the Ukraine, to visit COP 1 in Berlin 1995. Most active on the issue, however, has been the Forum U & E. The Forum's climate working group sees as one of its main tasks education of the public on the connection between the environment and development with the aim of motivating a broad section of the population to change consumption and production patterns.[38] It has accordingly published several positions papers on the issue. The Forum, in addition, has multiple contacts to organizations in developing countries and cooperates with VENRO (*Verband Entwicklungspolitik deutscher NROs*), an alliance of several German development NGOs, founded in December 1995.

Summing up, therefore, the environmental groups were the most active, followed by the industry groups and unions. As regards the latter two, it is remarkable that the general umbrella groups were politically more active than the selected issue-area-specific ones. The authoritarian organization under review was almost inactive.

In terms of political level of activity, all groups were primarily active in the national arena. However, most groups were also active at the international level. In the remainder of this part, I will give a few examples of the transnational work of the groups here investigated—starting with those most transnationally active.

At first, the DNR focused its activities on support for local initiatives such as, for example, energy saving measures within local communities. The UNCED process, however, drastically changed DNR's assessment of the relevance of international policy processes. Today, DNR is active on the national, European, and international level. The group manages the EU coordination of German NGOs in cooperation with the European Environmental Bureau (EEB)[39] and organizes the Forum U & E. The DNR is a founding member of the Climate Network Europe (CNE) which is one of the regional focal points of the global Climate Action Network (CAN). CNE was established in 1989 and was the first Climate Network organization, providing a coordinating role for its European member organizations. It supplements that coordination function by liasing with the other CAN focal points in Africa, Asia, Latin America, the United States, Canada, and Central and Eastern Europe. Since both CNE and CAN maintain contacts to the delegates of different countries in the FCCC negotiation process, the network operates as a communication point between NGOs and the international sphere—with CNE focusing on the EU. CNE liases regularly with the European UN delegates and supports the development of common NGO positions.[40]

DNR's active involvement in both CNE and CAN provides the organization with facilitated access to international level politics. Indeed, representatives of both DNR and the Climate Working Group of the Forum U & E are regularly present at international events. In relation to resource transfers (case 2), DNR's contacts to NGOs in developing countries through CAN are crucial. With the help of CAN, the views of recipient-country NGOs may be incorporated into policy proposals; representatives of these NGOs may also themselves present CAN proposals to the global public via the media. These unique networking possibilities give CAN members a major advantage at the international level.

The trade unions tend to rely on their transnational umbrella groups when it comes to international action. The DGB, for example, has cooperated with the European Trade Union Confederation (ETUC) and the International Confederation of Free Trade Unions (ICFTU) in its climate work and was also a participant in a pre-UNCED conference of trade unions in Sao Paulo. Via ICFTU, DGB and IG BCE are also taking part in the Commission on Sustainable Development (CSD), where unions hold the position of major groups as laid down in Agenda 21. In terms of resource transfers (case 2), the DGB and IG BCE are—if at all—mainly active in cooperation with ICFTU.

At the beginning of the policy process, the BDI focused mainly on the national sphere, working with, for example, the Interministerial Working Group or the national UNCED preparation committee. Since the Kyoto conference in 1997, however, BDI's European umbrella organization, the Union of Industrial and Employer's Confederations of Europe (UNICE), assumed greater importance. UNICE hosts a climate change working group, consisting of experts chosen from companies within its member federations. This working group follows the international policy process and produces consensus papers representing the European business position on relevant issues. The BDI also has direct representation in Washington, DC, through which, for example, the UNCED-PrepComs in New York were followed.[41] The activities of VDEW have also mainly been oriented at the national level. Nevertheless, it has cooperated with its European representatives EUR-ELECTRIC[42] and UNIPEDE[43] in Brussels, whose Joint Climate Change Working Group has drafted consensus papers expressing the view of European electricity industries.[44] European cooperation has, in fact, been a feature of the electricity industry since the early 1990s, during which time the liberalization of European energy markets was being discussed.

As a Federal party, the Greens were mainly active at the national level. Attempts have been made, however, to coordinate green parties across Europe and globally. At the European level, this effort is carried out by the green party attached to the European Parliament; globally, examples of coordination do exist, for example, common press statements are issued at COP meetings.[45]

Whereas IG BE was mainly active locally in German coal industrial areas, IG CPK was very active at the international level, mainly through ICFTU. Today's IG BCE, at the global level, is affiliated to ICFTU and to the International Federation of Chemical, Energy, Mine and General Workers' Unions (ICEM). Although ICFTU and ICEM are active on the issue of climate change, IG BCE has not been a strong supporter of or participant in their climate change activities.[46] As mentioned above, the Republikaner Party only took up the issue when they were confronted with it during discussions on implementation policies in regional parliaments where they were represented at the time. This mainly regional representation also explains their purely regional (and low intensity) activity with respect to the climate issue.

In sum, most internationally active were the DNR and the DGB—both organizations cooperating with their newly established or already existing transnational affiliations to involve themselves in international climate politics. The BDI and the Green party mainly concentrated their transnational efforts at the European level where they also operated through their existing European counterparts.

Spatiality. With regard to the territorial scope of regulation called for by the group, we look at whether, preferably at a time before the FCCC was signed, statements of the organization demonstrated a preference for national as against international CO_2 emissions targets and at what political level the organization thought that the relevant policies should be negotiated. For example, it is asked whether the group called for an international climate convention even before UNCED in 1992, and how the group assessed the development of internationally fixed CO_2 targets before Kyoto in 1997. In terms of the degree of denationalization of the group's proposals, their supranational versus intergovernmental nature is assessed. As to the territorial scope of the policy proposals made by the groups under review, it at first sight looks as if almost all groups unanimously opt for an international climate change mitigation strategy. With the exception of the Republikaner Party, all groups view the solution to the problem as being global in nature.[47] When one looks, however, at the degree of denationalization perceived appropriate by each group, interesting differences become apparent; it is at the level of these differences that the conflict lines of climate politics exist.

In relation to CO_2 emissions by industrialized countries (case 1), on one side of the spectrum are the green groups (the Green Party and the environmental organizations) and (although to a lesser degree) trade unions, which promote genuine international integration policies aimed at effective international regulation. The central focus of this coalition is the establishment of a binding international convention on climate change and the setting up of an international environmental regime with firm competencies. Some policy papers outline a multilevel model that incorporates action on each of the international, regional, national, and local level. Some proposals even suggest the formation of a strong supranational structure, involving the reform of the existing UN environmental institutions and the building of a new institution that has the specific mandate and the encompassing competencies to incorporate a global politics of sustainable development. This institution, it is argued, should take the form of, as per the DGB, a proportionally organized World Environmental Council (*paritätisch besetzter Weltökologierat*) or, as per the DNR, a World Council for Environment and Sustainable Development (*Rat für umweltverträgliche und nachhaltige Entwicklung*) as suggested at the UN General Assembly Special Session on Environment & Development in 1997:

> The Council should be able to decide on sanctions if international environmental law is breached.... The ruling of the

World Council for Environment and Sustainable Development
should take precedence over decisions of the World Trade
Organization (WTO).[48]

These groups moreover, rather than waiting for a multilateral response to
come about, are engaged at the national level with the goal of strategically
furthering an international regime.

DNR demands from the Federal Government of Germany to
increase the credibility of the negotiations for a greenhouse gas
reduction protocol by implementing its own CO_2 reduction objective of 25 percent until 2005.[49]

Likewise, the Green Party points out that in a globalized world economy international environmental agreements need political leadership.[50]
Thus, they specify national urgent action towards, and international middle
and long-term measures for, climate mitigation. Most unions support these
proposals, however their policy conceptualizations are less specific.

On the other side, the business associations prefer to talk in terms of
international harmonization of national climate policies. Because of international competition—BDI stresses—the German government should not act
unilaterally. Rather, international agreement is encouraged to secure the fair
sharing and utmost efficiency of CO_2 reduction measures:

Climate-Protection: as a global problem par excellence, this can
only be tackled by way of a concerted multilateral effort.... Thus it
is inappropriate to unilaterally attempt CO_2 emissions reductions,
an undertaking that despite exorbitant costs would only result in
the most limited reduction.[51]

VDEW, using the same argument strategy, also emphasizes the need for
international agreement on emissions reductions. They emphasize that even
a trans-European approach is not sufficient:

A policy limiting itself to Europe alone cannot meet the demands
of a working climate protection strategy. What is needed is a
global concept that draws together all industrialized nations, developing countries and threshold countries.... Intervention measures
have to be targeted where the means input will effect the greatest
efficiency output.[52]

For both organizations the efficiency argument is crucial. Their point is
that since further emission reductions are technically difficult to achieve and
extremely costly—a result of the fact that emission levels of facilities in
Germany are comparatively already very low—an international approach is

essential. Both industry organizations, therefore, were early supporters of an international climate convention, a convention which was clear and realistic in its terms and which provided certainty for future investment decisions. To these groups, such a convention was absolutely necessary to avoid national differences in environmental protection legislation forming a barrier to international market relations.

As already mentioned above, the Republikaner Party took up a somewhat outlying position. The Party rejects any sacrifice of national sovereignty to international organizations, and regards national measures as providing the only practical answer to the problem. The group in particular favors technological solutions that are expected to not only benefit the national economy but also provide the possibility of opening up an export market. The Republikaner Party does, however, admit that some international cooperation on particular global environmental problems is necessary.

> We, the *Republikaner*, still hold that the modern nation state, even now at the threshold of the 21st century, is the decisive subject of international relations. We therefore strongly oppose the attempt by certain German politicians to surrender the shaping of and responsibility for German politics to the supranational level, an attempt the effect of which is only to risk sacrificing our sovereignty as a nation state. At the same time, there are certain exceptional circumstances when the nation-state may seek to transfer a part of its sovereignty to certain international institutions (e.g., with respect to the ecological issues).[53]

Nevertheless, this authoritarian Party is very critical about the efficiency of international organizations.

The issue of resource transfers (case 2) elicits comparable responses. The DNR/Forum U&E, the Green Party, and the DGB[54] emphasize how important international cooperation is in solving global environmental problems, in particular in relation to the worldwide spread of sustainable technology and financial and technical support. Even before UNCED they advocated the financial support of environmental funds as well as the establishment of a specific climate fund. Following UNCED, they accordingly called for generous support of GEF and lobbied the German government to both raise bi- and multilateral overseas development aid and support the transfer to developing nations of environmentally sound technologies.

At a fundamental level, the DGB, Green Party, and DNR/Forum U & E are critical of the current global market structure. Their demands are far reaching:

> ...those elements of the global economic framework that are responsible for the environmental destruction of the Third World must be changed as soon as possible...[55]

They call on both government and international institutions, such as the IMF and World Bank to consider environmental concerns within development aid projects and debt relief policies and argue that certain minimum requirements for environmental protection and social safeguarding be introduced in the world trade regime. Sustainable development, they argue, should be the guiding principle of all international politics. In addition to calling for a reform of all major international institutions, including the WTO, the World Bank, the IMF, the UN and CSD, they also, as mentioned above, argue for the establishment of a "World Council for Environment and Sustainable Development" as the cornerstone of the global market governance structure. Membership in this Council, they argue furthermore, in contrast to the World Security Council, should be balanced between the North and the South to meet the needs of developing countries.[56]

In contrast to this strategy of strengthening international institutions, the BDI maintains that if a favorable investment climate is guaranteed, the problem will be solved by the international market. Given the appropriate conditions, it argues, industry will develop environmentally sound and efficient technologies and transfer such to the countries in need. A global scheme in which developing and threshold nations can participate is deemed necessary, but the question of whether these guarantees should be based on bilateral or multilateral development agreements is not specified by the group:

> Given a positive investment climate, German industry is willing to increase its initiative in the development and transfer of efficient and environmentally friendly technologies.... The North-South conflict, as exemplified by the current climate discussions, could be resolved to a certain extent by the willingness of German industry to cooperate and provide concrete technology based solutions.[57]

VDEW discusses the issue only in the context of joint implementation projects and in principle, welcomes bi- or multilateral cooperation. They promise to further develop their position on the issue as soon as the political process proceeds.

Again, the Republikaner Party adopts a national position. In its view, climate politics should indeed involve all countries, including developing countries, but it strongly opposes the channelling of aid through international or (transnational) nongovernmental organizations. It prefers to see projects coordinated on a bilateral footing and considers multinational cooperation advantageous only in relation to research on renewable energy technologies. It further argues that recipient countries should not be able to decide on the use of overseas development aid for environmental projects independently; rather it suggests that donor countries maintain strict control over the expenditures.[58]

Summing up on this spatiality dimension, then, in relation to CO_2 targets, the green groups display the most denationalized approach, followed by the trade unions and then the two business associations. The response of the Republikaner Party clearly situates it at the more national end of the spectrum. In relation to resource transfers, the DNR/Forum U & E, Green Party, and DGB call for strong international action to secure sustainable development in developing and threshold countries, while the BDI shows more confidence in a somewhat less denationalized combination of international harmonization and national policies that encourage private investment. Again, the Republikaner Party displays a national orientation.

Intervention. The question of intervention is investigated through two indicia. The first looks at the degree of intervention contemplated in the proposals of the group. Here of primary interest is what CO_2 emission targets or levels of resource transfers are deemed appropriate by the group. Whether the group demanded some form of redistribution, compensatory measures, or support for specific groups, for example, suggesting the exclusion of a certain circle of persons or economic sectors from CO_2 reduction or the establishment of special conditions for such groups is also considered relevant at this point. The second indicator is mode of intervention, which examines the instruments and subjects of governance favored by the group. The term "instruments of governance" refers to the type of policy instrument or instruments (regulation or market-based, hierarchical or nonhierarchical) called for by the group. For instance, a group may suggest the introduction of specific regulations covering power plants such as a Combined Heat and Power (CHP) Directive, for example, while another group may choose to rely on market mechanisms to address the problem, for example, by introducing fiscal incentives or energy taxes, or making use of JI or ET measures. The question raised by looking at the subject of governance is whether the group regards state action as most appropriate or whether it sees self-regulation as the more effective remedy.

The CO_2 reduction levels (case 1) debate is largely oriented along externally defined targets, whether they be scientifically determined, for example, by the Intergovernmental Panel on Climate Change (IPCC), or politically, for example, by the federal government or other governmental entity, such as the Alliance Of Small Island States (AOSIS). Only a few groups have developed their own ideas on targets, most groups' claims are limited, framed in terms of less or more than the publicly debated figures. Some groups do not state any precise policy on the matter, like the Republikaner Party, for example, whose comments on the matter have in fact been inconsistent, while others consider the issue as more a governmental concern rather than their own. It is along these lines that the various positions of the groups vary. The DNR, Green Party, and the DGB, in line with the national target of the federal government and in support of the global protocol proposal of AOSIS, each advocate a 25 per cent reduction target.[59] This figure, however, represents something of a compromise for some of these groups, in the past having called for even higher reductions and further measures in accordance with scientific findings of the time. In 1990, for example, the Green Party called for a 35 per cent reduction on emissions by 2005 and a 50 per cent reduction by 2010 (on the basis of 1987 levels).[60] Similarly, after UNCED, the DNR pressed for a 30 per cent reduction on European CO_2 emissions by 2005 (on the basis of 1990 CO_2 levels).[61] They later revised their policy to match the AOSIS proposal, and then, at COP 3 in Kyoto accepted the EU proposal of a 15 per cent reduction by 2010 as a minimum. Nevertheless, the German government is pressed to remain committed to its goal of a 25 per cent reduction by 2005, which it aims to achieve through reform of all energy related policy areas, such as, environmental tax reform, more energy efficient traffic and building policies, a program for renewable energy etc. The BDI supported the German government's reductions target, but also urged for the incorporation of no-regret measures, for example, measures focused on improvements of energy efficiency for its own sake and with the added benefit to reduce global warming. The VDEW declared that there was a potential to reduce CO_2 emissions within the public electricity sector, by 2015, by 25 per cent (calculated on 1987 base levels) or 12 per cent (with 1990 as the base level).

With regard to suggested levels of resource transfers (case 2), again the debate is often oriented along externally defined targets, such as the 0.7 per cent of GNP target as suggested by the UN—an aspirational target supported by DNR/Forum U & E, the DGB, and the Green Party. This proposal, and the discussion of transfer levels in general, occurs in the context of these groups' belief in the necessity for a structural reform of the world market, and more specifically, the transition from an economic model directed exclusively to economic growth to a model based on the principles of sustainable development, protection of the environment and a new global solidarity. Such reform is seen as the best way to achieve fair means and levels of resource transfers. Debt relief is also regarded as essential in this context, as is the concept, already embedded in the FCCC, of additionality of financial resources for climate mitigation, which includes funding for technology transfers or the support of the GEF.[62] The BDI, on the other hand, sees more potential in increasing energy efficiency in Eastern Europe, threshold countries and developing countries via the market. It therefore calls on the international system to create favorable conditions for private investment. Most other groups do not offer any specific proposals regarding transfer levels.

The issue of what is the appropriate mix of policy instruments for reducing CO_2 emissions (case 1) is one which is hotly debated. On the one hand, business associations are keen to see the introduction of market-based instruments as steering mechanisms, arguing that such instruments are more flexible and efficient than regulatory measures. They point to the fact of the still many uncertainties in climate science to justify this preference for a looser, more flexible approach. Moreover, in terms of the subject of governance, they regard business itself as being in the best position to determine the most effective means of achieving implementation. Thus business groups tend toward a preference for self-regulation and horizontal governance structures. Such approaches involve a sharing of responsibility, with the state taking responsibility for the overall policy framework (including CO_2 targets) and business deciding autonomously about how to implement those targets:

> The German business community requests the EC Commission and the German Federal Government to give priority to voluntary, efficient and economically sound measures in keeping with competition and free-market principles, instead of regulatory and fiscal regimentation....A free-market approach as demanded by the German business community means that government fixes realistic goals in agreement with the business community, but leaves enterprises free to decide for themselves where and by what means they want to achieve these goals.[63]

German business and industry associations thus sought the initiation of a voluntary initiative (VI) on CO_2 emission reductions. And in fact, in the run-up to COP 1 in Berlin 1995, a voluntary action agreement called the "German trade and industry declaration on precautionary climate protection measures" was negotiated between the BMWI (Federal Ministry of Economics and Technology) and the BDI in which German trade and industry organizations voluntarily declared their willingness to reduce their specific CO_2 emissions or their specific energy consumption by 20 per cent compared to 1990 levels.[64] VDEW and other sectoral business associations participated in this VI with individual emissions reduction targets for the different industrial sectors that were involved. In negotiating this agreement, the business sector hoped to prevent the introduction of energy taxes and other regulatory measures such as, for example, laws on combined heat and power. Other market instruments, such as joint implementation projects (JI) and emissions trading programs (ET), are also promoted by the two business groups. Generally speaking, taxes are rejected by these groups for the reason that they are considered inefficient as a means of regulation. The view of the BDI is somewhat different, it sees certain tax measures as preferable to other regulatory policies, but only if the tax regime remains flexible and is dominated by a steering as opposed to a revenue motive. Ultimately, however, and for a failure to meet these criteria, the BDI opposed the Eco-tax reform proposals, and called for a positive incentive regime:

German industry fears yet another wave of burdens, made up of a rather unfortunate mix of state directives expressed in detailed case by case specifications and revenue targeted taxes, and all in the disguise of "Eco taxes."...We call on the federal government, when defining and implementing its aims, to adopt market instruments such as voluntary self-commitment industrial agreements and investment incentives.[65]

This position has support from some unexpected allies. Whereas IG CPK, the former sector-specific union approved of certain fiscal measures to protect the environment, the IG BCE of today is strongly opposed to any environmental tax reform. IG BCE maintains that positive rather than negative incentives should be employed to encourage energy saving. It does not advocate leaving the market entirely to its own devices, but argues that excessive regulation would be counterproductive. Instead, in its opinion, the state should restrict itself to the provision of a transparent framework for action and support the self-regulating capabilities of the market. The Republikaner Party also takes the view that market-based instruments are more appropriate than formal regulatory measures, and rejects an environmental tax on the basis that it would place too much of a burden on German industry, trade and the citizen.

In contrast, the DGB and DNR, as well as the Green Party insist that VIs cannot replace legislation and other command and control options available to governments. According to these groups, VIs assume value only when they go beyond the legally obligatory baseline set by legislation. Consequently, these groups argue for a mix of policy instruments, including market instruments such as the Eco-Tax-Reform (*sozial-ökologische Steuerreform*)[66] and the abatement of environmentally harmful subsidies. The basic position of the DNR is that the only priority is attainment of CO_2 emissions reduction—the particular instrument used being secondary in consideration.[67] Nevertheless, the DNR refers to certain experiences with the different instruments and therefore regards the formal regulatory approaches preferable in certain contexts, one example being in the setting up of targets. The group sees ecological tax reform as a prime instrument for the reason that it is integrated into the market, such as, it steers the market in the direction of sustainable development by providing the right incentives. The group further argues that if soft instruments, like VIs, are employed, they should be designed in such a way as to ensure their effectiveness, that is, they should be legally binding, monitored along clearcut criteria, and inclusive of sanction mechanisms (for example, a statutory ordinance mandating heat efficiency standards) in the event of nonattainment of overall reduction targets. The Green Party also advocates a mix of instruments, starting with Eco-tax reform but also including positive incentives for the development and use of efficient and renewable energy technologies. The Greens criticize Germany's environmental policy making of the 1980s for its tremendous regulatory bias and simultaneous massive deficit in implementation. According to the Greens:

> The modern state, facing the huge challenge of finding new solutions within a globalized world economy, still needs to regulate economic activity, but it should not do so by imposing more bureaucracy. State activity is essential, and not only on a national level, if we want to solve our current environmental problems.[68]

The position of the trade unions is similar to that of the green groups, with perhaps more of a focus on the more classic forms of intervention. In addition, however, the trade unions also see it as their responsibility to ensure that the social dimension of environmental policy is clearly recognized and acted upon (Heins 1998). This social dimension embraces the question not only of who pays for climate protection, but who can afford to pay and what compensatory or redistributive policies and social support measures are required. This issue often arises in the context of the assumption that climate change mitigation policies could result in negative income and employment effects—an assumption which is, however, not universally held. The DGB, for example, expects that more positive than negative employment effects will result from such policies.

There is just as much disagreement amongst these two factions of groups (the business faction vs. the green faction) in relation to the question of instruments for effecting resource transfers (case 2). Particularly vexed is the issue of the use of market-based mechanisms such as JI or the CDM in this context. In general, market instruments as JI or the CDM are primarily discussed as efficient means for CO_2-reduction at home. In addition to this, the positive side-effect of clean technology transfers to developing countries is appreciated. Especially the BDI is in favor of the use of these mechanisms, as well as emissions trading and Debt-For-Nature-Swaps as possible instruments for the transfer of resources; these instruments are seen as encouraging private initiative and assuring efficiency, as already promoted in the UNCED documents. "Agenda 21 does not want state guidance, regulation of the economy, or a restriction of world-wide trade.... What is necessary is personal initiative and increasing technical efficiency."[69]

At the same time, the BDI puts some conditions on the design of these market instruments. For example, it argues that bureaucracy should stay lean but nevertheless provide an efficient project management and monitoring system and calls on the federal government to pay more attention to these matters. Ultimately, however, it regards the harmonization of public development and private investment initiatives as the central means of ensuring transfer of resources to developing countries:

...the principal task of any globally responsible policy must be to create a favorable investment climate with incentives for industry, thereby providing scope for the development of new and efficient technical processes and the transfer of know-how and efficient technologies to the developing and newly industrializing countries as well as to eastern Europe.[70]

The VDEW supports this view as well, specifically calling for financial and infrastructure support from the government for private business projects in developing and Eastern European countries. The Republikaner Party also regards market-based instruments as representing efficient means of technology transfer, approving of such instruments for the reason that they do not compromise the strength of domestic industry:

Our economy will be weakened even more by more regulations, new taxes and another increase in state levies...one has to focus on where one can gain the most sustained results with the smallest investment. This can only happen through market mechanisms, via the intelligent use of technology.[71]

On the other hand, the DNR/Forum U & E, DGB, and Green Party demand structural reforms of the world market and the general greening of development politics *(Ökologisierung der Nord-Süd-Politik)*. They regard JI and the CDM as merely possible supplements to bi- and multilateral development aid and not the primary tools of effective resource transfer. If market instruments are introduced, these groups argue, governmental organizations should ensure a strong framework for project monitoring and evaluation, including sanctions if targets are not met. DNR and Forum U & E are most critical of market instruments. While acknowledging that traditional development aid is limited,[72] they see the so-called flexibility mechanisms as opening up serious loopholes through which countries may avoid their domestic emission reduction obligations under the Convention. One example of such a loophole is the trading of hot air, for example, the trading of virtual CO_2 emissions by former Soviet bloc countries whose industry has broken down.[73] The exploitation of such loopholes is a matter of substantial concern for all environmental NGOs, who thus argue that a separate quantitative cap be placed on the use of the CDM.[74] In addition, accurate information and transparency are seen as essential for the effective operation of the CDM, including the setting up of viable verification, monitoring, auditing, and reporting processes. Provided these requirements are met and provided a sound system of governance is put in place, environmental NGOs are in favor of utilising the CDM to assist developing countries. In respect of the subject of governance all groups refer to the nation state as their preferred primary legislator. Most groups, in addition, advocate the strengthening of international organizations in the field, including not only the United Nations and its institutions, but also other international entities such as the WTO or EU. Overall, however, the groups seem to lack a certain amount of innovative imagination in considering alternative forms of governance without government.

Great Britain

Great Britain has been, to date, quite influential in global climate politics, a fact probably attributable to ambitious domestic climate change policies (Chasek 1996, 13). As mentioned in the introduction to this chapter, significant CO_2 emission reductions have already been achieved through a liberalization and restructuring of the energy sector, together with a shift away from the use of coal in favor of the more efficient, and less carbon dioxide producing, natural gas. This has, of course, shaped the approach of British lobby groups to future CO_2 reduction targets (case 1). For the British groups, the international COPs to the Climate Convention, and in particular COP 3 in Kyoto in 1997, were important catalysts for action. The problem of resource transfers (case 2), on the other hand, has not been given much serious attention, with most groups under study here taking the view that the issue is not of their concern and consequently, express no view on the subject.

Activity. Both the mode and intensity of activity differs significantly between the groups. Perhaps the only point of similarity is that all groups mainly focus on the issue of domestic CO_2 emissions reduction (case 1). If at all, the issue of resource transfers (case 2) is only mentioned in a group's policy platform as part of its more general attitude towards climate change, or more specifically, flexible mechanisms for the mitigation of climate change, for example, via measures implemented jointly (namely in this context, the CDM). In fact, until COP 3 in Kyoto, there were almost no developed concepts on how transfer policies could be put into effect. The activities outlined below, therefore, are centerd mainly on domestic emissions reductions, although, simply by nature of the problem, a concern for global development issues does figure at various points within the groups' responses.

Starting this time with the least active group, the AEEU has been entirely inactive on climate change, preferring to defer to the TUC on more general political issues. Instead, the AEEU has focused on more practical work; for instance, at the local level, AEEU organizes training seminars for its members on environmental protection within companies.[75] The Green Party has also been somewhat inactive on the issue. In fact, until 1998, climate change did not even figure as a major issue for the group. As mentioned above, because of a lack of resources, the Green Party has placed its reliance in relation to climate issues on the British Global Commons Institute (GCI), an institute founded in 1990 after the Second World Climate Conference, and highly active since then within the FCCC and IPCC processes.[76] The Green Party has, however, addressed the problem of climate change within the context of their work on other issues. For example, although the Party does not have a seat in Parliament, it has authored two Road Traffic Reduction Acts and another act on energy efficiency in local housing, and has succeeded in passing them through Parliament using Private Member's Bills.

The TUC, the CBI, and the EA have been roughly equal in terms of activity—however, there are variations between the groups in the intensity of their commitment over time. The TUC was very active at the beginning of the political debate on climate change, having started its work on the issue in 1989 with the establishment of an Environmental Action Group (EAG). This action group was highly active at the national level in the lead up to UNCED; it participated in the UNEP-UK National Committee, held meetings with Department of Environment officials on the UK contribution to the Summit, was involved in the preparation of the NGO national report on UK climate practices for UNCED and was invited to join the UK official delegation in Rio. In relation to resource transfers (case 2), TUC has involved itself in consultations with trade union centers in the developing world[77] and has engaged the EAG to investigate how the industrial world can "assist the third world to find a means of increasing living standards at the same time as protecting the stock of ecological assets."[78] After UNCED, TUC became a member of UNED-UK (United Nations Environment and Development—UK Section) and since 1995, has been a member of the UK Round Table on Sustainable Development, in a so-called "multi-stakeholder initiative." Although the TUC, after UNCED, undertook the task of maintaining its involvement in the follow-up process,[79] today TUC is not as active as it used to be. The CBI, by contrast, took up the climate issue very late in the process. The group was slightly active after UNCED, but its intense policy work did not start before the preparations for COP 3 in Kyoto began. Nevertheless, in dealing with the issue, CBI derives much of its approach from a general attitude to environmental issues that it had already developed in the mid-1980s with the slogan "Environment Means Business."[80] At that time, CBI established an Environmental Management Unit and an action plan for the 1990's was drawn up. CBI's main involvement has been in consultation processes.[81] CBI itself points out its unparalleled access to decision-makers in Whitehall, Westminster, and Brussels and the fact that it is frequently consulted informally before new proposals are published for full public debate.[82] In recent times, the CBI has become more proactive in its climate work. One such project was its support for an initiative of twenty-five British companies whereby a pilot project for domestic emissions trading was set up—this project being part of CBI's attempt to persuade the government that it should drop its plans for a carbon tax.[83] The EA started its climate related activities after the electricity industry was privatized in 1990, with the establishment of an Environmental Committee and a Working Group on environmental issues. In 1994, these two committees were integrated to form the Environmental Steering Group, within which representatives from member companies develop the EA's environmental policies. The EA was most active during 1997, the year in which both the second UN General Assembly Special Session on Sustainable Development and the third COP to the Climate Convention in Kyoto occurred. During this year, the group, according to a self-description, "lobbied extensively...to present the UK electricity industry's views and record on a range of climate change issues."[84] Most of its published materials, however, convey the impression that the EA is rather reactive to political processes at the national, European, and international level.[85] In its lobbying efforts, the EA presents itself as being very cooperative, assisting the UK government in fulfilling its obligations under the Convention.[86] This co-operative attitude is also shown in its approach to the issue of resource transfers (case 2). Projects undertaken abroad are presented as part of the industry's climate relevant activities: "[t]he industry is also investing in the modernisation of the energy industry abroad and consequently helping to lower CO_2 emissions globally."[87] The FOE and CAN UK were most active in relation to both issues. The UK branch of FOE was established in 1971 and claims to be the first NGO in Great Britain to take up the issue of climate change:

> Friends of the Earth has a long interest and involvement in climate change and related issues, campaigning on energy and transport for two decades. The organization first presented evidence on climate change to the House of Commons Environment Committee Enquiry on Air Pollution in March 1988.[88]

Since 1988, FOE has published a steady stream of reports on the issue of climate change; it has also campaigned widely on the issue, promoting sustainable energy policies.[89] Aside from lobbying and press work, FOE also supports local member groups in organizing more unconventional forms of action, such as flag protest marches, postcard campaigns exposing and embarrassing oil and car companies, and the "Global Climate Coalition."[90] It was not until December 1996, however, that the issue became top priority for FOE. FOE is also a member of CAN UK, an issue-specific network of several British environmental NGOs founded in 1989. CAN UK's main task is to facilitate coordination of member organizations' climate related work, and to this end, it coordinates regular meetings of the Greenhouse

Roundtable, a forum designed to facilitate information exchange and discuss strategy building for influencing government on important policy issues related to climate change. CAN UK also provides an information service for NGOs, the media and the public on emerging climate change policy developments as well as recent advances in climate science.

As to the political level of activity, all groups were active mostly at the national level. Nevertheless, as a result of relationships with European and international partner organizations, most of the groups are also involved at the European and international level. In the following section, a few examples for these transnational activities are given, starting with the organization least active at the international level.

The Green Party is a member of the European Federation of Green Parties, and according to the International Co-ordinator of the Party, this sphere of action is becoming more and more important.[91] So far, however, the Green Party has been active mainly at the national and even local level, where members lobby their local MPs. As for the EA, even though it has not been directly present at the international climate convention negotiations, some of its member companies have been. The lobbying activities of the EA are directed primarily at the UK government and national delegations to the climate conferences. The EA does have an office in Brussels and, like its German counterpart VDEW, EA is a member of EURELECTRIC[92] and UNIPEDE[93] whose Joint Climate Change Working Group represents the view of EU electricity industries at the European and international levels.[94] The CBI generally seeks to influence political decision making at all levels, including "[g]overnment and all those agencies, national and international, active in the field"[95] as well as "anyone who, in turn, can influence how business performs—at Westminster, in Whitehall and the UK regions, around Europe and beyond, within the trade union movement, and the general public."[96] Although through UNICE CBI has a hook in into European policy,[97] its access is best at the national level. Nevertheless, CBI has its own office in Brussels through which it involves itself in European climate politics whenever its position differs from that of UNICE. CBI is, moreover, a member of the International Chamber of Commerce (ICC), which coordinates business action at the UN and OECD level. In addition, some of CBI's member corporations (for example, BP) are themselves directly active at the international level.

Whereas CBI has become more and more active at the European level after Kyoto, the TUC was internationally most active during the preparation and followup of UNCED in 1992. The TUC coordinates political work on the European and international level with the help of the umbrella organizations ETUC and ICFTU.[98] As part of a broad range of activity in preparation for the Rio Summit, TUC contributed to the ICFTU "Report to the Summit on Environment and Development: the Trade Union Agenda" and was actively involved in the drafting of the section of the UNCED Agenda 21 entitled "Strengthening the Role of the Trades Unions." In addition, TUC's Environmental Action Group (EAG) consulted with the ICFTU and ETUC and sought to raise the issue of an international agreement on emissions targets with trade union centers in the developed and developing world.[99] The ultimate goal of this transnational coordination was to develop a "united trans-global union response to environment and development issues", as first stated in the context of the UN Economic Commission for Europe Bergen Conference in May 1990. The EAG has also participated in meetings of the UN's IPCC. Despite this early international involvement, at the moment, most of TUC's activities are focused at the national level.[100]

FOE UK has always been primarily a network of local groups, campaigning in 250 communities all over Great Britain. Hence, much activism takes place at the grassroots level, a focus which FOE emphasizes as providing a solid basis for effective national and international campaigning. The strategy of FOE has been, however, primarily to attempt to influence international level politics through the British government and so the group evidences a strong national focus in its activities.[101] At the same time, FOE has connections to Friends of the Earth International (FOEI)[102]—the largest international network of environmental groups in the world, represented in fifty-two countries—and is further affiliated internationally through the global CAN. As mentioned above, CAN UK's work is also mainly directed at climate change mitigation opportunities in the UK, but a significant part of its work is also on the international level. Thus it cooperates closely with the Climate Network Europe (CNE) in Brussels and other CAN focal points worldwide, and is involved in the Climate Action Watch Process, a regional monitoring process with reports prepared by member organizations of CAN within each country and published together by the global CAN.[103] CAN UK also plays a critical role for the global network as a whole by obtaining funding for the well-known ECO Climate Change Newsletter which is disseminated by the group to government, experts and the UK media.[104] Both FOE and CAN, moreover, have been continuing participants in the FCCC negotiations and have as a goal further activity on the international level.[105] With respect to the issue of resource transfers (case 2), both NGOs emphasize how important their transnational contacts with environmental NGOs in developing countries are. This coordination, they argue, lends credibility to their own positions on development issues.

Overall, with the assistance of their transnational networks the environmental NGOs are by far the most internationally active amongst the groups studied. TUC, in addition, was able to coordinate many activities through the ICFTU. The CBI, EA, and the Green Party have also cooperated, albeit to a lesser extent than the other groups and mainly at the European level, with their respective transnational umbrella organizations.

Spatiality. Despite the fact that all groups emphasize the need for international cooperation and harmonization in the setting up of measures targeting CO_2-emissions (case 1), the degree of denationalization supported by the British groups—compared to those in Germany—is at a somewhat lower level. The following discussion begins with the groups that have adopted the most denationalized approach.

FOE and CAN UK both support the introduction of firm international climate change mitigation legislation, to be implemented at the national level without delay. Even before UNCED, they pushed the British government to support the INC in its attempt to draft an international "climate convention with teeth"[106] and, after Rio, to ratify the FCCC as soon as possible.[107] Both environmental NGOs were explicit in calling for an international protocol attached to the existing convention with binding targets for reductions in emissions:

> The Government should recognize its international responsibility and work to encourage global adoption of these policies.[108]
> We have ... been calling for a protocol with the following key elements: be legally binding with an effective compliance and review mechanism; commitments to introduce policies and measures which require international coordination.[109]

In Kyoto, both NGOs confirmed their stance on strengthening the Framework Convention, and were highly critical of the agreement for falling short of the targets necessary for adequate protection of the environment.[110] Both NGOs called for "government action at an international and national level to build on the Kyoto deal and stop dangerous climate change."[111] The groups in addition addressed themselves to the domestic reductions policy agenda.[112] Generally, FOE and CAN UK are in favor of additional unilateral, self-binding actions to strategically advance an effective international regime. As a complement to this strategy, they support a coordinated European approach to accelerate international progress:

> We welcome the recent unilateral commitments made by Denmark, the Federal Republic of Germany, and the Netherlands, to cut their own carbon dioxide emissions, even before a treaty is finalised. ... If the Member States of the European Community adopt a common position which leads to reductions in carbon dioxide emissions, it will send a positive signal to the rest of the world.[113]

The environmental NGOs aim to incorporate all international institutions in mitigating climate change. CAN UK emphasizes that the WTO in particular should be involved in climate politics in order to deal with the problem of competitiveness and bring environmental concerns into economic decision making.[114]

The Green Party occupies a rather outlying position that is hard to evaluate in terms of spatiality. Somewhat contrary to the mainstream approach, their aim is, according to the title of their 1999 European election campaign, to "Protect the Local, Globally." Building on a massive critique of globalization, the Party argues against adjusting to the logic of denationalized problems with global policies,[115] suggesting rather internationally coordinated relocalization programs:

> What Does A "Protect the Local, Globally" Policy Entail?...Its essence is to allow nations and communities to retake control over their local economies and to make them as diverse as possible. It uses policies which ensure that...whatever goods and services can be provided locally are done so.... [It should] begin for example in Europe, it would be replicated in all regions of the world and allow for similar policies to be introduced globally.[116]

The Green Party maintains that this policy strategy is internationalist in scope, however it is difficult to escape from the fact that its focus is on the relocalization of economies and the attempt to stop and reverse the processes of globalization; it is aimed at strengthening local economies in order to reduce the amount of energy "wasted in transporting goods around the world."[117] The Green Party is also a supporter of the contraction and convergence concept developed by the British Global Commons Institute (GCI), a model based on regulating CO_2 emissions via internationally negotiated targets calculated on a per-capita basis:

> First, countries would set an internationally agreed global ceiling on CO_2 concentrations in the atmosphere for the next century. ...Second, countries would agree a global "carbon emissions budget" for each year of the next century in order progressively to reduce CO_2 concentrations to within the agreed ceiling.... Third, countries would agree to share out the annual CO_2 budget among each other on a per capita basis and with a view to per capita emissions converging by an agreed date.[118]

This rather demanding concept would require continuous international negotiation processes. The TUC, on the other hand, is more critical of the usefulness of unilateral action, preferring to adopt a multilateral approach:

> The Group [viz. TUC's EAG] accept that preventative action must be taken to combat the perceived risk of global warming. However, the Group also recognize that unilateral action would

achieve little. As such the Group calls for a multilateral response, with Western governments taking the lead.[119]

The business associations also call for multilateral coordination and international harmonisation of climate change policies. Thus, the CBI, for example, states:

> Business is ready to act now in partnership with government and others based on the following principles:...
>   • Greater co-operation between governments, supported by effective agreement, monitoring and enforcement...;
>   • Legally binding targets need powerful international institutions to administer and enforce agreements which do not exist at present;
>   • Securing worldwide agreement to policies and measures...[120]

Likewise, the EA "would certainly favor international programs" and "global agreements."[121] In contrast to the environmental NGOs, however, business associations are critical of the inflexibility of supranational structures and are wary of giving up too much policy control to international bureaucracies, in particular within the European Union. That is even true for voluntary initiatives:

> European Agreements would bypass national governments and their environmental programs and would not necessarily lead to effective or equitable solutions. We urge UK Government to oppose this approach. On the other hand national agreements, which could be developed within an EU framework but concluded at national level, could be a useful additional tool for implementing environmental policies, provided that the framework does not become bureaucratic or over-prescriptive.[122]

On the other hand, both CBI and EA strongly reject a purely national response, arguing that unilateral action would be damaging for the international competitiveness of British business as well as run the risk of driving business out of the country. These organizations are particularly opposed to the introduction of a unilateral carbon or energy tax:

> There are concerns that such a tax would result in increased import penetration and a loss of market share in non-taxed countries. Energy intensive users might also relocate their production facilities to avoid the tax, so continuing to emit as before.[123]

CBI and EA therefore demand that all climate change policies take into account UK business competitiveness as well as EU obligations.

With regard to the issue of resource transfers (case 2), the environmental NGOs (FOE, CAN UK and the GCI), the Green Party, and TUC are consistent in their general aim of strengthening and greening bi- and multilateral aid programs in order to enable developing countries take more control of their CO_2 emissions: "International action is thus essential, especially by the major industrial powers..., transfer of resources to the developing world is a prerequisite to any international agreement."[124]

The CBI also points to the necessity of worldwide agreement on international technological transfers, insisting moreover, on the participation of developing countries in the process—without which "there is little possibility of reducing global greenhouse gas concentrations to the extent that may be required."[125] As a peak business body, however, CBI is mostly interested in the ways that such technology transfer can benefit British business opportunities (the same could be said for EA). Until Kyoto in 1997, both CBI and EA had not really developed any specific concepts on how technology transfer could occur, although they did indicate that any governmental support for private initiative would be a step in the right direction:

> The transfer of clean technology to developing countries must form a key part of successful climate change policy...supporting international aid and sponsorship/partnering help for environment industries in overseas markets.[126]

Summing up, therefore, while the environmental groups push for strong governmental action at all political levels and promote supranational structures, and while TUC calls for multilateral over unilateral measures, the business groups argue in favor of international harmonization but warn against too much bureaucracy at the international level. As far as resource transfers are concerned, the environmental NGOs and TUC support a multilateral approach (combined with strong domestic commitments) with the aim of achieving sustainable development in developing countries. CBI, on the other hand, although not against the multilateral approach, seems to prefer bilateral projects for the reason that they minimise unnecessary bureaucracy.

Intervention. As in Germany, the CO_2 targets debate (case 1) in the UK has also been largely oriented along externally set lines. Also notable is that, like their counterparts in Germany, and perhaps even more so, the British groups have been somewhat inconsistent in their formulation of clear reductions targets policies. The following section discusses group responses in order of level of intervention proposed, starting with the high-degree of intervention end of the spectrum. Even before UNCED, FOE and CAN UK supported rigid national and international targets, with a focus on the necessity for a common European approach. In 1991, thus, they called for substantial early cuts in fossil fuel related carbon emissions by industrialized countries in the order of at least 25–50 per cent on 1990 levels by 2005 as well as cuts in global carbon dioxide emissions for the same period of around 20–35 per cent on 1990 base levels and 45–55 per cent (on 1990 levels) by 2050. These, they argued, represented appropriate emissions targets for the next few decades. In addition, they saw cuts in carbon dioxide emissions of 80–100 per cent after 2050 as essential in order to prevent climate destabilization beyond the end of the twenty-first century.[127] By the time of COP 3 in 1995, however, the groups came to accept, as a minimum, the 20 per cent reduction target as proposed at the Toronto Conference and subsequently by AOSIS; even though they still maintained the view that stricter cuts were necessary:

> Several OECD countries...already have national-level targets similar to the Toronto target, which makes incorporation into the Climate Convention a realistic way of implementing the convention obligation that industrialized countries should take the lead in combating climate change. CAN UK strongly encourages the UK Government to review its position and take the opportunity offered by the AOSIS proposal.[128]

The strategic importance of a common European approach and unilateral obligations is underlined. Thus, for example, in the context of a draft proposal by the Italian Presidency for a stabilization in CO_2 emissions at 1990 levels by the year 2000, CAN UK stated:

> We urge you to at least support this position, instead of sticking out the UK's current target proposal for a stabilization by 2005, in order that the European Community can adopt a common position. Though the environmental groups signing this letter believe that significant cuts in CO_2 emissions by the year 2000 are necessary to avert serious global warming, we also believe that an initial position of stabilization by the Community would have key political importance.[129]

The targets ultimately agreed on at Kyoto were the subject of much criticism by these groups; describing the 5.2 per cent reduction target in the Kyoto protocol as pitifully low. FOE, for example, went on to point out that such a target is "totally inadequate if one considers the 60 percent reduction needed by the middle of the next century to stabilize atmospheric concentrations at a level which would avoid dangerous climate change."[130] Aside from their activity in relation to targets, FOE and CAN UK were also highly involved in other aspects of the Kyoto process, including the finer points of its administrative aspects.[131] In addition, at the national level, they developed a series of comprehensive policy concepts, called the Fossil Free Energy Scenarios, which promote a combination of efficiency improvements, renewable energy technologies, and fuel switching to achieve long-term reductions in CO_2 emissions.[132]

The Green Party is also generally in support of the AOSIS' 20 per cent reduction target as a minimum. As mentioned above, however, the true thrust of the Green Party's approach is the suggestion that CO_2 emissions be regulated on a per capita basis, with global targets set according to pollution quotas which decrease over time in order to achieve converging emission levels:

> The most obvious equitable principle for allocating quotas is that each person in the world should be entitled to emit the same amount of carbon dioxide into the atmosphere which we must all share.... This would translate into an 80 or 90 percent cut in emissions.[133]

For industrialized countries, this system implies a fundamental change in both economic structures and lifestyle and thus represents an extremely high degree of intervention. Commenting on the issue of targets in 1990, the TUC was critical of the Thatcher Government's modest aim of stabilizing CO_2 emissions at 1990 levels by 2005, and argued instead for the more demanding target of the stabilization of 1990 carbon dioxide emissions by the year 2000.[134] Since that time, however, TUC has not been vocal on specific targets. The group instead cautions against blind activism and panic solutions, arguing rather for a "balanced integrated approach"[135] with cautious no regret measures such as, for example, improved energy conservation, an expanded program of afforestation, and the promotion of renewable energy resources.

The business associations were most outspoken on the issue of targets in the run up to, and aftermath of Kyoto in 1997. In the context of the negotiations of this period, the view of CBI was that a 10 per cent European reduction goal was a realistic and challenging objective, and it criticized as unreasonable the domestic target of a 20 per cent reduction in CO_2 emissions by 2010.[136] At COP 1, in Berlin, the EA supported the target of a 5–10 per cent reduction in CO_2 levels by 2010, and it maintained this view in the run-up to Kyoto, emphasising the need for realistic targets and timetables.[137] According to EA, the targets achieved at Kyoto were reasonably realistic, but a national reduction of 20 per cent by 2010 is seen as challenging, if not unrealistic—not only for the electricity sector but for Great Britain as a whole. On the national level, EA points to the fact that by investing in new gas-fired power stations, nuclear plants, and modifications to existing coal-fired plants, the electricity industry has already done much to reduce greenhouse gas emissions.[138] It therefore calls on other sectors to pull their weight in meeting reductions targets:

In the UK, the electricity industry is single-handedly delivering the national savings to meet the Government's commitment of returning CO_2 emissions in 2000 to 1990 levels.... This needs to be recognized in discussions on a possible protocol and any measures agreed should be aimed at those sectors which have yet to reduce emissions.[139]

As to the issue of resource transfers to developing countries (case 2), most groups are silent on the question of the exact magnitude of appropriate financial and technological support. Again, externally defined targets are a common point of reference. FOE and CAN, for example, support the UN-backed target of aid amounting to 0.7 per cent of GNP, in addition to calling for general debt relief for developing countries.[140] On a fundamental level, the equitable sharing of resources between North and South is suggested by these groups as a guiding principle for international cooperation in development and sustainability.[141] Even these NGOs, however, do not have a specific position on how large the UK's financial contribution to the GEF, for example, should be; their comments on the matter are limited to more general statements, such as that funds for sustainable development should be made available. The Green Party's position on how resource transfers to developing counties may be achieved is based on the contraction and convergence model. According to this model allocations of emissions entitlements to developing countries can be traded with industrialized countries, thus opening up revenue streams that developing countries could use to fund clean energy strategies. One result of this system is that developed countries in effect pay for the right to pollute, at a rate proportional to their over-consumption.[142] Referring to the UN target, TUC's EAG calls for an increase in environmental bilateral aid cooperation and technology transfer to the developing world:

> An international approach must be underpinned by a net transfer of resources from the industrialized world to the developing world as well as to areas of severe environmental degradation—notably Eastern Europe.... Official UK aid to developing countries remains at just over half the UN recommended minimum of 0.7 per cent of GNP.[143]

CBI and EA focus more on the need for domestic measures to encourage and support initiative in the private sector, such that technology transfer is voluntarily undertaken in the name of good business. CBI goes on to cite the following as key issues "the removal of trade barriers e.g., profit repatriation limits, limited intellectual property rights, export restrictions, foreign exchange restrictions and price fixing, which have discouraged private sector investment in developing countries."[144]

The question of which policy instruments are most appropriate is one that, as in Germany, has been much debated in Britain. Indeed, for the business associations, this issue is one of the most important concerns of the entire debate. In order to achieve the satisfaction of CO_2 reductions targets (case 1), CBI advocates the implementation of a policy mix that relies mainly on market instruments, these measures, it is argued, being superior in terms of cost effectiveness.[145]

> The CBI's aim is to assist the Government in achieving its commitment to international targets agreed at Kyoto in the most cost effective way.... Economic instruments, particularly the development of internationally-tradable permits, have an important role to play in climate change policy.... Other tools should include voluntary initiatives, sensible regulation and greater public awareness.[146]

Similarly, EA criticizes prescriptive regulation in principle[147] pointing out that the market itself is the most efficient regulator of industry. It supports, therefore, the liberalization of the gas and electricity markets as the most effective means of achieving CO_2 emissions reductions:

> Liberalization of energy markets... encourages improved efficiency and the wider use of cleaner electricity Generation technologies... we believe that an economic approach incorporating liberalization offers worthwhile and significant benefits in reducing carbon dioxide emissions globally.[148]

On the question of taxes, both organizations concede that green taxes may work in an advantageous manner for business in so far as they reward innovation and efficiency in individual companies. They caution, however, that such taxes have to be implemented in a reasoned and consistent manner, taking full account of the pressures of international competition.[149] Indeed, it is because of its effect on international competition that EA opposes a European or national energy tax:

> If the EU were to introduce new energy taxation without similar measures being implemented in other OECD countries, EU energy prices would be increased relative to those of other major trading blocks, product costs would be increased across the EU and the international competitiveness of EU industry would be damaged. This would encourage industry to relocate to countries outside the EU... which would simply shift CO_2 emissions away from the EU to other parts of the world. Furthermore, goods produced in countries not exposed to energy taxes or rigorous environmental controls would then enter European markets as cheap imports.[150]

Similarly, CBI calls on the British government to identify and remove those tax distortions which work against the broader objectives of reducing greenhouse gas emissions.[151] Both CBI and EA regard voluntary environmental agreements (VAs or EAs) as the most efficient means of regulation, for the reason that they allow business to minimise implementation costs. "Voluntary agreements (VAs) are a cost-effective, flexible tool to achieve specific goals such as energy efficiency targets and reductions in greenhouse gas emissions."[152]

These agreements, they argue however, should not be negotiated at the European level, but instead at the national, sectoral, or corporate level. One such voluntary measure, in the form of a public-private partnership, was the Energy Saving Trust which was established in 1992 by electricity and gas companies in cooperation with the government. The goal of the Trust is the efficient use of all forms of energy in the UK, with the ultimate aim of reducing total energy consumption and its attendant environmental impact.[153] To that end, the Trust has set up Local Energy Advice Centers which dispense all manner of energy efficiency advice.

Emissions trading is another least-cost instrument which both CBI and EA have indicated a strong interest in. Thus, CBI supported British business leaders in presenting a proposal for an emissions trading scheme to government ministers in October 1999.[154] In relation to all suggested market instruments, CBI and EA urge the government to "address the potential problems of compliance monitoring to avoid introducing unnecessary bureaucracy, which would counteract the aim of efficient market-based solutions."[155]

Discussing the advantages and disadvantages of different steering mechanisms, the TUC comes to the conclusion that a balanced policy mix is essential. In contrast to the business associations TUC stands firmly behind state intervention, arguing that the free market offers no solution to environmental problems, nor do low growth or no growth options:

> A completely laissez faire solution to the environment simply does not exist. Historically, it has been public intervention—whether to protect the health of the people from unsafe water, adulterated products, or unsafe housing—which has been found essential, even by governments whose ideological predisposition made that course unpalatable. The answer is more Government action not less.[156]

Nevertheless, the group comments that if market instruments are introduced, their adverse social effects must be countered with the help of redistributive measures:

> An unqualified "market forces" solution is unworkable. The income distributional and inflationary effects of over emphasis on market mechanisms is of particular concern. A mix of policy

instruments to meet targets is required with compensatory measures to counter adverse sectoral impact and social effects.[157]

The TUC also makes the point that enabling people to live more energy efficient lifestyles requires "structural-architectural change,"[158] for example, increasing investment in public transport to reduce vehicle emissions.[159] As mentioned above, the group is somewhat skeptical about the benefits of a carbon tax on the use of fossil fuels:

> Regulation is not always effective. . . . Taxes may not work at all if polluters can pass the tax on to the consumer in higher prices, as there is then no incentive to cut back on pollution.[160]

TUC further argues that such a tax introduced by Britain alone would threaten industrial competitiveness and damage energy producing industries.[161]

The environmental NGOs also advocate the importance of a policy-mix, arguing that a "combination of structural, regulatory and fiscal changes in the energy market, including the introduction of a small carbon tax [will] deliver substantial and cost-effective cuts in carbon dioxide emissions in the UK."[162] They are critical, however, of the government's current National CO_2 Program citing the reason that it lacks coherence both in its regulatory and financial aspects. FOE and CAN UK are not convinced of the effectiveness of voluntary agreements, insisting that such agreements do not work in the absence of a regulatory framework to provide incentives and establish sanctions:

> While Friends of the Earth welcomes, and indeed promotes, cost-effective voluntary action by individuals, local authorities, business and commerce to reduce emissions of CO_2, such actions have limited effect in the absence of "hands-on" support from Government creating an appropriate information, fiscal and regulatory framework. The adoption of the "voluntary approach" denies the failed history of industry self-regulation and individual action in the UK in relation to the vast majority of environmental objectives and is blind to the success of regulation in many other countries.[163]

They thus see the need for the more conventional approach of command and control regulation. At the same time, however, they do not regard this form of regulation as excluding the use of market instruments:

> As outlined in Jackson's[164] work for Friends of the Earth, the choice between regulation and economic instruments need not be seen as mutually exclusive . . . it becomes clear that both market-based policy mechanisms and regulatory instruments have vital roles to play in overcoming the full range of obstacles to the efficient operation of the markets in energy services and transportation.[165]

Therefore, they see domestic market instruments as supplementing regulatory measures. The use of market instruments at the international level, on the other hand, namely, joint implementation, emissions trading, borrowing or banking emissions, is criticised for the reason that they "cannot guarantee real reductions in greenhouse gas emissions...they distract from the real measures that could help to protect the climate."[166]

From the very beginning, the environmental NGOs supported the concept of an Eco-tax as one of a number of mechanisms to encourage the switch to less polluting energy supplies and greater efficiency in energy use.[167] Such a measure adheres to the polluter pays principle, which the environmental NGOs offer as the guiding principle of regulation. FOE and CAN UK further urge the government to review all existing regulation for its climate impact, and remove distortions in tax policy.

Most interventionist in terms of the measures considered necessary to stop global warming is the Green Party. In addition to arguing in favor of both regulation and taxes[168] they also call for an alternate political and economic system that controls globalization and places "limits on transnationals."[169]

> This Green Party...[proposes] to deal with globalization and climate change, by using policies to strengthen local economies, reduce the power of transnational corporations, encourage the use of renewable energy sources and phase out fossil fuel use.... Green MPs would introduce a policy of "site here to sell here" which would bring transnational corporations back under the control of governments.... We would introduce a carbon tax and we would also support the development of renewable energy sources.[170]

In relation to policy instruments for resource transfers to developing countries (case 2), the Green Party views official development aid as the main means of support. While initially opposing all forms of market instruments in the context of resource transfers, such as emissions trading (a position curiously at odds with GCI's contraction and convergence model, which as indicated above, includes such a concept),[171] at COP 4 it came to accept the idea of global emissions trading, provided that certain limitations (a legally binding global cap on total emissions) were built into the system. This cautious approach is shared by the TUC, FOE and CAN UK. Generally speaking, these groups argue that financial and technological transfers should not be left to the market alone. While emissions trading or the CDM are seen as possible means of ensuring "North to South transfers,"[172] the groups fear that by allowing countries to offset their targets by buying unlimited emissions rights the possibility is created of industrialized countries avoiding their emissions reductions commitments at home. They argue, therefore, that emissions trading or crediting through the CDM should be capped to ensure industrialized countries cannot avoid having to take substantive measures at the national level. Moreover, they insist that various control systems be incorporated into the scheme, such as a formal review process providing for accountability, equity, monitoring, and verification.

CBI and EA, on the other hand, call for state support in encouraging private sector investment in developing countries. This includes the examination and development of market instruments such as joint implementation or the CDM and tradable permits. Government should, CBI argues:

> ...promote the potential market opportunities in developing countries; fully analyse the potential for market instruments such as JI to encourage technical transfer internationally. The Government should: develop a framework giving UK business an incentive to engage in JI projects and explore the links for JI and trading in GHG emission permits.[173]

The EA is also critical of the fact that government does not support industry enough in making use of JI or the CDM and argues that this creates a comparative disadvantage for British industry:

> Because the UK is likely to meet its own emissions targets, there is less reason for the UK government to provide incentives to companies to carry out mitigating projects in other countries. By contrast, those countries which are not likely to meet their targets domestically will offer incentives to their business community to instigate such projects abroad, disadvantaging the potential UK competitors. Government should ensure that the competitiveness of UK industry is maintained.[174]

Although CBI and EA recognize the need for some kind of legal framework for these market based systems to operate, including compliance systems, supervisory and regulatory bodies and monitoring mechanisms, they warn that too much bureaucracy will hinder their functioning and discourage business from taking part.

Summing up, therefore, on the one side of the scale are the business organizations, who generally argue that mitigation of climate change will be most effectively achieved through the use of market-based mechanisms—that is, all market-based mechanisms that aim to bring about business-led voluntary action (for example, environmental agreements, emissions trading, and JI strategies). They argue that penalizing energy use with the help of negative incentives such as a carbon tax—although this also is supposed to be a market-oriented incentive—will not be as effective. On the other side of the scale are the environmental NGOs, the Green Party, and the TUC, who argue rather in favor of a policy mix that highlights firm governmental regulation as a framework for action. Although all groups view the national arena as the most important level of activity, they also see a multilevel system of governance as essential for the implementation of the relevant policies. In accordance with their preference for voluntary action and self-regulation, business associations could be assessed as being most in favor of nonhierarchical forms of governance.

Results and Response Patterns

The following section presents a summary of the results along each of the response dimensions, namely (1) activity, (2) spatiality and (3) intervention. These features are then analysed to determine generalized (4) response patterns according to which the groups can be characterized.

Activity. Most groups acted only in response to the policy process after it was already underway—driven by external agenda-setting through epistemic communities.[175] Indeed, the relatively low level of most organization's internal incentive or initiative to take up the problem of climate change is striking. The majority of organizations were, moreover, and in particular during the agenda-setting phase of the international policy process, somewhat lacking in innovative, or even specific, solutions to the issues raised. For example, if the old politics interest groups took up the issue at all, most did not even specify whether their preference was for a stabilization of, limited growth in, or certain percentage of reduction of CO_2 emissions. Rather, with the notable exception of the environmental NGOs, groups acted only in response to national initiatives; it was only after the government presented targets and timetables that groups actually commented on the issue, and even then did so without going beyond those particular subjects that were of special interest to them. The prevalence of this initially reactive and narrow-minded response is somewhat disappointing if one considers how intensely groups were invited to participate in the debate before UNCED in 1992 and how vigorously they vie for participation today.

Moreover, even though all organizations frame the problem as a global one, most of the organizations tend to limit their activity to the national arena; they hardly ever involve themselves in the political processes at the international level. Most groups, however, delegate the international aspects of climate politics to their existing European bureaus (e.g., UNICE or ETUC) or international umbrella organizations (e.g., ICFTU). The problem here is that the work of these transnational umbrella organizations does not necessarily feed back into national level politics, and thus genuine interest representation is often lost at some point. Most transnational cooperation is rather ad hoc, such as, on an occasional single-project basis. Only recently have there been attempts towards organizing international cooperative efforts which are more coherent and continual. The environmental NGOs—such as, the issue-specific new politics/emancipatory groups—are an exception in this respect. Aside from transnational association through international umbrella groups (e.g., FOE International or the European Environmental Bureau) they have managed to set up an issue-specific network, namely, the Climate Action Network (CAN). This network not only provides a means of access to the international policy process, but also enables member groups to include an international perspective in their national level work.

Spatiality. All organizations under review—even the German Republikaner Party which is generally opposed to any form of international integration—consider an international approach essential for the effective governance of the issue of global climate change. Beyond this general understanding, however, there are considerable differences in the design and content of the specific policies advanced as solutions to the problem. Business associations, for example, point out that unilateral policies may disadvantage the national economy by stifling competition. Thus, in their Declaration, first presented at COP 1 in Berlin in 1995, the German business community stated that measures taken to protect the climate must not distort international competition nor jeopardise Germany's position as an industrial location.[176] In accordance with this approach, business associations call for the international harmonization of policies while at the same time oppose, for efficiency reasons, the setting up of bulky supranational bureaucracies. In contrast, other groups do not accept that climate change policies represent a threat to competitiveness and the well-being of the national economy. Thus environmental NGOs and trade union umbrella organizations[177] argue that certain national measures—in particular policies aimed at improving energy efficiency—function rather as incentives for the modernization of the domestic economy and may even create new jobs. Therefore, and with the intent to strategically further a global climate protection regime, they encourage their national governments to stay in the vanguard of the struggle to protect the climate. Moreover these groups welcome giving firm competencies to supranational bodies to administer climate politics and policies.

Intervention. The question of how to go about solving the problem of climate change, in the sense of which policy approach would be most effective, is an important issue for most groups. Although the conventional and hierarchical form of regulatory control (i.e., legislation) is regarded by most groups as insufficient as a means of regulation, there is disagreement about the emphasis that a policy-mix approach could take. Trade unions and environmental NGOs view the emphasis as lying firmly on the side of tax incentives combined with state set regulation which lays down a strong framework for the further influence of market-based instruments. The British environmental groups in fact fairly intent on compensating for the lack of regulation[178] created as a result of the dominance of deregulation policy in the neo-liberal Thatcher-era, a policy that environmental groups see as having sent the wrong signals to the energy market.[179] On the other hand, taking up the efficiency argument again, business groups place the policy emphasis on voluntary agreements and the use of flexible market instruments such as joint implementation or emissions trading programs. Thus the business community in both Germany and the UK have been quite vocal in lobbying for priority to be given to private sector initiatives over regulatory and fiscal regimentation. At the same time, these groups call for government to bear the costs of administration and monitoring[180] of these flexible mechanisms—and keep bureaucracy at a minimum.

With the above in mind, one could say that all organizations still tend to adhere to the nation-state as the primary subject of governance. Nevertheless, different organizations call on government to do different things. Unions and environmental organizations appeal to the state to guarantee the protection of the environment by whatever means are necessary. To this end, they press for solid state control over the economy, affirming the authority and capacity of government to rule the market where it is not achieving sustainability. They argue that voluntary initiatives be permitted only in the shadow of state regulation. For these groups the precautionary principle, which states that preventative action be taken even in the absence of a final proof of the harmful effects of a particular environmentally suspicious cause, defines the appropriate degree of state intervention; even if there is uncertainty about the future impacts of climate change, all risk should be avoided.

Business associations, on the other hand, assign to the state the function of a moderator who provides a reliable framework for action, and both supports and monitors otherwise independently acting entrepreneurs, the role of whom being to negotiate with the state appropriate targets or transfers, but then decide independently on how to execute and implement such goals. The uncertainty of future climate change is used as an argument in favor of this flexible approach. Both sides of the debate present their approach as the only viable no-regret option. This conflict is almost inseparable from the issue of what is required in terms of target percentages, transfer support and the like, in other words, the degree of intervention. Here the range varies from high-level interventionism, including the appeal for a fundamental change in both lifestyle and basic economic structures, to low-level no-regret policies such as, for example, Eco-efficiency measures.[181]

Response Patterns. By drawing these results together, three response patterns emerge:

- The environmental NGOs (DNR, FUE, CAN UK, FOE UK) are clearly the most active and innovative organizations in the political debate surrounding global warming. They developed, very early on in the debate, substantial and relatively precise positions on climate policies at both the global and national level. Their goal is to influence government to effectively protect the environment—and in their view this requires a wide policy mix supported by a firm governmental framework.

- From the very beginning of the international policy process, these NGOs were active at all levels of climate politics. They formed dense transnational networks for information exchange and coordination of their international lobbying. This response pattern—in which high levels of spatiality and intervention are combined with a very high level of activity—could be characterized as the promotion of "global governance based on sustainable development." The peak trade union organizations (DGB, TUC) also support a multilateral and supranational approach. Although their focus is more on activity at the national level, their international umbrella organizations (ETUC, ICFTU) are quite active in the field of international climate politics. There are, however, differences between the approach of the trade unions and that of the environmental NGOs. First of all, since climate change is not their central concern, the policy work of the unions is of a more general nature, with a focus on social and employment issues. In this respect their task is made harder by the fact that they have the responsibility of representing the quite diverse interests of unions from a wide range of industries. Second, the unions are stricter than the environmental NGOs in their emphasis on classical hierarchical regulation. The response of the unions, therefore, could be regarded as a sub-type of the first response pattern, a response which places a somewhat stronger emphasis on state intervention within a supranational setting and with a focus on the social aspects of the issue. This approach could be described as global regulation for social and environmental sustainability. Both responses share the common objective of effective international re-regulation to regain political control over the problem of climate change.

- The approach of the business associations (BDI, VDEW, CBI, EA) may be characterized as that of intergovernmental harmonization as a framework for market-based public-private partnerships. Opposed to unilateral action on the national level as well as the conventional model of state dominated regulation, these groups call for international harmonization and the establishment of an intergovernmental framework with a low level of bureaucracy that supports voluntary action. The lobbying activities of these groups focus on the economic disadvantages of Eco-taxes at both the national and European level. In that context, business groups see targets and transfers being achieved best through the use of market-oriented instruments which provide positive incentives for voluntary action and ensure flexibility. This response pattern is thus characterized by a low level of intervention, a relatively high level of activity and an emphasis on an internationally coordinated framework.

- Two groups, but for very different reasons, show another type of approach, one which could be termed the re-nationalization or even re-localization approach. Both the Republikaner Party in Germany and the Green Party in the UK are critical of the processes of globalization and aim to restrengthen national competencies with the introduction of strict command-and-control type regulation. Beyond this similarity, these two groups differ very much indeed in both idea and intention. Nevertheless, their responses and preferred policy options show a common support for a national intervention state.

EXPLAINING POLITICAL GROUP'S RESPONSES TO CLIMATE CHANGE—SOME HYPOTHESES

The following section provides an attempt to explain these central features of the groups' responses within each of the response dimensions. It concludes with the formulation of hypotheses as to why the response patterns merged as they did.

Activity. The predominantly government-induced behaviour of the old politics groups (business associations and unions) can perhaps be explained by the fact that the issue itself is a complex one, and that traditional interest groups, generally speaking, tend to react only if the (non-)implementation of specific policies affects their special interests. It is only once the state takes up such an issue as climate change, and declares its intention of acting in such a manner as to affect the interests of the stakeholders these groups represent, that they will in fact react. This same explanation could also go towards understanding the difference in intensity of activity between the two issues of targets and transfers; while the regulation of CO_2 emissions (through the imposition of Eco-taxes, for example) directly affects the interests of those that the groups under study here represent, most groups do not see themselves as being responsible for the transfer of resources to other countries. In relation to such mechanisms as JI, the CDM, or ET, these instruments are conceptualized primarily as efficient means for the reduction of one's own industrial CO_2 emissions. Hence, if a governance challenge does not tackle the special interests of a group's constituency but represents an external common-good problem, the response of the group tends to be less pronounced. The activity of the environmental NGOs (DNR, FOE/CAN UK) seems to provide an antithesis, but one could also interpret common-good problems as the special interests of these groups. The climate issue goes to the heart of their concern, these groups perceiving the issue as presenting an urgent problem with high future risk-costs. Their value-driven ideals motivate determined action. Accordingly, the hypothesis could be made that issue-area NGOs will react proactively to complex denationalization challenges if the challenge strongly affects their nonmaterial interests.

The territorial scope of activity, on the other hand, seems to be more a function of whether there is an existing policy cycle at the relevant level; in other words, if, in relation to a particular issue, a policy process at the international level exists, organizations will be more likely to act at that level. This can be seen most clearly through a comparison of the two different global warming issues here investigated, namely, targets and transfers. Until Kyoto in 1997, the international climate debate was centerd around the issue of CO_2 reductions targets. Since Kyoto, however, resource transfers have become more of a concern at the international level, which has seen a corresponding increase in the number of groups taking up the issue at that level. The groups' affiliations also play an important role. All the groups under investigation are deeply rooted within the national social and political system; in relation to international activity, therefore, they tend to rely on their existing transnational linkages for representation. This has both positive and negative repercussions. On the one hand, such links enable internationally coordinated action even if the issue is not at the heart of the organization's concern (unions are a good example of this). In most cases, an existing environmental workgroup with representatives from the different national member organizations took up the new issue and organized the international lobbying. On the other hand, persisting path-dependencies and veto rights of conservative members (for example, of the coal lobby) within these transnational associations often hinder innovative action beyond a lowest common denominator. That being said, groups without transnational affiliations find it much more difficult to gain access to the international policy sphere. Where breaking into the international arena is important enough, however, new issue-centerd networks might evolve.

Compared to general purpose transnational associations, these issue-specific networks tend to be more flexible, competent, and capable of action since they focus on a single topic and as a result of the fact that members' interests tend to be more homogeneous. A case in point is the transnational Climate Action Network (CAN). In November 1989, with the assistance of a regional organization (the European Environmental Bureau) and the support of various national groups (among them the German DNR), the Climate Network Europe (CNE) was established. This network operates to connect environmental organizations throughout Europe, enabling the sharing of expertise and information amongst members. It also provides members who otherwise might not have the necessary resources to get access to the international sphere. Involvement with international organizations may also provide an opportunity for a group without much direct influence in national sphere politics to nevertheless play a greater role in the decision making process. This is a strategy that the Green Party in the UK made use of, exercising influence in the European Parliament through their Green affiliation there.

Spatiality. Climate is so much an analogue for global that almost all groups, readily accepting the denationalized problem structure, see general international coordination as essential for an effective solution.[182] As mentioned above, however, groups vary significantly in terms of the degree of denationalization they regard as appropriate. This variance may be explained with the way groups perceive and construct the challenges of climate change and the costs associated with these challenges, in other words, ultimately with their material or nonmaterial interests. On the one hand, motivated by their constituents' interests, business associations take up the concern of international competition and business opportunity. From this point of view, it is less the problems of climate change as an environmental phenomenon but rather the policies constructed to mitigate climate change that are perceived as a danger: because the costs of environmental protection are expected to be high, the fear of business is that such measures will compromise the competitiveness of the national economy. This threat represents the main challenge for the business community, and, as those most directly affected by the logic of international competition—which punishes economies with the most rigid environmental regulation—they do not want to pay an unfair share of the costs of preserving a global common good. The business organizations, therefore, argue for a solution to the problem which is internationally harmonized, and, for efficiency reasons, low on bureaucracy. On the other hand, environmental groups, though they recognize that environmental protection is cost intensive in the short term, argue that this is necessary to mitigate the even larger long-term costs of the main challenge, such as, global climate change and its potentially devastating consequences for the environment in the future.[183] They even make the point that swift efforts at environmental protection can lead to positive economic effects:

The economic impact of climate change will be enormous—billions of dollars and that the longer action to reduce emissions is delayed, the more expensive it will become.... Studies have shown that many of the first wave of actions to reduce energy consumption will be both energy and economically efficient.[184]

Environmental groups further argue for the establishment of a supranational environmental protection regime with teeth—one which is strong enough to ensure that all states do what is necessary to stem the tide of global warming and put environmental sustainability in place as a basic principle of development. These groups adopt cosmopolitan ideas which support international integration and a compromising of national sovereignty. The position of the various trade unions is largely a function of their evaluation of the policy costs involved, such as, their interests especially concerning employment. For example, the British union body, TUC, reserved its opinion on national carbon taxes as a result of several studies which suggested that up to 40 per cent of the UK's high energy consuming industries, responsible for employing nearly two million people, could be put at risk if such a tax was imposed unilaterally.[185] The German union DGB, by contrast, expecting positive employment effects as a result of such a tax, came out in favor of the measure. The DGB also points out that German industry should make use its current position to pioneer the field of environmental technologies such as to effect higher growth and employment.[186]

Intervention. The group's interests and ideas, in other words, the way that groups perceive the challenge of climate change and its associated policy costs, also goes towards explaining the degree and form of intervention which they promote. Since both the complexity of CO_2 reduction (in terms of the uncertainty of policy and risk costs), and its relevance for market competition, is high, all groups support, in principal, market-based measures and flexible instruments as means of intervention. For business groups, this should be the main thrust of all climate mitigation policies. They fear that if the typical form of unilateral hierarchical intervention is employed too rigorously, it will be ultimately damaging to the economy. Industry therefore supports the most economically advantageous methods of achieving climate policy goals, involving an emphasis on market-based instruments, a moderate degree of intervention and no-regret measures such as the improvement of energy efficiency. "Transparent and rigorous economic appraisal' must be employed to assess the range of possible instruments. The analysis should take into account second order effects, including impact on competitiveness...."[187]

There are certain business sectors, however, which expect new business opportunities to arise from future legislation:

> New business opportunities exist for the electricity industry as a consequence of... the development of environmentally clean technologies.... The implementation of environmental legislation will encourage the development and use of cleaner technologies. This is likely to open up new markets for electricity... [188]

The same difference in opinion across sectors, for instance, those that recognize the potential for profit in climate change mitigation policies and that do not, also exists amongst the trade union groups. A further demonstration of the difference in approach that arises from a differing perception of the problem lies in the response of the various groups to the uncertainties of climate change. Business associations argue that the high level of uncertainty attached to issue has to be recognized in instruments chosen to deal with it: "[i]f the scientific base is not fully proven, the nature of the uncertainty should be taken into account in the design of the instrument."[189] The environmental organizations, on the other hand, regard the very same uncertainty as requiring the maximum amount of precaution.

The principled ideas of each particular organization also affects its approach to intervention. Business groups start with the assumption that the free market guarantees an efficient, productive economy which in the long run benefits everybody; state intervention is therefore perceived as potentially harmful in its interruption of market forces. These groups see sustainability as arising from the capacity of the market to self-regulate.[190] The environmental groups, on the other hand, take the view that left to themselves, markets give rise to undesired effects as an unfair distribution of wealth or decay of the environment, and therefore insist on government intervention.

As to the issue of why groups still adhere to the nation state as the dominant addressee and locus of government, this might be explained by persisting path dependencies and the lack of mature international organizations in the field. Nevertheless, the more groups belief in self-regulatory capacities of the market, the more they are likely to promote nonhierarchical forms of governance as, for example, voluntary agreements.

The above cleavage lines are fairly consistent as between Germany and the UK; the most remarkable difference between these being the degree to which environmental issues are the subject of state intervention. Whereas in the past the approach of the German government has been somewhat interventionist, in Great Britain the logic of deregulation has been predominant. This variance in institutions could explain the difference in attitude that groups in both countries demonstrate toward the use of new instruments. In Germany, where the government has been criticised for being responsible for a "substantial regulatory overload with massive simultaneous deficits in implementation,"[191] groups are far more interested in new market-based measures. In Britain, on the other hand, groups reacting to the regulatory

gaps of the past call for an acknowledgement of "the value of much more significant Government activity to deliver necessary and cost-effective cuts in
UK CO_2 emissions" and recognition of the fact "that such activity will
involve applying both regulatory measures and financial incentives."[192]

Explaining Response Patterns: Hypotheses. The experience of the cases con-
firms that "actors will often fight for what they understand to be their preferred outcome" (Rowlands 1995, 158). Summing up, the attempt to
delineate hypotheses using these inferences provides us with the following as
three potential explanations for the response patterns outlined above.

(1) The call of environmental NGOs, representing the emancipatory side of new politics, for global governance based on sustainable development is mainly motivated by their ideas and
non-material interests. Their cosmopolitan and market-skep-
tical view combined with a concern for environmental protection at all costs results in the firm ideal of strong global
governance.[193] Unions support this concept of international
re-regulation, placing their trust in the notion of global regulation for social and environmental sustainability. An internationalist approach combined with a special interest in
employment issues leads unions to a position according to
which environmental concerns are best treated by positive
(i.e., market-regulating) international integration. Their aim
is to protect workers from the negative impacts of globalized
markets, whether this concerns employment or the environment. In line with their historical role, unions aim to extend
the model of the welfare state to the global level.

(2) Business associations follow the approach of intergovernmental harmonization as a framework for market-based public-
private partnerships because of the special business interests of
their members. These groups expect the policy costs of climate change mitigation to be exorbitant and thus fear to be
placed at a competitive disadvantage; as a result they call for
the international harmonization of all policies and opt for voluntary, efficient and economically sound measures in keeping
with competition and free-market principles. This approach is
based on ideas that see the market as self-regulating and
responsive to social and environmental needs.

(3) Organizations that promote re-nationalization or even re-
localization reject globalization as a dangerous development.
The two groups that adopted this approach here—the
German Republikaner Party and the British Green Party—

did so, however, for quite different reasons. Indeed it is interesting that clashing ideas nevertheless lead to the adoption of policies with remarkably similar characteristics. Both groups do not accept the status quo of the challenged nation state; accepting some form of international coordination, they call for the integrity, and capacity for self-determination, of the national and local community to be restored.

DISCUSSION: POLITICS FROM ABOVE OR BELOW?

The interests and ideas of an array of actors—governments, business, pressure groups, and other stakeholders—play a pivotal role in global climate politics. Studies on international cooperation, thus, should not be restrained to the systemic level; instead "in order to discover how interests are determined, the black box of the state should be opened" (Rowlands 1995, 156). So far, the impression of the cases is such that politics from above predominates, most groups only acted in response to state action in the past and limited their engagement to the evaluation of state policies. Even most of the agenda-setting was channelled through the UN-system.

However, since most groups now understand what's at stake, they—as stakeholders—demand more participation in both, the international negotiations themselves and the processes of national will-formation and decision-making. However, so far, there still exists no forum for such comprehensive involvement. Of course, there are the NGO parallel fora to the intergovernmental conferences, and the special role of NGOs in that issue-area has already been highlighted. And, of course, there is a lot of lobbying behind the scenes or protests on the street.[194] But what is really needed is an open, transparent and democratic system that involves societal groups in a process of global governance,[195] a forum for actors to develop, present and discuss their positions. This controversial input from below would be a necessary contribution to improve the democratic legitimacy of any system of global governance (Beisheim 2001).[196] Moreover, it could make use of the important contributions that groups have to make. Most groups possess significant financial, scientific, and management expertise to develop the kind of solutions needed in the future. They may, moreover, provide for private governance, as, for example, codes of conduct or voluntary initiatives. Such cooperative forms of policy-making could also involve negotiated decision-making between various governmental actors and organized interests. Within public-private partnerships societal groups may, for example, negotiate certain CO_2-reduction targets with the government but then decide for themselves how to administer and execute their implementation. Other NGOs may focus on monitoring these agreements. Hence, whereas the decision-making itself remains in the hand of the state, the latter governance tasks are being privatized.[197]

Global governance could serve as a means to cope with the politics of denationalization, such as, the new domestic and transnational cleavages and alliances discussed above. Such a cooperative and pluralist approach of a multilevel governance may create the necessary spirit of competition in the search for good environmental governance. Global governance, however, must not become special interest group politics and participation must not be limited to experts and organized actors. Since interest representation tends to be asymmetric, it remains the task of the state or of international organizations to assure the transparency and fairness of the processes. As regards the issue of climate change, this study shows that most societal actors support international cooperation to solve the problem. Differences occur mainly with regard to the best way to achieve sustainable development. An innovative and fair system of global governance may provide the tools to develop a consensus on this controversial issue.

NOTES

1. "European Charter on Environment and Health", adopted at the First European Conference on "Environment and Health" in 1989. For the assumption that one of the state's function is to protect its citizen's security, and therefore as well their natural environment, see Zangl and Zürn 1997.

2. That this is perceived as a significant governance challenge, consider the following statement published by the German federal government in 1991: "For a climate protection strategy to be effective, international agreement is essential. Global problems require global solutions. A unilateral national reduction of CO_2 emissions by 25–30 per cent equals, given the current status quo, a global reduction of approximately 1 per cent. Due to the growing global consumption of energy this reduction would be offset within six months.... Both the low impact of unilateral German CO_2 reduction measures and the potentially grave consequences for the world economy necessitate international action." BMWI 1991: Die Treibhausproblematik—eine globale Herausforderung. Bonn, p. 2 and 37 (translation: MB).

3. For the distinction between targets and transfers see also the two conflict lines in Oberthür 1993, 46f. See also Steffan 1994, 79–81, who distinguishes between two main conflicts: "reduction of greenhouse gases" and "financial and resource transfers", referring to each as the "North-North conflict" and "North-South conflict" respectively.

4. Attesting to the perceived relevance of this particular denationalization challenge is the following: "International action is essential to tackle the threat of climate change. No single country of group of countries can tackle the problem alone.... With anticipated increases in population and economic growth, emissions of

some gases from developing countries could double over the next twenty years and overtake those from the developed world.... Given the rates of economic and population growth in many developing countries, the Convention's objectives can only be realized if they play a full and active part in it." DOE / HSMO 1994: Global Climate Change, p. 11, 20.

5. For a further discussion see Breitmeier 1997.

6. For an insight into how these negotiations are progressing and the role of political groups within them see, for example, Mintzer (1994) or Rowlands (1995).

7. United Nations Framework Convention on Climate Change (UN FCCC) (A/AC.237/18(Part II)/Add.1), Art. 2.

8. United Nations Framework Convention on Climate Change (A/AC.237/18(Part II)/Add.1), Art. 4(2) a and b. This commitment applies to the so-called Annex I states, that is, the 24 original OECD-members, 11 former members of the Soviet bloc and the EU.

9. The overall 5 per cent target, applicable to the developed countries, is to be met in the European Union (EU) through cuts of 8 per cent. The EU has made its own internal arrangement so as to meet its 8 per cent target by distributing different rates to its member states. These targets range from a 28 per cent reduction by Luxembourg and 21 per cent by Denmark and Germany to an increase by 27 per cent for Portugal.

10. See the Prologue to and Art. 4(3) to 4(10), as well as Art. 11 of UN FCCC (A/AC.237/18(Part II)/Add.1). In these articles, the so-called Annex II countries, such as, the 24 original OECD-members and the EU, commit themselves to provide resources required for climate protection in developing countries. In addition, chapter 33 of Agenda 21 deals with "Financial Resources And Mechanisms" and chapter 34 with "Transfer Of Environmentally Sound Technology, Cooperation And Capacity-Building."

11. See Kyoto Protocol to the UNFCCC (FCCC/CP/1997/L.7/Add.1) of 10.12.1997, Art. 12.

12. The terminology attached to this strategy has changed somewhat since its introduction. At COP 1 in Berlin, the term "Activities Implemented Jointly" (AIJ) was used for a pilot phase to test the concept. Since COP 3 in Kyoto, however, the term "joint implementation" has been used to describe joint projects between developed countries, and the term "Clean Development Mechanism" (CDM) to describe joint projects with developing countries.

13. The 1997 Kyoto Protocol contains provisions for the international trading of permits for greenhouse gas emissions amongst developed countries only. For opinions of interest groups on this issue compare the empirical work in Chasek and Downie 1996.

14. Bundesministerium für Umwelt, Naturschutz und Reaktorsicherheit (BMU) 1997 @ http://www.bmu.de/ umweltziele/vorbem.htm (translation: MB) .

15. See, for example, the DPG's warning in the *Frankfurter Rundschau* No. 217, 19.9.1986, p. 15. See also *Der Spiegel* 40. Jg. No. 33 of 11.8.86; *Zeit-Magazin* No. 26

of 26.6.87; and *Natur* No. 8/87, Geo No. 9/89, where climate change takes the position of the front page story.

16. Such a Study Commission comprises both Members of Parliament and independent experts. Their task is to gather as much relevant information as possible on a given subject, thereby providing law-makers with a basis for decision-making on complex and important issues.

17. Kabinettbeschluß, 06/13/90, Bundestags-Drucksache 13/8936, p. 70.

18. Kabinettbeschluß, 11/07/90, Bundestags-Drucksache 13/8936, p. 72.

19. Enquete-Kommission "Schutz der Erdatmosphäre" des Deutschen Bundestages 1992: Klimaänderung gefährdet globale Entwicklung. Bonn; p. 5–17.

20. Compare quote in Fn. 2.

21. Decision of the Federal Government on the Climate Protection Program of the Federal Republic of Germany, on the Basis of the Fourth Report of the CO_2 Reduction Interministerial Working Group (CO_2 Reduction IWG), p. 4/13.

22. Enquete-Kommission "Schutz der Erdatmosphäre" des Deutschen Bundestages 1992: Klimaänderung gefährdet globale Entwicklung. Bonn; p. 180f (translation: MB) .

23. Kabinettbeschluß, 11/07/1990, Bundestags-Drucksache 13/8936, p. 77 (translation: MB). Statements of this sort have been frequently repeated: "The federal government considers it important to assist developing countries meet their energy requirements . . . in a way that safeguards the environment and climate", Kabinettbeschluß, 12/11/1991, Bundestags-Drucksache 13/8936, p. 86 (translation: MB) .

24. CCIRG: The Potential Effects of the Climate Change in the United Kingdom, First Report, 1991 @ http://www.doc.mmu.ac.uk/aric/ukimpact.html.

25. HSMO 1990: This Common Inheritance. White Paper on the Environment, London.

26. DOE/HSMO 19943: Global Climate Change; p. 11, 20. (2nd edition of 1991.)

27. Although Green Parties have not generally grown simply or directly out of strictly environmental movements, they are widely regarded as an important part of a broader green movement (Rootes 1995).

28. The positions of the DNR and the Climate Working Group of the Forum U & E are almost identical, one reason being an overlap in the person in charge. The position of the Forum U & E is therefore occasionally taken to represent the view of the DNR. This is particularly the case in relation to the issue of resource transfers.

29. The members of CAN UK are: the Association for the Conservation of Energy; Council for the Protection of Rural England; Foundation for International Environmental Law and Development, Friends of the Earth; Greenpeace; Green Alliance; Institute for European Environmental Policy; International Institute for Energy Conservation, National Society for Clean Air and Environmental Protection;

Royal Society for the Protection of Birds; Transport 2000; WWF UK; and The Wildlife Trusts.

30. Betz (1994) also does not name a right-wing populist (as opposed to right-wing extremist) party in Great Britain.

31. This Committee continued its work after UNCED as the "Nationales Komitee für Nachhaltige Entwicklung" (National Committee for Sustainable Development).

32. That is why in the following pages both cases are dealt with concurrently, and not separately as in the other chapters.

33. In context of that event, the Green Party drafted the *Wörlitzer Erklärung zum Klima-und Umweltschutz* (The Wörlitz Declaration on Climate and Environmental Protection) which was decided upon at a meeting of the Greens' parliamentary party in January 1997.

34. Further information on this is provided in the section on "Intervention."

35. For examples of such projects see VDEW 1996: Möglichkeiten wirksamer Klimavorsorge mit Hilfe von "Joint Implementation", Frankfurt a.M.

36. Going back as far as 1982, the DGB's annual "Environmental Forum" chose "Environment and Third World" as its topic.

37. For example, in the context of the special summit of the General Assembly of the UN in 1997, BDI launched a publication series with the title "Positions." This publication was supposed to provide a forum for German business to present and discuss their concepts of sustainable development. However, German industry seems to be in the phase of still developing such a position. This is also indicated by the fact that in context with the German "Umweltpreis" the BDI funded an award for studies on the issue of "Technological Transfers in developing countries and Eastern Europe."

38. See their mission statement @ http://www.oneworldweb.de/forum/.

39. The DNR is in fact the German focal point of the European Environmental Bureau (EEB).

40. @ http://sme.belgium.eu.net/climnet/aboutcne.htm

41. Other transnational partners of BDI are the International Chamber of Commerce (ICC) and the Business Council for Sustainable Development (BCSD). Thus, in the run-up to UNCED the BDI presented its position at ICC's "Industry Forum on Environment and Development" in Rio de Janeiro.

42. European Grouping of the Electricity Supply Industry.

43. Union of International Producers and Distributers of Electrical Energy.

44. See, for example, UNIPEDE/EURELECTRIC 1998: UN Framework Climate Change Convention. The Electricity Industry's Role, in: *WATT's new*, No. 0, Domain 4/01.

45. See, for example, European Federation of Green Parties: "Kyoto is just a little step." Statement by Green Party representatives and members of parliament present at Kyoto to the results of the climate summit, Kyoto, 11 December 1997.

46. However, the longtime head of IG BCE's environmental section has been very active at the CSD—but in his function as a representative for the ICFTU, not for IG BCE itself. Nevertheless, there are indications that positions formulated within the international umbrella organization are used to push for action on the national level.

47. Numerous policy papers outline this preference. To present just a few relatively early examples: BDI 1989: Vorsorge zum Schutz des Klimas. Eine Bestandsaufnahme der deutschen Industrie, Cologne; DGB 1992: UNCED muß zum Motor globaler Umweltpartnerschaft werden, press release 5/25/1992; Die Grünen 1990: "Extra" 9/90: Die Klimakatastrophe verhindern!; VDEW et al. 1991: Initiative der deutschen Wirtschaft für eine weltweite Klimavorsorge. IG CPK/Walter, Jürgen/Heins, Bernd 1993: UN-Konferenz für Umwelt und Entwicklung Rio de Janeiro 1992, Hannover.

48. DNR: Position Paper, UN General Assembly Special Session on Environment & Development, 1996 @ http://www.dnr.de/DNR_intern/un-sgv-e.htm.

49. DNR: Position Paper, UN General Assembly Special Session on Environment & Development, 1996 @ http://www.dnr.de/DNR_intern/un-sgv-e.htm.

50. Bündnis 90/Die Grünen 1997: Wörlitzer Erklärung zum Klima-und Umweltschutz; p. 1 (translation: MB).

51. R. Grohe, Head of BDI-Committee for Environmental Politics, Speech on the Forum "Umweltschutz als Wirtschafts- und Standortfaktor," 8/30/94, BDI-Drucksache No. 283, p. 32 (translation: MB).

52. VDEW et al. 1991: Initiative der deutschen Wirtschaft für eine weltweite Klimavorsorge; p. 1.

53. Bundesverband der Republikaner (without year): Parteiprogramm, Programmpunkt Europapolitik, p. 13 (translation: MB).

54. Although the former IG CPK did address itself to several issues on the international scale, currently IG BCE offers no substantial position on the issue.

55. Die Grünen 1990: "Tropenwald-Minderheitsvotum vereint Forderungen von Grünen, SPD und Regenwaldbewegung," press release No. 495/90, 31.05.1990 (translation: MB). Brought into the discussion are, for example, debt relief within an overall framework of poverty reduction and control mechanisms for transnational corporations. For similar arguments see also: Forum U & E 1997: Umwelt und Entwicklung. Eine Bilanz, Bonn.

56. Deutscher Naturschutzring (DNR): Position Paper, UN General Assembly Special Session on Environment & Development, 1996 @ http://www.dnr.de/DNR_intern/un-sgv-e.htm

57. BDI et al. 1991: "Wirtschaft fordert marktwirtschaftliche Alternative für Klimavorsorge," press release 163/91, 3.12.1991 (translation: MB).

58. Bundesverband der Republikaner (without year): Parteiprogramm, Programmpunkt "Entwicklungshilfe"; p. 96.

59. The AOSIS protocol proposal foresees a 20 per cent CO_2 reduction for industrialized countries by 2005 based on 1990 levels.

60. This position can be found in the Party's dissenting votes to the Report of the Enquete Commissions and in their questions to and motions within the German Parliament.

61. The DNR points out that on a global level CO_2 emissions will probably be reduced by one per cent annually until the middle of the next century. Therefore, according to the group, the CO_2 emissions of nonindustrialized countries must also be constrained.

62. Especially the DNR/Forum U & E presses for increased funds to support the GEF, see, for example, Forum U & E/Peter Wahl 1997: Finanzierung von Umwelt und Entwicklung, Bonn; Forum U & E 1997: Umwelt und Entwicklung. Eine Bilanz, Bonn.

63. BDI et al. 1991: Initiative of German Business for World-Wide Precautionary Action to Protect the Climate, in: BDI 1992: Inter-national Environmental Policy-Perspectives 2000, Cologne, p. 65.

64. At first the base year was 1987, this was revised in 1996.

65. R. Grohe, Head of BDI-Committee for Environmental Politics, Speech on the Forum "Umweltschutz als Wirtschafts-und Standortfaktor," 8/30/94, BDI-Drucksache No. 283, p. 31ff (translation: MB).

66. This reform, for example, involves the introduction of an energy tax (with a CO_2 component) and an increase in taxes on fuels and heating oil.

67. Interview with a representative of DNR, 3/4/1998.

68. Bündnis 90/Die Grünen 1997: Wörlitzer Erklärung zum Klima-und Umweltschutz; p. 2 (translation: MB).

69. BDI 1997: BDI-Position zu "Nachhaltiger Entwicklung," press release, 2/26/1997 (translation: MB).

70. BDI et al. 1991: Initiative of German Business for World-Wide Precautionary Action to Protect the Climate, in: BDI 1992: Inter-national Environmental Policy-Perspectives 2000, Cologne, p. 65.

71. Landtag of Baden-Württemberg, Plenary-protokoll, 06/24/93, Speech of Mr. Bühler from the "Republikaner"-fraction, p. 2309f (translation: MB).

72. "Destruction of the environment due to poverty and poverty due to destruction of the environment cannot be overcome only through the classical forms of private and state sponsored development aid...," Forum U & E 1997: Umwelt und Entwicklung. Eine Bilanz, Bonn, p. 9 (translation: MB).

73. It is worthwhile to note that in Buenos Aires BDI—but not its European partner UNICE—criticised plans for trading with hot air.

74. DNR/Forum U & E, for example, want to see a cap put in place such that at least 50 per cent of reductions are achieved domestically.

75. See, for example, AEEU's leaflet "Building Partnership to Reduce Waste and Save Energy. A How-To Guide."

76. See GCI @ http://www.gn.apc.org/gci/index.html#about

77. TUC 1991: Congress 1991—General Council Report and Report of Congress 1991, London, p. 81.

78. TUC 1989: Towards a Charter for the Environment. General Council Statement to the 1989 Trades Union Congress, London.

79. The General Council decided that the TUC should press for full involvement in the work of any machinery which follows up the UNCED. See TUC 1992: Congress 1992-General Council Report and Report of Congress 1992, London, p. 48.

80. See CBI (no year, presumable 1989): Managing The Greenhouse Effect. A business perspective, London.

81. For example in response to the establishment of an integrated climate impact assessment project by DETR, the CBI commented: "The CBI will liase with the DETR to establish business representation on the steering committee which will govern the integrated impacts assessment." See CBI 1997: Climate Change Policies and Measures. A Preliminary Note on CBI Priorities, London.

82. See the presentation of their policy work @ www.cbi.org.uk.

83. See "Top 25 UK Companies Seek Emissions Trading," in: *The Times of London*, 06/28/99.

84. EA 1997: Annual Review; p. 7.

85. See, for example, EA 1990: The Greenhouse Effect. Environmental Briefing No. 2.

86. "Actions by the electricity industry are enabling the Government to meet its sustainable development objectives in the following ways. Climate Change:...The Government's updated forecast in Energy Paper 65 (1995) expects that emissions from electricity generation will reduce by 18 MtC pa by 2000, whilst those from all other sectors increase by 10 MtC, which will more than meet the UK's commitment. This will be achieved by commercially sound actions carried out by the electricity generators in improving existing plant performance, switching from coal to gas for generation and increasing the output of nuclear plant," in: EA 1996: Sustainable Development. Meeting Our Obligations to Future Generations. Environmental Briefing. See also EA 1994: Global Warming. Climate Change Convention Implements Precautionary Approach. Environmental Briefing No. 17; EA: The Road From Rio—The Environment And The UK Electricity Industry Five Years On, press briefing PR07/97,04/02/1997.

87. EA 1994: Global Warming. Climate Change Convention Implements Precautionary Approach. Environmental Briefing No. 17.

88. FOE UK 1992/93: Friends of the Earth's Response to the Department of Environment's Discussion on "Climate Change. Our National Program for CO_2 Emissions," London; p. 2. In 1988 FOE also published their report, *The Heat Trap, The Threat Posed By Rising Levels of Greenhouse Gases.*

89. FOE UK / Jackson, T. / Roberts, S. 1989: Getting Out Of The Greenhouse. An Agenda for UK Action on Energy Policy; See also FOE UK/Karas, J.H.W. 1991: Back from the Brink. Greenhouse Gar Targets for a Sustainable World; FOE UK / Jackson, T. 1991: Efficiency without Tears. "No-Regrets" Energy Policy to Combat Climate Change; FOE UK 1992–1993: Friends of the Earth's Response to the Department of Environment's Discussion on "Climate Change. Our National Program for CO_2 Emissions," London.

90. The Global Climate Coalition (GCC) was an organization established in 1989 to coordinate business participation in the international policy debate on the issue of global climate change. It largely represented the view of grey US businesses, companies, and corporations.

91. Interview with a representative of the Green Party, 04/23/98.

92. European Grouping of the Electricity Supply Industry. "Our office in Brussels has proved invaluable in providing a constantly available contact point for our members.... Our lobbying efforts on European Union legislation are complemented by the EA's membership of Eurelectric," @ http://www.electricity.org.uk/about_ea/ea_brief.html.

93. Union of International Producers and Distributers of Electrical Energy.

94. See, for example, UNIPEDE/EURELECTRIC 1998: UN-Framework Climate Change Convention. The Electricity Industry's Role, in: WATT's new, No. 0, Domain 4/01.

95. CBI (no year, presumable 1989): Managing The Greenhouse Effect. A business perspective, London.

96. See CBI @ http://www.cbi.org.uk/cbi/htdocs/standard/info_on_cbi/

97. Interview with a representative of CBI, 04/30/98.

98. European Trade Union Council and International Confederation of Free Trade Unions

99. TUC 1991: Congress 1991—General Council Report and Report of Congress 1991, London, p. 81.

100. Compare, for example, TUC 1997: Congress 1997—General Council Report and Report of Congress 1997. London, p. 37.

101. Interview with a representative of FOE UK, 04/30/98. It was mentioned that the group has even attempted to utilise the special relationship between the UK and the US government to influence the latter's position on climate change.

102. "We innovate at all levels: from our participation in Friends of the Earth International to the work carried out by over 250 local groups, we are uniquely placed

to mobilize public opinion and campaign successfully—locally, nationally and internationally," @ http://www.foe.co.uk/fund/welcome/five_reasons.html

103. See, for example, US CAN / CNE 1995: Independent NGO Evaluations of National Plans for Climate Change Mitigation. OECD Countries. Third Review.

104. See Climate Action Network UK. The UK Center for an NGO Service on Climate Change Issues, London.

105. "Our next task at international level is to ensure that the review and compliance mechanism is tightened, and that rules for trading, sinks, JI and the CDM are environmentally driven. At a national level we will be watching and working to ensure that the UK Government implements policies to achieve its target," The View of CAN UK, in: *The Environment Council 1998: Business and Environment Program Background*, p. 31f.

106. CAN UK: Letter to MP Chris Patten, Secretary of State / DOE, 10/09/1990, see also CAN UK: Letter to MP Michael Heseltine, Secretary of State / DOE, 10/09/1991.

107. CAN UK: Letter to Prime Minister John Major and other MPs, as well as the national press, 11/27/1992.

108. FOE UK / Jackson, T./Roberts, P. 1989: Getting Out Of The Greenhouse. An Agenda for UK Action on Energy Policy; p. 12.

109. The View of CAN UK, in: *The Environment Council 1998: Business and Environment Program Background*, p. 31f.

110. CAN UK 1997: The Science and Politics of Climate Change. Kyoto and the Climate Convention Process.

111. FOE UK: Government Action! @ http://www.foe.co.uk/climatechange/aims.html.

112. See for example the policy recommendations in FOE UK / Jackson, T. / Roberts, S. 1989: Getting Out Of The Greenhouse. An Agenda for UK Action on Energy Policy; p. 12ff.

113. CAN UK: Letter to MP Chris Patten, Secretary of State / DOE, 09.10.1990.

114. Interview with a representative of CAN UK, 04/28/1998.

115. "The most significant aspect of the Government's review of the effects of global warming (climate change) on the UK went unnoticed. This frightening revelation became apparent as John Gummer talked about how Britain will need to adapt to the coming changes, that is, the Government has abandoned all pretence of trying to prevent global warming. It admits its totally inadequate target to cut CO_2 emissions can at best only slow down the process.", Green Party 1996: It's the end of the world as we know it. Global warming—Climate Change, in: *Green World*, No. 15, p. 7.

116. Hines, Colin: Protect the Local, Globally, in: *Green International* 1998.

117. Chris Keene, Anti-Globalization Campaigner, Green Party of England and Wales: Globalization And Climate Change, Report, May 1999.

118. Global Commons Institute/The Corner House for Globe UK 1997: Climate and Equity. An International Agenda. The Kyoto Papers, No. 1, London (presented by a representative of the British Green Party).

119. TUC 1990: Congress 1990—General Council Report and Report of Congress, London, p. 73–75.

120. CBI Industrial Policy Group 1997: An agenda for action. A CBI policy statement on climate change, London.

121. Interview with a representative of EA, 04/23/98.

122. EA 1997: Electricity Association Position Paper on Environmental Negotiated Agreements.

123. CBI 1998: Coming clean. Using market instruments to improve the environment, London.

124. TUC 1990: Congress 1990—General Council Report and Report of Congress, London, p. 73–75. For similar statements see TUC Energy Committee 1989: Memorandum to the House of Commons Select Committee Inquiry into The Greenhouse Effect, p. 6–7 and FOE UK / Jackson, T. / Roberts, p. 1989: Getting Out Of The Greenhouse. An Agenda for UK Action on Energy Policy; p. 12.

125. CBI Industrial Policy Group 1997: An agenda for action. A CBI policy statement on climate change, London.

126. CBI 1997: Climate Change Policies and Measures. A Preliminary Note on CBI Priorities, London.

127. FOE UK/Karas, J.H.W. 1991: Back from the Brink. Greenhouse Gas Targets for a Sustainable World; p. 2.

128. CAN UK: Brief an MP John Gummer (Secretary of State for the DOE), 01/20/95. See also CAN UK: Climate Groups challenge UK to implement Rio Convention, press release, 03/21/94.

129. CAN UK: Letter to MP Chris Patten, Secretary of State/DOE, 09/19/90. Here, already at the very beginning of the negotiations, in the run up to the Second World Climate Conference and the commencement of negotiations on a global climate convention, environmental NGOs pressed the British government to support the draft proposal from the Italian Presidency, for a stabilization in CO_2 emissions at 1990 levels by the year 2000.

130. FOE UK: Kyoto and Beyond @ http://www.foe.co.uk/climatechange/what kyoto.html.

131. CAN UK: Letter and Policy-Paper to MPs John Prescott (Deputy Prime Minister and Secretary of State for the DETR), Michael Meacher (Minister for the Environment and Countryside) and Robin Cook (Foreign Secretary) 10/14/97. Friends Of The Earth International Climate Change Campaign Policy Position, June 1997 @ http://www.foe.co.uk/climatechange/posit. html.

132. Compare FOE UK 1992/93: Friends of the Earth's Response to the Department of Environment's Discussion on "Climate Change. Our National

Program for CO_2 Emissions', London; p. 41ff, and Climate Action Network UK: Hot News. Special Report: Energy Efficiency in the UK, Issue 7, 1993.

133. Miriam Kennet (Campaigns Co-ordinator GP): A Response from the Green Party to the UK Government Consultation Paper on Climate Change.

134. TUC 1990: Congress 1990—General Council Report and Report of Congress, London, p. 73–75.

135. TUC Energy Committee 1989: Memorandum to the House of Commons Select Committee Inquiry into The Greenhouse Effect; p. 6–7

136. Industry Policy Group, CBI 1998: "The View of the CBI", in: The Environment Council: The Kyoto Protocol to the UN Framework Convention on Climate Change. Business and Environment Program Background, p. 31f.

137. EA 1996: The Electricity Industry and Climate Change. A Response to the Liberal Democrat Consultation Paper.

138. "The electricity industry's success in reducing greenhouse gas emissions... has made a significant contribution to a worldwide issue," EA: Industry Cuts Greenhouse Gases, press release, 03/11/1996.

139. EA 1996: The Electricity Industry and Climate Change. A Response to the Liberal Democrat Consultation Paper.

140. FOE UK: Earth Summit II—Online press briefing, 1997 @ http://www.foe.co.uk/climatechange/esii.html.

141. Friends Of The Earth International Climate Change Campaign Policy Position June 1997 @ http://www.foe.co.uk/climatechange/posit.html.

142. Global Commons Institute / The Corner House for Globe UK 1997: Climate and Equity. An International Agenda. The Kyoto Papers, No. 1, London (as presented by a representative of the British Green Party).

143. TUC 1990: Congress 1990—General Council Report and Report of Congress, London, p. 87–88.

144. CBI 1997: Climate Change Policies and Measures. A Preliminary Note on CBI Priorities, London.

145. See, for example, CBI 1998: Coming Clean. Using market instruments to improve the environment, London; EA 1998: Increased Challenges and New Business Opportunities. Trends In Environmental Legislation & Its Implementation. Environmental Briefing.

146. CBI 1998: Coming clean. Using market instruments to improve the environment, London.

147. More specific, the EA "recognizes and supports the need for regulation of those parts of the business which, of necessity, operate as a monopoly. The EA welcomes the introduction of full competition, and deregulation, in all other parts of the business. Where regulation is essential (e.g., in the transmission and distribution businesses), the EA supports the following regulatory principles: 1. Incentive

Regulation; 2. Regulatory Panel / Transparency; 3. Stability; 4. Electricity Regulator.", EA 1995: Regulation, Position Paper #2.

148. EA 1996: The Electricity Industry and Climate Change. A Response to the Liberal Democrat Consultation Paper. See also EA 1997: Electricity Association Position on the European Commission Proposal for a Council Directive on the Taxation of Energy Products.

149. CBI 1998: Coming clean. Using market instruments to improve the environment, London.

150. EA 1997: Electricity Association Position on the European Commission Proposal for a Council Directive on the Taxation of Energy Products.

151. As an example of the distortions that may arise with tax mismanagement, CBI refers to the differential tax treatment of fuels and energy efficiency products: "UK tax arrangements distort the market in favor of energy consumption as opposed to energy saving. Energy efficient products carry VAT at the full 17.5 percent, whereas VAT on domestic fuel is due to be reduced to 5 percent as announced in the July budget." CBI 1997: Climate Change Policies and Measures. A Preliminary Note on CBI Priorities, London.

152. CBI 1997: Climate Change Policies and Measures. A Preliminary Note on CBI Priorities, London. See also EA 1997: Electricity Association Position Paper on Environmental Negotiated Agreements.

153. See EA (no year): The Electricity Industry and the Energy Saving Trust: A Working Partnership; and EA 1994: Global Warming. Climate Change Convention Implements Precautionary Approach. Environmental Briefing No. 17.

154. "Top 25 UK Companies Seek Emissions Trading," in: *The Times of London*, 28.06.99. This was linked to an attempt to persuade the Government that it should drop its plans for a carbon tax: CBI calls on government to address serious concerns about energy tax (see press release, 06/09/1999).

155. EA 1996: The Electricity Industry and Climate Change. A Response to the Liberal Democrat Consultation Paper.

156. TUC 1989: Towards a Charter for the Environment. General Council Statement to the 1989 Trades Union Congress, London.

157. TUC 1990: Congress 1990-General Council Report/Report of Congress, London, p. 73–75.

158. Interview with a representative of TUC, 04/28/98.

159. TUC 1990: A Trade Unionists' Guide to Environmental Issues, London; p. 7.

160. TUC 1989: Towards a Charter for the Environment. General Council Statement to the 1989 Trades Union Congress, London.

161. TUC 1990: Congress 1990—General Council Report and Report of Congress, London, p. 86.

162. FOE UK/Jackson, T. 1991: Efficiency without Tears. "No-Regrets" Energy Policy to Combat Climate Change; pp. 6–7.

163. FOE UK 1992/93: Friends of the Earth's Response to the Department of Environment's Discussion on "Climate Change. Our National Program for CO2 Emissions", London; pp. 5–6.

164. FOE UK/Jackson, T. 1991: Efficiency without Tears. "No-Regrets" Energy Policy to Combat Climate Change.

165. FOE UK 1992/93: Friends of the Earth's Response to the Department of Environment's Discussion on "Climate Change. Our National Program for CO2 Emissions", London; p. 20–21.

166. CAN UK 1997: The Science and Politics of Climate Change. Kyoto and the Climate Convention Process.

167. FOE UK/Jackson, T./Roberts, S. 1989: Getting Out Of The Greenhouse. An Agenda for UK Action on Energy Policy; p. 13.

168. For a detailed discussion see Miriam Kennet (Green Party Campaigns Co-ordinator): A Response from the Green Party to the UK Government Consultation Paper on Climate Change, 1999 @ http://www.greenparty.org.uk/

169. Dawe, Steve 1998: Collision course. Corporate resistance to environmentalism, in: *Green World*, No. 21, p. 11.

170. Chris Keene, Anti-Globalization Campaigner, Green Party of England and Wales: Globalization And Climate Change, Report, May 1999.

171. The model introduces emissions trading between developing and industrialized countries. Revenue streams to developing countries could then be used to fund clean energy strategies. See Global Commons Institute/The Corner House for Globe UK 1997: Climate and Equity. An International Agenda. The Kyoto Papers, No. 1, London (Paper presented by a representative of the Green Party).

172. TUC 1990: Congress 1990—General Council Report and Report of Congress 1990. London, 73-75.

173. CBI 1997: Climate Change Policies and Measures. A Preliminary Note on CBI Priorities, London. See also: CBI 1997: Principles for Greenhouse Gas Emissions Trading. A Preliminary Note by the CBI, London.

174. EA 1996: The Electricity Industry and Climate Change. A Response to the Liberal Democrat Consultation Paper.

175. For the term and concept see Haas (1992) and (1993).

176. BDI 1996: Updated and Extended Declaration by German Industry and Trade on Global Warming Prevention, p. 3.

177. The position of national sectoral unions—as well as that of sectoral business associations—tends to vary according to the stakes of their member industries.

178. Interview with a representative of FOE UK, 04/30/98.

179. FOE/Roberts, S. 1993: The Government, The Monkey and Energy Efficiency, in: Climate Action Network UK: Hot News. Special Report: Energy Efficiency in the UK, Issue 7; p. 6.

180. There have been occasions, however, where monitoring was carried out by a nongovernmental institution, for example in Germany where the voluntary agreement on CO_2 emissions reduction was monitored by the Rheinisch-Westfälisches Institut für Wirtschaftsforschung (RWI). In that case, however, the government still retained the role of evaluating the monitoring activities of the institution.

181. For a more in-depth discussion of this, see section 5.3.

182. Moreover, the related ozone problem was being dealt with internationally quite effectively only shortly ago and—as stated in the interviews—this served for some groups as a model for action.

183. "The world's top climate scientists now agree that our climate is changing, and probably for the worse. Worse for people, worse for business and worse for the environment. More frequent storms, floods, hurricanes, hotter drier summers and wetter winters are predicted as a result of climate change caused by increased carbon dioxide and other polluting greenhouse gases in our atmosphere. Such changes could leave millions dead, homeless or impoverished", FOE UK: Climate Catastrophe Ahead! @ http://www.foe.co.uk/climatechange/catast.html.

184. CAN UK 1997: The Science and Politics of Climate Change. Kyoto and the Climate Convention Process.

185. "A recent conference in Cambridge on the 'UK Economy and the Green 1990s' predicted that up to '40% of Britain's high energy consuming industries employing some 1.7m people could be put at risk if Britain imposed a unilateral carbon tax on these industries ahead of other countries'." TUC 1991: Work and the Environment. The European Dimension, London.

186. Statement of Dr. H. Heuter, DGB 1996, as cited in: Schlegelmilch, Kai/Streckert, Christian 1997: Saving the Climate. That's My Job! Beschäftigungseffekte von Klimaschutzmassnahmen. Wuppertal Papers No. 70; p. 15–17 (translation: MB).

187. CBI 1998: Coming clean. Using market instruments to improve the environment, London. The improvement of energy efficiency is thus seen as a no regret policy: "Improving competitiveness and reducing costs are key issues for CBI members. Britain lags behind the best practice in energy efficiency which is to be found in the industry and commerce of our principal industrial competitors...." CBI 1989: The Greenhouse Effect and Energy Efficiency, London.

188. EA 1998: Increased Challenges and New Business Opportunities. Trends In Environmental Legislation & Its Implementation. Environmental Briefing.

189. CBI 1998: Coming clean. Using market instruments to improve the environment, London. At the beginning of the policy process, business associations questioned the existence of future climate change all together. By the time of the second IPCC report at the latest, however, this attitude was largely given up (with a few exceptions, that is: The Global Climate Coalition and the so-called "Climate Skeptics" still question the science of climate change.)

190. "The full liberalization of EU energy markets will provide a far greater incentive for efficient power generation than the setting of specific EU targets for different

forms of electricity generation", EA 1998: Commission Communication On A Community Strategy To Promote Combined Heat And Power (CHP), Position Paper #7.

191. Bündnis 90/Die Grünen 1998: Antrag, Bundestags-Drucksache 13/10010, 03/03/98 (translation: MB).

192. FOE UK 1992/93: Friends of the Earth's Response to the Department of Environment's Discussion on "Climate Change. Our National Program for CO_2 Emissions'; p. 5f. The argument is expressed even more strongly in the following: "These [energy conservation] signals are not in place at the moment and, because of the systemic failure of policies since World War II to provide them, the signals will not spontaneously appear without Government action.... Government action is needed because its own policies have created many of the 'wrong' signals in the existing energy market." FOE / Roberts, S. 1993: The Government, The Monkey, and Energy Efficiency, in: *Climate Action Network UK*: Hot News. Special Report: Energy Efficiency in the UK, Issue 7; p. 6.

193. An exception to this are the NGOs which promote resistance to globalization processes; instead of global governance, they encourage a de-globalization and a re-localization of politics.

194. As Seattle and Prague have shown, those groups that promote resistance to globalization set off pressure politics from below.

195. "Governance" refers to the processes and institutions, both formal and informal, that guide and restrain the collective activities of a group (Keohane and Nye 2000b, 12). See also Zürn 1998 for his "project of complex world governance."

196. For further discussion see, among many others, Held 1995 and McGrew 1997.

197. Of course, some forms of government intervention will continue to be necessary. For further discussion see Brühl et al. 2001, Haufler 1993, Reinicke 1998 Reinicke et al. 2000, and Rosenau and Czempiel 1992.

Chapter 6

Conclusions

The Politics of Denationalization

Gregor Walter and Michael Zürn

INTRODUCTION

How do national interest groups respond to political challenges associated with globalization? In raising this question, this volume has targeted three shortcomings of mainstream research into the effects of globalization. These shortcomings were identified as follows: first, that the definitions of both globalization and its assumed consequences are often either rather vague or limited to economics only; second, that in most cases the nation-state remains the basic unit of analysis despite the claim of fundamental change—something we call methodological nationalism—and third, that the actual process of policy-formulation, in other words, the very basis of what politics is about, has in our view largely been ignored.

The design of our study was specifically oriented toward avoiding these pitfalls. In respect of the first mentioned shortfall, we have built on the notion of societal denationalization rather than globalization as a working definition. This notion is based on the fact that areas of dense social transaction are no longer confined by national borders. In our view, societal denationalization exists to the extent that the traditional dominance of intranational over transnational transactions is challenged. The affected transactions are not confined to economics only. Thus, based on this definition and on empirical considerations, we singled out communication (viz, the Internet), migration and climate change as areas particularly worthy of investigation. Though each of these areas demonstrate marked levels of transnational interaction, amongst them there is still a degree of variance in their extent of denationalization.

In addition, (in respect of the second above mentioned shortcoming) we deliberately moved below the level of the nation-state. We looked at nationally constituted political groups closely tied to politics within the nation-state as we know it. At the same time, we selected these groups from countries at the core of the OECD world. While looking at issue areas evidencing a high level of denationalization, therefore, we otherwise followed a double-hard case design. That is to say, our focus was on groups with a national focus in countries widely regarded as examples of the successful modern state. Our reasoning behind this was that if political processes concerning these issue areas remains indistinct from politics as usual, there is very little reason to expect that the politics of denationalization brings anything new. We thus intentionally did not include new transnational entities[1] or countries well removed from the notion of the model modern state in our inquiry.[2] The logic behind this design was to ensure sufficient sensitivity to change but without being oversensitive or reacting too easily to marginal variation.

The core of our investigation therefore lies in the reactions of nationally constituted political groups faced with governance challenges in areas showing a high degree of denationalization. Our focus is on the political process, that is, the negotiation between an array of different policy possibilities, rather than on political outcomes (our response to the third shortcoming identified above). In this way, we circumvent the structural shortcuts of macrocorrelative attempts to link globalization directly to policies. We are not concerned with the immediate policy outcomes of denationalization, but rather with the political processes which it triggers. The fundamental question is: is there such a thing as a politics of denationalization? And if so, what does it look like?

Chapters 3 to 5 have already established there are various aspects of politics in the respective fields that constitute interesting results in their own right. On the one hand, some responses of nationally constituted interest groups' responses were outside the realm of politics as usual. In the Internet cases, the groups from the New Left join the issue-specific groups on the Right in demanding only very soft and weak forms of intervention, thus making up for strange bedfellows following a strategy of deregulation. The Climate cases support the notion that policy debates on international fora directly lead to politics beyond the nation-state. Many groups were active on the international level and almost all groups asked for some form of international policies. National policy-making fora thus proved to be subordinated to international policy-cycles. And in the labor migration case, unions—seen by many as most heavily bound to the national constellation—could be portrayed as the most internationalized actor. All that points to politics of denationalization as something specific, quite different from politics as usual. On the other hand, however, in both migration cases, it is traditional domestic interests that drive the responses to denationalized issues. The problems of cryptography produced similar patterns. Those who do not like the status quo, merely employ international arguments to get rid of disliked national regulations. And while business sometimes accepts the need for international regulation as in the climate issue, they always try to get the cheapest deal. In these respects, our cases pretty much look like politics as usual.

The purpose of this concluding chapter is to integrate these findings by systematically comparing the cases with the aim of generating some generalized statements about the politics of denationalization. In order to do so, we compare group reactions with a somewhat stylized picture of politics as usual in advanced capitalist democracies. While it will become apparent there are interesting general trends, there is also considerable variation in the findings. In order to account for these results, we analyse these differences along the dimensions of case, group type, and country. This chapter proceeds as follows: first, drawing on consensual elements of research in comparative politics, we present our conceptualization of what we call politics as usual, outlining the main characteristics of politics in advanced capitalist societies in the twentieth century. We then systematically compare this model with the results from our case studies, making use of a standardized coding procedure. Having established that there are indeed significant differences between our results and politics as usual, we then attempt to summarize and condense our results in such a way as to represent what could be called a model of the politics of denationalization. We then delve deeper into the politics of denationalization and evaluate some hypotheses about its outcomes; in particular, we look at the role of new political divisions, the significance of state intervention, and the relevance of new steering mechanisms.

As mentioned in the introduction, this study followed an abductionist logic. Although it has an hypotheses-generating thrust, the observations are structured by theoretical expectations. On the one hand, we use the politics as usual blueprint in order to highlight the changes that are taking place in descriptive terms. On the other hand, the generation of hypotheses explaining the variation in societal responses to denationalization challenges is guided by a preselected number of independent variables, which were presented and discussed in the introduction and especially in chapter 2. Accordingly, group responses can vary along three dimensions: cases, countries, and groups. For each of these three dimensions, we identify one or two independent variables. The five ensuing independent variables form a pool on which we draw in order to interpret the data. In the concluding section we summarize the findings. We hope to have demonstrated by then that the politics of denationalization looks quite different from politics as usual. It is characterized by a remarkable role for transnational policy-demands and even activities of nationally constituted interest groups beyond the nation-state. Obviously, external constraints play an important role and often set national and international policy cycles into motion. These external constraints do however not structurally predetermine the response patterns, moreover, the external constraints can be changed by coordinated political responses. In addition, there is a still latent triangular cleavage structure that may become typical of the politics of denationalization. Moreover, we show that the Old Right with its preference for deregulation is put into a privileged position in the politics of denationalization. On the other side, the Left has to overcome both the deregulatory default option and disadvantages in organizing itself transnationally. Yet the Right cannot permanently escape its counterforces by moving to the level beyond the nation-state. In fact, the New Left in many respects turns out to be the spearhead of political denationalization. This suggests that political regulation beyond the nation-state can be as market-correcting and as traditional in the employed steering mechanisms as we know it from the national constellation. With the final reflections, we return to the larger picture of the postnational constellation as sketched in the introduction and ask for further avenues of research.

Politics as Usual

In sketching an ideal typical model of politics as usual, we do not intend to provide a comprehensive account of politics in the national constellation. All that is required in the present context is to establish general indicators of national politics that are empirically observable and consistent with the approach used in our case studies. We therefore employ the three basic dimensions that were used to structure group responses (see chapter 2). What does politics as usual look like in terms of intervention (i.e., attitudes to market regulation), spatiality (i.e., attitudes in respect of appropriate levels of governance), and activity (i.e., patterns of group activity)?

Intervention

The issue of government intervention is at the very core of politics as usual. There is significant disagreement among those engaged in the political sphere as to both the degree to which governments should be allowed to intervene in the free play of market forces and as to the most appropriate set of policy instruments this intervention can make use of. The lines of this conflict are shaped by a wide array of factors including national tradition, path dependencies, and favored economic paradigms. In spite of this variation, however, it is class conflict that forms the most important cleavage in this context. The dominance of this cleavage over other national divisions is relatively firmly institutionalized in all advanced capitalist democracies, albeit in different ways.[3] Although more recent times have witnessed the emerging importance of an alternate cleavage—that between libertarians (New Left) and authoritarian traditionalists (New Right)—this new cleavage has merely reinforced the binary nature of the intervention debate. The new emancipatory movements are most often found in support of the Left in relation to distributional issues, and unions and social democratic parties usually join these movements—often, however, with some delay—in relation to emancipatory issues (Kriesi 1999). The relationship between the New Right and established Right is somewhat more complicated, but still does not question the binary Left-Right coding of politics as usual.

By and large, it is fair to say that within national politics, leftist groups tend to demand a high degree of state intervention with clear-cut, hierarchical provisions, while Right-oriented groups tend to regard intervention as introducing inefficiencies into the market and agree to policy instruments only if they are strictly in conformity with market conditions. Generally, Right-oriented groups adopt a preference for strict hierarchical mechanisms only in relation to social deviance, while in such cases, the Left is more liberal.[4]

In the context of our study, it is important to keep in mind that the cases under consideration resemble more the first type of issue than the second. In the case studies presented here, it is market intervention (such as restricting cryptographic products, regulating labor standards and conditions of acceptable CO_2 emissions) which is at stake. Whereas Right-oriented groups may be active on levels beyond the nation-state in creating markets and contexts for free exchange, they can be expected to be less interested in regulating them. The reverse is true for those on the Left. It follows that if our cases reflect politics as usual, we should see differences in opinion in relation to intervention taking on a binary character with Left-oriented groups favoring intervention and Right-oriented groups opposing it.

Spatiality

Intervention may be highly contested within national politics, but spatiality is not. In fact, general consensus on the idea of the nation-state as the appropriate level of governance is one of the defining characteristics of the national constellation. The reason for this lies in the fact that there is ordinarily agreement amongst those involved in the political sphere that it is meaningful to subject transactions (most of which are domestic) to national (or subnational) rule. There is thus little need for governance beyond the nation-state. Whatever the goods to be achieved by policies are, these are delivered by national governments. International politics is—at best—an additional tool used at these governments' discretion to improve the effectiveness of policies at the national level.[5] Politics as usual is thus marked by the fact that—across the board—political groups share a vision of governance according to which the nation-state is the centerpoint of politics.

This should hold all the more for the groups under investigation, as these nationally constituted groups, as we have termed them, were specifically formed in order to influence public policy at the national level—a task they have fulfilled all too well. Indeed, some go so far as seeing the twentieth century as the century of interest groups and this omnipresence has not been welcomed by all. When, for example, the German political scientist Theodor Eschenburg (1955), spoke of the rule of interest groups, it was not with great enthusiasm. Later, a re-evaluation of interest groups took place, with analysts discovering the merits of corporatism (e.g., Lehmbruch and Schmitter 1982) and private interest governments (Streeck and Schmitter 1985). Recent literature on the role of interest groups, however, has not only emphasized their productive role in policy-making, but also the fact that the functional distinction between state and society, and between governments and interest groups, is eroding (Grande 2000). Be that as it may, it remains the defining characteristic of interest groups that they are "organizations separate from, though often in close partnership to government" (Wilson 1990, 3), such as, national government. The whole relationship, therefore, between interest groups and governments is conceived within national confines and function in reference to national policy-making. In this sense, national policies are the central focus of politics as usual.

Activity

The fact that politics as usual mainly revolves around national policies also implies that the national political arena is the main focus of political activity. It is within the national political system that most policy cycles are initiated and maintained. This also implies it is the national government that is responsible for pursuing national interests in the international sphere. Governments have become the exclusive, authorized agents representing national interest groups in the anarchy of the international domain. Hence, if nationally constituted interest groups become affected by international affairs, they are expected to approach their national government to defend their interests in the international arena. In the national constellation, national interest groups are not expected to carry out lobby work at international fora themselves, as this would undermine the exclusivity of national interest representation by national governments.[6] National governments are thus the exclusive targets of all lobbying, even if the source of dissatisfaction is outside the territorial boundaries of the state. The unconditional orientation of interest groups towards national policy-making fora and the national political system, even if the problems at hand are of an international character is thus another feature of politics as usual.

Summary. The typical characteristics of politics as usual can thus be represented by the following: a binary cleavage between Left and Right in relation to state intervention; an overall vision of governance that is clearly anchored to national governments; and a political process unconditionally orientated towards national political systems and national policy fora. Correspondingly, deviations from this model occur to the extent that:

- the binary nature of the intervention conflict becomes blurred;
- notions of governance beyond the nation-state gain prominence;
- the government's monopoly of national interest representation on the international level is challenged even by nationally constituted interest groups.

BEYOND THE USUAL

How do the results of our inquiry sit with these indicators? Does the politics of denationalization show any systematic deviation from politics as usual? In this section we analyse our findings across case, group type, and country to discern possible changes in policy demands and political activity compared to politics as usual. Such an aggregate analysis is made possible by the fact that the case studies use a common analytic framework that yields a relatively high number of points of observation. In order to keep the analysis manageable, however, we significantly simplify the findings of our study. The dependent variable consists of three dimensions, each of which with some subcategories. Thus, whenever possible we reduce the analysis to consider only the broad dimensions of intervention, spatiality, and activity rather than each of their component parts. In addition, we standardize the results into a binary scale, making use of this simplicity to present the dimensions either on their own as single digits or in combination with other dimensions. The results are either presented as single digits (0 or 1) representing a single dimension, or in patterns of two or three representing a correlation between the dimensions (for example, 10 or 101).[7]

Intervention: Blurred lines of conflict and the role of external constraints

As we saw above, one of the features of politics as usual is the dominance of institutionalized forms of class conflict, a conflict which finds political expression in attitudes towards state intervention. Considering the three dimensions of the dependent variable—such as, spatiality, intervention, and activity—the Left-Right cleavage of politics should resonate most strongly with intervention. Typically, those on the Left argue that market outcomes need to be corrected by government intervention, while those on the Right oppose such interference.

At first glance, looking at the combined elements of the intervention dimension,[8] the results of our study appear to reproduce this familiar pattern,[9] with Left and Right strongly split. Across both case and country, almost two thirds of the responses of right-oriented groups reveal a preference for a low degree of intervention and softer steering mechanisms, while two thirds of the responses of Left-oriented groups go the other way.[10] Thus it appears that a group's position in the Left-Right cleavage determines its stand on intervention. As Marianne Beisheim pointed out in the context of the climate cases (chapter 5), for example, business groups start with the assumption that the free market guarantees an efficient and productive economy, while Left-oriented groups take the view that left to themselves, markets give rise to socially undesirable outcomes—such as the decay of the environment. This is more or less a direct reproduction of politics as usual.

The results become more complex, however, once the distinctions between the general and specific groups and between the Old Politics and New Politics groups are taken into consideration. Surprisingly enough, the general-specific split is almost as significant as the Left-Right cleavage. Almost two-thirds of general groups favor higher levels of intervention and traditional steering mechanisms, while only one-third of specific groups take this approach. The illegal content and cryptography case studies demonstrate this pattern most clearly: in both Canada and Germany specific business organizations and specific groups from the Old and New Left were remarkably similar in their preferences while a coalition of general groups (be they Old or New, Left or Right), tended to take a contrasting approach. This squarely contradicts the typicalities of politics as usual; once on the same side of the Left-Right cleavage, normally the positions of groups converge strongly and it hardly matters whether a group is general or specific in its focus on a particular issue.

An additional breakdown according to the Old-New distinction provides further insight. Most groups representing the Old Right behave as we would expect them to; they favor lower levels of intervention and softer steering mechanisms. The specific New Right groups also adopt this approach. General New Right groups, however, tend to go in the opposite direction, resembling the standpoint of the general left groups. In fact, the strongest interventionists are found in the general Left and general New Right camps. At the same time, the specific left groups—whether from New or Old Politics—are rather mixed in their approach, with some groups favoring intervention and others taking the attitude of laissez faire. Thus, apart from the reaction of the Old Right, conflict lines are far more complex than the politics as usual scenario. The New Right is split and general Left groups can not count on the undisputed solidarity of their respective specific group counterparts. Moreover, there is little systematic variance in this pattern between the countries. This also contradicts notions of politics as usual, where we would expect a much stronger demand for governmental intervention to occur in countries with corporatist and thus more interventionist traditions in CMEs (such as Germany) than countries with pluralist and much more liberal traditions in LMEs (such as the United States).

The variance between case studies is more significant. The illegal content, political asylum and resource-transfers case studies more or less resemble the fifty-fifty default that can be expected from an aggregation of all cases.[11] The cryptography case, on the other hand, shows a remarkable concentration of low intervention approaches, while in the immigration and labor standards, and CO_2 reduction case studies, higher levels of intervention and traditional steering mechanisms are more common. The feasibility of certain interventionist measures, therefore, seems also to depend on the particular issues at hand, a factor which is likely to dominate over other sources of variance. This observation can be interpreted as indicating a certain role of external constraints on interventionism in the age of denationalization. By their very nature, some cases seem to make interventionist measures more or less plausible than others.

Indeed, even in those cases where calls for both deregulation and the maintenance of intervention balance each other, the proponents of deregulation rely heavily on the presence of external constraints to justify their position. A good example derives from the Internet content case study, where certain groups adopted the position that what cannot be implemented online cannot be prohibited offline either. This is essentially an argument for liberalizing content control without saying why the liberalization of content control is a good thing as such. Apparently, it is the very nature of the Internet challenge rather than any substantial argument that suggests the liberalization. Similarly, in the context of the asylum case study, no one really questions (with the exception of some extreme rightists) the normative value of asylum as an institution. Many do argue, however, that a change in asylum practices is necessary because the number of asylum seekers and the policies of neighboring states have changed. In general, in most of the case studies, a policy change is called for not because the value of policy goals has been reevaluated, but because the cost and effectiveness of a given national policy has changed as a result of an external challenge. External challenges do exist; they are perceived as such and thus constitute constraints over the political process set in motion to deal with that challenge.

These presence of these international constraints do not, however, necessarily mean that each country reacts in the same way—as was pointed out in chapter 1 in the discussion of the convergence hypothesis. What tends to occur, however, is that deregulation forces become stronger and pressure is placed on the solidarity of the Left. The more difficult it is to maintain higher levels of intervention in the face of the external challenge, the more likely a division within the Left is to take place. Typically, in such a situation, both specific and general New Left groups, together with specific groups from the Old Left, tend to opt for lower levels of intervention, while general Old Left groups stick to traditional notions of interventionism. In other words, the main effect of external constraints is the promotion of internal divisions within, and therefore the weakening of the Left.

In sum, the cases under investigation reveal more variation with regard to intervention across groups than would be expected from a basic application of the convergence hypothesis. The Left-Right cleavage still plays a major role in setting group agendas regarding intervention, but that is not all. Specific Left-oriented groups show signs of questioning traditional Left preferences while general Old Left groups tend to stick to the interventionist approach—with, however, the added support of general New Right groups. If we assume that the specific groups, being closer to the relevant issues, are better informed as to their nature, the external constraint argument receives added support. It appears, moreover, that cases of extreme denationalization tend to compel groups that are typically in favor or interventionism against such a stance. The pattern, which results from this series of interlinked factors, does not exactly indicate a neutralization or reversal of the traditional Left-Right split we are used to in national politics, but nonetheless, it does point to a muddying of the waters.

Spatiality: The New Left as the spearhead of political denationalization

The very questioning of levels of governance outside of the nation-state represents a move beyond the realm of politics as usual. In the national constellation appropriate levels of governance are hardly contested. In the case studies, however, it was often the case that groups adopted responses that brought into question appropriate levels of governance. Indeed, in each of the cases there were examples of groups developing extremely detailed proposals involving a sophisticated interplay between international (re-)regulation and national measures. The climate cases stand out particularly in this respect, with groups from the New Left calling for the establishment of multilevel institutions headed by a supranational body to facilitate implementation, monitoring, and enforcement of a global policy of sustainability. Similarly, in the migration cases, Sabine Dreher has shown that even unions—regarded by many as most closely bound to the nation-state—developed policy demands that were remarkably internationalist in character. Proposals such as these could turn out to be a stepping stone on the way to the realization of multilevel governance.

While the qualitative results show that demand for an international approach to the relevant issue at hand existed in all cases, an aggregate analysis shows significant variation in responses by group type. Thus, it is interest-

Table 6.1. Binary simplified group responses on intervention by different variations of group type, case study, and country

Group	Left	Right	Total
0	14 (34)	21 (64)	35
1	27 (66)	12 (36)	39
Total (max 48)	41 (100)	33 (100)	74

Group	General	Specific	Total
0	14 (35)	21 (62)	35
1	26 (65)	13 (38)	39
total (max 48)	40 (100)	34 (100)	74

Group	NP-L-S	NP-L-G	OP-L-S	OP-L-G	OP-R-G	OP-R-S	NP-R-G	NP-R-S	Total
0	5 (50)	3 (27)	4 (50)	2 (17)	7 (78)	8 (80)	2 (25)	4 (67)	35
1	5 (50)	8 (73)	4 (50)	10 (83)	2 (22)	2 (20)	6 (75)	2 (33)	39
Total (max 12)	10 (100)	11 (100)	8 (100)	12 (100)	9 (100)	10 (100)	8 (100)	6 (100)	74

Case	1: Illegal Content	2: Cryptography	3: Labor Migration	4: Pol Asylum	5: CO_2 Reduction	6: Resource Transfers	Total
0	8 (53)	10 (67)	4 (36)	4 (44)	4 (33)	5 (42)	35
1	7 (47)	5 (33)	7 (64)	5 (56)	8 (67)	7 (58)	39
Total (max 16)	15 (100)	15 (100)	11 (100)	9 (100)	12 (100)	12 (100)	74

Country (and case no.)	DE (1/2)	CA (1/2)	DE (3/4)	US (3/4)	DE (5/6)	GB (5/6)	Total
0	9 (60)	9 (60)	5 (45)	3 (33)	5 (36)	4 (40)	35
1	6 (40)	6 (40)	6 (55)	6 (67)	9 (64)	6 (60)	39
Total (max 16)	15 (100)	15 (100)	11 (100)	9 (100)	14 (100)	10 (100)	74

Figures are presented in absolute numbers representing the number of groups adhering to that position, percentages are provided in brackets. Key: OP = Old Politics, NP = New Politics, L = Left, R = Right, G = general, S = specific, max = theoretical maximum of column totals, where the difference between the theoretical maximum number and the actual column total indicates the number of missing values.

ing to note that overall, the Left-Right cleavage is at least as significant on the (aggregated) dimension of spatiality as it is in relation to intervention.[12] Two thirds of all Left-oriented groups produce spatiality responses with a highly internationalist slant while three quarters of Right-oriented groups go in the opposite direction.[13] This is not so surprising if it is considered that the cases mainly concern a governmental response that is market-correcting (i.e., positive) in nature.[14] As the Right is generally opposed to intervention, it can hardly be expected to champion a reinstitutionalization of intervention on a level above the nation-state. The challenges apparently result in de facto deregulation something the Right prefers while the Left wants to reestablish intervention on the international level. The cases at hand thus strengthen the notion that societal denationalization favors business interests by default.[15]

The response patterns that emerge on the spatiality dimension do not, however, simply replicate those relating to intervention. Thus, on spatiality, neither the Old Left nor the specific Old Right groups show a clear-cut majority for or against policies with an extended spatial reach. In fact, it is the New Left alone that is responsible for the overall position of the Left in the Left-Right split. The Old Left is evenly split over the issue, while the record of the New Left is quite striking. Across all the case studies, it is the New Left that stands out for its engagement with the international sphere and for its political expertise and solid recommendations in this respect. Making up less than a third of the groups under investigation, responses of the New Left accounts for more than half of all demands for policies with a high spatiality aspect: seventeen out of twenty-one New Left responses score highly on this dimension. For the specific groups of the New Left, the ratio is even higher: nine out of ten.

On the other hand, Right-oriented groups show a strong preference for policies with a low spatial implication, with the exception of the specific Old Right groups, who are almost evenly split on the issue. Looking at a spread of the various groups, therefore, we have the New Left taking the lead, the Old Left and specific groups of the Old Right covering the middle ground, followed by general Old Right groups and then the New Right.

Comparing the results across case and country yields surprisingly little systematic variation. There is a slight majority of high spatiality positions in the cryptography case study, while in the political asylum case study, demands with a low spatial implication are slightly more common. Other than these general observations, no other case-based or country-based trend emerges. This finding suggests that while the nature of the issues under question leads to increased demand for policies beyond the nation-state, there is no uniform, direct relationship between challenge and response. The perception of and the response to the challenge depends primarily on the character of each particular group—in other words, each group's motivating interests and ideals. A second point to make is that the national origin of the

Table 6.2. Binary simplified group responses on spatiality by different variations of group type, case study and country

Group	Left	Right	Total
0	13 (33)	21 (75)	34
1	26 (67)	7 (25)	33
Total (max 48)	39 (100)	28 (100)	67

Group	New Left	Old Left	O. Right	N. Right	Total
0	4 (19)	9 (50)	11 (69)	10 (83)	34
1	17 (81)	9 (50)	5 (31)	2 (17)	33
Total (max 24)	21 (100)	18 (100)	16 (100)	12 (100)	67

Group	NP-L-S	NP-L-G	Total
0	1 (10)	3 (27)	34
1	9 (90)	8 (73)	33
Total (max 12)	10 (100)	11 (100)	67

Group	OP-L-S	OP-L-G	OP-R-S	OP-R-G	NP-R-G	NP-R-S	Total
0	3 (50)	6 (50)	5 (56)	6 (86)	6 (75)	4 (100)	34
1	3 (50)	6 (50)	4 (44)	1 (14)	2 (25)	0 (0)	33
Total (max 24)	6 (100)	12 (100)	9 (100)	7 (100)	8 (100)	4 (100)	67

Case	1: Illegal Content	2: Cryptography	3: Labour Migration	4: Pol. Asylum	5: CO_2-Reduction	6: Resource Transfers	Total
0	7 (50)	4 (40)	6 (55)	6 (67)	6 (50)	5 (55)	34
1	7 (50)	6 (60)	5 (45)	3 (33)	6 (50)	6 (45)	33
Total (max 16)	14 (100)	10 (100)	11 (100)	9 (100)	12 (100)	11 (100)	67

Country (and case no.)	DE (1/2)	CA (1/2)	DE (3/4)	US (3/4)	DE (5/6)	GB (5/6)	Total
0	6 (50)	5 (42)	6 (55)	6 (67)	6 (43)	5 (56)	34
1	6 (50)	7 (58)	5 (45)	3 (33)	8 (57)	4 (44)	33
Total (max 16)	12 (100)	12 (100)	11 (100)	9 (100)	14 (100)	9 (100)	67

Figures are presented in absolute numbers representing the number of groups adhering to that position, percentages are provided in brackets. Key: OP = Old Politics, NP = New Politics, L = left, R = right, G = general, S = specific, max = theoretical maximum of column totals, where the difference between the theoretical maximum number and the actual column total indicates the number of missing values.

political group appears to be largely insignificant in predicting how that group might respond to a denationalization challenge. This finding is significant if it will be recalled that in our study Germany was chosen as a country of special focus for its supposedly postnational character (Sørensen 2001). On our results, however, German groups do not really stand out compared to groups in other countries in terms of an international orientation. Nor is there any remarkable difference between countries with LMEs and countries with CMEs in this respect.

To sum up, it is clear that a significant number of groups turn their attention to policies at a level beyond the nation-state. Spatiality, however, remains contested in all countries and in all cases. There is no default connection between a specific challenge and a higher frequency of denational political demands. It appears therefore, that a deviation from politics as usual in the context of this dimension depends largely on the interests and ideals of each particular group. While the New Right is its most obvious opponent, the New Left stands out as the spearhead of the politics of denationalization.[16]

Activity: New Political Opportunity Structures

Politics as usual is national politics. The political process is centerd around the national arena and international activities are more or less the exclusive domain of the state. The results of our study indeed show that the national arena remains dominant in terms of group activity. Almost two-thirds of the groups under consideration acted mainly or exclusively on the national level.[17] From a political science perspective, this implies that theories predicting the end of the nation-state (Guéhenno 1995; Ohmae 1996) may be greatly exaggerated. As long as nationally constituted interest groups remain the primary form of interest representation, our findings indicate that the nation-state will remain a vital political institution for some time to come.

At the same time, while the national system retains its dominance our results show it is no longer the exclusive domain of political action. The denationalization challenges presented here motivated more than a third of groups to engage in a significant amount of activity beyond the nation-state—on either a macroregional or international level. This is all the more relevant given that the groups under consideration are nationally constituted political actors (i.e., their very raison d'être is to influence national public policy). Looking at the results on a case by case basis reveals that patterns of activity beyond the nation-state are strongly affected by the nature of the relevant policy cycle at hand. Thus international activity was rare in the two Internet cases and totally absent in the political asylum case—case studies in which the process of policy making took place on the national level only if at all. By contrast, the labor standards and climate cases evidence an almost 50 per cent rate of international activity, being cases marked by prominent

Table 6.3. Binary simplified group responses for political level of activity by different variations of case study, group type and country

Case	1: Illegal Content	2: Cryptography	3: Labor Migration	4: Pol. Asylum	5: CO2-Reduction	6: Resource Transfers	Total
0	8 (73)	6 (67)	6 (55)	9 (100)	6 (50)	6 (55)	41 (65)
1	3 (27)	3 (33)	5 (45)	0 (00)	6 (50)	5 (45)	22 (35)
Total (max 16)	11 (100)	9 (100)	11 (100)	9 (100)	12 (100)	11 (100)	63 (100)

Group	NP-L-S	NP-L-G	OP-L-S	OP-L-G	OP-R-G	OP-R-S	NP-R-G	NP-R-S	Total
0	4 (40)	7 (78)	4 (67)	4 (40)	6 (75)	6 (60)	7 (100)	3 (100)	41 (65)
1	6 (60)	2 (22)	2 (33)	6 (60)	2 (25)	4 (40)	0 (00)	0 (00)	22 (35)
Total (max 12)	10 (100)	9 (100)	6 (100)	10 (100)	8 (100)	10 (100)	7 (100)	3 (100)	63 (100)

Country (and case no.)	DE (1/2)	CA (1/2)	DE (3/4)	US (3/4)	DE (5/6)	GB (5/6)	Total
0	8 (67)	6 (75)	8 (73)	7 (78)	7 (50)	5 (56)	41 (65)
1	4 (32)	2 (25)	3 (27)	2 (22)	7 (50)	4 (44)	22 (35)
Total (max 16)	12 (100)	8 (100)	11 (100)	9 (100)	14 (100)	9 (100)	63 (100)

Figures are presented in absolute numbers representing the number of groups adhering to that position, percentages are provided in brackets. Key: OP = Old Politics, NP = New Politics, L = left, R = right, G = general, S = specific, max = theoretical maximum of column totals, where the difference between the theoretical maximum number and the actual column totals indicates the number of missing values.

international policy cycles. Thus our results go towards supporting the thesis that group activity is to a large extent dependant on the political opportunity structures that are available (Kriesi et al. 1995; Tarrow 1999). Once policy-making processes have been initiated at levels beyond the nation-state, a significant number of nationally constituted groups no longer rely on their national governments for representation. Rather, they themselves step forward into the international arena. In some cases, national interest groups even operate to initiate policy cycles beyond the nation-state. In these cases, it is not so much the existence of policy cycle, but the nature of the individual challenge, that encourages groups to go international.

Comparing the results across the different countries does not yield any significant variation—this operates to reinforce the relevance of policy cycles by showing that, by and large, the respective proportions of nationally versus internationally active groups are equal within the same cluster of cases. Once more, the variation between countries is small, indicating that with regard to group activities Germany also does not exhibit characteristics of the first postnational state. Moreover, our data presents no indication that the Left is less active on levels beyond the nation-state than the Right. On the contrary, the Left is distinguished in terms of its international activity. In the case of the Old Left this is probably due to long-established transnational institutions and channels of influence, while for the New Left, this seems to be mostly the result of a great deal of political innovation. One significant point that arises out of this finding is that international political processes, at least in terms of participation, are not necessarily biased in favor of business interests, suggesting that new political opportunity structures contain new opportunities for all, not only for business.

Summary

It appears that the question with which this section began can be answered quite unambiguously. Our results indicate a significant departure in group responses from the sketch of politics as usual we introduced above. First, conflicts over the question of state intervention do not follow the simple binary structure of a unified right against a unified left. The primary cleavage structure attending national constellation politics is not simply reproduced in denationalization politics. Second, the concept of political regulation beyond the nation-state has well and truly been accepted even by interest groups that are closely tied to the nation-state. These groups no longer concern themselves exclusively with national policy making; instead, there is increasing demand for political coordination beyond the national level. Third, nationally constituted political groups no longer see themselves as bound to the national political fora. They engage themselves in activities beyond the national arena and are even active in initiating policy cycles at the international level. All in all, it seems fair to say that our model of politics as usual does not adequately capture what is going on at a political level when governance challenges are created as a result of societal denationalization.

AN IDEAL TYPE OF POLITICS OF DENATIONALIZATION

Do these deviations from politics as usual suggest a new pattern of political activity? Do denationalized governance challenges lead to a political process that can be captured by another model, an ideal form of politics of denationalization? To be sure, a process of change hardly lends itself to the construction of an ideal type. At the same time, looking at our results in this way can serve the purpose of bringing to fore a number of interesting observations. In order to inductively derive a model politics of denationalization we move beyond the separate analysis of spatiality, intervention, and activity and look at response patterns, in other words, simultaneous combinations of values for all three dimensions. In doing so, we build on the fact that our binary simplification of the scales keeps the number of possible patterns manageable. If a single binary value is assigned to each of the three dimensions, we arrive at response patterns such as 001 with the first digit representing the combined elements of spatiality, the second representing the combined elements of intervention, and the third representing the three elements of activity.[18]

Using this terminology, how would we expect response patterns to be distributed in the model politics as usual? We have argued above that politics as usual is marked by demands for policies with an exclusively national reach (viz, spatiality), a state intervention conflict structure which is divided by the Left-Right cleavage, and political activity anchored to the national political system. politics as usual should thus be mainly structured by demands for national intervention—advocated by the Left—and national deregulation—championed by the Right. Thus the first digit of the response patterns—representing spatiality—remains 0 for all groups, while the second digit—representing intervention—should vary equally between the Left and Right. The activity dimension (i.e., the last digit), is also expected to vary between groups but with a low (i.e., 0) value being the more common, as international activity cannot at all be expected.[19] In terms of response patterns, therefore, groups from the Left should show 011 or 010 while groups from the Right should feature 001 or 000.

Table 6.4 summarizes, by response pattern and group type, how a single hypothetical case, coded according to the standards of our framework, should look like if it represented the model politics as usual.

In order to derive a model politics of denationalization, we start out with an aggregate summary of our results following the same schematics that was used above for the politics as usual. Table 6.5 summarizes all our results by

Table 6.4. Hypothetical distribution of politics as usual in terms of binary simplified response patterns for a single case measured against group type (percentages provided in brackets).

Group Type	New Left	Old Left	Old Right	New Right
000			3 (75)	3 (75)
001			1 (25)	1 (25)
010	3 (75)	3 (75)		
011	1 (25)	1 (25)		
100				
110				
101				
111				
Total	4 (100)	4 (100)	4 (100)	4 (100)

Table 6.5. Binary simplified response patterns measured against group type (max = theoretical maximum of column totals; difference from actual column totals indicates number of missing values).

Group Type	New Left	Old Left	Old Right	New Right
000	0 (00)	2 (11)	1 (06)	2 (18)
001	1 (05)	0 (00)	8 (50)	0 (00)
010	3 (14)	4 (22)	2 (13)	5 (45)
011	0 (00)	3 (17)	0 (00)	2 (18)
100	1 (05)	0 (00)	1 (06)	1 (09)
110	2 (10)	2 (11)	0 (00)	1 (09)
101	6 (29)	3 (17)	3 (19)	0 (00)
111	8 (38)	4 (22)	1 (06)	0 (00)
Total	21 (100)	18 (100)	16 (100)	11 (100)
(max 24)				

response pattern and group type across all cases and countries. The single digit numbers in the table represent the numbers of groups falling in at that position across all case studies. The numbers in brackets are percentages, while salient figures are highlighted.

It appears that the politics of denationalization is not exactly the opposite of politics as usual but is nonetheless quite different. Thus while the Old Right remains chiefly interested in deregulation, it shows itself to also be willing to actively pursue its interests on the international level (001 and 101). Similarly, the Old Left, while also showing a tendency towards its old paradigm (011 and 010), can also be seen to show a move towards acceptance of strong international institutions on varying levels of intervention (111 and 101). In this respect, the Old Left partly coalesces with the New Left, which shows itself to be strongly focused on international regulation while remaining more or less evenly split over the appropriate level of intervention (111 and 101). At the same time, though the New Right does not exactly merge with the Old Right, it appears to be the group type that sticks most adamantly to national intervention while remaining passive in most cases (010 and 011).

Simplifying and condensing these results, a model politics of denationalization could be represented as follows:

Table 6.6. Ideal typical distribution of "politics of denationalization" according to coded response patterns measured against group type (single numbers represent number of groups at that position; bracketed numbers represent percentages).

Group Type	New Left	Old Left	Old Right	New Right
000				
001			3 (75)	
010		1 (25)		3 (75)
011		1 (25)		1 (25)
100				
110				
101	2 (50)	1 (25)	1 (25)	
111	2 (50)	1 (25)		
Total	4 (100)	4 (100)	4 (100)	4 (100)

Of course, this summary—constructed from our results with an abductionist logic—involves some significant simplifications. Yet, it brings together some interesting features of the results collected by our study and allows us to compare individual case results against a unified model. To effect this comparison, we use vector mathematics to first calculate and then pool deviations between actual group responses on the case level and the model responses in table 6.6.[20] This results in a single number for each case representing the overall deviation of the case from the model. Figure 6.1 depicts these deviations, with the shape of the diagram deriving from the fact that deviations range between a minimum of 0° and a maximum of 90°.

In explaining this figure, the first point to note is that although the politics of denationalization model is derived from an aggregate of all cases, individual cases still differ significantly from the model. In other words, there is considerable variance as between the individual cases and the aggregate.[21] Another point to note is that the hypothetical politics as usual distribution—while not representing the total opposite of the politics of denationalization—is nonetheless significantly removed from it.[22] As can be seen in the diagram, the results indicate remarkable variance as between individual cases and the model. More specifically, the labor migration case comes closest to the ideal type of the politics of denationalization, followed by CO_2 reduction and illegal content. Resource transfers, cryptography, and political asylum are further detached from the politics of denationalization but lie rather close to each other.

Can we account for this variation by the type of denationalization challenge? As was explained in chapter 1, the strength of a denationalization challenge is linked to three factors: whether the challenge involves transborder production as opposed to transborder exchange, whether the issue is global as opposed to merely regional, and whether the challenge causes

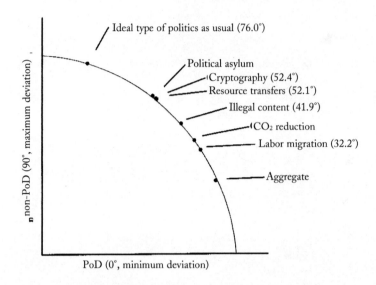

Figure 6.1. Deviation of individual case studies, aggregate results and the ideal type of politics as usual from the ideal type of the politics of denationalization. Deviation angles for summary vectors, corrected for missing data.

externality as opposed to competitiveness problems. Illegal content, CO_2 reduction and resource transfers cases represent a transborder production problem, appear on a truly global scale and cause mainly externality problems.[23] On the other hand, the migration cases represent transborder exchange issues (i.e., of human beings), are largely regional, and are linked in political discussion primarily to national competitiveness problems while the cryptography case, although a transborder production problem, is usually also framed as a competitiveness issue in the OECD setting (i.e., in a regional context). One would expect, therefore, the illegal content, CO_2 reduction and resource transfers cases (cases one, five, and six) to elicit stronger denationalization responses as compared to the migration and cryptography cases (cases two, three, and four).

This ranking matches our findings in terms of proximity to the ideal type of politics of denationalization with one major exception: ranking second, third, and fourth, the three more denationalized challenges (i.e., cases five, one, and six) are indeed closer to the model than cases two and four. This leaves only case three, the immigration and labor standards case, as the exception: how is it that this case, based on a relatively less intense denationalized challenge, ranks first in terms of proximity to the model? Two exceptional features in the case suggest an explanation. First, the New Right almost perfectly conforms to the model of the politics of denationalization in insisting on national intervention which significantly lowers the overall deviation of the case. Second, the New Right is joined in its demands by a group of the New Left. While this squarely contradicts the notion of politics of denationalization, it hardly affects the overall deviation of the case study since this group from the New Left was the only one that could be observed and missing values result in a discount of deviations.[24] In other words: There are features of the case that fit the ideal type rather well while those that do not are discounted due to missing values. It thus appears that the exceptional character of the case study is at least partly explained by data problems. It seems safe to conclude, therefore, that the strength of the denationalization challenge at hand is still useful in explaining proximity to the ideal type of politics of denationalization. Global challenges of the transborder production type resulting in externality problems are particularly likely to show elements of the ideal type of politics of denationalization.

HYPOTHESIZING THE POLITICS OF DENATIONALIZATION

As we have seen, denationalized governance challenges lead to political processes that differ significantly from politics as usual. The responses and response patterns of nationally constituted interest groups to denationalization issues indicate a marked difference from patterns of behavior that we are used to seeing. Indeed, our findings suggest the presence of an ideal-type politics of denationalization which operates quite apart from politics as usual. True it is that none of the cases in this volume perfectly match this ideal type of denationalization politics; they merely approach it to different degrees. Yet, the ideal type may nonetheless be use in describing and explaining policy processes in the postnational constellation. For the remainder of this chapter this is exactly what we aim to investigate. On the basis of our empirical findings, we aim to generate some hypotheses about the politics of denationalization.

Salient Response Patterns and New Cleavages

Salient Response Patterns
Nationally constituted interest groups act in an environment that is structured by political cleavages, formed and institutionalized as a result of a series of historical conflicts over time (Lipset and Rokkan 1967). These conflicts have created distinct and highly durable group identity structures as well as patterns of social conflict, in particular in relation to class. Does the politics of denationalization involve new lines of conflict, new political coalitions? Some see internationalization and globalization as processes that undermine the predominance of the political struggle between the Left and the Right.

On the one hand, there are those who argue that in a denationalized world, opportunities are no longer systematically linked to class.[25] Frieden (1991), for instance, postulates that in world of global finance sectoral conflicts will come to dominate over class conflicts.[26] On the other hand, it is argued that class divisions have shifted, a result of the fact that internationalization has created a new set of winners and losers. Contrary to these hypotheses Marks and Wilson (2000) have pointed out that the cleavage structures remain stable and that, for example in the context of European integration, new issues simply become assimilated into the old structures.

In order to probe these competing hypotheses, we try to identify response patterns that stand out in our findings, on the assumption that these dominant patterns represent basic positions in the sphere of denationalization politics.. As outlined above, the response patterns are a combination of the spatiality, intervention, and activity dimensions according to a binary code. Following the coding procedure we have used, there is a total of $2^3 = 8$ theoretically possible response patterns. Table 6.7 presents the distribution amongst groups of these eight possible response patterns.[27] As it can be seen from the table, almost 60 per cent of responses fall into only three patterns, namely, 010, 101, and 111. These, then, we assume, represent salient response patterns.

Table 6.7. Number of groups falling into each binary coded response pattern

Pattern	Total	
000	5 (08)	
001	9 (14)	
010	**14 (21)**	national intervention
011	5 (08)	
100	3 (05)	
110	5 (08)	
101	**12 (18)**	transnational (de-) regulation
111	**13 (20)**	transnational (re-) regulation
Total (max 96)	66 (100)	

Aggregate results with percentages provided in brackets; max = theoretical maximum of column total, where the difference between the maximum number and the actual column total indicates the number of missing values; bold indicates salient figures.

The first salient response pattern (010) accounts for 21 per cent of all group responses and can be labelled national intervention. It is characterized by the demand for a relatively high level of state regulatory action by means of traditional policy instruments (i.e., a high value on intervention), an exclusive policy focus on the national sphere (a low value on spatiality), and a group activity level which is largely low-key, reactive and directed almost exclusively at the national level (a low value on activity). An example of a group adopting this response pattern would be the German Republikaner Party in response to illegal content on the Interent. The group called for a rigorous ban on violence and pornography in all electronic media, argued against any international treatment of the issue and remained largely passive throughout the debate.

The second salient response patterns, which we call transnational (de-) regulation (101) is more or less an exact opposite of the first. This pattern accounts for 18 percent of group responses and is characterized by the promotion of a low degree of state regulatory activity and/or policy controls that conform to market requirements (low value on intervention), a preference for regulation with a wide spatial scope including a significant role for international institutions (high value on spatiality), and a high level of group activity in all respects, in other words, the group responds early and intensively at all levels (high value on activity). Here, the case study on immigration and labor standards provides a good example. After an initial rejection of any state intervention, the German Old Right groups actively advocated international legislation while insisting on the principles of the Liberalized Common Market for Services. Employers' organizations thus utilized the interplay between the different levels of governance in furtherance of their own interests. The German BDA demonstrated quite openly how they emphasized and adhered to primarily market-making international regulations in order to prevent regulations against the undermining of national social standards.

The last of the three salient patterns represents 20 per cent of group responses and scores high on all three dimensions of the dependent variable (111). We call this pattern transnational reregulation. Groups falling into this pattern demonstrate a strong belief in state regulatory action and traditional policy instruments (high value on intervention), the preference for a wide spatial scope and involvement of international institutions (high value on spatiality), and a high level of activity that goes beyond the national level (high value on activity). The responses of the New Left in both climate cases provide good instances of this type of pattern. In response to the issue of CO_2 emissions the German Green Party, for example, involved itself actively in lobbying and parliamentary work and pressed for international environmental CO_2 agreements with strong reduction targets for CO_2-emissions and backed up by government command and control measures.

Triangular Cleavage Structure?
The relative dominance of these three response patterns, creating what we would term a "triangular cleavage structure," points to the possibility of a new configuration of social forces that may replace the binary Left-Right conflict structure dominating politics in the national sphere. To the extent that this new triangular structure is visible not only at the aggregate level but

Table 6.8. Binary simplified response patterns by case study

Case	1: Illegal Content	2: Cryptography	3: Labor Migration	4: Pol. Asylum	5: CO_2-Reduction	6: Resource Transfers	Total
000	3 (21)	0 (00)	0 (00)	0 (00)	1 (08)	1 (09)	5 (08)
001	1 (07)	1 (11)	1 (09)	1 (11)	**3 (25)**	**2 (18)**	9 (14)
010	**3 (21)**	**2 (22)**	**3 (27)**	**4 (44)**	1 (08)	1 (09)	**14 (21)**
011	0 (00)	0 (00)	2 (18)	1 (11)	1 (08)	1 (09)	5 (08)
100	0 (00)	1 (11)	1 (09)	1 (11)	0 (00)	0 (00)	3 (05)
110	1 (07)	1 (11)	0 (00)	0 (00)	2 (17)	1 (09)	5 (08)
101	**3 (21)**	**4 (44)**	**2 (18)**	**2 (22)**	0 (00)	1 (09)	**12 (18)**
111	**3 (21)**	0 (00)	**2 (18)**	0 (00)	**4 (33)**	**4 (39)**	**13 (20)**
Total (max 16)	14 (100)	9 (100)	11 (100)	9 (100)	12 (100)	11 (100)	66 (100)

The single digits indicate the numbers of groups adopting a particular pattern, percentages for columns provided in brackets; max = theoretical maximum of column total where the difference between the theoretical maximum and the actual column total indicates the number of missing values; bold indicates salient figures.

also in the individual cases is a further indication of the possible applicability of this new structure.

Looking at the individual cases, these three dominant response patterns are clearly present in the illegal content and immigration and labor standards cases (cases 1 and 3)[28]—two cases which are high in proximity to the ideal type of politics of denationalization (compare with Fig. 6.1). In the cryptography and political asylum cases (i.e., cases two and four), the transnational deregulation and national intervention response patterns figure most prominently, indicating a shift towards the international sphere but with the binary interventionism conflict still intact. In the climate cases (cases five and six), transnational reregulation and a national variant of the deregulation pattern (i.e., 001) are numerically dominating. In this latter pattern, policy demands center on the national level, we would suggest, more because of an emphasis on deregulation than on an avoidance of the international sphere per se. In other words, in these cases it appears that groups from the Old Right see high spatiality as leading directly to some kind of intervention and thus resort to 001 rather than 101, suggesting that the 001 pattern becomes the option of choice because the relevant policy cycles are strongly geared towards international institutions in any case. It thus seems safe to assume that the political conflict in these cases is still largely removed from the national sphere.

Nonetheless, what can safely be said is that even though in some cases a binary conflict structure of some sort remains, our results indicate the potential for this new triangular cleavage structure to reveal itself; that is, our results hint at a latent triangular cleavage structure in denationalization politics. Moreover, it seems that the more the case approaches the denationalization model in terms of the overall distribution of group responses, the more clearly the triangular structure stands out. We would thus suggest that the old class conflict is assimilated into the new structure, rather than the other way around, as Gary Marks and his colleagues would suggest. Thus, while this hypothesis obviously needs further testing, we would venture the cautious conclusion that in denationalization politics the binary shape of political conflict is replaced by a latent triangular structure. That is to say, while conflict lines are still too fluid to talk of a newly institutionalized cleavage structure, the triangular potentiality has begun to reveal itself. Whereas we do not support the end of class thesis, our results suggest that political cleavages in the politics of denationalization are less stable and more flowing.

Strange bedfellows?

The question that follows is what types of new factions form in the politics of denationalization with a potential triangular cleavage structure?[29] To begin with, the more or less stable coalitions between the Old and New Left, and between the Old and New Right are not to be found in the politics of denationalization.

As we saw earlier, the New Right shows a clear preference for national regulation, while the Old Right—not surprisingly—is most often found in active
support of deregulation (thirteen out of sixteen Old Right responses feature a
low value on intervention) primarily on the national level (001).[30] In addition,
whereas the Old Left is difficult to pin down in terms of a particular response
pattern, the New Left is actively committed to denationalized policies, but
remains split over the appropriate level of intervention (101 and 111).

Some of the Old Left groups join the New Left in their drive towards
denationalization politics, others, however, remain attached to their traditional focus on national regulation (010 and 011), thus in effect siding with
the New Right. The strange coincidence between the policies of the Old
Left and the New Right is even more apparent once the results in table 6.5
are analysed row-wise instead of column-wise (i.e., by pattern instead of by
group type). The Old Left and New Right together make up for nine of the
fourteen occurrences of national intervention.

Despite the fact that the Old Left is somewhat split in its approach,
however, it is still closest to the New Left when it comes to transnational
reregulation. Out of the thirteen groups responsible for this response pattern, twelve are accounted for by the New and Old Left. Though less surprising than the other coincidences, it is remarkable nonetheless that this
response pattern comes to be common ground for the Old and the New
Left. At the same time, when the New Left does accept some weaker form
of regulation therefore falling into the transnational deregulation programme, they are often joined by groups on the Right. In the Internet cases,
for example, the similar response patterns of the New Left and specific Old
Right groups stood out quite prominently, indicating the presence of some
new coalition-building.

Overall, therefore, it appears that the politics of denationalization has a
modification effect on the alignments typical in politics as usual. In doing so,
it produces some strange bedfellows, most notably the Old Left and New
Right, and the New Left, Old Left and Old Right.[31]

Positive Governance Beyond the nation-state?

That governance beyond the nation-state can overcome the current
deficits of national governance is a notion that has been fairly widely criticized by theories of both international institutions and the democratic
welfare. This critique is based on the claim that the effectiveness of international institutions is highly conditional on prerequisites that are very
unlikely to be met outside of the national context. It is admitted that
international institutions do play a role, but it is argued that this role is
restricted to the creation of markets and the facilitation of free cross-
border exchange. Measures that attempt to regulate this exchange in favor

of workers, consumers, or environmental interests, so the argument continues, are only possible within a hierarchical national structure. In other words, the welfare state is a national institution which is incompatible with the international level. Thus, it is argued that the structural problem with governance beyond the nation-state is that economic efficiency is prioritized while market control and distributive justice are systematically neglected (see e.g., Streeck 1995a, 1995b).

Asymmetric Representation beyond the nation-state?

There are three questions which are often raised in relation to the possibility of effective positive international regulation. The first question concerns the possibility of effective interest representation beyond the nation-state. There is the argument that fast policy-making is hampered at the international level because business groups can, following the logic of collective action, much more easily organise themselves on levels beyond the nation-state than other groups. Subsequently, the superior financial and informational resources of business groups could help them to dominate the policy-making process (see e.g., Offe 1985b). Our data, on the other hand, points away from this supposition. With the exception of the New Right (for whom, in our case studies, international activity is very rare), activity beyond the nation-state is in evidence across all group types.[32] There are two possible reasons for this. First, the EU and other international organizations actively encourage the activities of groups representing a diversity of interests beyond the national level (see e.g., Pollack 1997), and second, it may be that collective action issues do not figure as prominently internationally, having already been overcome in domestic politics (see Jordan 1998).

While it can be shown that denationalization is responsible for a significant proportion of nationally constituted political groups taking action on the international level, it would, however, be inappropriate to conclude that all groups can easily do so. In the context of our study, this becomes visible once the political level of activity is correlated with spatiality.[33]

Overall, there is a positive correlation between spatiality and political level of activity, for example, groups tend to act on their preferred level of governance.[34] This correlation, interestingly however, is weighted significantly in favor of the low spatiality value; in other words, groups who prefer policies on the national level also stick to other aspects of politics as usual, such as, domestic lobbying.[35] By contrast, only little more than half of the responses that rank relatively high on spatiality (11 and 10) are voiced on a level beyond the nation-state (seventeen out of thirty-two). Thus, almost 50 per cent of groups prefer denationalized policies, but leave it to the state to negotiate them on the international level. The state thus retains to some extent its representative function, but is increasingly supplemented in its activities by nationally constituted political groups taking matters into their

Table 6.9. Correlation of binary simplified group responses on spatiality and political level of activity by group type

Group Type	New Left	Old Left	Old Right	New Right	Total
00	3 (16)	3 (20)	9 (56)	8 (80)	23 (38)
01	0 (00)	3 (20)	2 (13)	0 (00)	5 (08)
10	8 (42)	4 (24)	1 (06)	2 (20)	15 (25)
11	8 (42)	5 (33)	4 (25)	0 (00)	17 (28)
Total	19 (100)	15 (100)	16 (100)	10 (100)	60 (100)
(max 24)					

Single digits represent numbers of groups adopting the relevant pattern, percentages for columns provided in brackets, max = theoretical maximum of column totals, where the difference between the theoretical maximum and the actual column total indicates the number of missing values.

own hands at the international level. Analyzing these results by group type allows for a further refinement of the above findings.

As seen above, about 80 per cent of responses from the New Left and about 50 per cent of responses from the Old Left show a preference for relatively high levels of spatiality. These results are visible here as well; in relation to the New Left, sixteen out of nineteen, that is, 84 per cent of responses, show 10 or 11, while in relation to the Old Left these patterns account for nine out of fifteen, or, 57 per cent of responses.[36] Given that there is a tendency for groups to act on their preferred level of governance, one would expect groups from the Left to be more prominent in terms of international activity. Comparing international activity with spatiality, however, reveals an interesting result: only half of the groups from the New Left who call for denationalized policies manage to organize themselves on the international level, while in relation to the Old Left, this is the case for five out of nine responses. On the other hand, if groups from the Old Right call for denationalized policies (which is the exception), four out of five become active on the international level. One can see reflected in these findings, therefore, evidence of the organizational advantage which groups from Old Politics in general, and groups from the Old Right in particular, have.

To conclude, business groups may, on the one hand, indeed be in a privileged position, owing to their superior financial and informational resources, to instrumentalize the interplay of different governance levels for their own purposes. On the other hand, they cannot escape their political opponents by moving beyond the nation-state. The representatives of the new social movements and some unions reveal themselves to be very articulate in demanding multilevel network governance for problem solving in denationalized issue areas, and act to an increasing extent on the international level. What we appear to be witnessing, therefore, is a coevolution of both the role of nationally constituted interest groups and governance beyond the nation-state—a process, however, which implies a larger effort for Left-oriented groups than business groups.

Weak Transnational Re-regulation?

Another question raised in the context of international governance concerns the depth of intervention possible at the international level. Thus there is the argument that regulation on the international level must necessarily, because of difficulties associated with achieving consensus on market-correcting policies, fall short of what we are used to in the national constellation (Scharpf 1999, chaps. 2 and 3). Our data allows us to examine whether such considerations effect group responses. If international institutions are unable to intervene in market exchanges to the same degree as national governments, this should—at least to some extent—be taken into account by interest groups in their views on international regulation. This means that spatiality and the depth of intervention should be negatively correlated; political groups placing their hopes on international institutions to overcome the challenges of denationalization, should—as a rule—propose relatively low levels of intervention. Conversely, groups most comfortable with national solutions should be most likely to demand higher levels of intervention. In terms of our coded result patterns, this should translate into a greater prominence of the 10 and 01 patterns in a correlation of spatiality and depth of intervention. Empirically, however, this is not the case.[37] In the aggregate, positively and negatively correlating patterns are distributed about evenly and further analysis shows that this generally holds in a breakdown by group type and country.

Significant correlations can be observed, however, once the results are broken down by case. Both migration cases as well as the cryptography case do indeed show a clear predominance of negative correlations. In the cryptography case, the 10 pattern, such as, high spatial demands combined with low levels of intervention, stands out particularly clearly, while in the immigration and labor standards case, the 01 pattern, for example, intense national regulation, is dominant. In the political asylum case, moreover, both patterns occur with equal frequency. By contrast, in the illegal content case, the positively correlating patterns are most prominent. This is even more pronounced in the environment cases, where the positively correlating patterns are clearly the most frequent. In other words, in these cases—which together come relatively close to the ideal type of politics of denationalization—groups either call for highly denationalized policies and a high degree of state intervention or the opposite in respect of both dimensions.

It follows—at least on the results of this study—that the politics of denationalization is not necessarily characterized by low levels of intervention. Whereas some cases point to such a relationship, others clearly do not. The variation may again be the result of differences in the underlying type of denationalization challenge. The underlying problems in the illegal content and climate cases are inherently more denationalized in character than the migration challenges. Confronted with a challenge which is highly denationalized, it may be that groups appreciate that calling for a low degree of spatiality coupled with a high degree of intervention is rather meaningless. A single nation-state is relatively helpless in the face of truly denationalized issues. It follows that those who believe in some form of intervention are compelled to reach for international forms of regulation, while those who are opposed to intervention, remain committed to the primacy of the nation-state. In an interesting twist, the hypothesis with which this section began is inverted: the more denationalized the issue at hand, the more likely it is that political demands will not show a zero-sum relationship between spatiality and depth of intervention. This suggests that in the face of issues which are lower on the denationalization scale, some may see national regulation as sufficient, while others use the zero-sum assumption strategically, for exam ple, to disguise resentment against intervention. In the context of highly denationalized problems, a relatively large number of groups appear to be very much aware of the fact that international institutions without teeth will not solve the problems at hand.

Soft Instruments beyond the nation-state?

A further question concerns the mode rather than the level of intervention that is most likely to be effective on the international level. Thus it is argued that governance beyond the nation-state is a prime opportunity to consider new, more lenient steering mechanisms that rely on partnerships with private actors and implementation mechanisms that conform to market require- ments rather than on hierarchical steering controls. The depth of interven- tion may, it is argued, be maintained on the international level, once appropriate methods of intervention are used. According to this line of rea- soning, there is a certain affinity between the level of governance and the methods of intervention employed. Thus while traditional hierarchical steer- ing mechanisms will remain the domain of the nation-state, so the argument goes, on the international level softer modes of intervention will prevail. In conformity with market requirements, instruments geared towards self-regu- lation will increasingly blur the line between the public and private sphere constituting a new form of governing without government ushering in an era of global public policy (Reinicke 1998; Reinicke and Deng 2000). Given that policy outcomes are reflected in group demands, if this argument reflects the nature of what is actually occurring we should again expect a strong negative correlation, or even zero-sum relationship, between spatiality and steering mechanism / locus of governance. Groups who favor regulation close to or at the national level should prefer traditional steering mechanisms while groups who advocate a high degree of political denationalization should prefer softer and less hierarchical instruments.

Indeed, on our results negative correlations are slightly more common than positive correlations.[38] However, the margin is so small that it seems safe to conclude that also the second affinity hypothesis is far from dominat- ing group responses. Moreover, on a breakdown of the results by pattern it appears that groups which favor policies on the international level are also more likely to demand traditional intervention measures (11 vs. 10)—a find- ing quite contrary to the notion of a new form of global public policy.[39] In fact, the choice of policy instruments seems to be hardly contested at all: 75 per cent of all groups investigated show a preference for traditional steering mechanisms.[40] Of more importance are these instruments' appropriate level of application (01 vs. 11), and an analysis by case supports this conclusion: in four out of five cases,[41] the dominance of either negative or positive correla- tion is due to patterns that show no variance with regard to a preference for traditional steering mechanisms. The illegal content case is the only one in

Table 6.10. Correlation of binary simplified group responses on spatiality and depth of intervention by case study in terms of group numbers, percentages provided in brackets while bold indicating salient figures.

Case	1: Illegal content	2: Cryptography	3: Labor Migration	4: Pol. Asylum	5: CO_2-Reduction	6: Resource Transfers	Total
pos. Corr.	**8 (57)**	3 (30)	3 (27)	1 (14)	**9 (90)**	**8 (80)**	32 (52)
neg. corr.	6 (43)	**7 (70)**	**8 (73)**	**6 (86)**	1 (10)	2 (20)	30 (48)
Total (max 16)	14 (100)	10 (100)	11 (100)	7 (100)	10 (100)	10 (100)	62 (100)

Case	1: Illegal content	2: Cryptography	3: Labor Migration	4: Pol. Asylum	5: CO_2-Reduction	6: Resource Transfers	Total
pos. 00	**4 (29)**	2 (20)	1 (09)	1 (14)	**4 (40)**	**3 (30)**	15 (24)
11	**4 (29)**	1 (10)	2 (18)	0 (00)	**5 (50)**	**5 (50)**	17 (27)
neg. 01	3 (21)	2 (20)	**5 (45)**	3 (43)	1 (10)	1 (10)	15 (24)
10	3 (21)	**5 (50)**	3 (27)	3 (43)	0 (00)	1 (10)	15 (24)
Total (max 16)	14 (100)	10 (100)	11 (100)	7 (100)	10 (100)	10 (100)	62 (100)

which spatiality is negatively correlated with regulation type. Here, most groups adopt either traditional instruments on the national level (01) or innovative steering mechanisms on the international level (10).

Why is the illegal content case special in this regard? In answering this question it is helpful to recall the rationale used by groups in stating their policy preferences in the case. Many groups pointed out that a single dissenting state would render ineffective any form of international cooperation—as the source of illegal content would simply migrate to the uncooperative country leaving the content as accessible as before. In the environment cases, by contrast, the relevant problems are considerably mitigated if a significant number of states agree on certain measures. In other words, for interstate cooperation to be successful, the illegal content case requires unanimous consent, something that groups in that case considered rather unlikely. Thus the predominance of a negative spatiality / mode of intervention correlation in the case seems to be a result of the fact that groups seeking to tackle the problem on the international level are forced by practicality into considering new, non-hierarchical steering mechanisms.

In sum, contrary to the above hypothesis, there seems to be no direct link between denationalized problems and innovative methods of intervention. Rather traditional state intervention remains the option of choice for most groups. Nonhierarchical steering mechanisms only enter the picture if traditional methods of (inter-) state cooperation and intervention are considered to be potentially ineffective or unlikely to be applied.

To conclude this section, our results do not indicate any significant correlation between political denationalization and a lower degree or softer forms of intervention. On the contrary, the more denationalized the issue at hand and the more the political process resembles the ideal-type politics of denationalization, the more likely it is that groups which adopt a high spatiality approach will also prefer strongly interventionist measures. Moreover, no matter what the preferred level of governance is, demands for nonhierarchical steering mechanisms are not as widely advocated as more traditional methods of state intervention. Apparently, the former type of measure is only considered if groups come to the conclusion that traditional forms of intervention cannot or will not be implemented on the international level. Finally, while business groups do appear to have organizational advantages on levels beyond the nation-state, Left-oriented groups are nonetheless able to find a voice and become active on levels beyond the nation-state.

SUMMARY AND OUTLOOK

In the introduction to this book, we criticized the race to the bottom debate as a poor structure within which to study the political effects of globalization.

Table 6.11. Correlation of binary simplified group responses on spatiality, steering mechanism and locus of governance by case study. Group numbers, percentages provided in brackets; bold indicates salient figures.

Case	1: Illegal content	2: Crypto-graphy	3: Labor Migration	4: Pol. Asylum	5: CO_2-Reduction	6: Resource Transfers	Total
pos. Corr.	5 (36)	1 (25)	4 (36)	3 (33)	**9 (75)**	**6 (55)**	28 (46)
neg. corr.	**9 (64)**	**3 (75)**	**7 (64)**	**6 (67)**	3 (25)	5 (45)	33 (54)
Total (max 16)	14 (100)	4 (100)	11 (100)	9 (100)	12 (100)	11 (100)	61 (100)

Case	1: Illegal content	2: Crypto-graphy	3: Labor Migration	4: Pol. Asylum	5: CO_2-Reduction	6: Resource Transfers	Total
pos. 00	3 (21)	0 (20)	1 (09)	0 (00)	3 (25)	0 (00)	7 (11)
11	2 (14)	1 (10)	3 (27)	3 (33)	**6 (50)**	**6 (55)**	21 (34)
neg. 01	**4 (29)**	2 (20)	**5 (45)**	**6 (66)**	3 (25)	**5 (45)**	25 (41)
10	**5 (36)**	1 (50)	2 (18)	0 (00)	0 (00)	0 (00)	8 (13)
Total (max 16)	14 (100)	4 (100)	11 (100)	9 (100)	12 (100)	11 (100)	61 (100)

On one side of the debate is the view that globalization leads to a neoliberal convergence of national policies, a position we regard as limited by an overly structuralist line of argumentation: globalization is appropriately conceived as at best a challenge that becomes consequential only to the extent that political systems respond to it. On the other side of the debate is a position that emphasizes the persistence of divergence, an approach we consider also to be limited insofar as it is bound to methodological nationalism: it overlooks the changes that are taking place, because, focused as it is on national policies, it ignores the dependence of such policies on movements in politics beyond the nation-state. Against both these approaches, we studied the responses of nationally constituted interest groups to governance challenges attributed to societal denationalization. Our main findings can be summarized as follows.

External challenges do not translate directly into political outcomes. Nationally constituted interest groups respond to governance challenges even if they are due to international developments. Indeed, most of the groups under investigation responded to the challenges presented with articulately formulated proposals of how the challenge should be met. Some groups even proactively helped to identify the relevant denationalization problem and bring the issue into the political agenda. Some groups, it goes without saying, are more active in this respect than others, with the actions of the New Left, standing out particularly in this regard. In general, the response of a group in the face of a denationalization challenge is a function of that group's particular ideas and interest foci, and to the extent that ideas and interests differ amongst groups, so their political responses differ as well. These differences lead to political struggles creating a context outside of which political outcomes cannot be truly comprehended. In other words, the nature of these outcomes can never be properly understood from a mere appreciation of the problem at hand. Political processes matter just as much as both challenge and outcome.

Our study demonstrates that all types of nationally constituted interest groups, but to varying degrees, have developed notions of governance beyond the nation-state and are active in international policy-making forums. The New Left appears to be leading in this new internationalism or political denationalization, but other groups stand out as well. Business groups, for example, often make use of market-based agreements on the international level in order to avoid intervention on both the national and international fronts. The unions, in addition, while without any clear-cut orientation in aggregate terms, have nonetheless developed, in certain cases, responses that bring into play international regulatory forces. This demand for policies beyond the nation-state, together with the transnational activity that these groups engage in, demonstrate that nationally constituted interest groups are increasingly setting out to work on the international institutional environment, not only in order to provide solutions, but also to change and mitigate the challenges themselves. External challenges can therefore not only be responded to in different ways, they themselves can be transposed and altered. Once, as a result of such efforts, an international policy cycle is initiated, the political opportunity structure changes. The more developed an international policy cycle is, the more nationally constituted groups become active on levels beyond the nation-state. In this sense, interest groups follow political opportunities and authority. Studies that are build on methodological nationalism miss all that. In times of societal denationalization, however, political outcomes cannot be understood without reference to political processes beyond the nation-state.

A mere comparison between the national policies of different countries tends to overlook the most significant changes. The persistence of differences in the national policies of different countries does not mean that societal denationalization creates no constraints on policy-making. The absence of a convergence of national policies does not indicate the absence of constraints. On the contrary, societal denationalization is accompanied by choice constraints; political groups realize these constraints and respond to them. In extreme cases, when constraints persist even after being addressed by international efforts, groups tend to reanalyse their choices and look for second-best solutions. An example of this can be seen in the illegal content case study, where groups ultimately opted for soft transnational steering mechanisms when it was clear that more severe international regulation would most likely be impossible.

Moreover, the new constraints created by societal denationalization work in favor of the Right. Since challenges to the effectiveness of national interventionist policies lead in effect to deregulation—the preferred outcome of the Old Right—the Left is forced into a position where it must struggle for reregulation beyond the nation-state. Because the default outcome privileges the Old Right, they can in most cases lean back and pursue a wait and see approach. At the same time, they can focus their efforts on international market-building institutions, deepening their structural advantage. In this respect, constraints due to societal denationalization are mainly a problem for those who want to correct market outcomes by way of intervention. The more difficult it is to maintain higher levels of intervention, the more a division within the Left can be observed.

These constraints do not, however, directly translate into a neoliberal convergence of national policies. Rather, these constraints trigger new political processes which clearly deviate from politics as usual. Surprisingly, country differences seem to play almost no role in how groups respond. We did not find any significant differences in response patterns of interest groups among countries, be they pluralist or corporatist, CMEs or LMEs, German, or Anglo-Saxon. Instead, differences in political processes seem to be mainly the result of different denationalization challenges. This finding indicates why traditional approaches to comparative politics cannot account for the political processes triggered by the relevant constraints; being bound to methodological nationalism, such studies treat each national political system as independent of each other and seek to compare national policies without reference to the nature of the processes that produce them. The politics of denationalization can only be understood if methodological nationalism is overcome.

The politics of denationalization is a new game, quite different from politics in the national constellation, with new rules and sometimes new teams. Denationalization challenges do not lead to the dissolution, but rather to a reconfiguration, of national politics—to a reinvention of politics (see Beck 1996b).

First, the cleavage structure of politics in the national constellation seems to undergo a change when faced with strongly denationalized issues. Thus, our results indicate that the binary cleavages typical in national politics are replaced by a latent triangular structure in the politics of denationalization. The extent to which this latent structure comes into the open largely depends on the type of challenge: the more denationalized the governance challenge, the more likely is the triangular conflict structure to manifest itself. Thus, the politics of denationalization brings out crosscutting conflict lines which vary significantly from one issue to another. This does not, however, point to the end of institutionalized conflicts through traditional interest groups; the division between the Left and the Right remains crucial and clearly will play an important role for some time to come. At the same time, what is also clear is that the politics of denationalization brings with it the beginning of more complicated structures of political alliance. Crosscutting conflict lines seem to grow, especially along sectoral lines, while the issue-overarching triangular cleavage often does not come into the open.

Second, as mentioned above, the new rules of the politics of denationalization give political groups that favor deregulation a comparative advantage. At the same time, while it is more difficult for the Left to organize itself transnationally our results indicate an increasing tendency for Left-oriented groups to seek to overcome these difficulties. In fact, our cases show that, as a rule, the Left is more active on levels beyond the nation-state than the Right. Indeed, one thing that our study shows clearly is that the New Left has taken a position at the vanguard of political denationalization. It therefore cannot come as a surprise that there is no strong relationship between levels beyond the nation-state on the one hand and weak regulations with soft-steering mechanisms on the other. To the contrary, it is precisely when an issue is strongly denationalized, that groups demand international reregulation and ask for deep interventions with traditional instruments.

What do these findings imply for the development of a postnational constellation? And what stands out as challenges for future research in this area? Our findings are clearly compatible and indeed do support to some extent the notion spelled out in the introduction that in the age of denationalization the dimensions of statehood, which were hitherto closely interwoven within the framework of the nation-state, gradually drift apart. While states are able to maintain and protect their resources even when they are confronted with denationalization challenges, the formulation of policies has shifted to the international level and the process of recognition of legitimate political authority seem to have partially shifted to the transnational level. These developments indicate a movement towards a postnational constellation. National pressure groups have at least partially already adapted to the new constellation. They increasingly think global and act on international levels if it helps them to pursue their interests. Politics in the postnational constellation is not just politics on another level; it is a new game, with new rules and new coalitions.

One important challenge for future research is to account for much more details of this new game. For most of these purposes, it is insufficient to just look at the positions of national interest groups or political parties. While this study has moved forward our understanding in that it departs from mere survey analysis of levels of societal support for European and international institutions and thus may be seen as a second generation endeavor (Marks 2004, 28), future research should also take into account interaction between among national interest groups and between them, transnational NGOs and nation-states. This is to say, third generation research in this area should look more closely on the process of policy-making in order to understand the politics of denationalization. A number of important questions about politics in the postnational constellation can be analyzed in this way. We want to mention only three of the aspects mentioned in the introduction in order to illustrate the argument. First, it would help to grasp the role of the state in the postnational constellation more precisely. Is it true that states are reduced to a territorial form of interest organization, existing side by side with functionally segmented forms of interest organizations? Or are they privileged in that they can structure the interplay between NGOs, national interest groups, and nation-states? A focus on the process of policy-making in the postnational constellation could help to answer these questions. Second, the modes of decision-making and the sources of influence in the postnational constellation need to be studied more closely. What are the modes of decision-making, what creates argumentative influence and what creates bargaining power? In assessing the relative influences of national interest groups and transnational NGOs on postnational policies, questions like these must be answered more conclusively. Third, the postnational polity contains functional differentiation. World politics became a political sphere in which all actors and all states do not have similar functions. But what functions exactly are taken over by which actors and how do they interact with each other?

Studies like this would improve our understanding of politics in the postnational constellation. It would move away the modern study of international institutions from issues of problem solving capacity and effectiveness and raise issues of a postnational polity. It would see the postnational constellation as a new game and would give political scientists the assignment to explore the underlying rules of the games. This is more than just a descriptive exercise. By exploring the rules, there is necessarily an element of shaping them. Moreover, any normative analysis and critique of politics in the postnational constellation, be in on grounds of lacking democracy or on grounds of rising inequality, would definitely benefit from a better understanding of how politics works in the postnational constellation.

TECHNICAL APPENDIX

Mapping group responses

Our case design is structured in such a way that each of the six case studies looks at two countries with a selection of eight groups in each. Due to problems of group selection, however, the maximum of (6 x 2 x 8 =) ninety-six points of observation is not achieved.[42] Still, there is a total of eighty-five group responses that provide the empirical basis for the aggregate analysis. Group responses in the case studies are generally conceptualized as having three dimensions with two to three elements each. This results in a total of seven elements making up the dependent variable.[43] Various scales are used in order to quantify results, enabling a comparison across case and country. For the purposes of this chapter, however, we simplify both the dimensions of the dependent variable and the scales that apply to them. This simplification is carried out in order to reduce the complexity of the analysis.

The scales are standardized to range between 0 and 1 and then collapsed into a binary division in order to maximise the contrast between different responses. For the binary simplification itself, we use a uniform algorithm that transforms all values below or equal to 0.5 into 0 and all values above 0.5 into 1. One thing that has to be kept in mind, however, is that due to our initial coding procedure, the actual number of scale points for each element varies. Thus there are three fixed scales which we use for a number of the different elements (a six-point and two four-point scales) as well as a series of other scales the result of the fact that some elements are coded relatively (see chapter 2), that is, the groups in a specific case and a specific country are ranked. Identical rankings and a varying number of missing values form an additional source of variation with regard to the number of scale points. Table 6.12 illustrates the connection between the results of the binary simplification and scale type.[44]

Table 6.12. Binary simplification of the elements of the dependent variable depending on scale type.

	0 = m.v.							0.5							1
8-point scale (0)	1/8	2/8	3/8		4/8	5/8	6/8		7/8		8/8				
7-point scale (3)	1/7	2/7		3/7	4/7		5/7		6/7		7/7				
6-point scale (18)		1/6	2/6		3/6		4/6		5/6		6/6				
5-point scale (6)			1/5	2/5		3/5		4/5		5/5					
4-point scale (42)			1/4		2/4		3/4		4/4						
3-point scale (4)			1/3			2/3		3/3							
2-point scale (8)					1/2			2/2							
1-point scale (3)								1/1							

Number of actual occurrences of the respective scales given in brackets. The dotted vertical lines represent the scale points that were assigned to 0. The straight vertical lines represent scale points that were assigned to 1. m.v. = missing value.

In addition to binary simplification, we also combine the different elements of the dimensions in order to arrive at a unified value for each particular dimension. In this manner, a single value for spatiality is derived by summarizing its two elements, degree of denationalization and territorial scope. Similarly, the unified intervention value combines depth and mode of intervention, while the activity value summarizes mode, intensity and political level of activity. When the binary value for each of the respective elements is identical, a combination of values is straightforward; where the values for the individual elements are different, however, we follow a decisive factor weighting. Thus, on spatiality the degree of political denationalization is considered to be the decisive factor in the dimension as this element is considered to be closer to the core of spatiality than territorial scope of demands. On intervention, depth of intervention is considered to be the decisive factor, while on activity—with three elements—we use the arithmetic mean of all the elements (rounded off) to provide the unified value.[45] If values are missing for one or more elements, the other element(s) define the overall value for the dimension. The following table gives an overview of how the seven elements are simplified.

Table 6.13. Combination of different elements of group responses

Element	Dimension
Degree of political denationalization	Spatiality
Territorial scope of demands	
Depth of intervention	Intervention[46]
Steering mechanism and mode of governance	
Mode of activity	Activity
Intensity of activity	
Political level of activity	

Overall, this procedure allows us (1) to assign a binary value to each element of a group's response and (2) to assign a binary value to each corresponding dimension of group responses. Taking these single variables one step further, we also look at response patters. Thus, we are not only interested in finding out—for instance—that a given type of group usually demands international cooperation, strictly prohibitive measures or acted on a level beyond the nation-state, we also want to know whether these different aspects of the dependent variable are covariant; in other words, single variables are also seen as part of a larger constellation (see Ragin 2000). This form of analysis is greatly assisted by binary simplification as this significantly reduces the number of combinations of results across different elements of the dependent variable.[47] The patterns may take on the form of simple correlations between two elements and/or dimensions or all three dimensions, combining all elements.

This process of simplification thus produces results with the simple form of 1 or 0,[48] or in the form of patterns such as 10 or even 101—depending on the number of elements or dimensions considered.[49] In most cases, we present the distribution of the results by either group type, case or country.[50]

Calculating deviations from the ideal type of politics of denationalization

In order to compare the distribution of response patterns with the model politics of denationalization (fig. 6.1), we interpret the former for any given group type as a mathematical vector. Any representation of group responses by group type and response pattern (such as the ideal type in table 6.6) thus consists of four eight-dimensional vectors, defined by the frequencies of the patterns in the four columns. Each of the four vectors of the ideal type corresponds to a vector in one of the actual distributions of group responses on the case level. For instance, the distribution of response patterns of the New Left in the model corresponds to the actual distribution of response patterns of the New Left in any given case study. We are then able to calculate the angle between the corresponding vectors using the formula below:

$$\cos(\alpha) = \frac{\sum x_i y_i}{\sqrt{\sum x_i^2 \sum y_i^2}}$$

X denotes the frequency of the response pattern i for a given group type in the ideal type, and y_i the corresponding frequency of the response pattern i in one of the cases; α is the angle between the two vectors.) This procedure results in four angles of deviation per case study[51] (one for each group type) and can be applied to both the aggregate results (using the data in table 6.5) and the model politics as usual (using the data in table 6.5). The results are summarized in table 6.14.

In order to derive a single deviation value for each case we perform another vector operation which simultaneously allows us to correct for missing values. The four deviation angles are construed as angular characteristics of four new vectors. In order to correct for missing values, the length of these four vectors is defined as the number of observation points for each respective group type.[54] For instance, there are three points of observation for the Old Left in the cryptography case study while the distribution of response patterns for this group type deviates from the model distribution by an angle of 69°. The corresponding vector would thus be defined by an angle of 69° and a length of 3. The more points of observation we have for any given group type, the greater the length of the corresponding vector. For each case study, the four deviation vectors of varying length are added to derive a single summary vector, with the result that longer vectors have a stronger influence

Table 6.14. Deviation angles between the ideal typical distribution of response patterns and actual distributions in the cases. Values in degrees, minimum deviation = 0°, maximum deviation = 90°).

	New Left	Old Left	Old Right	New Right
Case Study #1 (Illegal content)	0.0	69.3	43.1	56.8
Case Study #2 (Cryptography)	47.9	69.3	26.6	90.0
Case Study #3 (Labor migration)	90.0	35.3	43.1	8.1
Case Study #4 (Political asylum)	69.3	45.0	90.0	26.6
Case Study #5 (CO_2 reduction)	47.9	54.7	25.8	18.4
Case Study #6 (Resource transfers)	47.9	30.0	31.9	90.0
Aggregate results[52]	22.6	23.2	17.3	24.7
Ideal type of politics as usual[53]	90.0	50.8	72.5	90.0

on the resulting summary vector; that is to say, empirically better founded results have a stronger influence on the overall result. Fig. 6.2 illustrates this procedure for the cryptography case study.

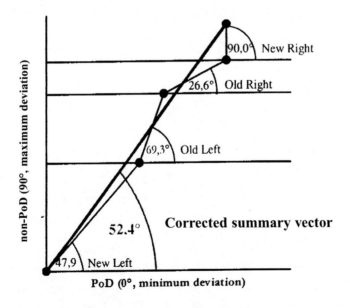

Figure 6.2. Schematics of vector addition, resulting in a single summary deviation vector for the cryptography case study.

Table 6.15. Number of points of observation by group type and case study and corrected summary deviation angles. Absolute values and values in degrees, minimum deviation = 0°, maximum deviation = 90°.

	New Left	Old Left	Old Right	New Right	Corrected summary deviation angles
Case study #1 (Illegal content, max. 4)	4	4	3	3	41,9
Case study #2 (Cryptography, max. 4)	4	2	2	1	52,4
Case study #3 (Labor migration, max. 4)	1	4	3	4	32,2
Case study #4 (Political asylum, max. 4)	4	2	1	3	53,7
Case study #5 (CO_2 reduction, max. 4)	4	3	4	4	35,5
Case study #6 (Resource transfers, max. 4)	4	3	3	4	52,1
Aggregate results (max 24)[55]	21	18	16	19	22,1
Ideal type of politics as usual (max 4)[56]	4	4	4	4	76,0

Ultimately, this procedure results in a single corrected summary deviation vector for each case that gives on overall impression of the deviation of the respective case study by its angle. Table 6.15 presents the number of points of observation used to construct the respective deviation vectors as well as the corrected summary deviation angles that were graphically depicted in Figure 6.1.

NOTES

1. See the growing literature on NGOs, see Princen and Finger (1994), Wapner (1995), Risse et al. (1999) and Hummel (2001). Risse (2001) provides a thorough overview.

2. Politics in Somalia, to take an extreme example, always differed significantly from the model form of politics in the national constellation. Thus, we implicitly follow Sørensen's (2001) distinction between pre-Westfalian, Westfalian and post-Westfalian states and focus on the extent to which politics in post-Westfalian states differs from politics in Westfalian states. Pre-Westfalian states are not considered in the study.

3. In the varieties of capitalism literature, a vast range of different typologies have been suggested in attempting to come to terms with the institutional features of this cleavage. A more recent distinction is that between business-coordinated market economies (CMEs), for example, in much of Northwestern Europe, Japan and Korea, and liberal market economies (LME) as can be seen in the United States and Great Britain (Kitschelt et al. 1999b).

4. Giddens (1995, chap. 1) points out that this deviation from the hands-off approach by the Right indicates a fundamental contradiction in the conservative-liberal project. According to Giddens, the ongoing marketization of society systematically produces values and norms that are incompatible with conservatism thus requiring an increasing need for state interventionism.

5. In political science, this central role of national governments is analytically reflected in what we have called "methodological nationalism." It represents the fundamental the assumption that nation-states are the basic units of all politics.

6. In Germany in the 1970s, signs of an increased foreign policy role of *Länder* (states), interest groups and the opposition were heavily criticized for exactly that reason. This intolerance of about international activity by political organizations other than the national government is an expression of the national constellation. Today however, the role of transnational and sub-national actors on levels beyond the nation-state is increasingly accepted.

7. For the methodological details of the analysis, see the technical appendix.

8. The combination of depth of intervention and steering mechanism can be justified by the fact that there is a clear positive correlation between the two. Almost 70 per cent of all group responses show either high or low values on both elements.

9. For all data on intervention see table 6.1. It presents a summary of group responses on the intervention dimension by group type, case study, and country; in each table, 0 represents the preference for a low degree of intervention and soft steering mechanisms, while 1 represents the preference for a high degree of intervention and traditional forms of government control.

10. In the aggregate (i.e., across Left and Right) the split is almost 50/50. This, however, is partly due to the coding procedure as the dimension intervention combines the elements depth and mode of intervention with the former being coded relatively. Relative coding, however, tends to produce 50/50 splits after binary simplification. See technical appendix, n. 48.

11. See technical appendix, n. 48.

12. The combination of degree of political denationalization and territorial scope is based on a strong positive correlation between the two elements. More than 75 per cent of all group responses show either 11 or 00 after binary simplification of the respective scales.

13. For all data on spatiality see table 6.2. It presents our simplified results on the spatiality dimension. In each table, 0 represents a preference for policies with a low spatiality reach, while 1 represents a preference for policies marked by an extended spatial scope.

14. Positive international regulation obliges states to actively undertake certain activities and intervene in markets in line with a coordinated strategy, whereas negative international regulation contains an agreement that states refrain from certain activities. This distinction goes back to Tinbergen (1965), who distinguishes between positive and negative economic integration and Pinder (1968), who applied it to European integration. Here, we utilize this conceptual distinction in a regulatory sense, maintaining that integration processes, as well as international regimes, may contain both positive and negative aspects. See Corbey (1995, 263) for a recent employment of this distinction that is very similar to its use here.

15. This finding is very strongly supported by a finding of a project on the attitude of political parties toward European integration headed by Gary Marks and Marco Steenbergen. In the introductory chapter Marks (2003, 2) writes: "In the 1980s, European integration was essentially a market-making project, favored by the Right, less so by the Left. By the turn of the century, the situation was reversed as Left-leaning policies, such as environmental policy, social policy, and employment policy came on the agenda."

16. This again is replicated by the Marks-Steenbergen study about party positions on European integration (see Marks 2003, 13).

17. For all data on the political level of activity see table 6.3. In this table, 0 represents purely national activity or mainly national activity, while 1 refers to significant macroregional or international activity. For the results on the total aggregate see the last column.

18. 001 would thus represent a group that opts for low levels of political denationalization, favors low intensity regulation and/or nonhierarchical steering mecha-

nisms but is high on the activity scale—that is, it engaged itself in the issue early on in the policy cycle, was intensely active during debate and/or involved itself in the international arena.

19. In the following table, this expectation is quantified by assuming a 3:1 ratio in favor of 0 over 1 for the last digit.

20. For the mathematical detail of these calculations, see the technical appendix.

21. It is important to note that the aggregate does not represent an average of the cases. It is simply a summary representation of all results on the case level and thus is not determined in its deviation relative to the individual cases.

22. In interpreting table 6.7, it should be kept in mind that deviations from the politics of denationalization model do not necessarily imply any proximity to politics as usual. The two models do not lie on the same scale. Due to the multidimensionality of the information underlying the model, deviations from politics of denationalization can exist in numerous forms (see technical appendix for the mathematical detail).

23. The regulation of climate change may be hindered by problems of economic competitiveness, but at its core, it is mainly an externality problem.

24. According to our methodological procedures empirically, poorly grounded results on the group type level affected overall deviations to a lesser degree. For details see the technical appendix.

25. See Esping-Anderson (1999) for a good survey and a critical discussion.

26. In opposition to the factoral models based on the classic theories of Heckscher-Ohlin and Stolper-Samuelson, Frieden's approach assumes that production factors are specific to particular economic sectors and that thus policy preferences reflect the competitiveness of individual sectors rather than the scarcity of factors. See also Iverson (1999) and Schwartz (2001).

27. Please note that only complete patterns were considered in this analysis. If a value for one of the dimensions was missing, the whole pattern was excluded from the investigation (the number of missing values is thus highest for this type of data analysis as opposed to the single or double dimensional patterns used elsewhere in this chapter). Also important to note is that an equal distribution of response patterns between groups would result in a 12.5 per cent hit rate for each response pattern.

28. For individual case results see table 6.10.

29. For all results on the group level compare with table 6.6 above.

30. In interpreting these results, it has to be kept in mind that we are dealing with positive rather than negative regulation. In a market creation rather than market correction context the Old Right could be expected to tend to the 101 pattern.

31. A compatible finding from the Marks and Steenbergen project can be reported in this regard as well. They find between Left / Right position and European integration an inverted U-curve relationship. This describes support for European

integration among centrist parties and opposition among parties towards the extremes of both Left and Right, dependent upon the issues at stake (Marks 2003, 5).

32. This finding replicates the results of similar studies carried out in the context of the European Union. For instance, Alasdair Young (1998, 149) demonstrates that "consumer groups are among the better resourced organisations in Brussels."

33. For all data on the relationship between spatiality and political level of activity see table 6.9; for aggregate results see the last column. The first digit represents spatiality, the second political level of activity.

34. 23 + 17 = 40 out of 60 responses (i.e., two-thirds) show either 00 or 11.

35. There are twenty-eight cases with a low spatiality value (00 and 01); twenty-three of these are 00.

36. The slight differences in these results compared to those presented are due to the varying number of missing values; see n. 49.

37. For all data on the relationship between spatiality and depth of intervention, see table 6.11; for aggregate results see the respective last columns.

38. For all data on the relationship between spatiality and steering mechanism / locus of governance see table 6.12; for aggregate results see the respective last columns. The first digit is for spatiality, the second for steering mechanism / locus of governance; in respect of the steering mechanism / locus of governance value, 0 represents new steering mechanisms and 1 represents hierarchical control mechanisms.

39. Despite its low score, it is interesting to take a closer look at the groups that opt for the 10 pattern, in other words, those groups that call for the application of innovative steering instruments on the international level. Although theorists such as Reinicke (1998, 228) have emphasized the special role of the global corporate community in taking on public policy functions our results indicate no single group type for which the 10 pattern is more prevalent. Right-oriented groups do favor negatively correlating patterns, but the 01 pattern (i.e., traditional national intervention) is much more common than the 10 pattern (fourteen versus four occurrences). Among those groups who do adopt the 10 pattern, it is the specific groups from the Old Right and New Left that are most prominent; they account for five out of eight instances of the pattern. Thus it would seem that it is the specialized groups on both sides of the Left / Right, Old / New cleavage that are most likely to take on the global public policy idea.

40. This implies that traditional steering mechanisms are considered most appropriate on the national level as well, and in fact, such an attitude is exhibited by twenty-five of the thirty-two groups indicating a preference for low spatiality levels (i.e., 00 and 01). Apparently, denationalization does not lead to an increased tendency towards societal self-regulation on the national level. (See in this context research carried out by the Max Planck Institute for Societal Research in Cologne; e.g., the contributions in Mayntz and Scharpf 1995).

41. The number of missing values in the cryptography case study is so high (twelve out of sixteen) that we prefer to exclude it from the analysis.

42. It should be noted that missing values due to group selection are not equally distributed across the types of groups under consideration. Groups are missing only from the New Right—most particularly issue-specific New Right groups—in the climate cases (i.e., in chapter 5). These considerations have to be kept in mind when interpreting the conclusions.

43. Social inclusiveness forms an eighth element, but as this element is particular to the migration case studies (i.e., chapter 4) it can not be used in a comparison across all cases.

44. In the original scales 0 was only assigned to missing values. Zero thus lies outside the unsimplified scales. A further point to be noted is that the procedure described above implies a bias towards 1 for all scales with an uneven number of scale points. In the case of the seven-point scale, for example, the upper four-scale points are transformed into 1 whereas only the lower three are assigned to zero. There is, however, no unbiased way to simplify scales with an uneven number of scale points in a binary manner, as the middle-point always has to be forced in one direction. The problem is most severe in case of the single-point scale. It occurs when all groups under consideration are ranked equally. Uneven scales in general and one-point scales in particular are empirically relatively rare, however, limiting the coding error. Out of eighty-four scales (i.e., six cases, two countries each in respect of seven elements), only sixteen have an uneven number of scale points and only three are one-point scales. To further reduce coding error, the single point scales are checked individually in a qualitative manner. We check whether a 1 classification can be justified for the respective element on substantive grounds. Thus in relation to two one-point scales, the result is manually remapped to zero because it is apparent that a 0 classification is more appropriate. The remapping effects four group responses, all of them in the United States in the political asylum case.

45. The procedure used for rounding off is the same that is used for binary simplification of the standardized 0–1 scales, i.e., all values below or equal to 0.5 are assigned to 0, all others to 1.

46. Social Inclusiveness, a further element of intervention, could not be incorporated into cross-case comparisons since it was special to the migration cases.

47. It has to be kept in mind that the number of possible response patterns increases exponentially with the number of scale points for each element in the pattern. For example, assuming that the number of scale points is identical for each element, the total number of possible patterns is given by xy, with x standing for the number of scale points and y representing the number of elements. Our original seven elements coupled with an average number of scale points of about five would thus result in the fantastic number of $5^7 = 78125$ possible response patterns.

48. In interpreting the results, it should to be kept in mind that the coding procedure leads to a 50/50 split in the distribution of 1 and 0 in the case of relative scales with an even number of scale points. If an even number of groups is ranked and the resulting ordinal scale is then split into two, the number of groups recording 0 will be the same as the number of groups recording 1. (Exceptions occur only when groups are ranked equally.) Rankings are constructed in a case and country specific manner

(building on the assumption that a comparison between responses is most meaningful within one policy-cycle; see chapter 2). A bias towards a 50/50 split thus occurs only in aggregations on the case or country level, whereas group type aggregations are not affected. Therefore, it should be considered that (a) total aggregates and (b) country and case-specific aggregate results that cover relatively coded data (e.g., spatiality) are most interesting to the extent that they deviate from the 50/50 default.

49. It should be noted that the number of missing values is not constant across these different forms: this number increases with the complexity of the response pattern considered. This is because, for a pattern such as 101 to be constructed, values for all three dimensions have to be present. By contrast, for a one-digit result data on one of the dimensions suffices. As it turns out, in the complex three-dimensional patterns, missing data occurs most frequently in relation to groups from Old Politics, the general groups in particular, and general-Right groups specifically. This is somewhat counter-intuitive as old, Right, and general can be assumed to be factors that should increase the resources available to the group. We would thus expect such groups to be more likely than others to have had the opportunity to form opinions on the issues and make their voices heard. Apparently, resources alone do not adequately predict the likelihood of significant activity in the cases under investigation.

50. In the presentation of results missing values are generally excluded from the analysis. The percentages given thus do not include missing values.

51. Since we are dealing with positive values only (all frequencies are necessarily positive), the above formula implies that the maximum angle of deviation can not exceed 90°.

52. This represents the deviation between the aggregate results reported in table 6.6 and the ideal type of the politics of denationalization (see fig. 6.1).

53. This represents the deviation between the hypothetical politics as usual model depicted in table 6.5 and the ideal type of the politics of denationalization (see fig. 6.1).

54. It should be noted that the number of points of observation is reduced by (a) missing values due to group selection (see n. 42) and (b) missing values due to missing data (i.e., responses were too vague to construct a pattern). For conceptual reasons, in defining the length of the deviation vectors, the maximum number of points of observation (4) was only reduced by the number of missing values due to missing data. If a group could not be meaningfully selected, then the remaining groups of that type constitute an accurate representation of all groups of that type. Errors in group selection thus necessarily imply deviations from the model as the model implies an ideal group selection. Deviations are also a test for the plausibility of our group selection procedures (see chapter 2).

55. This represents the deviation between the aggregate results reported in table 6.6 and the ideal type of the politics of denationalization (see fig. 6.1).

56. This represents the deviation between the hypothetical politics as usual model depicted in table 6.5 and the ideal type of the politics of denationalization (see fig. 6.1).

Bibliography

Abromeit, Heidrun. 1993. *Interessenvermittlung zwischen Konkurrenz und Konkordanz. Studienbuch zur Vergleichenden Lehre politischer Systeme.* Opladen: Leske and Budrich.

Aggarwal, Vinod K. 1985. *Liberal Protectionism. The International Politics of Organized Textile Trade.* Berkeley: University of California Press.

Albert, Mathias, and Lothar Brock. 2000. "Debordering the World of States: New Spaces in International Relations." In *Civilizing World Politics: Society and Community Beyond the State*, edited by Mathias Albert, Lothar Brock, and Klaus Dieter Wolf, 19–44. Lanham, MD: Rowman & Littlefield.

Albrow, Martin. 1996. *The Global Age: State and Society Beyond Modernity.* Cambridge, MA: Polity Press.

Aldrich, John, Claire Kramer, Peter Lange, Renan Levine, John Ratcliff, Laura Stephenson, and Elisabeth Zachmeister. 1999. "Racing the Titanic: Globalisation, Insecurity and American Democracy." Paper presented at the Conference of the American Political Science Association, Atlanta, GA, September, 2–5.

Altvater, Elmar, and Birgit Mahnkopf. 1996. *Grenzen der Globalisierung: Ökonomie, Ökologie und Politik in der Weltgesellschaft.* Münster: Westfälisches Dampfboot.

Appadurai, Arjun. 1996. *Modernity at Large: Cultural Dimensions of Globalization.* Minneapolis: University of Minnesota Press.

Aspinwall, Mark, and Justin Greenwood. 1998. "Conceptualising Collective Action in the European Union. An Introduction." In *Collective Action in the European Union: Interests and the New Politics of Associability*, edited by Justin Greenwood and Mark Aspinwall, pp. 1–30. London: Routledge.

Barro, Robert J. 1996. *Getting It Right: Markets and Choices in a Free Society.* Cambridge, MA: MIT Press.

Baumann, Zygmunt. 1998. *Globalization: The Human Consequences.* Cambridge, MA: Polity Press.

Beck, Ulrich. 1996a. "Das Zeitalter der Nebenfolgen und die Politisierung der Moderne." In *Reflexive Modernisierung: Eine Kontroverse*, edited by Ulrich Beck, Anthony Giddens, and Scott Lash, 19–112. Frankfurt am Main: Suhrkamp.

———. 1996b. *The Reinvention of Politics: Rethinking Modernity in the Global Social Order.* Cambridge, MA: Polity Press.

———. 1997. *Was ist Globalisierung?* Frankfurt am Main: Suhrkamp.

Beck, Ulrich, ed. 1998. *Perspektiven der Weltgesellschaft.* Frankfurt am Main: Suhrkamp.

———. 2003. *Macht und Gegenmacht im globalen Zeitalter: neue weltpolitische Ökonomie.* Frankfurt am Main: Suhrkamp.

Beisheim, Marianne, Sabine Dreher, Gregor Walter, Bernhard Zangl, and Michael Zürn. 1999. *Im Zeitalter der Globalisierung? Thesen und Daten zur gesellschaftlichen und politischen Denationalisierung.* Baden-Baden: Nomos.

Beisheim, Marianne, and Gregor Walter. 1997. "Globalisierung— Kinderkrankheiten eines Konzeptes." *Zeitschrift für Internationale Beziehungen* 4, no. 1: 153–80.

Beisheim, Marianne, and Michael Zürn. 1999. "Transnationale Nicht-Regierungsorganisationen: Eine Antwort auf die Globalisierung?" In *Neue Soziale Bewegungen—Impulse, Bilanzen und Perspektiven*, edited by Ansgar Klein, Hans-Josef Legrand, and Thomas Leif, 306–19. Opladen: Westdeutscher Verlag.

Beisheim, Marianne. 2001. "Demokratisierung einer klimapolitischen Global Governance durch NGOs? Chancen und Probleme der 'Legitimationsressource NGO.'" In *NGOs als Legitimationsressource. Zivilgesellschaftliche Partizipations- und Handlungsformen im Globalisierungsprozess*, edited by Achim Brunnergräber, Ansgar Klein, and Heike Walk. 415–36. Opladen: Leske and Budrich.

Berking, Helmuth. 1998. "'Global Flows and Local Cultures': Über die Rekonfiguration sozialer Räume im Globalisierungsprozeß." *Berliner Journal für Soziologie* 8, no. 3: 381–92.

Bernauer, Thomas. 2000. *Staaten im Weltmarkt: Zur Handlungsfähigkeit von Staaten trotz wirtschaftlicher Globalisierung.* Opladen: Leske and Budrich.

Betz, Hans-Georg. 1993. "Krise oder Wandel? Zur Zukunft der Politik in der postindustriellen Moderne." *Aus Politik und Zeitgeschichte* B11/93: 3–13.

——. 1994. *Radical Right-Wing Populism in Western Europe*. New York: St. Martin's Press.

Bowles, Paul, and Barnet Wagman. 1997. "Globalisation and the Welfare State: Four Hypotheses and Some Empirical Evidence." Paper presented at the 38th Annual Convention of the International Studies Association, Toronto, March 18–22.

Breitmeier, Helmut. 1997. "International Organizations and Global Environmental Governance." In *Global Governance: Drawing Insights from the Environmental Experience*, edited by Oran R. Young, 83–107. Cambridge: Cambridge University Press.

Breuilly, John. 1994. *Nationalism and the State*. 2nd ed. Chicago: University of Chicago Press.

Brühl, Tanja, Tobias Debiel, Brigitte Hamm, Hartwig Hummel, and Jens Martens, eds. 2001. *Die Privatisierung der Weltpolitik. Entstaatlichung und Kommerzialisierung im Globalisierungsprozess*. Bonn: Dietz.

Busch, Andreas, and Thomas Plümper, eds. 1999. *Nationaler Staat und internationale Wirtschaft. Anmerkungen zum Thema Globalisierung*. Baden-Baden: Nomos.

Butt Philip, Alan. 1994. "European Union Immigration Policy: Phantom, Fantasy or Fact?" In *The Politics of Immigration in Western Europe*, edited by Martin Baldwin-Edwards, and Martin A. Schain, 168–92. London: Cass.

Buzan, Barry, Charles Jones, and Richard Little. 1993. *The Logic of Anarchy: Neorealism to Structural Realism*. New York: Columbia University Press.

Castles, Stephen, and Mark J. Miller. 1998. *The Age of Migration. International Population Movements in the Modern World*. 2nd ed. London: Macmillan.

Cerny, Philip G. 1995. "Globalization and the Changing Logic of Collective Action." *International Organization* 47, no. 2: 175–205.

——. 1996. "International Finance and the Erosion of State Policy Capacity." In *Globalization and Public Policy*, edited by Philip Gummett, 83-104. Cheltenham: Edward Elgar.

Chasek, Pamela, and David Downie. 1996. "European Union Views on International Greenhouse Gas Emissions Trading." Environmental Policy Studies Working Paper 3, School of International and Public Affairs, Columbia University.

Clark, Ann Marie, Elisabeth J. Friedman, and Kathryn Hochstetler. 1998. "The Sovereign Limits of Global Civil Society: A Comparison of NGO Participation in UN World Conferences on the Environment, Human Rights, and Woman." *World Politics* 51, no. 1: 1–35.

Clinton, William J. 1994. *Accepting the Immigration Challenge: The President's Report on Immigration.* Washington, DC: U.S. Government Printing Office.

Cooper, Richard. 1986. *Economic Policy in an Interdependent World.* Cambridge, MA: Massachusetts Institutite of Technology Press.

Copeland, Emily A. 1997. "Industrialized States Responses to Emerging Refugee Flows: Industrialized Actions, Coordinated Responses." Presented at the 38th Annual Convention of the International Studies Association, Toronto, March 18–22.

Corbey, Dorette. 1995. "Dialectical Functionalism: Stagnation as a Booster of European Integration." *International Organization* 49, no. 2: 253–84.

Della Porta, Donatella, Hannspeter Kriesi, and Dieter Rucht, eds. 1999. *Social Movements in a Globalizing World.* London: Macmillan.

Deutsch, Karl W. 1969. *Nationalism and Its Alternatives.* New York: Random House.

Deutsch, Karl W., and Alexander Eckstein. 1961. "National Industrialisation and the Declining Share of the International Economic Sector 1890–1959." *World Politics* 13, no. 2: 267–72.

de Swaan, Abram. 1994. *Social Policy Beyond Borders: The Social Question in Transnational Perspective.* Amsterdam: Amsterdam University Press.

Dickerson, Kitty G. 1991. *Textiles and Apparel in the International Economy.* New York: Macmillan.

Diffie, Whitfield, and Martin E. Hellman. 1976. "New directions in cryptography." Institute of Electrical and Electronic Engineers (IEEE), *Transactions on Information Theory* 22: 644–54.

Dreher, Sabine. 2001. "Neoliberalism and Migration: An Inquiry into the Politics of Globalization from a Neo-Gramscian Perspective." Dissertation, University of Bremen.

Eckstein, Harry. 1975. "Case Study and Theory in Political Science." In *Handbook of Political Science*, edited by Fred I. Greenstein, and Nelson W. Polsby, 79–138. Reading, MA: Addison-Wesley.

Eichhorst, Werner. 1998. "Europäische Sozialpolitik zwischen nationaler und supranationaler Regulierung: Die Entsendung von Arbeitnehmern im Rahmen der Dienstleistungsfreiheit innerhalb der Europäischen Union." Dissertation, Universität Konstanz.

Eising, Rainer. 2000. "Assoziative Demokratie in der Europäischen Union?" *Polis* 47/2000, Fernuniversität Hagen.

Eising, Rainer, and Beate Kohler-Koch. 1999. "Governance in the European Union: A Comparative Assessment." In *The Transformation of Governance in the European Union,* edited by Beate Kohler-Koch, and Rainer Eising, 266–84. London: Routledge.

Elkins, David J. 1995. *Beyond Sovereignty: Territory and Political Economy in the Twenty-First Century*. Toronto: University of Toronto Press.

Eschenburg, Theodor. 1955. *Herrschaft der Verbände?* Stuttgart: Deutsche Verlagsanstalt.

Esping-Andersen, Gøsta. 1999. "Politics Without Class? Postindustrial Cleavages in Europe and America." In *Continuity and Change in Contemporary Capitalism*, edited by Herbert Kitschelt, Peter Lange, Gary Marks, and John D. Stephens, 293–316. Cambridge: Cambridge University Press.

Faist, Thomas. 1995. *Social Citizenship for Whom? Young Turks in Germany and Mexican Americans in the United States*. Avebury: Aldershot.

Faist, Thomas, Klaus Sieveking, Uwe Reim, and Stefan Sandbrink. 1998. *Ausland im Inland. Die Beschäftigung von Werksvertragsarbeitnehmern in der Bundesrepublik Deutschland*. Baden-Baden: Nomos.

Fernández Kelly, Patricia M. 1989. "International Development and Industrial Restructuring: The Case of Garment and Electronics Industries in Southern California." In *Instability and Change in the World Economy*, edited by Arthur MacEwan, and William K. Tabb, 147–65. New York: Monthly Review Press.

Flora, Peter. 2000. "Einführung und Interpretation." In *Staat, Nation und Demokratie in Europa: Die Theorie Stein Rokkans aus seinen gesammelten Werken rekonstruiert und eingeleitet von Peter Flora*, edited by Peter Flora, 14–119. Frankfurt am Main: Suhrkamp.

Fragomen, Austin T. 1997. "The Illegal Immigration Reform and Immigrant Responsibility Act of 1996: An Overview." *International Migration Review* 31, no. 2: 438–60.

Franck, Thomas M. 1992. "The Emerging Right to Democratic Governance." *American Journal of International Law* 86, no. 1: 46–91.

Frankel, Jeffrey A. 1993. *On Exchange Rates*. Cambridge, MA: Massachusetts Institute of Technology Press.

Frieden, Jeffry A. 1991. "Invested Interest: the Politics of National Policies in the World of Global Finance." *International Organization* 45, no. 4: 425–51.

Frieden, Jeffry A., and Ronald Rogowski. 1996. "The Impact of the International Economy on National Policies: An Analytical Overview." In *Internationalisation and Domestic Politics*, edited by Robert O. Keohane, and Helen V. Milner, 25–47. Cambridge: Cambridge University Press.

Frost, Mervyn. 1998. "Migrants, Civil Society and Sovereign States: Investigating an Ethical Hierarchy." *Political Studies* XLVI: 871–85.

GAO: see United States General Accounting Office.

Garrett, Geoffrey. 1998a. *Partisan Politics in the Global Economy*. Cambridge: Cambridge University Press.

————. 1998b. "Global Markets and National Politics: Collision Course or Virtuous Circle?" *International Organization* 52, no. 4: 787–824.

George, Alexander L. 1979. "Case Studies and Theory Development: The Method of Structured, Focused Comparison." In *Diplomacy: New Approaches in History, Theory and Policy*, edited by Paul Gordon Lauren, 43–68. New York: Free Press.

Giddens, Anthony. 1990. *The Consequences of Modernity*. Stanford, CA: Stanford University Press.

————. 1995. *Beyond Left and Right: The Future of Radical Politics*. Cambridge, MA: Polity Press.

Gill, Stephen. 1993. "Gramsci and Global Politics: Towards a Post-Hegemonic Research Agenda." In *Gramsci, Historical Materialism and International Relations*, edited by Stephen Gill. pp. 7–18. Cambridge: Cambridge University Press.

Gilpin, Robert. 1981. *War and Change in World Politics*. Cambridge: Cambridge University Press.

Glasmeier, Amy, Jeffery W. Thompson, and Amy J. Kays. 1993. "The Geography of Trade Policy: Trade Regimes and Location Decisions in the Textile and Apparel Complex." *Transactions* (Institute of British Geographers) 18: 19–35.

Godwin, Mike. 1995. "The Shoddy Journalism." Hotwired, Special Report. http://hotwired.lycos.com/special/pornscare/godwin.html (accessed 12/14/1998).

Goldmann, Kjell. 2001. *Transforming the European Nation-State: Dynamics of Internationalization*. London: Sage.

Goldstein, Judith, and Robert O. Keohane, 1993. "Ideas and Foreign Policy. An Analytical Framework." In *Ideas and Foreign Policy. Beliefs, Institutions, and Political Change*, edited by Judith Goldstein, and Robert O. Keohane, 3–30. Ithaca, NY: Cornell University Press.

Gorenburg, Dmitry. 2000. "Not with One Voice: an Explanation of Intragroup Variation in Nationalist Sentiment." *World Politics* 53, no. 1: 115–42.

Grande, Edgar. 1994. "Vom Nationalstaat zur europäischen Politikver-flechtung: Expansion und Transformation moderner Staatlichkeit—untersucht am Beispiel der Forschungs–und Technologiepolitik." Habilitationsschrift (Professoral Thesis), Universität Konstanz.

Grande, Edgar. 2000. "Verbände und Verbändeforschung in Deutschland." In *Unternehmerverbände und Staat in Deutschland*, edited by Werner Bührer, and Edgar Grande, 15–22. Baden-Baden: Nomos.

Grande, Edgar, and Anke Peschke. 2000. "Organizing Science in Europe: Interest Groups and the Problem-Solving Capacity of European Science and Technology Policy Making." Unpublished manuscript.

Grande, Edgar, and Thomas Risse. 2000. "Bridging the Gap: Konzeptuelle Anforderungen an die politikwissenschaftliche Analyse von Globalisierungsprozessen." *Zeitschrift für Internationale Beziehungen* 7, no. 2: 235–66.

Grande, Edgar, and Volker Schneider. 1991. "Reformstrategien und staatliche Handlungskapazitäten. Eine vergleichende Analyse institutionellen Wandels in der Telekommunikation in Westeuropa." *Politische Vierteljahresschrift* 32, no. 3: 452–78.

Guéhenno, Jean-Marie. 1995. *The End of the Nation-State.* Minneapolis: University of Minnesota Press.

Haas, Ernst B. 1964. *Beyond the Nation-State: Functionalism and International Organization.* Stanford, CA: Stanford University Press.

Haas, Peter M. 1992. "Obtaining International Environmental Protection through Epistemic Consensus." In *Global Environmental Change and International Relations,* edited by Ian H.Rowlands, and Malory Greene, pp. 38–59. Basingstoke: Macmillan.

Haas, Peter M. 1993. "Epistemic Communities and the Dynamics of International Environmental Co-Operation." In *Regime Theory and International Relations,* edited by Volker Rittberger, pp. 168–201. Oxford: Clarendon Press.

Habermas, Jürgen. 1998. *Die post-nationale Konstellation: Politische Essays.* Frankfurt am Main: Suhrkamp.

Hafner, Katie, and Matthew Lyon. 1998. *Where Wizards Stay Up Late. The Origins of the Internet.* New York: Touchstone.

Hall, Peter, and David Soskice, eds. 2001. *Varieties of Capitalism. The Challenges Facing Contemporary Political Economy.* Oxford: Oxford University Press.

Harrison, Trevor. 1995. *Of Passionate Intensity. Right-wing Populism and the Reform Party of Canada.* Toronto: University of Toronto Press.

Hasenclever, Andreas, Peter Mayer, and Volker Rittberger. 1997. *Theories of International Regimes.* New York: Cambridge University Press.

Haufler, Virginia. 1993. "Crossing the Boundary between Public and Private. International Regimes and Non-State Actors." In *Regime Theory and International Relations,* edited by Volker Rittberger, 94–111. Oxford: Clarendon Press.

Haus, Leah. 1995. "Openings in the Wall: Transnational Migrants, Labor Unions, and U.S. Immigration Policy." *International Organization* 49, no. 2: 285–313.

Heins, Bernd. 1998. *Soziale Nachhaltigkeit.* Berlin: Analytica.

Held, David, and Anthony G. McGrew. 1993. "Globalization and the Liberal Democratic State." *Government and Opposition* 28, 2: 261–285.

Held, David. 1995. *Democracy and the Global Order: From the Modern State to Cosmopolitical Governance.* Cambridge, MA: Polity Press.

Held, David, and Anthony McGrew, eds. 2002. *Governing Globalization: Power, Authority, and Global Governance.* Cambridge, MA: Polity Press.

Held, David, Anthony McGrew, David Goldblatt, and Jonathan Perraton. 1999. *Global Transformations: Politics, Economics and Culture.* Cambridge, MA: Polity Press.

Helleiner, Eric. 1994. *States and the Reemergence of Global Finance: From Bretton Woods to the 1990s.* Ithaca, NY: Cornell University Press.

Hellmann, Kai-Uwe. 1999. "Paradigmen der Bewegungsforschung." In *Neue soziale Bewegungen. Impulse, Bilanzen und Perspektiven*, edited by Ansgar Klein, Hans-Josef Legrand, and Thomas Leif, 91–113. Opladen: Westdeutscher Verlag.

Hirsch, Joachim. 1995. *Der nationale Wettbewerbsstaat: Staat, Demokratie und Politik im globalen Kapitalismus.* Berlin and Amsterdam: Edition ID-Archiv.

Hirst, Paul, and Grahame Thompson. 1996. *Globalisation in Question: The International Economy and the Possibilities of Governance.* Cambridge, MA: Polity Press.

Hobsbawm, Eric J. 1992. *Nations and Nationalism since 1780: Programme, Myth, Reality.* 2nd ed. Cambridge: Cambridge University Press.

Holm, Hans-Henrik, and Georg Sørensen. 1995. "Introduction: What Has Changed?" In *Whose World Order? Uneven Globalisation and the End of the Cold War*, edited by Hans-Henrik Holm, and Georg Sørensen, 1–17. Boulder, CO: Westview Press.

Hummel, Hartwig, ed. 2001. *Die Privatisierung der Weltpolitik. Entstaatlichung und Kommerzialisierung im Globalisierungsprozess.* Bonn: Dietz.

Hurd, Ian. 1999. "Legitimacy and Authority in International Politics." *International Organization* 53, no. 2: 379–408.

Inglehart, Ronald. 1977. *The Silent Revolution. Changing Values and Political Styles among Western Publics.* Princeton, NJ: Princeton University Press.

Inglehart, Ronald. 1990. *Cultural Shift in Advanced Industrial Society.* Princeton, NJ: Princeton University Press.

Iverson, Torben. 1999. *Contested Economic Institutions. The Politics of Macroeconomics and Wage Bargaining in Advanced Democracies.* Cambridge: Cambridge University Press.

Jachtenfuchs, Markus, and Beate Kohler-Koch. 1996. "Regieren im dynamischen Mehrebenensystem." In *Europäische Integration*, edited by Markus Jachtenfuchs, and Beate Kohler-Koch, 15–44. Opladen: Leske and Budrich.

Jacobson, David. 1996. *Rights Across Borders. Immigration and the Decline of Citizenship*. Baltimore, MD: John Hopkins University Press.

Jessop, Bob. 1994. "Post-Fordism and the State." In *Post-Fordism: A Reader*, edited by Ash Amin, 251–79. Oxford: Blackwell.

Joppke, Christian. 1998. "Asylum and State Sovereignty: A Comparison of the United States, Germany, and Britain." In *Challenge to the Nation-State. Immigration in Western Europe and the United States*, edited by Christian Joppke, 109-152. Oxford: Oxford University Press.

Jordan, Grant. 1998. "What Drives Associability at the European Level? The Limits of the Utilitarian Explanation." In *Collective Action in the European Union*, edited by Justin Greenwood, and Mark Aspinwall, 31–62. London: Routledge.

Josephson, John R. 2000. "Smart Inductive Generalizations are Abductions." In: *Abduction and Induction. Essays on Their Relation and Integration*, edited by Peter A. Flach, 31-44. Dordrecht: Kluwer.

Junne, Gerd. 1996. "Integration unter den Bedingungen von Globalisierung und Lokalisierung." In *Europäische Integration*, edited by Markus Jachtenfuchs, and Beate Kohler-Koch, 513–30. Opladen: Leske and Budrich.

Kahler, Miles. 1995. *International Institutions and the Political Economy of Integration*. Washington, DC: Brookings Institution Press.

Kahn, David. 1969. *The Codebreakers: The Story of Secret Writing*. New York: Macmillan.

Katzenstein, Peter J. 1975. "International Interdependence: Some Long-term Trends and Recent Changes." *International Organization* 29, no. 4: 1021–34.

Katzenstein, Peter. ed. 1978. *Between Power and Plenty: The Foreign Economic Policies of Advanced Industrial States*. Madison: University of Wisconsin Press.

Katzenstein, Peter J. 1987. *Policy and Politics in West Germany: The Growth of a Semisovereign State*. Philadelphia: Temple University Press.

Kaufmann, Franz-Xaver. 1997. *Herausforderungen des Sozialstaates*. Frankfurt am Main: Suhrkamp.

Kearney, A. T. 2003. "Measuring Globalization: Who's Up, Who's Down." In *Foreign Policy* 134: 60–73.

Keohane, Robert. 1993. "Sovereignity, Interdependence and International Institutions." In *Ideas and Ideals: Essays on Politics in Honor of Stanley Hoffmann*, edited by Linda B. Miller, and Michael Joseph Smith, 91–107. Boulder, CO: Westview Press.

Keohane, Robert O, and Joseph S. Nye. 2000a. "Globalization: What's New? What's Not? (And So What?)." *Foreign Policy* 118: 104–19.

Keohane, Robert O. and Joseph S. Nye. 2000b. "Introduction." In *Governance in a Globalizing World*, edited by Joseph S. Nye, and John D. Donahue, 1-41. Cambridge, MA and Washington, DC: Brookings Institution Press.

Kitschelt, Herbert. 1986. "Political Opportunity Structures and Political Protest: Anti-Nuclear Movements in Four Democracies." *British Journal of Political Science* 16, no. 1: 57-85.

———. 1994. *The Transformation of European Social Democracy*. Cambridge: Cambridge University Press.

Kitschelt, Herbert, Peter Lange, Gary Marks, and John D. Stephens. 1999a. "Introduction." In *Continuity and Change in Contemporary Capitalism*, edited by Herbert Kitschelt, Peter Lange, Gary Marks, and John D. Stephens, 1-8. Cambridge: Cambridge University Press.

———. 1999b. "Convergence and Divergence in Advanced Capitalist Democracies." In *Continuity and Change in Contemporary Capitalism*, edited by Herbert Kitschelt, Peter Lange, Gary Marks, and John D. Stephens, 427-60. Cambridge: Cambridge University Press.

Kittel, Bernhard, Herbert Obinger, and Uwe Wagschal. 2000. "Die 'gezügelten' Wohlfahrtsstaaten im Vergleich: Politisch-Institutionelle Faktoren der Entstehung und Entwicklungsdynamik." In *Der gezügelte Wohlfahrtsstaat: Sozialpolitik in reichen Ländern*, edited by Herbert Obinger, and Uwe Wagschal. pp. 329-64. Frankfurt am Main: Campus.

Klingemann, Hans-Dieter, Richard I. Hofferbert, and Ian Budge. 1994. *Parties, Policies, and Democracy*. Boulder, CO: Westview Press.

Koch, Jürgen. 1991. "The Completion of the Internal Market and its Impact on the Building Sector in Europe." In *Restructuring a Traditional Industry: Construction Employment and Skills in Europe*, edited by Helen Rainbird, and Gerd Syben, 263-83. Oxford: Berg.

Köbele, Bruno, and Gerhard Leuschner, eds. 1995. *Dokumentation der Konferenz "Europäischer Arbeitsmarkt -Grenzenlos mobil?"* März 6-8 in Bonn. Baden-Baden: Nomos.

Köbele, Bruno, and Karl-Heinz Sahl, eds. 1993. *Die Zukunft der Sozialkassensysteme der Bauwirtschaft im Europäischen Binnenmarkt*. Cologne: Bund-Verlag.

Kobrin, Stephen J. 2001. "Territoriality and the Government of Cyberspace." In *Journal of International Business Studies* 32 no. 4: 687-704.

Kohler-Koch, Beate. 1993. "Die Welt regieren ohne Weltregierung." In *Regieren im 21. Jahrhundert. Zwischen Globalisierung und*

Regionalisierung, edited by Carl Böhret, and Göttrik Wewer, 109–141. Opladen: Leske and Budrich.

Kohler-Koch, Beate. 1999. "The Evolution and Transformation of European Governence." In *The Transformation of Governance in the European Union,* edited by Beate Kohler-Koch, and Rainer Eising, 14–35. London: Routledge.

Krasner, Stephen D. 1978. *Defending the National Interest. Raw Material Investments and U.S. Foreign Policy.* Princeton, NJ: Princeton University Press.

Krasner, Stephen D. 1994. "International Political Economy: Abiding Discord." *Review of International Political Economy* 1, no.1: 13–20.

Kriesi, Hanspeter. 1991. "The Political Opportunity Structure of New Social Movements: Its Impact on Their Mobilization." Discussion Paper FS III 91–103. Berlin: WZB.

Kriesi, Hanspeter. 1999. "Movements of the Left, Movements of the Right: Putting the Mobilization of Two New Types of Social Movements into Political Context." In *Continuity and Change in Contemporary Capitalism,* edited by Herbert Kitschelt, Peter Lange, Gary Marks, and John D. Stephens, 398–423. Cambridge: Cambridge University Press.

Kriesi, Hanspeter. 2001. "Nationaler politischer Wandel in einer sich dena-tionalisierenden Welt." *Blätter für deutsche und internationale Politik* 46, no. 2: 206–13.

Kriesi, Hanspeter, Ruud Koopmans, Jan Willem Duyvendak, and Marco G. Giugni. 1995. *New Social Movements in Western Europe. A Comparative Analysis.* London: UCL.

Krugman, Paul. 1994a. "Competitiveness: A Dangerous Obsession." *Foreign Affairs* 73, no. 2: 28–44.

Krugman, Paul. 1994b. *Peddling Prosperity.* New York: W. W. Norton.

Krupat, Kitty. 1997. "From War Zone to Free Trade Zone." In *No Sweat. Fashion, Free Trade, and the Rights of Garment Workers,* edited by Andrew Ross, 51–78. London: Verso.

Lacher, Hannes. 2004. *The International Relations of Modernity: Capitalism, Territoriality and Globalization.* London: Routledge.

Lehmbruch, Gerhard, and Philippe C. Schmitter, eds. 1982. *Patterns of Corporatist Policy-Making.* Beverly Hills, CA: Sage.

Leibfried, Stephan, and Elmar Rieger. 2003. *Limits to Globalization. Welfare States and the World Economy.* Cambridge: Polity Press.

Levy, Steven. 1993. "Crypto Rebels," *Wired,* May/June.

Lindblom, Charles E. 1977. *Politics and Markets: The World's Political-Economic Systems.* New York: Basic Books.

Lijphart, Arend. 1977. *Democracy in Plural Societies: A Comparative Exploration.* New Haven, CT: Yale University Press.

Lijphart, Arend. 1984. *Democracies: Patterns of Majoritarian and Consensus Government in Twenty-One Countries.* New Haven, CT: Yale University Press.

———. 1999. *Patterns of Democracy: Government Forms and Performance in Thirty-Six Countries.* New Haven, CT: Yale University Press.

Lipset, Seymour Martin, and Stein Rokkan. 1967. *Party Systems and Voter Alignments: Cross-National Perspectives.* New York: Free Press.

Lösche, Peter. 1992. "Interessenorganisation." In *Länderbericht USA II. Gesellschaft, Außenpolitik, Kultur, Religion, Erziehung,* edited by W. P. Adams and E. O. Genpiel, 919–41. Bonn: Bundeszentrale für Politische Bildung.

Lowi, Theodore. 1972. "Four System of Policy, Politics and Choice." *Public Administration Review* 32, no. 4: 300–10.

Luhmann, Niklas. 1971. "Die Weltgesellschaft." *Soziologische Aufklärung,* vol. 2. Opladen: Westdeutscher Verlag. 51–71.

Marks, Gary, Liesbet Hooghe, and Kermit Blank. 1996. "European Integration from the 1980s: State Centric vs. Multi-level Governance." *Journal of Common Market Studies* 34, no. 3: 341–78.

Marks, Gary, Leonard Ray, and Carole J. Wilson. 2002. "National Political Parties and European Integration." *American Journal of Political Science* 46, no. 3: 585–94.

Marks, Gary, and Carole Wilson. 2000. "The Past in the Present: A Cleavage Theory of Party Response to European Integration." *British Journal of Political Science* 30, no. 3: 433–60.

Marks, Gary. 2004. "Conclusion: European Integration and Political Conflict." In *European Integration and Political Conflict,* edited by Gary Marks, and Marco R. Steenbergen, 235–53. Cambridge: Cambridge University Press.

Marshall, Thomas H. 1992. "Staatsbürgerrechte und Soziale Klassen." Chapter 3 in *Bürgerrechte und soziale Klassen. Zur Soziologie des Wohlfahrtsstaates.* Frankfurt am Main: Campus.

Martin, Hans-Peter, and Harald Schumann. 1997. *Die Globalisierungsfalle: Der Angriff auf Demokratie und Wohlstand.* Reinbek: Rowohlt.

Martin, Lisa L., and Beth A. Simmons. 1998. "Theories and Empirical Studies of International Institutions." *International Organization* 52, no. 4: 729–57.

Martins, Herminio. 1974. "Time and Theory in Sociology." In *Approaches to Sociology. An Introduction to Major Trends in British Sociology,* edited by John Rex, 246–94. London: Routledge.

Massey, D. S., J. Arango, G. Hugo, A. Kouaouci, A. Pellegrino, and J. E. Taylor. 1993. "Theories of International Migration: A Review and Appraisal." *Population and Development Review* 19: 431–66.

Mayntz, Renate, and Fritz Scharpf. 1995. *Gesellschaftliche Selbstregelung und politische Steuerung*. Frankfurt am Main: Campus.

Mayntz, Renate. 2001. "Politikwissenschaft in einer entgrenzten Welt." In *Politik in einer entgrenzten Welt*, edited by Christine Landfried, 49–68. Köln: Verlag Wissenschaft und Politik.

Mazur, Jay. 2000. "Labor's New Internationalism." *Foreign Affairs* 79, no. 1: 79–93.

McAdam, Doug. 1982. *Political Process and the Development of Black Insurgency, 1930–1970*. Chicago: University of Chicago Press.

McGrew, Anthony, ed. 1997. *The Transformation of Democracy? Globalization and Territorial Democracy*. Cambridge, MA: Polity Press.

Mills, Kurt. 1998. *Human Rights in the Emerging Global Order: A New Sovereignty?* New York: St. Martin's Press.

Milner, Helen V., and Robert O. Keohane. 1996. "Internationalisation and Domestic Politics: An Introduction." In *Internationalisation and Domestic Politics*, edited by Robert O. Keohane, and Helen V. Milner, 3–24. Cambridge: Cambridge University Press.

Mintzer, Irving M., ed. 1994. *Negotiating Climate Change: The Inside Story of the Rio Convention*. Cambridge: Cambridge Universitiy Press.

Müller, Harald, and Thomas Risse-Kappen. 1990. "Internationale Umwelt, gesellschaftliches Umfeld und außenpolitischer Prozeß in liberaldemokratischen Industrienationen." In *Theorien der internationalen Beziehungen. Bestandsaufnahme und Forschungsperspektiven, PVS-Sonderheft 21*, edited by Volker Rittberger, 375-400. Opladen: Westdeutscher Verlag.

Narr, Wolf-Dieter, and Alexander Schubert. 1994. *Weltökonomie: Die Misere der Politik*. Frankfurt am Main: Suhrkamp.

Neyer, Jürgen, and Martin Seeleib-Kaiser, eds. 1995. "Bringing the Economy Back" In: *Economic Globalisation and the Re-Commodification of the Workforce*. Bremen: Zentrum für Sozialpolitik.

Nölke, Andreas. 2000. "Regieren in transnationalen Politiknetzwerken? Kritik postnationaler Governance-Konzepte aus der Perspektive transnationaler (Inter-) Organisationssoziologie." *Zeitschrift für Internationale Beziehungen* 7, no. 2: 331–58.

North, David S. 1994. "Enforcing the Minimum Wage and Employer Sanctions." *Annals of the American Academy of Political and Social Science* 534: 58–68.

Oberthür, Sebastian. 1993. *Politik im Treibhaus: Die Entstehung des internationalen Klimaschutzregimes.* Berlin: Edition Sigma.

Offe, Claus. 1985a. *Disorganized Capitalism.* Oxford: Polity Press.

———. 1985b. "New Social Movements: Challenging the Boundaries of Institutional Politics." *Social Research* 52, no. 4: 817–69.

———. 1998. "Demokratie und Wohlfahrtsstaat: Eine europäische Regimeform unter dem Streß der europäischen Integration." In *Internationale Wirtschaft, nationale Demokratie: Herausforderungen für die Demokratietheorie,* edited by Wolfgang Streeck, pp. 99–136. Frankfurt am Main: Campus.

Ohmae, Kenichi. 1996. *End of the Nation State: The Rise of Regional Economies.* London: HarperCollins.

Organization for Economic Cooperation and Development (OECD). 1994. *The OECD Jobs Study: Facts, Analysis, Strategies.* Paris: OECD.

Ougaard, Morten, and Richard Higgott, eds. 2001. *The Global Polity.* London: Routledge.

Overbeek, Henk. 1995. "Towards a New International Migration Regime: Globalization, Migration and the Internationalization of the State." In *Migration and European Integration. The Dynamics of Inclusion and Exclusion,* edited by Dietrich Thränhardt, and Robert Miles, 15–37. London: Pinter.

Overbeek, Henk, and Kees Van der Pijl. 1993. "Restructuring Capital and Restructuring Hegemony: Neo-Liberalism and the Unmaking of the Post-War Order." In *Restructuring Hegemony in the Global Political Economy,* edited by Henk Overbeek, 1–27. London and New York: Routledge.

Palan, Ronan, and Jason Abbott. 1996. *State Strategies in the Global Political Economy.* London: Pinter.

Panitch, Leo. 1994. "Globalization and the State." In *Between Globalism and Nationalism, Socialist Register 1994,* edited by Leo Panitch, and Ralph Miliband, 60-93. London: Merlin Press.

Pierce, Charles S. 1878. Deduction, Induction, and Hypothesis. In *Popular Science Monthly* 13, no. 8: 470–82.

Pierson, Paul. 1996. "The New Politics of the Welfare State." *World Politics* 48, no. 2: 143–79.

Pinder, John. 1968. "Positive and Negative Integration. Some Problems of Economic Union in the EEC." *World Today* 24, no. 3: 88–110.

Piore, Michael. 1979. *Birds of Passage.* Cambridge: Cambridge University Press.

Piore, M. J. 1986. "The Shifting Grounds for Immigration." *Annals of the American Academy of Political and Social Science* 485: 23–33.

Piore, Michael. 1997. "The Economics of the Sweatshop." In *No Sweat. Fashion, Free Trade, and the Rights of Garment Workers*, edited by Andrew Ross, 135–42. London: Verso.

Pollack, Mark A. 1997. "Representing Diffuse Interests in EC Policy-making." *Journal of European Public Policy* 4, no. 4: 572–90.

Pontusson, Jonas. 2001. *Social Europe versus Liberal America: Employment, Inequality and Social Welfare*. New York: Century Foundation, i.p.

Princen, Thomas, and Mathias Finger. 1994. *Environmental NGOs in World Politics: Linking the Local and the Global*. London: Routledge.

Ragin, Charles. 2000. *Fuzzy-Set Social Science*. Chicago: University of Chicago Press.

Reinicke, Wolfgang. 1998. *Global Public Policy. Governing without Government?* Washington, DC: Brookings Institution Press.

Reinicke, Wolfgang H., and Francis Deng, (with Jan Martin Witte, and Thorsten Benner). 2000. *Critical Choices. The United Nations, Networks, and the Future of Global Governance*. Ottawa: IDRC Publishers.

Richardson, Jeremy J., ed. 1993. *Pressure Groups*. New York: Oxford University Press.

Rieger, Elmar, and Stephan Leibfried. 2003. *Limits to Globalization: Welfare States and the World Economy*. Oxford: Polity Press.

Risse-Kappen, Thomas. 1995. "Introduction: Bringing Transnational Relations Back." In *Non-State Actors, Domestic Structures and International Institutions*, edited by Thomas Risse-Kappen, 3–33. Cambridge: Cambridge University Press.

Risse, Thomas. 2001. "Transnational Actors, Networks, and Global Governance." In *Handbook of International Relations*, edited by Walter Carlsnaes, Thomas Risse, and Beth Simmons, 255–274. London: Sage.

Risse, Thomas, Stephen C. Ropp, and Kathryn Sikkink, eds. 1999. *The Power of Human Rights: International Norms and Domestic Change*. Cambridge: Cambridge University Press.

Rittberger, Volker. 2000. "Globalisierung und der Wandel der Staatenwelt: Die Welt regieren ohne Weltstaat." In *Vom Ewigen Frieden und vom Wohlstand der Nationen: Dieter Senghaas zum 60 Geburtstag*, edited by Ulrich Menzel, 188–218. Frankfurt am Main: Suhrkamp.

Rittberger, Volker, and Michael Zürn. 1990. "Towards Regulated Anarchy in East-West Relations." In *International Regimes in East-West Politics*, edited by Volker Rittberger, 9–63. London and New York: Pinter.

Robertson, Roland. 1992. *Globalization: Social Theory and Global Culture*. London and Beverly Hills: Sage.

Rodrik, Dani. 1997. *Has Globalisation Gone too Far?* Washington, DC: Institute for International Economics.

Rokkan, Stein, and Derek W. Urwin. 1983. *Economy, Territory, Identity: Politics of West European Peripheries.* London: Sage.

Rootes, Chris. 1995. "Britain—Greens in a Cold Climate." In *The Green Challenge. The Development of Green Parties in Europe*, edited by Dick Richardson, and Chris Rootes, 66–90. London and New York: Routledge.

Rosecrance, Richard, and Arthur A. Stein. 1973. "Interdependence: Myth or Reality?" *World Politics* 26, no. 1: 1–27.

Rosecrance, Richard, Alan Alexandroff, Wallace Koehler, John Kroll, Shlomit Laqueur, and John Stocker. 1977. "Whither Interdependence?" *International Organization* 31 no. 3: 425–72.

Rosenau, James N. 1986. "Before Cooperation: Hegemons, Regimes and Habit-Driven Actors in World Politics." *International Organization* 40, no. 4: 849–94.

Rosenau, James N. 1990. *Turbulence in World Politics: A Theory of Change and Continuity.* Princeton, NJ: Princeton University Press.

Rosenau, James N. 1992. "Governance, Order, and Change in World Politics." In *Governance without Government: Order and Change in World Politics*, edited by James N. Rosenau, and Ernst-Otto Czempiel, 1-29. Cambridge: Cambridge University Press.

Rosenau, James N. 1997. *Along the Domestic-Foreign Frontier: Exploring Governance in a Turbulent World.* Cambridge: Cambridge University Press.

Rosenau, James N, and Ernst-Otto Czempiel, eds. 1992. *Governance without Government. Order and Change in World Politics.* Cambridge, MA: Lexington Press.

Rosenberg, Justin. 1994. *The Empire of Civil Society. A Critique of the Realist Theory of International Relations.* London and New York: Verso.

Rowlands, Ian H. 1995. *The Politics of Global Atmospheric Change.* Manchester and New York: Manchester University Press.

Rucht, Dieter. 1994. *Modernisierung und neue soziale Bewegungen: Deutschland, Frankreich und USA im Vergleich.* Frankfurt am Main: Campus.

Sahl, Karl-Heinz, and Brigitte Stang. 1996. "Das Arbeitnehmer-Entsendegesetz und die Europäische Entsenderichtlinie." *Arbeitsrecht im Betrieb* 11: 652–61.

Sansom, Gareth. 1995. *Illegal and Offensive Content on the Information Highway.* Background Paper, Industry Canada (Long Range Planning & Analysis, Spectrum, Information Technologies and

Telecommunications Sector). http://insight. mcmaster.ca/org/efc/ pages/doc/offensive.html (accessed 10/14/98).

Sassen, Saskia. 1988. *The Mobility of Labor and Capital: A Study in International Investment and Labor Flow.* Cambridge: Cambridge University Press.

———. 1996. *Migranten, Siedler, Flüchtlinge. Von der Massenauswanderung zur Festung Europa.* Frankfurt: Fischer.

———. 1998. *Globalization and Its Discontents: Essays on the New Mobility of People and Money.* New York: New Press.

Scharpf, Fritz W. 1987. *Sozialdemokratische Krisenpolitik in Europa.* Frankfurt am Main: Campus.

Scharpf, Fritz W. 1996a. "Negative and Positive Integration in the Political Economy of European Welfare States." In *Governance in the European Union,* edited by Gary Marks, Fritz W.Scharpf, Philippe C. Schmitter, and Wolfgang Streeck, 15-39. London: Sage.

———. 1996b. "Politische Optionen im vollendeten Binnenmarkt." In *Europäische Integration,* edited by Markus Jachtenfuchs, and Beate Kohler-Koch, 109–40. Opladen: Leske and Budrich.

———. 1999. *Governing in Europe.* Oxford: Oxford University Press.

Scharpf, Fritz W., and Vivien A. Schmidt. 2000. *Welfare and Work in the Open Economy.* 2 Bde. Oxford: Oxford University Press.

Schmidt, Manfred G. 1995. *Wörterbuch zur Politik.* Stuttgart: Kröner.

———. 2000. Demokratietheorien. 3rd ed. Opladen: Leske and Budrich.

Schmitter, Philippe C. 1974. "Still the Century of Corporatism?" *Review of Politics* 36: 85–131.

———. 1979. "Still the Century of Corporatism?" In *Trends Towards Corporatist Intermediation,* edited by Philippe C. Schmitter, and Gerhard Lehmbruch, 7-53. Beverly Hills, CA: Sage.

Schmitter, Philippe C., and Gerhard Lehmbruch, eds. 1979. *Trends Towards Corporatist Intermediation,* Beverly Hills, CA: Sage.

Schneider, Volker. 2003. "Komplexität und Policy-Forschung: Über die Angemessenheit von Erklärungsstrategien." In *Die Reformierbarkeit der Demokratie. Innovationen und Blockaden,* edited by Renate Mayntz and Wolfgang Streeck, 291–317. Frankfurt am Main and New York: Campus.

Schönwälder, Karen. 1999. "'Persons Persecuted on Political Grounds Shall Enjoy the Right of Aslyum—But not in Our Country': Asylum Policy and Debates about Refugees in the Federal Republic of Germany." In *Refugees, Citizenship, and Social Policy in Europe,* edited by Alice Bloch, and Carl Levy, 76-90. Houndmills: Macmillan.

Scholte, Jan Aart. 1993. *International Relations of Social Change.* Buckingham: Open University Press.

———. 2000. *Globalization. A Critical Introduction.* New York: St. Martin's Press.

———. 2003. "What is Globalization? The Definitional Issue—Again." Working Paper Series, Institute on Globalization and the Human Condition, Hamilton, Ontario.

Schwartz, Herman. 2001. "Round up the Usual Suspects! Globalization, Domestic Politics, and Welfare State Change." In *The New Politics of the Welfare State*, edited by Paul Pierson, 17–44. Oxford: Oxford Univesity Press.

Seeleib-Kaiser, Martin. 2001. *Globalisierung und Sozialpolitik: Ein Vergleich der Diskurse und Wohlfahrtssysteme in Deutschland, Japan und den USA.* Frankfurt am Main: Campus.

Shade, Leslie R. 1996. "Is There Free Speech on the Net? Censorship in the Global Information Infrastructure." In *Cultures of the Internet: Virtual Spaces, Real Histories, Living Bodies*, edited by Rob Shields, 11–32. London: Sage.

Smith, Anthony D. 1979. *Nationalism in the Twentieth Century.* Oxford: Martin Robertson.

Sørensen, Georg. 2001. *Changes in Statehood: The Transformation of International Relations.* New York: Palgrave.

Soskice, David. 1999. "Divergent Production Regimes: Coordinated and Uncoordinated Market Economies in the 1980s and 1990s." In *Continuity and Change in Contemporary Capitalism*, edited by Herbert Kitschelt, Peter Lange, Gary Marks, and John D. Stephens, 101–34. Cambridge: Cambridge University Press.

Steinmann, Rolf, and Günter Haardt, eds. 1996. *Die Bauwirtschaft auf dem Weg zum Dienstleister. Neue Anforderungen an das Baumanagement.* Baden-Baden: Nomos.

Steffan, Martin. 1994. *Die Bemühungen um eine internationale Klimakonvention. Verhandlungen, Interessen, Akteure.* Münster: LIT.

Stephens, John D., Evelyne Huber, and Leonard Ray. 1999. "The Welfare State in Hard Times." In *Continuity and Change in Contemporary Capitalism*, edited by Herbert Kitschelt, Peter Lange, Gary Marks, and John D. Stephens, 164–93. Cambridge: Cambridge Univesity Press.

Strange, Susan. 1982. "Cave! Hic Dragones: A Critique of Regime Analysis." *International Organization* 36, no. 2: 479–96.

———. 1996. *The Retreat of the State: The Diffusion of Power in the World Economy.* Cambridge: Cambridge University Press.

Streeck, Wolfgang. 1995a. "German Capitalism: Does It exist? Can It survive?" Discussion Paper, Cologne: Max Planck Institute for Societal Research.

Streeck, Wolfgang. 1995b. "From Market-Making to State-Building? Reflections on the Political Economy of European Social Policy." In *European Social Policy: Between Fragmentation and Integration*, edited by Stephan Leibfried, and Paul Pierson, 389–431. Washington, D.C.: Brookings Institution.

Streeck, Wolfgang, ed. 1998. *Internationale Wirtschaft, nationale Demokratie. Herausforderungen für die Demokratietheorie.* Frankfurt am Main: Campus.

Streeck, Wolfgang. 1999. *Korporatismus in Deutschland. Zwischen Nationalstaat und Europäischer Union.* Frankfurt am Main: Campus.

Streeck, Wolfgang, and Philippe C. Schmitter, eds. 1985. *Private Interest Government. Beyond Market and State.* London: Sage.

Taplin, Ian M. 1994. "Strategic Reorientations of U.S. Apparel Firms." In *Commodity Chains and Global Capitalism*, edited by Gary Gereffi, and Miguel Korzeniewicz, 205–22. Westport: Praeger.

Tarrow, Sidney. 1995. "Bridging the Quantitative-Qualitative Divide in Political Science." *American Political Science Review* 89, no. 2: 471–74.

Tarrow, Sidney 1999. *Power in Movement: Social Movements and Contentious Politics.* Cambridge: Cambridge University Press.

Tinbergen, Jan. 1965. *International Economic Integration.* 2nd ed. Amsterdam: Elsevier.

Tomei, Veronica. 1997. *Europäische Migrationspolitik zwischen Kooperationszwang und Souveränitätsansprüchen.* Bonn: Europa Union Verlag.

Tsebelis, George. 1995. "Decision Making in Political Systems." *British Journal of Political Science* 25, no. 3: 289–325.

Tulmein, Oliver. 1999. "Materielles Recht und virtueller Raum. Strafrecht, Strafprozeßrecht und Internet." In *Neue Medienumwelten. Zwischen Regulierungsprozessen und alltäglicher Aneigung*, edited by Eike Hebecker, Frank Kleemann, Harald Neymanns, and Markus Stauff, 151–65. Frankfurt am Main: Campus.

Underdal, Arild. 2002. "One Question, Two Answers." In *Environmental Regime Effectiveness. Confronting Theory with Evidence*, edited by Edward Miles, Arild Underdal, Steinar Andresen, Jørgen Wettestad, Skjærseth, and Elaine Carlin, 3–46. Cambridge, MA: MIT Press.

United States General Accounting Office (GAO). 1988. *'Sweatshops' in the U.S. Opinions on Their Extent and Possible Enforcement Options.* Washington, DC: General Accounting Office.

United States General Accounting Office (GAO). 1994. *Garment Industry. Efforts to Address the Prevalence and Conditions of Sweatshops.* Washington, DC: General Accounting Office.

Vogel, Steven K. 1996. *Free Markets, More Rules: Regulatory Reform in Advanced Industrial Countries.* Ithaca, NY: Cornell University Press.

Vogel, David. 1997. "Trading Up and Governing Across: Transnational Governance and Environmental Protection." *Journal of European Public Policy* 4, no. 4: 556–71.

Voswinkel, Stephan, Stefan Lücking, and Ingo Bode. 1996. *Im Schatten des Fordismus. Industrielle Beziehungen in der Bauwirtschaft und im Gastgewerbe Deutschlands und Frankreichs.* Munich: Rainer Hampp Verlag.

Walter, Gregor, Sabine Dreher, and Marianne Beisheim. 1999. "Globalization Processes in the G7." *Global Society* 13, no. 3: 229–55.

Walter, Gregor, and Michael Zürn. 2003. "Into the Methodological Void: Drawing Causal Inferences on Systemic Consequences of International Regimes." In *Regime Consequences: Methodological Challenges and Research Strategies*, edited by Arild Underdal, and Oran Young, 307–34. Dordrecht: Kluwer.

Waltz, Kenneth N. 1979. *Theory of International Politics.* New York: Random House.

Walzer, Michael. 1983. *Spheres of Justice.* New York: Basic Books.

Wapner, Paul. 1995. "Politics Beyond the State: Environmental Activism and the World Civic Politics." *World Policy Journal* 47 April: 311–40.

Waters, Malcolm. 1995. *Globalization.* London: Routledge.

Weiner, Myron. 1995. *The Global Migration Crisis.* New York: Harper Collins.

Wilson, Graham. K. 1990. *Interest Groups.* Oxford: Basil Blackwell.

Windhoff-Héritier, Adrienne. 1987. *Policy-Analyse: Eine Einführung.* Frankfurt am Main: Campus.

Weiss, Linda. 1998. *The Myth of the Powerless State: Governing the Economy in a Global Era.* Cambridge, MA: Polity Press.

Wolf, Klaus Dieter. 2000. *Die neue Staatsraison—Zwischenstaatliche Kooparation als Demokratieproblem in der Weltgesellschaft.* Baden-Baden: Nomos.

World Society Research Group 2000. "Introduction: World Society." In *Civilizing World Politics: Society and Community Beyond the State*, edited by Mathias Albert, Lothar Brock, and Klaus Dieter Wolf, 19–44. Lanham, MD: Rowman & Littlefield.

Young, Alasdair. 1998. "European Consumer Groups: Multiple Levels of Governance and Multiple Levels of Collective Action." In *Collective Action in the European Union. Interests and the New Politics of Associability*, edited by Justin Greenwood, and Mark Apinwall, 149–75. London: Routledge.

Young, Oran R. 1978. "Anarchy and Social Choice: Reflections on the International Polity." *World Politics* 30: 241–63.

———. 1999. *The Effectiveness of International Environmental Regimes. Causal Connections and Behavioral Mechanisms*. Cambridge, MA: Massachusetts Institute of Technology Press.

Zangl, Bernhard, and Michael Zürn. 1997. "Die Auswirkungen der Globalisierung auf die Sicherheit in der OECD-Welt." In *Sicherheit in der unsicheren Gesellschaft*, edited by Ekkehard Lippert, Andreas Prüfert, and Günther Wachtler, 157–87. Opladen: Westdeutscher Verlag.

Zevin, Robert B. 1992. "Are World Financial Markets More Open? If So, Why and With Which Effects?" In *Financial Openess and National Autonomy*, edited by Tariq Banuri, and Juliet B. Schor, 54–73. Oxford: Clarendon Press.

Zolberg, Aristide R. 1991. "Bounded States in a Global Market: The Uses of International Labour Migrations." In *Social Theory for a Changing Society*, edited by Pierre Bourdieu and James S. Coleman, 301–25. Boulder, CO: Westview Press.

Zolberg, Aristide R. 1994. "Changing Sovereignty Games and International Migration." *Global Legal Studies Journal* 2, no. 1: 153–77.

Zolberg, Aristide R., Astri Suhrke, and Sergio Aguayo. 1989. *Escape from Violence: Conflict and the Refugee Crisis in the Developing World*. Oxford: Oxford University Press.

Zürn, Michael. 1998. *Regieren jenseits des Nationalstaates. Denationalisierung und Globalisierung als Chance*. Frankfurt am Main: Suhrkamp.

———. 2001. "Political Systems in the Postnational Constellation: Societal Denationalizaton and Multilateral Governance." In *Global Governance and the United Nations System*, edited by Volker Rittberger, 48–87. Tokyo: United Nations University Press.

———. 2002a. "Politik in der postnationalen Konstellation. Über das Elend des methodologischen Nationalismus." In *Politik in einer entgrenzten Welt*, edited by Christine Landfried, 181–203. Köln: Verlag Wissenschaft und Politik.

———. 2002b. "Societal Denationalisation and 'Positive' Governance in the OECD World." In *The Global Polity*, edited by Morten Ougaard, and Richard Higgott, pp. 78–103. London: Routledge.

Contributors

Marianne Beisheim holds a PhD in Political Science; her thesis investigates whether interest groups are "Fit for Global Governance" (2003). Marianne Beisheim worked for several years as a research associate at the University of Bremen and is now with the Free University of Berlin. She also works for the German Parliament, initially for the Enquete- Commission "Globalization" and now at the office of the Chairman of the Environment Committee, Dr. Ernst Ulrich von Weizsäcker. Her work and her publications focus on globalization and privatization, global governance and forms of soft law, questions of democratic legitimacy, the role of NGOs, and on environmental politics, especially climate change.

Sabine Dreher received her MA degree from York University in Toronto, Canada and her Diploma in Administrative Sciences from Constance University in Germany. She was formerly a research associate at the Institute for Intercultural and International Studies (InIIS) at the University of Bremen, where she completed her PhD in Political Science, and is now Assistant Professor for International Relations and International Political Economy at Near East University in Nicosia, Cyprus. Her research focuses on migration, wage and labor standards and questions of citizenship and democracy in the global political economy. She is currently completing a book manuscript on "Neoliberalism and Migration: An Inquiry into the Politics of Globalization."

Gregor Walter received an MA in Political Science, Macroeconomics and Public Law from the University of Tübingen and also completed an MA in Political Science at the State University of New York in Stony Brook, USA. He worked for several years as a research associate at the Institute for Intercultural and International Studies (InIIS) at the University of Bremen, and published various contributions on issues related to globalization and global governance. In summer 2003 he concluded his PhD on state reactions to governance challenges induced by the Internet. He is currently working as Head of Curriculum Development for the Hertie School of Governance, a newly established European Professional School for Public Policy, in Berlin.

Michael Zürn, formerly Professor of International Politics and Transnational Relations at the Institute of Political Science, University of Bremen and Director of the Special Collaborative Research Centre on "Transformations of the State" at the University of Bremen, is now Director at the Science Center Berlin and Founding Dean of the Hertie School of Governance, Berlin. He is author of *Frieden und Krieg* (coauthored with Bernhard Zangl; 2003), *Regieren jenseits des Nationalstaates* (1998), *Gerechte internationale Regime* (1987) and *Interessen und Institutionen* (1992). He has contributed to numerous academic journals including *World Politics, European Journal of International Relations, International Studies Quarterly, Zeitschrift für Internationale Beziehungen,* and *Politische Vierteljahresschrift* as well as edited volumes on such issues as international institutions, globalization and denationalization, and theories of international relations.

Index